SIGNED to the
Band leader
Artie Shaw

For Artie —

With twenty years of
fond memories —

Do you still want
twenty more?

[illegible]

Critical Comments on Ted Berkman's Work:

Cast A Giant Shadow:

"A remarkable and moving biography that illuminates not only the man but the times in which he lived."--- Robert Kirsch, Los Angeles *Times*. "A wonderful book."--- Leon Uris.

To Seize The Passing Dream:

"A many-splendored delight. . . . does far more for Whistler than *Lust for Life* did for Van Gogh."--- St. Louis *Globe-Democrat*. "We end up with a full understanding of Whistler's work and a deep sympathy for the man, a rare combination for anyone to have with Whistler."--- Frank Getlein, Washington *Star*. "A masterpiece."--- Camden *Courier*.

Fear Strikes Out:

"A solid hit. Educates the heart with compassion and understanding."--- *Time* Magazine.

My Prisoner:

"Touching and informative; a moving story that I couldn't put down."--- Atlanta *Journal-Constitution*. "Absorbing . . . few readers will remain unmoved."--- *Publishers Weekly*.

The Lady and the Law:

"Coherent, compassionate and penetrating; a remarkable biography."--- St. Louis *Post-Dispatch*. "Berkman writes superbly, with an exquisite sense of timing, humor and wit."--- *Best Sellers*.

Sabra:

"Vivid and fascinating."--- New York *Times*. "Unforgettable."--- Miami Public Library. "An affecting, sometimes too painful look at the ordinary Israeli. Berkman has a flair for the fast, vivid vignette."--- *Publishers Weekly*.

Decision (Harry Truman):

"A rich, human slice of history."--- New York *Daily News*.

(All that and — *Bedtime for Bonzo*)

$15-

Around the World in 80 Years

Newsrooms, Soundstages, Private Encounters and Public Affairs

Ted Berkman

Manifest Publications
Carpinteria, California
1 9 9 8

Around the World in 80 Years

Newsrooms, Soundstages, Private Encounters and Public Affairs

by Ted Berkman

Published by:
Manifest Publications
P.O. Box 429
Carpinteria, CA 93014-0429 U.S.A.

Printed in the United States of America

Library of Congress Cataloging-in-Publication Data

Berkman, Ted.
Around the world in 80 years : newsrooms, soundstages, private encounters, and public affairs / Ted Berkman.
p. cm.
Includes index.
ISBN: 0-9627896-1-5 (alk. paper)
1. Berkman, Ted--Biography. 2. Novelists, American--20th century--Biography.
3. Journalists--United States--Biography. 4. Voyages and Travels. I. Title.
PS3552.E724Z463 1998
813'.54--dc21
[B] 98-17479
CIP

Contents

— Author's Note —

Although I have taken no liberties with the facts recorded in these pages, in a very few cases involving non-central figures I have used fictitious names.

Preface

"Speak up, young man! I can't hear you!"

The voice at the other end of the line was tired, harsh, almost grating, shorn of the rolling cadences that had thundered through the British Parliament and electrified the world. Nonetheless it was unmistakable. I felt a chill of recognition. I was on the phone to Winston Churchill. The prime minister of embattled England had come to the White House, a mile away, in mid-May of 1943 to confer with President Roosevelt.

At my elbow, earphones clamped to his head, my colleague Dave Goodman was churning out a simultaneous translation of a speech by Adolf Hitler being shortwaved from Berlin. As daytime wire chief at the U.S. Foreign Broadcast Intelligence Service, I had been delegated to edit Goodman's copy for Churchill on the run, filling in a word where necessary, modifying a phrase, deciding whether to wait for a thought to be completed.

At 29, I was the agency's youngest editor, a newcomer to the world of radio frequencies and high-powered transmitters. I was then, and remain today a paragon of technical incompetence whose helplessness before machinery has confounded my colleagues for sixty years. Trying to repair a lamp fixture, I once plunged half a city block into darkness.

But I was good with words. Big words, little words. Homer's words. Hitler's words . . .

The Fuehrer was trying to rally support for the annual German Red Cross campaign. Transposing Dave's copy, I declaimed into the telephone: "All the privations and sacrifices of the Homeland cannot be compared with the superhuman hardships under which our soldiers are fighting in the east."

"What kind of ships?" inquired the Prime Minister. He sounded edgy.

"Hardships, sir." My heart was doing a tap dance in my chest. "Difficulties."

"Ah, yes. I'm not as young as you are!"

Hitler maundered on. My distinguished listener, no longer demanding higher decibels, absorbed the rest of the Nazi leader's appeal in silence. A clipped "Thank you," and my colloquy with greatness was over.

I headed for the water cooler. Dave was already there. We turned to find Ed Hullinger, deputy director of the agency, beaming at us. "Great job, fellas. The White House is very happy."

So was I. With the Churchill episode, a private problem had been resolved. I had found my long-sought wartime *métier*, one likely to take me overseas. I was carving a fresh path on what was already an unconventional journey.

CHAPTER 1

First Row, First Seat

History for me begins in the early years A.D. That's "After Dodgers," meaning the period in the third decade of the twentieth century when the Brooklyn baseball club, weary of colorless eons as the Superbas or Robins, adopted the sobriquet under which they would become a national legend.

I loved the Dodgers with a reckless passion. Every afternoon I scrambled down to the local candy store to catch the late-inning scores in the Brooklyn *Daily Eagle*.

When I was growing up, the media were a gentle supplement to living, not an overwhelming presence. People read the morning and evening papers, *Collier's* magazine and the *Saturday Evening Post*. Movies were Sunday serials of Douglas Fairbanks, Sr. leaping from parapets. Television was a remote juvenile joke, something that would let us peek into other people's homes (man on telephone to woman friend emerging from shower: "Boy, I wish we had television!"). Radio was still an esoteric novelty, something like surfing the Net in the 80s. Jack Benny and Fred Allen would begin trading quips on the air a few years later, and the Lone Ranger would be tracking down the bad guys, but the real potential of the medium would not be hinted at until President Roosevelt, under pressure from a hostile press, took his case directly to the public in his intimate, powerful "fireside chats."

So I counted on the *Eagle* to keep me abreast of the day's baseball developments. If there was no game, I invented one.

I forgave the Dodgers their trespasses, which were many. Pitchers got lost on their way to the ball park. Runners stumbled into disastrous collisions. The lower they sank, the more firmly I defended them. I have always been a patsy for the underdog.

I loved the Dodgers so fiercely because, other than my grandmother's sponge cake, in my pre-teen years I loved little else. As a youngster, I hated what and where I was: brightest, shiniest ornament on a spreading family tree. I squirmed under the stares of a dozen pairs of eyes fixed relentlessly, albeit affectionately, upon me: first grandson in the New

World, first son of two emotionally starved parents, first nephew of a competitive auntly squadron, each determined to put her stamp on me. I was the embodiment of long-cherished immigrant fantasies, the reluctant inheritor not only of wild hopes but of deep insecurities. Someone was always pawing me, surveying me. I woke one morning to find three females hovering over me: "Who's your favorite aunt?"

Family had a high priority in the pre-television era. So did friends. Most of our recreation and diversion was provided by ourselves: strolling in the park, singing around the piano, playing poker with round, colored "Necco" wafers as chips. The very notion of some outside element invading and even overrunning our homes was unthinkable.

Domestic unions were expected to be permanent. The marriage of my parents, although intermittently loving, brought together a bitterly frustrated man, nursing a moribund dream, and a Cinderella of fierce but hitherto squelched ambition.

My father, Sam Berkman, had by high school age acquired several academic prizes and a firm determination to serve humankind in what he considered the noblest of professions: as a physician. Well on the path to medical school, he was abruptly informed that the high tuition costs involved were beyond his family's means. They could, however, scrape up enough for the shorter curriculum of dentistry.

Enroute to Paradise, Sam had been bounced off the train. He never did get back on. Nor did he ever reconcile himself to the compromise and embrace dentistry seriously, so that while he became an excellent technician, frequently consulted by his peers, he was a lifelong failure as a business man, indignantly rejecting kickbacks, constantly scrambling for loans. My father once referred a patient to a specialist, who sent him a substantial check. Sam Berkman returned it untouched. The other dentist framed the check to commemorate a once-in-a-lifetime experience.

But my father never gave up on the dream, either. He simply tucked it away, for transfer to me. One day his son would fulfill his broken career. To crown his fantasy, he would return to complete his studies . . . as my medical school classmate.

That much he confided to me, and little else. It was a relationship which I would one day recreate on film between Anthony Perkins and Karl Malden in *Fear Strikes Out*. Black-moustached, smartly shod, my father maintained a conventional facade. But he continued to live in the unreality that had led him to abandon a prospering early practice for a tour of the concert halls and museums of Europe. Like an astronomer scanning the skies, I was constantly monitoring him for clues. But all my life Sam Berkman, stocky and massive-headed as Beethoven, would remain a remote, tormented figure whose terse staccato speech seemed to be torn in fragments from his mouth.

Voraciously curious—he once bought an encyclopedia set with money earmarked for rent—he was also extremely proper. Other people farted; Sam Berkman "effluviated." Sexual discussion was out of bounds. What little information I gleaned, I got from my mother.

Money was his scourge. I remember his nightly walk through the apartment, dousing lights: "I don't have to support Thomas Edison!" And too many mornings when, with the school trolley approaching, I held out my hand.

"I gave you a dime yesterday."

"I had to buy a notebook."

I heard the jiggle of coins as he reached hesitantly into his pocket. "Is a nickel enough?"

At this point my mother would emerge from the kitchen, dish towel in hand. "For God's sake, Sam, give the boy some money!"

That generally did it—until the next day. The hangover from those tense little clashes would color my approach to money for the rest of my life.

Once, to my astonished delight, my father came to sponge my back at a handball finals match. He never made even that much of a gesture toward my sister Helen, three years younger. And when he stunted on the beach, hc turncd his handsprings alone.

My mother's early years were equally shadowed. Eldest in a family of nine children, two of them invalids, Bertha Holtzmann had soon been drafted to surrogate motherhood, feeding, bathing and counseling a steady cycle of new babies. Plump and pretty, beloved "policeman" of a brawling household, Bertha took piano lessons at twenty-five cents an hour in order to relay them to neighbors at a profitable fifteen cents each. As soon as she was big enough to camouflage her age, she got a secretarial job. When her brother Jacob, spiraling upward in the law with the backing of ex-president Theodore Roosevelt, landed a publishing contract for a book on Municipal Court practice, it was Bertha who, suppressing her own yearnings for a career, served as his unpaid typist and unofficial editor. She had all the responsibilities of motherhood, with none of the rewards.

My arrival meant still another child—but with a monumental difference. This one was all her own, to mold as she saw fit. Her son would get the recognition she had been denied, by charging through school with gargantuan leaps, perennial occupant of the coveted "first row, first seat."

Toward this end I was under my mother's constant scrutiny, prodded to better performance, compared regularly and unfavorably with the neighborhood "model boy," one Lloyd Seidman. Since I could not hate my mother—needing such crumbs of support as she provided in the face of my father's silent frowns—I hated Lloyd Seidman with all my heart.

My mother left little question about who literally wore the pants in our family. I remember her at a Catskill summer resort, daringly outfitted in white slacks, puffing away smartly on a cigarette. When Teddy Roosevelt broke away from his fellow-Republicans in 1912 to form the renegade Bull Moose party, she filed its incorporation papers. She was a militant suffragette.

Her aplomb was astonishing. Years later, visiting me in England where I was writing movies, she was addressed by an autograph hunter as Mary Pickford. She graciously signed the star's name.

I was totally in her thrall: fascinated, adoring, intimidated. One evening I reported to her that the class bully, failing in an attempt to snatch my lunch box, had threatened to "get even tomorrow." She looked at me indifferently: "Go fight your own battles." I retreated to my room, blinking back tears, my emotional universe shattered. I remember running from her, up three flights of stairs, when faced with a dose of castor oil (the cure for everything in the 1920s). She caught me on the top landing and dragged me down by the collar. And the time when a store owner caught me slipping a *Tarzan* novel into my briefcase—an act that today would be diagnosed as a cry of desperation. I begged the man to impose any punishment he wished—"but don't tell my mother."

"Skipping" was my mother's obsession. Under her prodding, I bypassed no less than four grades in elementary school, thereby landing at the age of twelve instead of the normal fourteen in Boys' High School, a proudly (or notoriously) demanding institution. At Boys', my mother spurred me to clip six months off the four-year curriculum in order to graduate in June, thus qualifying for college in September. To advance my chances for a State Regents' scholarship, she wheedled permission from the high school principal for me to retake two of the Regents' tests. I obliged with the requisite improvements. But the process was draining.

By high school, propelled by my leap-frogging of grades into the company of older, more worldly boys, I found myself overmatched outside the classroom: last to be chosen for sandlot punchball games, first to be taunted into fights. I took refuge in *Tarzan*, the *Rover Boys*, *Tom Swift*, all pitifully naive and starry-eyed by today's standards. I thumbed through the *Saturday Evening Post* and *Collier's* backlogs in my father's office.

I had no inkling of Dr. Freud's theories, but I chafed under a feeling of separateness, isolation; of a secret self lost in the shadows, while the scarred achiever marched onward and upward. Other people were defining me, burying my personal nature under their various agendas. I was dimly aware of a nascent, half-formed inner man longing for expression. Instinctively I found sanctuary in the make-believe world of sports games, where alone in my room I could in my imagination chart the action. From there it was a short step, around my twelfth birthday, to writing.

My predilection for letters was of long standing. At the age of eight months, I am informed on reliable authority, I crawled into the cellar of my grandmother's home in Brooklyn, there encountered an ancient Underwood typewriter, and proceeded methodically to dismantle it, key by key.

My first poem, celebrating "the crack of the horsehide against the ash, the hit, the error—the homeward dash" won me a major league baseball. In high school, I advanced to reviewing plays.

Encouragement in these leanings came with the unexpected entry into my life of my Aunt Fanny, a dozen years my senior. A pint-sized dynamo with huge brown eyes, Fanny was determined to overcome her also-ran status in a large family where there was rarely enough money and never enough love to go around. She had slashed a solo path through night law school—the only girl in her class at Fordham—landed a job with a Broadway firm, and while still in her pigtails actually made serious inroads on the arts-and-entertainment scene. Her clients included Clifton Webb, ballet queen Alicia Markova and, across the Atlantic, sculptor Jacob Epstein. Fanny would make her bid for control of my soul—but not yet.

For an impressionable youngster, her mid-Manhattan suite was a smorgasbord of unpredictable delights. Traversing the marbled corridors of the Bar Building, I might trail behind matinee idol Leslie Howard or hear musical comedy star Gertrude Lawrence trilling a few bars on her way to rehearsal. I would find a Romanoff prince waiting for Fanny one day; the novelist Louis Bromfield the next.

Fanny herself might be on the phone talking in clipped British accents to His Majesty's ambassador in Washington, then shifting to earthy Yiddish to lay down the law to Broadway producer Max Gordon.

I was always welcomed with a flourish, then spirited past a smiling ticket-taker at a nearby matinee; Fanny was on easy terms with everybody on Broadway from stage door attendants to the brothers Shubert. At fifteen, I saw her as a fairy princess able to summon up unpurchasable intimacies at the touch of her wand; she once took me backstage to the *Band Wagon* dressing room where a quite bald Fred Astaire was removing his make-up.

Decades later, in my biography of Fanny, *The Lady and the Law*, I would devote nearly 400 pages to a study of her character and exploits; but in those formative adolescent years she was simply the siren of show business glamour for me, a siren against whom my father with his inarticulate protests on behalf of medicine was hopelessly outgunned.

The subterranean rivalry between Sam and Fanny erupted into a bitter argument one frosty, snow-blown afternoon as my father and I were tramping through the Botanical Gardens across Eastern Parkway from our apartment.

"You join a noble fraternity," he said suddenly.

"What?"

"When you enter medical school. Serving mankind. Their most basic need."

"I'm not so sure. Suppose there's a shipwreck, maybe fifty people cast away. "

"All right. What is their first concern? Food—and health."

"What about their need for emotional nourishment? It's artists who make life livable, laughable, who draw people together!"

"Artists!" A gust of wind blew my father's fur cap from his head. Bending to retrieve it, he shouted back over his shoulder. "Bums, half of them. Drunkards, lunatics!"

We were in a full-blown blizzard. My father, never at his best in verbal combat, paused to wipe the snow from his glasses. But he wasn't ready to abandon the field. "What good is music if you're too sick to enjoy it?"

"What good is health if there's nothing to enjoy?"

Neither of us mentioned the unspoken subtext, my father's longing to have me redeem his broken dream, his fear that I was being subverted by Fanny. We trudged on together in silence.

Curiously enough, for all our differences, I absorbed my father's insistence on honesty and his fundamentally dissident, reformist outlook on the world.

Pinned between combatants, I yearned to escape. A couple of hundred miles away, in the verdant hills above Lake Cayuga, stood Cornell University, its very name a chant of strength and dignity. Kids from Eastern Parkway did not normally aspire to the Ivy League. But Cornell offered a batch of scholarships through annual exams; and I had a sense of a private destiny, an unseen purpose, that might be nourished there.

Buckling down for once in my own interest, I breezed through the tests, finishing fourth in the state. Coupled with a Regents' award, the scholarship totally covered my tuition.

I started checking the train schedules to Ithaca. My father protested vehemently. "You can get just as good an education here, at City College. Without the living expenses!"

"Uncle Jack says he'll send me expenses. Seventy-five dollars a month."

Jack had swooped into some of the vacuum left by my father—at a price.

Jack had his own hollows to fill. Arriving in the United States at the age of nine as a greenhorn without a word of English, he had torn through the public schools and by nineteen had earned a law degree, successfully defended an accused murderer, and won the attention of ex-president Theodore Roosevelt. Carefully decked out in pince nez and high collar, he had barely missed election to Congress under the Bull Moose anti-trust banner.

But he had little personal life, and jumped at the chance to play uncle. It was Jack who in tribute to his patron dubbed me Teddy instead of the Edward on my birth certificate. Bent on weaning me away from my father's more firmly leftist politics—Sam leaned toward "socialized medicine"—Jack bought me banana splits and urged me to "go with the tide." I took the confection but not the advice. He wangled me free gym privileges at the Brooklyn Jewish Center, and took me to his box seat at Ebbets Field to cheer for my beloved Dodgers. He also saddled me with his own anxieties about looking and dressing right in a Gentile world, constantly adjusting my ties and criticizing my haircuts.

But Jack's intervention for Cornell was decisive. I made a mollifying concession to my father: my enrollment upstate would be as a pre-medical student.

In September of 1929 I arrived in Ithaca, at fifteen-and-a-half a husky youngster, thick-lipped and black-haired, with large brown eyes whose myopia I had concealed by memorizing the test chart at school. To the Holtzmann family, metaphorically perched on my shoulder, I was a doughty Lancelot carrying the ancestral banner into the fray.

To myself I was an outcast, unloved and unlovable, a boy who could win acceptance only by performing; an alien Jew, part of a hunted and haunted race, without financial resources. And something of an impostor to boot: in order to claim the university scholarship I had won at Cornell, which had a minimum entry age of sixteen, I had to fake my birth date by a year, moving it back to 1913.

I knew I had something to say—if I could dig down far enough to say it. I had a sense of a latent talent, a dimly perceived creative force, destined to leave an imprint on a highly imperfect world. But for the moment I was on my own, a bewildered adolescent who had been largely sheltered from the rough-and-tumble street life of his peers.

A month later the stock market collapsed; soon nearly a quarter of the country was out of work. Although Jack Holtzmann was hard hit, he never faltered in his commitment. I did, however, face chimeras of my own.

Cornell was one of the eight eastern Ivy League colleges, at a time when only a handful of other institutions had comparable status. The class of 1933 had in many cases been big frogs in their local puddles, and were now bent on staking out equal space in the national pond. The atmosphere was charged with rivalry, envy, and not a little snobbery.

I entered this arena with some odd lacunae. Although I later became a fair horseman, I had never learned to ride a bike. Nor could I brew coffee, sew a button, or charge a battery, making me a perfect target for campus pranksters who assured me galoshes were worn directly over socks. I was nearly forty before I discovered that banks would pay interest for the use of my money.

Freshmen scrambled for membership in a good "house," i.e. Greek-letter fraternity. The campus nurtured a caste system worthy of a medieval Japanese court. Delta Kappa Epsilon, for example—Deke—would be at or near the top of every list, certain to boast varsity lettermen, social bluebloods and editors of the Cornell Daily *Sun*. There were no Jews in Deke; ethnic segregation was absolute. Jewish students had their own fraternities, carefully rated in mimicry of the Gentile hierarchy.

Although Ezra Cornell had stipulated his desire to "found an institution where any person" could find instruction in any subject, it was understood that Jews were at Cornell on sufferance, subject to the will of the "white" majority. White meant Christian; it had nothing to do with blacks, who were virtually non-existent.

The tensions were subtle but real, and I was cruelly unprepared for them. Invited to my first fraternity rushing dinner, I completely fumbled an introduction to their star athlete and after dessert took refuge behind a *New Yorker*. I was not invited to become a brother.

Defying the portents, I tried out for the Glee Club. The auditions accompanist, a thin lemony man in his forties, led me through a series of ascending arpeggios. A sour smile crept across his face. "That's quite a baritone. Have you sung in public?"

"Summer camps and such. Do I qualify?"

"Musically, yes." He looked embarrassed. "But there isn't always room in the club for everyone who can sing." He hit a crashing dissonance. "I wouldn't count on it."

This was the climactic blow to a freshman year that was ninety percent pain. Not pursued by the best Jewish fraternities, I cultivated a protective net of Gentile friends, but never felt completely comfortable among them. My enrollment as a pre-med student meant lab courses in Comparative Anatomy and Physics. I was miserable in both.

My emotional life was correspondingly nil. This was the era of Tin Pan Alley's "Betty Co-ed," whose lyrics proclaimed that she had, among other things, "lips of red for Cornell." I was madly but surreptitiously infatuated with one Betty Andrews, the oh-so-Gentile willowy blonde campus queen, the epitome of remote, unattainable beauty; admission to her bed would obliterate my loathsome Jewishness. In the 1930s girls were quartered far across the campus, not across the hall. Undergraduate males were nearly all virginal; the occasional sophisticate who had reportedly bedded a local waitress or "town bag" was regarded with awe. Sex life for most freshmen was confined to evenings around a record player, where we clutched at our loins in mock ecstasy while Ruth Etting moaned "Cryin' for the Carolines."

At the end of the school year I pulled down a C in Comparative Anatomy, a barely-passing D in Physics—and a letter of rebuke from my father, my first and only correspondence from him during four college years. By contrast, my arts-college grades were all A's or B's. That summer, Sam Berkman bowed to the inescapable: his son was not destined for medicine.

Fanny, perhaps scenting victory, observed a discreet silence. But from every foray into Hollywood she would bring home autographed photos of such national goddesses as Clara Bow, known as the "It" girl, and Norma Shearer to ornament the walls of my dormitory room . . . and not incidentally to water my ambitions in writing and music.

My second year went better; I discovered Gershwin.

Music had always been part of my life. My mother sang, my father plucked a melancholy mandolin. Both were opera buffs. As a toddler, I perched on a piano bench beside my Aunt Stella who earned lunch money improvising keyboard accompaniment to silent movie melodramas. I sang folk songs and spirituals all through high school. My own piano studies, after running afoul of a crusty classics instructor, had flourished when I switched to the popular song field under the tutelage of Sylvia Fine.

Sylvia, the daughter of a family friend, was a feisty, bosomy brunette: not the long-legged golden blonde of my adolescent fantasies, but a skilled musician, prodigiously gifted lyricist and good company. I took her to my senior prom at Boys' High. Sylvia in turn asked me to several get-togethers where a tall, loose-limbed young man with theatrical ambitions invariably lurked in the background until prodded by Sylvia to display his vocal wares. His name was Daniel Kominski—but not for long. Danny Kaye and Sylvia Fine would be recurring motifs in my life.

A couple of months later I drifted off to college and the Berkman-Fine romance, always regarded more hopefully by the families concerned than by its principals, faded away.

But Sylvia's perceptive instruction didn't, enabling me to hear in Gershwin a fresh, powerful and singular voice. My introduction to the "Rhapsody in Blue" came in a downtown record store; it left me tingling, exhilarated, skirting the clouds. I walked the steep hill back to the campus in a daze (in later years I would reel under similar aftershocks after seeing *Journey's End* on Broadway and Michelangelo's Boy David statue in Florence). Gershwin's was a voice that spoke to me, and made me want to answer in kind. I couldn't wait to enroll in a harmony class.

I started composing, and in my junior year landed several tunes in the varsity show. As a full-fledged dramatic arts major, I reveled in the company of Aristophanes and Molière, the witty effronteries of Congreve and the scathing ironies of Strindberg. Willie Strunk, whose handbook on style would later be immortalized by E.B. White, hammered home a respect for words as living entities. It was a time when teachers still had a passion for teaching, before hands-on involvement gave way to considerations of tenure, research, and guest appearances on television.

Once, home for the holidays, I listened to the Cornell-Ohio State football game with my father. Radio was still in a prolonged infancy, associated mainly with Edgar Bergen's dummy Charlie McCarthy and "Amos 'n Andy," a broad dialect comedy series that used white actors to ridicule alleged black mannerisms. Radio drama, later a compelling theatrical form, was so little known that when Orson Welles in 1938 broadcast his adaptation of the H.G. Wells classic *War of the Worlds*, thousands fled to the hills in panic.

Somewhere around this time (my idea? my uncle's?) I decided I wanted to be a reporter. I loved to write, I was curious about the world, and I had visions of knightly service à la Lincoln Steffens, the turn-of-the-century muckraker.

My social life, previously limited to occasional invitations to fraternity dances, expanded to group auto excursions in which we wrestled on back seats with town girls, optimistically arming ourselves with condoms but having no opportunity to use them. For these adventures we all affected the camouflage of pseudonyms; I became "Ted Porter," in dubious tribute to the *soigné* Broadway composer.

At long last, with two classmates, I took my virginity to the town bordello, Carrie Jackson's, where a huge, gloomy and palpably bored Italian woman of advanced age (perhaps forty) helped me to accomplish the necessary rites. It was a strained, wretched and disillusioning experience, and probably the source of a subsequent lifelong distaste for mountainous thighs. However, by the start of my senior year I had developed sufficient self-confidence not only to acquire a co-ed girl friend, but to handle a comedy acting stint in *Boy Meets Girl*.

What I had not yet been able to deliver, with the D grade from my freshman year, was the Phi Beta Kappa key craved by my uncle Jack. Hurling myself into academic combat, I racked up seventeen hours of A's and vaulted into the coveted circle.

On the whole, college was finishing on a high note. There were the thrills of being young and merry and feeling we were the world's next leaders; of scrambling down from a morning in the library stacks overwhelmed by the beauty of knowledge; of stepping trim and vital from the Old Armory after a workout with the wrestling team.

It was a tremendous kick, an undreamed-of intoxication, to hear people humming my songs in the corridors, playing them on the concert grand in Willard Straight Hall. I had no inkling, of course, that Dorothy Sarnoff, capering through my operatic parody of a domestic crisis, would one day be raising her rich contralto on Broadway as Yul Brynner's wife in *The King and I*, or that Hildegarde would be performing my words and music at Eisenhower's White House. But I felt a welling-up of creativity, a crystallization of goals.

I even arrived at a kind of truce with my father who came up for his only visit to Ithaca. I worried shamelessly when, disregarding warnings about his "athletic heart," he trudged up the steep hill to my dorm; and I was choked with pride at the unexpected note of respect in the voices of my neighbors when they acknowledged introduction to Doctor Berkman.

I had tasted the Ivy League fruits of my ivory tower. My next stop would bring me down to earth.

CHAPTER 2

City Room

"This is it, Mr. Berkman." My uncle's chauffeur slid the long black Packard to a halt before a tall building on East 45th St. in Manhattan, and darted around to open the passenger door for me.

I hoped nobody was looking. In the dog days of the depression, the underpaid employees at my new job would not have been gratified by the trappings of my arrival. I loosened the collar around my bull neck, whisked an imaginary speck of dust from my right shoe, and like the tough reporters in gangster movies snapped down the brim of my gray fedora. I entered the Hearst Building and the world of newspapers.

Had my uncle Jack's corporate clients included the New York *Times*, my exposure to the scabrous underside of city life might have been considerably delayed; the *Times* was such a sprawling giant that its neophytes were often either sheltered from strife or lost in far-flung branches. As it happened, after the 1929 crash the newspaper client acquired by my mother's brother in the process of rebuilding his fortune was A.J. Kobler, publisher of the Hearst chain's *Daily Mirror*.

William Randolph Hearst, the best known if least admired newspaper tycoon in the nation, ruled over a publishing empire that at its zenith would include eighteen newspapers in twelve cities, nine magazines including *Good Housekeeping* and *Cosmopolitan*, the *American Weekly* syndicated supplement, and service organizations supplying news, features and photos. Rabidly conservative, without visible conscience, he was widely credited—or charged—with instigating the inflammatory press campaign that drove the United States into war with Spain over Cuba.

Bucking him in brawling competition for the New York market were seven other papers, each with a clear political alignment. The *Evening Sun* was as arch-Republican as the *World-Telegram* was liberal. Each side had its champion columnist: the lean, sardonic Westbrook Pegler on the right, roughly the equivalent of today's William F. Buckley; on the left, laying the groundwork for the future Ellen Goodmans, was rumpled, mountainous Heywood Broun, whose prose was as sparkling as his wardrobe was dreary. Only the *Times* pretended a pious objectivity—while prudently concealing certain staff affiliations.

The city had three tabloids, all direct descendants of the "yellow" journals which had fought the bitter circulation wars of the 1890s with wildly trumped-up stories and shrieking headlines. What the New York tabloids added was photography: copious, inventive and as sensational as they could get away with.

The *Mirror*, where my apprenticeship would begin was a rowdy, reckless newspaper whose pages reveled in sex, crime and gossip. As a scandal sheet it was surpassed in lurid detail only by the New York *Graphic*, and in circulation by its arch-rival, the *Daily News*. All three penny tabloids were big on photo coverage, and not inclined to be fussy about how they got it. A *Mirror* cameraman clambering down a skylight into a Ziegfeld Follies dressing room was likely to find a competitor from the *News* there ahead of him.

Pictures screamed for attention from the front and back pages of the *Mirror*. Intense coverage was devoted to the activities of "socialites," who lived on Park Avenue or in Newport and, to judge from the *Mirror*, occupied themselves largely with domestic squabbles. So popular among *Mirror* readers were the antics of these "fashionables" that one of the paper's major attractions was the Society column of Barclay Beekman, a name compounded of two snob-district telephone exchanges.

Crime, bred by hard times and bootlegging, found a hearty welcome in the tabloids. Killers like John Dillinger, "Baby Face" Nelson, "Dutch" Schultz and Bonnie and Clyde paraded across our front pages, vying with typical American delight in primacy for the title of Public Enemy Number One. The only limitation on murder coverage, I soon learned, was that the principals had to be white. Homicide in Harlem was a non-event.

Most other space was reserved for city politics, sentimental slobber by a trio of sob sisters, racetrack tips, comics, and gossip by-liners like Walter Winchell. The recently elected president, Franklin D. Roosevelt, might be turning the country upside down with his dynamic New Deal program; the *Mirror*, faithful to instructions from San Simeon, snorted at FDR's "Raw Deal" and either misrepresented or spiked its details.

Ultimately I found ways to pass along some of Hearst's more outrageous chicaneries to George Seldes, publisher of the peppery journal *In Fact*. A slow man with a compliment, Seldes got around to acknowledging the service fifty years later in a letter to the *Atlantic Monthly*.

Green as a Dartmouth College banner, I got off to an uneasy start, very aware of envious stares from office boys who had been haunting the city room for four or five years, hoping for a crack at a staff job, only to be by-passed in favor of a raw college kid who probably thought the composing room was a hang-out for musicians. Bar-hopping at 2 a.m., trying desperately to be one of the boys, I ordered a sherry flip, evoking cries of derision.

As the paper's most recent recruit, I was handed its least coveted job: the 6 a.m. morning desk, where I had to sift through all eight New York dailies and prepare a world-at-a-glance summary for the city editor. It was here that I caught my first whiff of the not-quite-believable Walter Winchell.

Winchell, like Ronald Reagan after him, symbolized an era. Dapper and glib, a tap-dancer turned gossip-monger turned pundit, he soared from the back alleys of Broadway to the confidential chambers of official Washington, forging links to FBI chief J. Edgar Hoover and the Roosevelt White House, reaching his zenith during World War II with Sunday night radiocasts to "Mr. and Mrs. America and all the ships at sea."

Winchell had a breezy air, a breathless delivery, and a knack for brisk staccato phrases—in which he was greatly abetted by clever press agents eager to plant the names of their clients in his widely syndicated (fifty million readers!) column.

In exchange for a contributed *bon mot* (which of course Winchell would present as his own), the flack's customer would be mentioned in some trumped-up context of achievement or romance. The columnist was colorful, unreliable, and like all rampant egomaniacs, desperately insecure.

On a blustery January morning in 1934, I had descended at 5:30 a.m. to an icy Brooklyn subway platform, just in time to hear one of the rare express trains vanishing in the distance; then, after a long shivery wait, been transported to Grand Central station, from which five blocks of trudging through heavy snow took me to the office. There, after plowing through piles of overnight teletype copy, I was plucking items out of the other papers for my summary when I heard quick footsteps in the hall.

Winchell bounced in, tie askew, fedora tipped back in the cocky newshound image popularized by the movie of *The Front Page* . . . nonetheless, in his camel's hair coat and sharply creased trousers, floating an aura of show business. He had been on his usual nocturnal prowl of haunts like the Stork Club where he gleaned most of his column material—and he couldn't wait to tell somebody about it. "That showgirl-ship owner honeymoon is over, kid. Nobody will admit it but she slipped out of their dream igloo on Sutton Place at three o'clock this morning; Sally will be suing for two million, saying she gave up a great career as a dancer. If you ask this reporter, her greatest folly was leaving the Follies." He beamed at me and moved on. It made no difference whatever to him that his audience was a callow twenty-year-old submerged in a story about mounting unrest in central Europe. Having unloaded his bulletin, he vanished into his cubicle nearby.

In succeeding weeks he would frequently drift in, sometimes in evening clothes, to regale me with tales of his night's adventures. But he gave no sign of even knowing my name until a year later when, promoted to a night rewrite desk, I was ordered to take a story being phoned in by Winchell—some sort of marital squabble—and whip it into shape under his by-line. I mimicked the bravura Winchell style well enough to elicit a thank you phone call.

I tried to parlay this minor recognition into an approach to Winchell's Girl Friday, Ruth Cambridge, who undulated languidly across the city room like a sex-hungry lioness, her insinuating hips inflaming the working staff (later she married the dancer/actor Buddy Ebsen). My gambit didn't work. Winchell and his entourage were an aloof circle, out of bounds for the hired help, beyond appeal or reproof—until his clash with Jacques Lait.

The columnist's free-wheeling innuendoes and careless handling of facts had caused occasional grief for Hearst's attorneys. But Winchell sold a lot of papers; as the *Mirror's* star attraction he was treated like an errant princeling whose breaches of accuracy, literacy and taste were to be, if not welcomed, overlooked. His effusions were not subjected to the customary scrutiny by the copy desk, but were cleared personally by the *Mirror's* burly, profane Executive Editor, Jacques Lait.

Among Winchell's bag of tricks was a once-a-week mix of rumors, gossip and speculation to which he gave the swaggering title, "Private Papers of a Reporter." In crusty humor on a hot afternoon, Lait ran a red pencil through the line. Appearing unannounced in Winchell's office, he bent low over the ex-hoofer's desk, iron jaw jutting. "When did you become a reporter, Walter?"

"Why, uh, I guess I've been with the paper about—"

"A reporter, I said! When did you ever cover a fucking fire, sit through a police line-up, interview the survivors of a plane wreck? That's what reporters do, Walter." The message was clear: Winchell had never earned the spurs he jangled so freely. Lait plunked down the offending page. The weekly heading would have to be changed.

Enraged, Winchell sulked and snorted for an hour. Then it was his turn to storm into Lait's sanctum and fling his copy on the desk. A single word had been inserted; the world would hereafter share the private papers of a *cub* reporter.

Lait initialed the change without comment. He had made his point.

Although I had my own problems with the cantankerous Lait, I had to admire his Jacques-the-giant-killer egalitarianism. I never knew him to pull rank except in the matter of the call-girl—or she might have been an ardent amateur—who occupied an apartment across the street from the news room and frequently left her drapes open, affording the night staff an evening's entertainment. Here Lait always asserted his authority; whoever held the prime observation post at the window always fell back to make way for the boss.

The *Mirror* boasted a lofty pyramid of editors, with a dizzying series of overlapping titles. On any given afternoon the high-priced bosses were likely to outnumber the copy boys; the city room echoed with the clang of brass stumbling over each other. Tight-fisted with his lower-echelon employees (I started at fifteen dollars a week), Hearst spared no expense in hiring some of the most illustrious names in pre-electronic journalism. Near the top of the heap glowered the legendary Walter Howey, tough and monosyllabic, who as a Chicago firebrand had served as the model for Walter Burns, hard-bitten city editor of the Ben Hecht-Charles MacArthur theater classic *The Front Page*.

Directly below Howey stood Managing Editor Stanley Walker, a laconic Texan who had risen to national prominence as city editor of the New York *Herald-Tribune*. Hearst had simply swept Walker aboard, much as he imported medieval chapels, by brandishing an enormous checkbook; it was some months before both men discovered there was nothing for Walker to do in the *Mirror's* crowded executive suite, where additional colorful figures like Paris-born Lait vied for attention. And at the stratospheric summit, on the very edge of the imperial throne, perched a personal favorite of the satrap of San Simeon, popular commentator Arthur Brisbane. Small and sour, Brisbane was best known for a column dismissing the country's two leading heavyweight boxers as no match, together, for a gorilla.

In the noisy, cluttered city room, a far cry from today's computer-fed mausoleums, I felt as if I had a box seat at a royal conclave. It was a thrill just to be in the ambiance of such mythic figures. I gaped as Howey, heading for the men's room like any ordinary mortal, passed within a foot of my desk. I froze in awe when Brisbane invited me to ride downtown with him in his chauffeured limousine.

Descending almost to the working level at the *Mirror*, one encountered handsome, gray-thatched Hinson Stiles, the Assistant Managing Editor. Stiles turned up once or twice a day at odd hours, preferring to spend his time at Tim Costello's bar around the corner on Third Avenue. Apart from its drink-cadging possibilities, Costello's was graced by a huge James Thurber mural depicting a young woman in football uniform galloping down field, bestowing a vicious stiffarm on a frustrated male tackler. The caption read something like "Wellesley 38, Yale 0." Late at night Stiles might be in one of the racier Broadway night clubs, whose press agents freely roamed the city room. They got lots of space in the paper's amusement section, and Stiles got lots of on-the-cuff entertainment.

Eyeing Stiles with quiet contempt was the man I worked for, George Clarke. A puckish, flamboyant Irishman, described by *Time* magazine as "the fastest city editor in town," Clarke lit up the news room from the moment he arrived, gliding to his desk with enormous strides despite a severe limp. His deep blue-eyed glance held a lurking humor; I thought his hawklike broken nose made him look like a pirate.

One of my 6 a.m. chores was to give Clarke a wake-up call at home. It became his whim, upon learning of my musical interests, to whisper "Sing me a little tune;" later he would introduce me to Ferde Grofé, composer of "Grand Canyon Suite" and orchestrator of "Rhapsody in Blue."

Far more importantly, in succeeding weeks he rescued me from the early beat and sent me out on every imaginable assignment: police stations, courts, beauty contests, riots. I had a fling at City Hall, where Mayor La Guardia, squat and sharp-tongued, eyed me belligerently. La Guardia had a reputation for eating fledgling newsmen alive. He was indeed a daunting figure, a feisty little bullfrog of a man hunched forward at his desk behind heavy black-rimmed glasses, a mop of black hair falling across his forehead. "What paper are you from?" he demanded.

"The uh, *Mirror*."

I thought he was going to place me under arrest. But he nodded and moved on.

I interviewed Senator Huey Long, the blustering dictator of Louisiana. Sprawled on a hotel bed in stockinged feet, large and bucolic, "The Kingfish" lectured me on the evils of Roosevelt's New Deal. Listening to his oratorical flourishes—his favorite phrase was a booming *ipso facto*—I could sense his appeal to redneck millions. A year later, aspiring to a fascistic takeover of the White House, Long was assassinated.

I covered suicides, and shuddered through the arrival at the morgue of ice-caked bodies after a disaster at sea.

As I began to feel at home, I looked forward to the unpredictable drama of each new day. The very air of the city room was charged with excitement. Everything was heightened here, more real than everyday reality. I felt we were at the heart of the volcano.

From my vantage point, the best thing about the *Mirror* was its chronic shortage of personnel. Gaps in the rewrite staff gave me opportunities to fashion my own stories.

However, space limitations forced economy of language. Writers for the *Times* could ramble all over the map, confident that its bulging columns would accommodate their reveries. At the *Mirror* you had to zero in on the essence fast; had to learn what information was vital so that if a harassed make-up man lopped off the last half of your story, what was left would still make sense. Either you got the meat-and-potatoes message or your copy wound up on the "overset," the columns of type matter that no reader ever saw. I particularly admired the paper's rewrite ace, Jim Whitaker. Placid and dignified as a walrus, he seemed somehow able to stay aloof from the *Mirror's* seedier side. And his prose sang like a Vivaldi chorale.

Less of a literary model was Bernard Sobel, the *Mirror* drama critic, who after years of extravagant tub-thumping as publicity man for Florenz Ziegfeld was incapable of expressing himself in anything but friendly superlatives. His fulsome hyperboles delighted producers, but were a questionable guide for playgoing readers. On a night that had two simultaneous Broadway openings, Clarke let me cover one of them; he pronounced my report "the first literate play review we've ever carried."

Still, even with Clarke's support I had crises of self-doubt. I experimented with elevator shoe-lifts to increase my five foot-eight inch height; worried about an incipient bald spot. At college I had reluctantly become reconciled to the need for glasses; now I discarded them, sometimes perilously, whenever possible. My romantic forays were few and too anxiety-ridden for pleasurable consummation.

Clarke was consistently amusing. After assigning one of his reporters to a somewhat ribald exposé of a nudist colony, he decided the author of the piece would be safer if his true identity remained unknown. So Jim Bishop became James De Priest.

Filling in as assistant city editor one afternoon, I tossed a short piece of copy onto his desk: "Five beautiful showgirls were sexually assaulted yesterday in the lobby of the Plaza Hotel by a clique of millionaire brokers."

Expressionless, Clarke penciled the page and flipped it back. He had given it a 2-1-18 headline, the minimum treatment accorded to harmless fires, petty thefts and routine weather reports.

I never knew why Clarke stayed on the *Mirror*. He moved easily in New York's creative circles. Unlike Arthur Brisbane or Walter Howey, he had no inside track to the gold vaults at Hearst Castle. I heard rumors of a past bout with alcoholism, but nothing tangible ever surfaced.

The single most memorable lesson of my *Mirror* years came on a hot August afternoon in 1934 when a sudden strike closed down New York's bustling garment district. Orders began piling up, picket lines were attacked, tempers flared.

Dispatched to the lower West Side, I scurried from union offices to manufacturing headquarters, covering wads of copy paper with defiant quotes. Back in the city room, I was turned over to rewrite man Arthur Mefford, a flinty scowling ex-police reporter. As I started reciting my statements, Mefford shoved an evening newspaper in my face. Banner headlines screamed of a violent clash that, while I had been collecting interviews, had erupted in Times Square. "Your first job," bawled Mefford, "is to find out what's happening! After that, what somebody says about it."

That simple summation would help me penetrate many a political fog in decades to come, and to separate the reality of an event from a self-serving press release about it. With this awakening came a gradual realization that newspaper work was more than a craft, more even than an exhilarating way of touching life at its core. It carried also an obligation to record the experience as honestly as possible, a relentless pursuit of facts, an insistence on checking things out, a refusal to settle for the agreeable façade. That in turn dictated a whole new way of observing: developing an x-ray eye for distinguishing between appearances and realities, along with a keen ear for the spurious phrase and polite fiction, whether in a campaign speech or a war communiqué. Officials had no monopoly on information or wisdom. Nobody was above suspicion—or at least skepticism. Facts had to be rooted out, pious public postures exposed, a tough-minded insulation against phoniness cultivated.

That unspoken newsmen's code pervaded the humblest and shabbiest of newsrooms. On the night in spring of 1940 when the German army invaded Denmark, even Hinson Stiles, our resident lazy *bon vivant*, snapped to attention, summoning up the ghost of a lost integrity. Like Molière's *Médicin Malgré Lui*, he became a newspaperman in spite of himself, once more a spirited member of the Fourth Estate, that unruly band of free spirits nurtured in pre-revolutionary France which previously had known only the three established "estates of the realm": aristocracy, clergy and common people.

American newspaper tradition took the French precedent even higher. We were the eyes and ears of an informed electorate, a keystone of democracy. New York newspaper publisher Peter Zenger, imprisoned in 1735 for his attacks on corrupt officialdom, was successfully defended by Alexander Hamilton. A hundred years later, abolitionist Elijah Lovejoy gave his life to defend his presses in Illinois. And in between, Thomas Jefferson declared he would prefer newspapers without a government to a government without newspapers.

Half a century ago this torch, however dimmed, still burned, something subliminal whose faint aroma one breathed in the air of every newsroom. And the newsman's way of perceiving has been a gift to me far transcending the inadequacies of one sloppy little newspaper, an indispensable antidote in a world where puffery has become ubiquitous. Roaming the corridors of the United Nations, the skies over Jerusalem, the lush dreamland of Hollywood, part of me never left the city room of the New York *Mirror*.

One of my ritual tasks at my Winchell-haunted dawn desk was a hunt through the Communist columns of the *Daily Worker* in search of likely photo stories; the *Worker* bristled with notices of upcoming parades and demonstrations.

It also bristled with fiery editorials. I was intrigued, if not then or ever converted, by the *Worker's* broadsides against the inequities of industrial society. Soon Steinbeck was creeping into my consciousness, along with Erskine Caldwell and the Italian author of *Bread and Wine*, Ignazio Silone. Their anger fell on fertile soil, fed by Sam Berkman's interest in socialized medicine and his wife's suffragette stand.

Fueled by their indignation, I wrote a long passionate piece about a court trial I had been covering every day, growing out of the ejection of a Polish-American farmer from his land by the Public Service Corporation of New Jersey. It wound up in the June, 1936 issue of the mildly leftist *American Spectator*: my first appearance, other than a few short fiction pieces sold to Hearst's King Features syndicate, in a national publication. I found a fierce satisfaction in tracking the story down, a sense of rightness, strongly felt if rarely articulated, that for decades to come would define my wellspring as a writer: a passion for truth regardless of consequences; to propound it, defend it, and where it was violated, to expose the violation relentlessly. As my career expanded, I would get sidetracked occasionally by ambition or circumstance, but I never stayed away long.

One of those excursions occurred shortly afterward, when my journalistic career was abruptly interrupted by Mary Astor. Miss Astor, a brunette screen siren of considerable renown and far-flung amatory interests, had recorded the intimate details of her love life in a journal which after being slavered over by tabloid editors as the "Mary Astor Diary" had acquired a more devoted following than anything since *Uncle Tom's Cabin*; a much-quoted passage provided an enthusiastic box-score of the successive climaxes she had enjoyed with tall, skinny playwright George S. Kaufman, hitherto regarded as a likelier candidate for cadaver than for Casanova.

The diary surfaced during an ongoing court battle between Miss Astor and a former husband for custody of their small child. Since the lady moved, or gyrated, in Hollywood's most eminent circles, the daily excerpts from her musings rocked the film colony. Some famous heads stirred uneasily in their connubial chambers, fearful of unwelcome reviews of their off-the-set extramarital performances. Other, less celebrated former lovers scanned the Astor lists eagerly, hoping for a mention that would catapult them to national attention.

None of this was lost, of course, on the scandal-splashing New York tabloids. At the *Mirror*, always a step behind the *News* in circulation, voluminous wire service reports on the steamy diary were turned over to a member of the rewrite staff for tender cultivation of their erotic possibilities, then published as a "Special to the *Mirror*" dispatch under a Hollywood dateline, as if we had a live correspondent on the scene.

Which is what I briefly became, thanks in part to my enterprising Aunt Fanny. During my college years, Fanny had kept up a discreet drumbeat of photos, postcards and matinee tickets, meanwhile accumulating as clients Fred Astaire, Noel Coward and the brilliant director of *Grand Hotel*, Edmund Goulding. Now she had an inspiration: "I've got a couple of contracts to clean up on the West Coast, Teddy. Why don't you come along? I'll get a tax write-off on your railroad fare. You might meet a producer or two."

I hesitated. I was just beginning to hit my stride as a literary crusader. On the other hand, maybe there was gold and glory in them thar Hollywood hills.

George Clarke threw in the clincher: "We'll pay you double space rates for anything you can dig up on the Mary Astor story."

Actually, the *Mirror* didn't owe me a thing. It had helped me break out of the suffocating embrace of family, cut through the smokescreen of appearance to the naked core of reality, and take my first tentative steps toward self-sufficiency. Its pungent if disreputable aroma might persist even in the glittering jungle of Fanny's Hollywood.

CHAPTER 3

The Industry

I was eager to taste the wonders of the movie world, but dubious about their price tags. For a couple of weeks I filed stories to the *Mirror* on the Mary Astor case, unblushingly supplied by its judge, Goodwin Knight, who would soon be bucking for governor. I basked in the spurious glory of having ostensibly peeked in her diary (which I had not).

Fanny launched my exploration of the film colony with a visit to the Walter Wanger lot on Melrose Avenue. Dartmouth-educated Wanger, a short but rather dashing figure in natty polo togs, took great pride in his status as the only college man among the major producers. He made a point of reading two books a week, hired prominent left-wingers like Group Theater playwright Clifford Odets, and had just bought the rights to gadfly newsman Vincent Sheean's *Personal History*. But he never followed through on Odets's sizzling screenplay of the Spanish Civil War, *The River Is Blue*; and his approach to Sheehan's thoughtful autobiography submerged it in Hollywood heroics. To crown his ambiguities, the half-Jewish producer sported on his desk a huge autographed photo of Benito Mussolini.

After an exchange of Ivy League pleasantries, Wanger tossed a script in my lap and invited me to attend a story conference at his home that evening. Carolwood Drive, a quiet tree-lined road off Sunset Boulevard, spiraled up to his predictably baronial mansion. There I found Wanger with two other conferees: the German director Fritz Lang and a man of undefined function named Arthur Ripley.

I looked down the hall. "Are we going to wait for the fellows who did the script?"

Wanger threw me a patronizing glance. "They'd only get in the way." That was the first hint I had of the writing fraternity's rank on the Hollywood totem pole. I looked over at Lang, who seemed grimly amused.

Lang, famous for a half-dozen cinematic landmarks including the 1926 silent classic *Metropolis*, was stocky and somber, very deliberate of speech, wary-eyed behind heavy tortoise-shell glasses. *Metropolis* projected a dictatorial future in which faceless workers dwarfed by machines became machines themselves in order to better serve their masters. Films had a more serious impact in Europe than in America. When Lang followed up a few years later with the anti-Nazi *Treatment of Dr. Mabuse*, he was invited to a meeting with Dr. Joseph Goebbels, Hitler's Minister of Propaganda, who offered him sovereignty over the entire German film industry. Lang replied that he was "tickled pink," deeply honored—then promptly packed everything he owned and left for Paris. His wife, the aristocratic Thea von Harbor, stayed behind and became a dedicated Nazi.

Oddly enough, I found Ripley more intriguing. A lanky, lugubrious graduate of the silent comedy school (he had directed one of Chaplin's few rivals, the doleful, pathetic Harry Langdon), he was totally miscast for the role of man-about-Hollywood. He rated zero in small talk and buttering up the boss; all he had going for him was native intelligence and mastery of the film craft—neither quality highly prized in the studio world. Wanger kept him on salary—a pitiful salary, I would discover—as an insurance policy against the transgressions of the high-priced duo who had perpetrated the script under discussion, *You Only Live Once*.

Starring Henry Fonda, Sylvia Sidney and William Gargan, this was the story of a three-time loser falsely accused of a major robbery, who in a desperate jail break accidentally killed the prison chaplain. The script I had read, while inherently theatrical, was fuzzy in characterization and motive and appallingly long.

The setting in Wanger's home was plush—heavy curtains, splendid carpeting—as befitted a Hollywood pasha.

Lang fixed an eye on me. "You understand vot the story says, the theme?"

"Sure. Fonda never has a chance. He's a victim of society."

Wanger, the Mussolini fan, frowned. "What did society ever do to you?" He reached over for a briefcase and hauled out a script. "Everybody up to date on this? The new yellow pages?"

Nods. "Ja."

"What do you think of the rewrite on the opening, Fritz?"

"Is better."

"Rip?"

"It gives Fonda a clearer motivation."

"So the audience will be rooting for him?"

Ripley shook his long, melancholy head. "Only if your dialogue is stronger. Right now it's movie dialogue, not the way people talk."

Wanger toyed with a gold medallion strung around his neck. "Five thousand a week I'm paying my writers, and he doesn't like their dialogue!" He turned to Lang. "You were worried about balance, Fritz. How much footage we could sustain after the jail break."

"Balance is okay now. First act, second act, ending . . . "

"I don't think so, Mr. Lang," I found myself saying. After all, I had studied dramatic structure at Cornell. He was merely the most famous director in Europe.

The German looked startled. "You don't sink so. Vy?"

"Because the climax is so powerful. Once Fonda kills the chaplain, nobody's going to sit around for the long, slow wind-up in the script."

Wanger stared. "How would you write it?"

"Shorter and tighter. You can't slide down from a mountaintop to a valley."

Ripley uncoiled his gaunt frame and lighted a cigarette. "The man has a point, Walter."

Long silence. Lang took off his glasses, put his hand up to his chin. "Let me sink about it."

After the meeting broke up, I reflected on my folly. Yes, the questionable status of writers in Hollywood was dismaying. But not insurmountable. Good pictures were somehow slipping past: *The Informer*, *All Quiet on the Western Front*, *Stagecoach*, and delicious comedies like *It Happened One Night* and the Marx Brothers' *Day at the Races*.

And I saw infinite potential for more. The medium was bigger than its current exploiters. Film, with its universal language of movement, transcended differences of wealth and culture, could galvanize masses in undeveloped corners of the world.

I had been handed a rare opportunity, allowed into the very front lines of movie-making. Why had I blown it by sounding off like a cocky schoolboy?

The next morning, Wanger called. Lang had been impressed, if not entirely persuaded. I could join Wanger's payroll at a lordly hundred dollars a week (equal to a thousand today) as back-up man to Arthur Ripley, the studio's gloomy ghost. I reported this coup to George Clarke in New York, who promptly granted me an open-ended leave of absence. Chalk up Round One for Fanny.

After expanding my wardrobe with a couple of floppy-collared sports shirts—*de rigueur* for screen writers—I was ready for action. Ripley took me out for coffee and a somber briefing. "Back East," he said, "You didn't get much money but you got respect. Here, Harry Warner calls writers 'schmucks with Underwoods.'"

"Without the 'schmucks' there wouldn't be any movies!"

"That's why they can't forgive you." He bit into a bagel. "Writers are considered unavoidable nuisances to be milked, squeezed dry and discarded. Working on a script, they're juggled and combined like chefs in a restaurant, one to lay out the plot line or main course; a dialogue specialist for garnishing; a team of anonymous gag writers for final spicing."

"So they must have some prestige. After all—"

Rip shook his head. "You don't understand the system." According to Rip, the movie world observed a rigid pecking order. In majestic seclusion at the top were the studio moguls, a small clique largely unhampered by taste or conscience, furiously promoting the main business of The Industry, the marketing of magic profiles.

Next in importance to the owners of the profiles were the hirelings entrusted with maximizing their charms: directors able to infuse their performances with some semblance of reality; cameramen skilled in manipulating lights and finding flattering angles; hairdressers and make-up men; costume designers; publicity staffs.

Moving up the ladder were agents like Charlie Feldman, who boasted of having had "a verbal talk" with Zanuck. Writers? An afterthought.

Ripley and I were to perform anonymous clean-up scripting services for Wanger's two official star authors, Gene Towne and Graham Baker. The assignment reminded me of the Sanitation Department plows in Brooklyn sweeping up the copious horse-droppings after a parade.

As new pages drifted in from Wanger's five-thousand-dollars-a-week team, the image proved all too apt. I promptly (but privately) dubbed the team Clown and Faker. Gene Towne had reportedly been an underwear salesman in the Midwest, an association which he never totally shed; it was his habit to work clad only in sandals and undershorts. Dumpy and balding, with a fire-engine red mustache, he looked like a circus clown caught in an offguard moment.

At best semi-literate, Towne never resorted to pencil or typewriter, dictating his inspirations loudly to a stenotypist, counting on her to rectify his more glaring abuses of language. This didn't matter since his communication with Wanger was entirely spoken and ad libbed, most effectively from a barefooted perch atop the producer's desk. "It's the difference between shit and ice cream!" he would bawl of a proposed dialogue change. Rumor, which I have no reason to doubt, said Towne was the model for the zany screenwriter in the Sam and Bella Spewack comedy classic, *Boy Meets Girl*. Wanger found his tactics captivating; the college-proud producer thought nothing of committing himself to an expensive story purchase on the strength of a flight of oratory by the ex-underwear salesman. In fairness to Towne, he did have a gift for the one-shot spectacular situation. But at that point his contributions ended; he passed the baton to his partner.

Graham Baker, a genial, fatherly-looking former rewrite man for the Brooklyn *Daily Eagle*, was as conservative and methodical as Towne was mercurial. His job was to transform Towne's eruptions into plausible prose, and to add dialogue which if not scintillating was at least an improvement over Towne's embarrassing effusions. The screenplays (screen ploys might have been more nearly accurate) resulting from this emulsion of eccentricity and mediocrity were invariably lumpy, requiring the intervention of nameless craftsmen like Rip and the occasional hiring of additional-dialogue specialists like David Hertz, who fashioned the memorable love scenes in *History Is Made At Night*. But this chaotic, patched-together assembly line approach to movie-making was precisely the style in vogue in a town where newcomers were all but announced according to rank as they arrived at parties: "Ted Berkman, ghost second class, Wanger, one hundred dollars a week."

History Is Made At Night grafted an international romance (Paris-accented suave Charles Boyer, cherubic Jean Arthur) onto a Titanic-like disaster at sea (Boyer, I was pleased to note, had no scruples about supplementing his Continental charm with high-heel lifts). Half-way through the shooting, with new pages constantly altering the climactic sinking scene, director Frank Borzage decided he'd had enough. Wanger turned over the camera reins to Ripley; the actors would be handled by a promising young dialogue director from the Princeton Triangle Club named Joshua Logan.

Beefy and energetic, his features obscured by a bushy moustache, Logan leaped onto the set, roaring my wild lines for the iceberg-collision crisis with a gusto that gave me an electric jolt. His uninhibited shriek-from-the-lungs—"Flooding aft of bulkhead forty-five! All hands stay forward of forty-five!"—was my first experience of how a strong performance could magnify and even transform the written word. Logan would have a brief fling at movie-making, then move on to a major Broadway career as writer-director, identified particularly with *South Pacific*.

For a twenty-two-year-old from New York, Hollywood had its blissful aspects: balmy orange-scented air, cozy cottages nestled among towering palms, tennis under a bright January sun. Smog had not yet settled over the Los Angeles basin; Hollywood Boulevard was decades away from its present tawdry mimicry of Times Square; there were more restaurants and flower shops along the Sunset Strip than drug-dealers and hookers.

Girls there were galore: girls from Dubuque and New Orleans and Apple Creek, Maine, haunting the famous soda fountain at Schwab's drug store, hoping to be discovered; car-hopping in tight skimpy halters (hoping to be discovered), patrolling the talent agencies and studio casting offices.

But I was ill-equipped to explore this sexual smorgasbord. My few successes in New York had been among ordinary mortals. Who was I to compete in this league of iridescent beauties, male and female? I had no confidence in my own appeal; and without confidence there are few conquests.

What rescued my personal life—although not without cost to my sense of social adequacy—was the presence in Hollywood of two ex-buddies from the *Mirror*, Ring Lardner, Jr. and Ian McLellan Hunter.

Both were strapping six-footers, fellow-dropouts from Princeton, polished and sophisticated, hard drinkers. Although both would win Oscars—Ian for *Roman Holiday* and Ring for *Woman of the Year* and *M*A*S*H*—each suffered terribly when his fervent political idealism took him afoul of the Red scare in the 1950s. I wore my two Princeton giants as talismans shielding me from my invisible yellow star of Jewishness.

Ring, the son and namesake of one of America's most celebrated humorists, was the first of our trio to reach Hollywood, as a publicity operative for David O. Selznick. At the time of my arrival he had already done his stint of successful ghosting, working with Budd Schulberg to revamp the Dorothy Parker-Alan Campbell script of *A Star Is Born* (neither neophyte, of course, received any credit). An extremely good-looking young man who insisted he wore glasses only to fend off frenzied pursuers, Ring was in a romantic quandary, unable to decide which of Selznick's two secretaries enthralled him the most. To both he penned a note: "Dearest Corinne and darling Sylvia, I couldn't love you more if there were twilvia." (He also came up with a rhyme pegged to his grandiose boss, something to the effect that not even Philadelphia's Independence Hall, "with its famous bell's nick," could rival the glory of David O. Selznick).

Ring was in the mogul's office when the news came over the radio that the Prince of Wales was abdicating to marry Wallis Simpson.

"My God!" ejaculated Selznick. "The Empire is ruined."

A strange sentiment, Ring observed, for a citizen of Pittsburgh, Pennsylvania.

Ring and I decided to take an apartment together. Fanny, unable to restrain her managerial impulses, found something better: a small stone house, complete with pool, surrounded by a walnut grove in Tarzana, now a crammed mini-metropolis, then a virtual wilderness. Ring was the most delightful of roommates, indolent (a beer can was always on the table, within reach, when he played ping-pong; he would spend fifteen minutes corkscrewing his way out of a garage rather than walk a block for his cigarettes) and unpredictable (one escapade ended with Ring and a donkey guiding each other carefully up four flights of stairs). He claimed to be working on a book—*Swimming, Drinking and Communism*—but I never saw any pages.

Twice he delivered unsolicited but still-remembered compliments. As we were juggling story ideas one evening, he remarked on the improvisations with which I embellished a theme: evidence, he declared, of the most fertile imagination he had ever encountered. More importantly, on another occasion he volunteered to share a batch of treasured letters from his father. He read them tenderly; I felt most honored. I have often reflected since on the egotistical practice of calling an offspring junior—surely an unfair burden, especially when senior has a reputation. Recently I posed the query to Wolcott Gibbs, Jr., a novelist whose father was a renowned drama critic for *The New Yorker*; had he ever thought of commenting on the subject? Gibbs paused, then grimaced: "Cuts too close to the bone," he said.

Ring and I had one domestic crisis. The most compassionate of men, he had, after attending a union rally in San Pedro, brought home a striking dock worker to take over our kitchen. George's meals were tasty enough, but his grocery bills were rocketing, and his employers were both getting visibly fat. One afternoon we stayed home to watch: George cooked mainly with butter, emptying it by the cup into every pot. It was an impasse: he was lost without his butter; we'd be lost if we kept consuming it. We flipped a coin to see who would give him the bad news. Ring had to struggle through the unhappy assignment.

Ian Hunter—he used the "McLellan" to distinguish himself from a screen actor of the period—was the epitome of debonair charm, from the languid purr of his slight English accent to the studied abandon of the handkerchief in his breast pocket. The son of a World War I captain in the British Navy, he wore rugged tweed jackets from De Pinna that accented his beefy country-squire good looks. Ian had been a two-hundred-pound tackle on the Princeton freshman football team, although it was hard to imagine him suffering the discipline of a training table. He had lived with his family on Park Avenue in New York, where in time-honored aristocratic fashion he borrowed regularly from the doorman; however proletarian his politics, he never lost his patrician aura and was rarely parted from his upper-class aplomb.

Ian had been signed as a junior writer by MGM at the recommendation of Ben Hecht, whom he met on a Latin American cruise ship. The studio had paired him with a friendly illiterate—somebody's cousin—

who quickly agreed to a companionable division of labor: the cousin would bring in firewood, fetch sandwiches, and replenish when necessary the supply of Johnny Walker Black Label; Ian would write "their" scripts.

Like Ring, Ian liked a couple of drinks at lunch and dinner, and sometimes in between. Big men, they were both proud of their capacities. One Saturday afternoon the three of us were at Don the Beachcomber's, where customers were restricted to two drinks each of the mixed-rums special. I, notorious as a cheap drunk, got about halfway through my first sampling of the powerful concoction. My two friends polished off their double rations, finished my drink and then split the refill . . . after which Ian refused to let me drive home. "No condition for it, old boy." He and Ring stood up, ramrod-straight, and led me to the exit. The homeward drive, in Ian's battered roadster, was enlivened by an eccentricity peculiar to the car: at every right turn the horn bleated twice and the right door flew open.

Meanwhile, I was training a well-honed reportorial curiosity on the star system. My first brush with a box-office hero came in the cavernous darkness of the indoor pool at United Artists, an elongated bathtub surrounded by a cluster of dressing rooms. Scrambling up from the water, I found myself face to face with a tall, painfully skinny toothpick of a man, his skin sickly white under a flickering fluorescent light: very naked, very unheroic of chest and biceps—and very unhappy with my presence.

Henry Fonda lost no time in communicating his displeasure to Walter Wanger, who notified me that pool privileges were reserved for performers, not mere writers. The line between studio royalty and the hired help would not be drawn again so sharply for me until more than a year later, when I stumbled onto terrain set aside for Shirley Temple.

But the star-gazing continued. Invited to the Hollywood Athletic Club one weekend by Fanny's client Eddie Goulding, I was changing into gym clothes when a strikingly handsome young man with electric blue eyes turned up at the next locker, quickly stripped out of workout gear and headed for the showers, leaving at my elbow a pair of blue shorts and a white jock strap. I needed no program notes to identify Robert Taylor, whose sculpted profile, accompanied by the screaming legend "Garbo Loves Taylor," adorned billboards all over the country.

I stared at the athletic support. Nothing could be more intimate, close to—should one say, the essence?—of Robert Taylor. If I pocketed this sweaty souvenir, what would it fetch from his admirers at auction, and what statement would that make about American values, circa 1937? In later years I have read of Madonna's sneakers fetching $4,500, an asking price of $25,000 for Marilyn Monroe's bed, the sale of Judy Garland's ruby slippers for $165,000. I shall never know what fortune escaped my clutches in 1937.

Still another leisure-hours encounter involved Johnny Weismuller, the Olympic swimming ace who metamorphosed into the first (and best) Tarzan. He was clowning at a pool frequented by Arthur Ripley. Weismuller was a magnificent physical specimen, a Greek discus thrower sprung from statuary to life, disconcertingly outsize but perfectly proportioned. As John Huston was to say of Marilyn Monroe, he was "like Niagara Falls," an unrepeatable, once-in-a-million accident of nature. Ripley and I, looking up at this smiling giant, shook our heads in awe.

But what I most remember is that the awe was mutual. Johnny had apparently heard somewhere of Rip's early work, and all but genuflected before him in tribute. When Rip introduced me as a "bright new writer from New York," the swimming champion unhesitatingly expanded the halo to make room for me. "Writers!" he exclaimed. "Boy! that's really something. I just don't see how you guys do it!" His wonderment was as direct and sincere as that of a child.

Which is precisely, according to writer-director Norman Panama, what all actors basically are: people who, unnerved by the complexities of growing up, have opted instead to remain in a Peter Pan world of make-believe.

Linda Fiorentino, a recently anointed cinema queen, told an interviewer she preferred to have her photo taken in character: "I'm very nervous being me—whoever that is." And I can think of a half-dozen others, not least of them Ronald Reagan, who, caught without scripts, without the separation of footlights or the confident authority of authors, wriggled and flopped like fish out of water: the venerable British idol John Gielgud in his dressing room after strutting as Benedick through *Much Ado*, collapsing toupee-less and silent before his make-up table; Fred Astaire backstage at *The Bandwagon* in a similar Samson mode; Zero Mostel fidgeting restlessly beside me at a Broadway opening; Eli

Wallach disintegrating into shallow self-puffery as we shared a speakers' platform.

Yet this generalization, like others, must be qualified. On that same platform sat Peter Ustinov, gracious and considerate, the very soul of civilized urbanity. Anthony Quinn, for all of his macho posturing, is a concerned and thoughtful world citizen, as is Jonathan Winters; both are fine painters. Jimmy Cagney in particular lingers in memory, an avid reader of John Ruskin essays, a man whose interests ran from literature to cattle.

For a uniquely local diversion, I tuned in on my party line in Laurel Canyon over which two neighboring females whom I never saw, evidently upper-class concubines, kept score on the prowess of various Hollywood studs, handing out ratings like book reviews or—occasionally—Academy Awards. I particularly remember their contemptuous dismissal of Clark Gable's performance in the sack: "strictly a face man."

After two frenzied clean-up jobs with Rip on Towne-Baker scripts I was ready, Wanger decided, for higher things. But he wasn't about to give me a free hand on an original. He had acquired a slick magazine story called "Summer Lightning": Hollywood ritual decreed that its adaptation be assigned to two separate writing teams, each unknown to the other.

My designated partner was Del Andrews, co-adapter of the unforgettable *All Quiet on the Western Front*, a frightened, gifted alcoholic who was being given one last chance for a screenwriting comeback. For a week Del showered on me an invaluable education in screen structure. "I'm a carpenter," he would insist, "not a writer. I build scenes." Then, despite every effort by well-wishing guardians—we locked him in a third-floor cubicle, hid his car keys, took away his pants—Del toppled off the wagon. I was left with two choices: to drop out of competition or finish my treatment alone. I opted to scribble on—and thereby entered the tempestuous orbit of William Kerrigan Howard.

Wanger had just hired Bill Howard, Hollywood's fabled "five-thousand-a-week Red," and was leaving it up to Bill to judge the rival scripts. Bill was the quintessential untamable Irish rebel: thick sprawling black hair, keen blue eyes, wit and charm enough for a regiment . . . along with a darker side, hidden a few drinks beneath the surface, of suspiciousness and Catholic guilt.

His career in movies had been spectacular. With the silent epic *The Thundering Herd* he won an immediate reputation, enhanced two years later by another western, *White Gold*. This was distinguished by one of the most mesmerizing scenes in film history, in which a libidinous ranch-hand lulls to sleep the husband of his quarry through deft relentless repetition of mounting close-ups: shuffled cards, a swaying lantern, piled-up chips . . .

The advent of talkies in the late 1920s brought to Hollywood a spate of converted stage plays. Bill's *Transatlantic* in 1931 was the first picture to restore a balance between camera and speech; his long wordless opening on the departure of an ocean liner—deep-throated horns, shrill whistles, the crash of cargo and roar of engines, mingled with daring boom shots and sharp vignettes of the crowds, was a breathtaking, convention-shattering tour de force. Afterward came such successes as Spencer Tracy's *The Power and the Glory*. Bill had just brought Laurence Olivier and Vivien Leigh to the screen in the London Films epic, *Fire Over England*.

But he was a political and social renegade in a tight, jealously guarded Establishment. Although a staunch Catholic who qualified every reference to the future with a "God willing," he openly espoused the cause of the Loyalists in Spain, donating to them a fully-equipped ambulance (the glory days of the Spanish Church, he told me, belonged to the long-departed "mission padres plodding up their mountain trails"). He declined to pay tribute, verbal or material, to such local icons as gossip queen Louella Parsons, before whose Beverly Hills mansion the caravans bearing Christmas gifts regularly rumbled to rest.

Nonetheless publisher Billy Wilkerson of the *Hollywood Reporter*, a man who hardly shared Bill's liberal views or unbridled ways, wrote an editorial reminding everybody that Bill Howard could go out into the empty desert with a couple of actors and a camera and always "come back with a movie."

The moguls nodded glumly. They couldn't harness Bill but they were afraid his brilliance would be snatched up by a rival. So by the Wangers of the world he was simultaneously condemned and courted.

Seated barefoot in his office, carefully clipping his toenails, Bill Howard explained to me why he had preferred my script treatment: the structure made sense (thanks, Del!) and the patches of dialogue had a good natural flow.

The problem was—and we both knew it—with the magazine story Wanger had bought. "Summer Lightning" was formula claptrap, the tribulations of a vapid heroine and her stalwart lean-jawed pursuers.

"Mr. Wanger said," I ventured, "that he liked the devices."

"De vices," grunted Bill, "far outweigh de virtues."

"Okay, so it's a sappy story. Can we make a movie out of it?"

"Maybe—if we throw away the original."

"Why did Wanger buy it?"

"Because he was afraid someone else might. Fear is what runs this town. Little men, aware of their limitations, terrified that they won't keep up with the competition . . . He tossed his scissors aside. "They don't like to hear plain truths. So I've stopped sounding off. It hurts me here"—he patted his head—"and here." He touched his wallet pocket. "Let's go out for a drink."

Bill Howard was a gift to me from the gods of drama, a fellow outsider who had easy access to the insiders: creative, imaginative, idealistic . . . in short, everything I hoped to be. A rumor, apparently floated by Bill's agent, trickled into the studio: the volatile director was thinking of exercising a clause in his contract that would permit him to return to the scene of his recent triumph with Olivier and Leigh in London.

Wanger called me in. "You're an organization man, aren't you?"

I nodded automatically, not sure where the conversation was going. He soon let me know. "I've got a hunch Bill Howard has the hots for a girl he left behind in London," Wanger said. "A Russian girl who was in his last picture. I want you to sound him out, find out what he's got on his mind—and report back to me." Class dismissed.

Now I knew what an organization man, Wanger-style, was. I also knew that I didn't want any part of it.

The next time I saw Bill I told him about the incident and my reaction to it. He raised a dark eyebrow, looked at me quizzically for a moment, and smiled; we dropped the subject. Before the week was out he had left for London.

A few days later Wanger announced he had run out of projects for me. Crushed, I paid no attention when Fritz Lang quickly invited me to move in with him and develop several original story ideas on which we would share credit. Technically, I was still on leave of absence from the *Mirror*, free to return there. But I couldn't face going back to the city room branded a failure, a Hollywood flunk-out in my freshman year.

I had barely adjusted to getting the boot—in fact was still feeling its sting—when a cheery cable arrived from London. Fanny and Bill Howard had run into each other at the Savoy Hotel, had conspired to descend together on their mutual friend Alexander Korda, a lean, pensive Hungarian intellectual who with his brothers Zoltan and Vincent, had captured British film-making. They had come up with a contract for me at Korda's London Films, where Bill was to start shooting on *The Squeaker*, an Edgar Wallace mystery, in a week. Afterthought: there was no script, so I'd better come on the run.

The prospect of working with Fritz Lang, heavy and Germanic, I could resist. Hollywood's mercurial "five-thousand-dollars-a-week-Red" I could not.

Ring emptied his coffers to finance my plane ride east. Clutching a copy of *The Squeaker*, I stumbled aboard the Queen Mary.

I hated mystery novels, never read them, even took a condescending view of people who apparently enjoyed them. I had no patience with their calculated mayhem, the parade of erratic millionaires and omniscient butlers, the folderol of Aztec rubies gleaming in kewpie doll navels.

The Squeaker had all of these and more, tangled together in a murky plot about stool pigeons in the London underworld. It was a bumpy crossing for me, that April of 1937, in more ways than one.

To meet a financial commitment, Korda had to get into production at once, ready or not. We were decidedly not. A few hours after I arrived Bill and I were sprawled on the living room floor of the town house he had rented in Mayfair, trying to flesh out the role of the detective who would be our central character. Wallace's novel had focused on an elderly garrulous Scottish reporter, hardly a suitable role for our jaunty leading man, Edmund Lowe. The first scene we wrote was for a barroom interior, because that was the only set thus far constructed by Korda's designer brother Vincent.

Early the next morning, typed pages in hand, we were speeding through a rolling green countryside to Korda's studio at Denham,

Buckinghamshire, where our leading man waited, a jump ahead of us, and twice as nervous. Edmund Lowe, his ruddy good looks topped by a rakish mustache, had swashed and buckled his way through a dozen features, including *What Price Glory* as the belligerent sidekick of Victor McLaglen. But he had passed his peak and needed increasing embellishments—a corset around his belly, a supportive patch added to his thinning hair, unobtrusively elevated heels—to keep his celluloid image intact.

For a certified Royal Personage, Lowe was pleasantly democratic. But he irritated me on two counts: he referred to all dialogue as the jokes—writers can get touchy about that sort of thing—and he wanted all the best jokes for himself. "Remember, fellas"—a cross between a whine and a command—"I'm the guy who has to carry this one at the box office."

Another complication in an untidy set-up was the presence of Edgar Wallace's son Bryan—lean and secretive, of hawklike mien—as my official collaborator on the screenplay. Bryan was not fond of Yanks. He resented, understandably, the daily extemporizations to which we were forced and he rarely shared my approaches to the story, to the point where he and I were submitting alternative scenes anonymously for Bill Howard's decision. The fact that Bill generally gravitated toward mine did not improve Anglo-American relations.

Korda remained scrupulously aloof. He was a curious amalgam of artist, or at least artistic sympathizer for whom the concept of taste was not confined to barbecue sauce, and business man. Tall, loose-limbed, with thick gray hair and a thicker Hungarian accent, Korda had style. Under constant siege for jobs from unemployed countrymen marooned in London, he hung a sign over his door: "To be Hungarian is not enough." When I stupidly miscomputed the exchange rate on pound sterling for my salary, he declined to argue the point, making me seventy-five dollars a week richer.

On the other hand, he hounded us relentlessly about keeping on schedule. He wanted the requisite number of reels in the can, no matter what was on them.

Our script, never having enjoyed the benefits of leisurely reflection, was subject to constant changes that required my presence on the set.

This, like the space squeeze at the *Mirror*, had its educational rewards: I was obliged to pay attention. And paying attention to Bill Howard provided a course in film craft that couldn't be bought at any university. Half a century later I would still be spouting to students some of the verities absorbed from Bill.

Moving pictures had to be exactly that: strips of film that projected physical action, and that were also moving in the sense of arousing strong feelings. Every scene had to justify itself either by advancing the story, illuminating character, or getting a laugh.

Bill loathed on-the-nose announcements of plot, preferring to lure his audience up to the screen through interesting characters, and to keep them there by inventive surprises. Instead of opening a scene on the close-up ringing of a telephone, he would come in on a youngster hurtling down the stairs to answer the ring. Something—either the camera or an actor—was always flowing, leading the spectator's eye. He gave his players bits of business—for instance, the watering of a plant by a police inspector—to enhance the illusion of reality and add a humanizing touch.

A new way of seeing became automatic for me. Whenever I view a movie, my eyes in effect become the camera, registering every nuance of its position or movement: low-angle, slow pan, high boom shot, close up. Conversely, in drafting a scene I draw upon the same reflex, envisioning what the camera will pick up.

English actors were more approachable than their Hollywood counterparts, less preoccupied with their public images: Renée Ray, a top-drawer film star, lived with her composer husband in a third-floor walk-up. I formed several rewarding friendships. Johnny Mills, then a Cagneyesque song-and-dance man, now the illustrious Sir John Mills, taught me to play and sing the melting Irish ballad, "Maire My Girl."

Meaty, country-plain Robert "Bobby" Newton, *Treasure Island's* glowering Long John Silver, solemnly explained to me over double whiskeys why at his farming cottage outside Oxford he preferred the company of animals. "My wife and her aristocratic friends are interested in nothing but clothes and sailing. My donkey, he's civilized. I bring him in, we sit together before the fireplace; I talk and he listens." Bobby wasn't kidding, I discovered a couple of weeks later when I attended a party at his house. Bored by the sophisticated chit chat, he coaxed one of the farm pigs into the parlor, where the new guest vented his nervousness on an outraged duchess. Bobby and his bride parted soon afterward.

Most striking of the thespian crew at Denham were Bill's stars from the Elizabethan *Fire Over England*, Vivien Leigh and Laurence Olivier, already thoroughly engrossed in 1937 but not yet married. The future Scarlett O'Hara of *Gone With The Wind*, Vivien, dainty and elegant as a Tanagra figurine from ancient Greece, strolled through the corridor recounting how she had flabbergasted a newspaper interviewer. "He wanted to know my favorite recreation. I told him, 'Fucking.'"

Olivier, whatever the subterranean tremors later revealed in his autobiography, was all glitter and panache—high cheekbones, dark eyes and hair—with a brittle, devil-may-care charm. His greatest accomplishments still lay ahead, but already his very presence had an arresting magic.

For closer access to the studio, Bill leased a splendid estate in Buckinghamshire near Chalfont St. Peter, the scene of Thomas Gray's "Elegy Written in a Country Churchyard." Here was pastoral English life at its most privileged: lovely rambling gardens, an *en-tout-cas* tennis court, the cool tang of apple orchards in September.

I had everything a young man could desire—except a warm personal life rooted in a firm sense of self. Bill, under pressure from Korda's timetables, kept me on a tight rein. Fanny lingered in London, drafting me for escort duty at parties. I had the uncomfortable suspicion that I was being converted from nephew to satellite, that in fleeing my demanding parents I had fallen into a more tortuous, powerful vortex.

I felt vaguely ill at ease in Bill's circle. At twenty-three I wasn't the peer of such Howard cronies as Jed Harris, the scowling contemptuous production wizard of Broadway, and I knew it.

Another of Bill's friends was Paul Lukas, a tall, imposing Hungarian actor, quite irresistible to women with or without his hairpiece. I challenged Paul to a set of tennis, presumably on the premise that by conquering the conqueror I would establish my masculine status. The big Hungarian clobbered me.

Although the studio was swarming with attractive bit players, my ventures into the sexual arena were few and not fruitful. When Alice

Marble, the blonde and comely American tennis champion, stayed at Bill's mansion during the 1937 Wimbledon competition, I was all thumbs and awkward silences. When John Sutro, one of Korda's backers at Prudential Life, turned up with a couple of ravishing sex kittens, I pursued them so hungrily that Bill cut me down: why wasn't I drafting the new scene for Eddie Lowe?

Tensions on the picture really exploded when, just as we were wrapping up, Bill's mother died in Ohio and he returned there for the funeral. Korda, viewing a rough final cut, decided our opening was too oblique and understated. He wanted the most gripping scene in the picture, a ghostly transaction along the fog-shrouded bank of the Thames, revised and yanked up front and asked me in Bill's absence to direct it. I sought cues for camera angles from Jack Dennis, our American cutter (today they're called film editors) and did the best I could.

It wasn't very good. That was obvious at the screening we held in London on the afternoon of Bill's return. To meet Korda's strictures I had written lamentably plot-laden dialogue that made Bill visibly wince.

Wordlessly he walked with me to the car that would take us back to Buckinghamshire. Then he blew up: "How could you do that opening, Ted?"

"Korda wanted it, Bill. And you were out of reach."

"Every critic in New York will be jumping on me. They expect something fresh from William K. Howard, something inventive. You've ruined not only the picture but my reputation!"

"I'm sorry, Bill. It was a lot of pressure for a guy 23 years old."

"Norman Krasna was on Broadway in his twenties (Krasna's *Louder, Please* had been produced a few years earlier). Why can't you be like him?"

I groaned inwardly. It had been my mother's habit to compare me regularly and unfavorably with the neighborhood "model boy," one Lloyd Seidman, an irreproachable paragon who reportedly was never late to class, kept his clothing spotless, thumped out his piano exercises with religious zeal, and wasted no time in frivolous pursuit of baseball scores. My mentor had stirred bitter memories.

"I'm me, Bill. I'm not Norman Krasna."

"I'll say you aren't!"

He ripped open the passenger door of the car and I crept in. Never close with his money, Bill had bought a beautiful low-slung white Jaguar, a race horse refashioned in steel. He reached for the clutch and set off at a full gallop in grim, terrifying silence on the wildest ride I have ever had, careening through narrow, winding country lanes at breakneck speeds. If we had met any traffic from the opposite direction, the crash would have been horrendous. He wanted, of course, for me to beg for mercy; I was determined not to.

I would not be forgiven for my sins until the following month, when Korda asked Bill and me to rescue from his vaults an unreleasable melodrama based on a Graham Greene original story, *Four Dark Hours*. Korda thought a few judicious cuts and added scenes might save his investment. I managed to come up with a crackling new climax between Johnny Mills and Renée Ray that jolted Korda out of his Hungarian languor. Bill too was impressed. Preparing to leave for Hollywood to honor an old commitment, he asked Johnny and Renée to do the scene live at his farewell party.

I could feel the electrical impulse circling the room as the pair faced off, Johnnie as a hunted gangster, Renée trying to pry him loose from the underworld. I had an unfamiliar but welcome sense of power, of major talents placed in my hands to manipulate. This was a new dimension of creativity, using my words to shape believable people out of nothingness.

I never did hear the critical or public response to *The Green Cockatoo*, our reworking of *Four Dark Hours*. But oddly enough *The Squeaker*, under its American title of *Murder on Diamond Row*, turned up forty years later in Berkeley, California as part of a movie classic series at the University of California; and "He's Gone," a song I contributed to the picture, suddenly produced ASCAP royalties from, of all places, Australia.

Korda wanted me to stay on in England, on a fresh deal that would keep me at his right hand as associate producer involved in the full panorama of film-making. It was a tempting offer. Overseas producers were relatively free to develop themes that in California had to be wrestled or smuggled past the studio tycoons.

But blind instinct—the protesting inner man—said I was a writer, or would be some day, would put my own stamp on something—words, or perhaps music. Fanny, sensing a potential familial ally in her lonely ascent of the heights, was determined not to let my movie fever subside. She insisted that with my new formal screenwriting credits, I would be a cinch for an improved contract in Hollywood. I had barely enough sense to take a few weeks' vacation on the Continent—exercising my French (and little else) at the World's Fair in Paris, contemplating (all too briefly) the serious study of music in Vienna, before joining her on the West Coast.

Promptly upon my arrival in Hollywood my body let me know how acute was my conflict and how deep my despair. Not only was I listless and without appetite, dragging at Fanny's heels like a reluctant puppy; my systolic blood pressure had dropped to an alarming ninety-two. Today this would be considered a signal of crisis ranking with an ambulance siren; in 1938 it merely led Fanny to prescribe a couple of weeks in the cool, dry desert terrain of Victorville, where we would wait out word about a contract from 20th Century-Fox.

At Victorville the air was bracing, the pension-style retreat serene. I walked the hard flat desert in cowboy boots, with nothing more on my mind than the diverting challenge of avoiding rattlesnakes. Within a week my appetite was back and my blood pressure had returned to a normal 120.

A few days later the summons came to return to Hollywood. In the course of our hundred-mile drive, the pressure reading dived again to ninety. My nerves and muscles were doing everything but sky-writing the message of unconscious resistance. I wanted out.

Instead, Fanny and I debated a response to Fox, where the only immediate opening was to work on an original for nine-year-old Shirley Temple, then at the zenith of an unrivaled career. Breaking into pictures three years earlier with *Stand Up and Cheer*, the curly-haired, dimpled moppet with the disgustingly winsome smile had been literally keeping the studio afloat with the annual five million dollars gross from her pictures. Could I "write cute" for America's miniature goddess? I had my doubts. But at Fanny's urging I plunged on. Looking back, it seems incredible that I would have been content to be maneuvered like a pawn across my aunt's crowded chessboard. But I was reluctant to return to Brooklyn in defeat.

Working with Hal Long, an affable young southerner, I churned out a treatment for *The Little Nugget*, a Western comedy-drama in which La Temple, as the orphaned child of a deceased gold miner would be reluctantly adopted by her daddy's surviving sidekick, a brawling, whiskey-soaked Victor McLaglen. An actor of vast muscle but limited talent, McLaglen had been coaxed and hammered into an immortal performance by director John Ford two years earlier in *The Informer*.

The next step in the 20th Century routine was what I called the "script tease," or waiting-for-Zanuck. Thus far I had seen Zanuck only once, at a distance and literally surrounded by his circle. Said circle had gathered around him on the lot outside Sound Stage Four after their master had announced he wanted to relieve his bladder. With military precision, the attendants and their topcoats went into formation to screen him from public view. If a flunky or two was splattered in the proceedings, that was the price of loyalty. To royalty.

It was the studio chief's lordly pleasure to schedule reviews of work-in-progress from time to time by some mysterious process that had nothing to do with the order in which scripts were received. A writing team might be called in the day after submission or left dangling for weeks.

At long last I had an opportunity to pursue other interests. But away from the sanctuary of the typewriter, I was still a frightened rabbit. When Eddie Lowe phoned to invite me for an afternoon at the racetrack with Bing Crosby, I backed away, knees shaking.

"Come on," said Eddie. "We'll have some laughs. I've told Bing about you."

Despite ten minutes of persistent coaxing I continued to duck, thereby wiping out what might have been a priceless opportunity to advance my composing ambitions.

Ring Lardner and Ian Hunter, by virtue of past familiarity, were less threatening. Ring had opted to marry the chubbier and livelier of Selznick's two secretaries, Sylvia Shulman. Ian tumbled into matrimony a few months later with Sylvia's best friend, a bold-featured, green-eyed blonde named Alice Goldberg. Their son is the acclaimed young director Timothy Goldberg Hunter—a name that has never ceased to enchant me.

Since my days at Wanger's, political issues had heated up. In Spain, American volunteers were rallying to the support of the embattled Republic, among them Ring's younger brother Jim.

And friction was mounting locally between the studio czars and the highly-paid serfs in their Writers' Buildings. Ian and I, attending an in-house screening of Temple's *Rebecca of Sunnybrook Farm*, jested merrily through the proceedings, throwing in our own derisive dialogue to enliven the picture's more banal moments. As soon as the lights went up a Zanuck henchman was at our throats. Ian was obliged to display his MGM credentials; I was subjected to dark warnings of retribution by the front office. They never materialized, but there was no mistaking the J. Edgar Hoover atmosphere at the studios. Fateful days and searing adventures lay ahead for Hollywood's leftists.

My own involvement with the radical wing in Hollywood was peripheral: sympathetic but not dedicated. I shared their concerns about aggression in the Far East and Europe, went all-out in the struggle for a Guild, but had reservations about the philosophy and tactics of Marxism, its accent on goals over methods. To me, the group who would become known as the Hollywood Ten and their colleagues combined the noblest of intentions with a political naiveté that made me feel sophisticated.

Of Ring's integrity there could be no question, then or now; if anyone can show me a subversive frame of footage, or a line of Red propaganda in any of his films, I'll be glad to eat it. His brother Jim was killed fighting in Spain. Ring, appearing before the committee in October of 1947, never faltered. He could tell them what they wanted to hear, he said, exonerate himself, betray his friends, "but I'd hate myself in the morning." Convicted of contempt of Congress, he was sentenced to a year in jail.

The bars that fell across Ian's career were less visible but just as crippling. Not numbered among the Unholy Ten, he was nonetheless blacklisted and forced for survival to ghost scripts from Mexico.

In later years, upon encountering sudden strange antipathies I would refer to myself, not entirely jocosely, as "number thirteen in the Hollywood Ten." I have often wondered how, if I had stayed in Hollywood and become embroiled in the hearings, I would have responded. I like to think that, like Ring, I would have stood my ground. But, in the absence of particular circumstances and specific pressures, one can never be sure.

Hal and I waited with diminishing zeal. By the start of our fourth week, I left in mid-afternoon to drive golf balls. That was the day Zanuck chose for his conference on *Little Nugget.*

Happily, he never noticed my absence. After a quick look around, in which he spotted Hal Long, he apparently decided that another of the motley crew on hand must be Berkman, and launched into his commentary on our treatment: promising concept, could use more romantic subplot and some broad Western comedy types. We were to discuss revisions with Harry Joe Brown, one of the studio's major producers.

Brown's reaction was more equivocal. He thought the treatment needed a feminine touch. "There's this woman writer on the lot . . . "

I took our pages to Bill Howard. "This is good stuff," he said. "Warm and funny. I could take it out and start shooting tomorrow. Stand your ground."

We did, and promptly had it cut from under us. Curiously enough, I found dismissal liberating. For me, disenchantment had set in. Hollywood was a Taj Mahal built on quicksand. I hated its shallow values, its pretensions, its bland indulgence in organized lying. I saw no realistic place for me in its social scheme. Even Ring and Ian, although momentary props to my self-esteem, in the long run only confirmed my sense of inferiority to and dependence on strong Gentile companions, my vulnerability to devastating self-comparisons.

Before entraining for New York, I had a phone call from Dashiell Hammett. The celebrated mystery writer had heard (from Ring? Ian?) that I was leaving Hollywood. He urged me to reconsider: articulate men of conscience were few and vanishing fast. Could we talk about it at lunch?

I was flattered but unmoved. I didn't know where I belonged or where I was heading, but for the time being at least, The Industry was more than I could handle, and less than I wanted.

CHAPTER 4

Coming Back

On a dank, gloomy afternoon in December of 1938, oblivious to a blinding blanket of snowflakes, I trudged through the slush-filled paths of the Brooklyn Botanical Gardens, every step pounding out a melancholy rhythmic refrain: "No place in the world for me, no place . . . "

Returning east, determined to recapture the personal voice I had let slide into the Hollywood swamp, I had spent six exhilarating weeks in New England with my novelist friend Don Wayne, tramping through village greens, drafting sketches.

I came back to Brooklyn to confront an empty scene. At the *Mirror*, George Clarke had left to take a job as a columnist in Boston; Hinson Stiles was "fully staffed." I scoured the want ads, called friends, reviewed my credentials. I took out my handball medals and put them back. Mercifully, I have no clear memory of the days that followed.

After what seemed like an eternity of lonely rambles—actually, it was about a month—a call came from Stiles. He had a temporary opening on the night side; "Nothing permanent, you understand; just a fill-in."

I hustled down to East 45th Street. With luck and labor, I managed to stretch the "temporary opening" into a full-time rewrite job.

Soon it was with better pay. Newspaper employees all over the country were jumping aboard the militant labor movement sparked by John L. Lewis's CIO. William Randolph Hearst, accustomed to bringing home a medieval drawbridge or a glittering Roman bath to amuse Marion Davies, had never extended the same largesse to his employees. Working by flashlight—Stiles was on a constant hunt for subversives—I churned out the first issue of our union paper, *Copy*.

The enthusiasm in the newsroom was not unanimous. George Buchanan, a veteran rewrite man, twirled his moustache and snapped, "Unions are for workers. I'm a professional." Others were frankly unwilling to tangle with the Lord of San Simeon.

Our union clique charged on. We were bucking a man who tossed millions around like confetti, although never in our direction; who commanded a legion of noisy newspapers all over the country; and whose ruthlessness was a personal trademark. We detested him and would have been happy to throw darts at his florid face if we had been able to post it in the men's room.

We got to the edge of a strike. Hearst snarled and threatened, but we hung on.

Seven weeks later when the smoke cleared, the Newspaper Guild was in place. My salary was doubled to seventy dollars a week; not Hollywood numbers but respectable. As a newspaperman again, I had more sense of belonging than I ever felt in Hollywood.

News vendors, nightly bawling their sing-song of early a.m. editions—"Noose-Amurrikin-Mirror"—were doing a lively business. In 1939, the West reeled under the Hitler-Stalin pact. Within weeks the Nazis and the Soviets carved up Poland. Europe bristled with declarations of war and hastily improvised alliances.

Ironically, for pacifist Sam Berkman's son things were looking up. With the flood of wire service copy pouring in from Europe, I was promoted to the night foreign news desk, from which I was detached only for major rewrite stints. I garnered a page one by-line on the 1940 Republican nomination of Wendell Wilkie for president, and another big splash the following year when my cherished Brooklyn Dodgers won the National League pennant. For a club known even to its most fervent admirers as "Dem Bums," this was quite a feat. With *Mirror* sports columnist Dan Parker and Tin Pan Alley-wise Bud Green, I had patched together "Leave Us Go Root for the Dodgers, Rodgers," which was sung over the NBC radio network by Dodger manager Leo Durocher, who had slightly less voice than Rex Harrison.

For Sam Berkman, things were not so cheery. His sun was going down. I can still remember the pain as I watched him leave three mornings a week, stubby legs struggling doggedly along, for the county clinic job a former patient had obtained for him where he had to take orders from a cocky supervisor fifteen years his junior. He had no choice; his practice at home had all but faded away, and with it his morale.

My mother fumed at his apathy, one morning unloosing a tongue-lashing that I could not help overhearing. I sat with one sock in my hand, wanting to leave, unable to move, as she delivered a relentless recital of his failures as breadwinner, father and husband, and climaxed it by the terrible judgment, "You're nothing but a piece of shit!" I wince again as I type the line.

A younger sister of my father always insisted that Bertha killed him. Familial hyperbole? Within the year, in April of 1940, my father crumpled to the floor of his office while working on a patient, dead of a heart attack. My mother's grief was enormous and genuine; they had known good times and high hopes before the bitterness. Guarding his lifeless body until the mortuary people arrived, I mourned not only his death but the chasm that had developed between us, my failure to ease his disappointments. Life forced cruel choices. How could I have fulfilled his dream without sacrificing my own? On my father's tombstone I put a paraphrased quotation from Thomas Paine: "The world is my country; to do good my religion."

Soon after my sister married, and I moved with my mother to smaller quarters on Manhattan's upper West Side. It was a restless time for me. I had been reading among the rebels and iconoclasts: Thorsten Veblen's *Theory of the Leisure Class*, Harold Laski's *The Danger of Being a Gentleman*, and fiction like *Studs Lonigan*, *Tobacco Road* and *Brave New World.* I turned out a few short stories for King Features; nothing earthshaking, but happily remote from Temple's curls or Zanuck's tantrums. Independence felt good.

Saul Colin, secretary to the late Luigi Pirandello, introduced me to Erwin Piscator, an elegant, white-haired avant garde theater director who had moved his celebrated talent from Hitler's Germany to more hospitable shores. I asked Piscator why, as a socialist, he had not chosen to work in Moscow. Piscator grinned his little-boy grin. "Socialism," he confided as he speared an asparagus stalk, "is in heaven."

With his svelte, stylish wife, Maria Ley, Piscator had just established a drama school in New York. He had recently staged Karel Capek's antimilitarist satire, *Schweik the Good Soldier*, adapted by the dramatist-poet Ernst Toller, in Berlin. However Capek, as if bored with his masterpiece, had neglected to end it with any kind of dramatic flourish; and Toller too had been stumped. Would I try my hand at a Broadway version?

I did, and came up with a third-act ending that crystallized Capek's theme. Piscator was much impressed. It was an association hardly dampened by Maria's habit of pressing her breasts gently into my flesh as she read over my shoulder.

In the spring of 1940, Hitler's tanks exploded across western Europe. *Schweik*, in which Jack Pearl had agreed to star on Broadway, was cancelled; there was no audience for anti-war themes. But Piscator's praises had restored my faith in my dramatic powers. I had been complimented by a theater authority outranking Harry Joe Brown or even—gasp—Darryl Zanuck.

Meanwhile, on the other side of the globe, Japan had expanded its pillage of China to a ruthless campaign for a Tokyo-controlled "Greater East Asia Co-Prosperity Sphere." Washington countered by placing an embargo on shipments of oil and scrap iron.

A diplomatic dance of negotiations ensued, with tension rising, but few people took seriously the rumors of Japanese armed action. In November, a retired naval officer occupying the locker next to mine at the 92nd St. YMCA roared merrily at the notion: "They'd be crazy to tangle with the American navy. Our carrier pilots would blow their fleet out of the water. The whole thing would be over in a couple of hours." He was right about one thing: the length of the first engagement.

On Sunday, December 7, I was rounding out a long free weekend with a somewhat special date. Sally, a former cheerleader at Texas Christian University was one of those genteel Southern types who breathe fresh-faced innocence but secretly yearn for carnal abandon. I had invited her to my hotel apartment on Riverside Drive to meet my mother at dinner. Sally was on her way up from her apartment in Greenwich Village when the phone rang.

Glenn Neville, the *Mirror's* night editor, was on the line. "Can you come in right away, Ted?"

"What's up? I've got kind of a big date tonight."

"The Japs have bombed Pearl Harbor. I'm calling everybody in."

I still didn't get it. "Can I come down later, after dinner?"

"This is war in the Pacific. Heavy casualties. Do what you want." He hung up.

Half an hour and a wild cab ride later I was in the city room for a long night of bulletins, maps, charts and replate editions.

Before evening half of the American air arm in the Philippines had been destroyed. The United States was at war.

As the sole support of my mother, I was placed in 3A by my draft board—a neither-fish-nor-fowl status that increased my edginess. Unlike Ring Lardner's brother Jim, I had sat on the sidelines during the Spanish civil war. I did not intend to sit this one out. But as a reserve infantryman at Cornell I had been rated a dumbbell in weaponry and a near-sighted unreliable marksman. I felt better equipped to deal in intelligence. But would the army, notorious for miscasting, put me there? Meanwhile, guilt haunted me.

Physical symptoms were not far behind: low blood pressure, general malaise. My Uncle David prescribed Gertrude Lawrence's doctor, a droll little man named Harvey Rubin. ("Gertrude Lawrence need vitamins? Forget it. Vitamins need Gertrude Lawrence.") Rubin prescribed getting away from Bertha. "Nothing wrong with you physically," he assured me. "But too much mama, too close."

In March of 1942, thumbing through the Newspaper Guild journal, I ran into a quiet paragraph: the newly-formed Foreign Broadcast Monitoring (later changed to Intelligence) Service was looking for editors with experience in foreign affairs; an extra language or two would be a bonus. The following week I was in Washington for an interview. A week later I was saying good-byes on East 45th Street.

CHAPTER 5

Listening In

I clambered down from the train at Union Station, suitcase in hand, into a maelstrom of purposeful humanity: soldiers and scientists, aerial engineers and administrators, waves of wide-eyed secretaries from Cedar Rapids and Pacific Grove and Atlanta pouring out of high white government palaces. Half a century ago Washington was still a beautiful city, glorying in its architectural heritage from Paris; crime and drugs and decay had not yet overtaken America's capital.

The stately office buildings housed an alphabet soup of overlapping agencies. I felt stranded, bewildered, a stranger in my own capital. Where would I fit in this supercharged beehive? More immediately, where was I going to hang my hat?

As usual, Fanny had come up with a suggested contact; eager to get her off my back, I had ignored it. After a week of futile hunting, I checked her man out. David Karr proved to be an affable civil servant of about my age, with political connections reaching into the White House; he was a protégé of David Niles, FDR's adviser on Jewish affairs. Karr knew the capital ropes. More important in 1942 Washington, he had a room in the center of town with an available alcove. I grabbed it.

Washington was the hub of an enormous network for gathering and disseminating information. Overnight I found myself thrust into a key quasi-military operation. The Foreign Broadcast Intelligence Service, where I took over the morning shift, had been created—and was still being pieced together—out of grave necessity. An army, true to the Napoleon dictum, marches on its stomach, but it plans operations on the basis of its accumulated intelligence reports. If these are sketchy—or worse, inaccurate—the most formidable, highly trained military force can exercise its muscle in the wrong direction and incur terrible casualties.

With the expansion of the war, radio moved to center stage. The speed of the Nazi blitz had cut off the Western allies from many normal sources of information: government decrees, diplomatic channels, professional secret agents, enterprising news people. Europe's occupied regimes were under tight Nazi lock and key. However, in order to impose their rule effectively the Germans needed radio: not so much the shortwave broadcasts beamed overseas as the medium and longwave frequencies of the domestic networks. These were the quickest channels for spreading the word about curfews, military call-ups, cabinet changes, food and fuel rationing, the whole paraphernalia of occupation. And radio could not be strictly confined within national borders; to ensure full coverage of outlying areas, a certain amount of overlap was inevitable.

Here was something on which the allied powers could capitalize. A monitoring post, able to pick up much of the domestic output of the Continent, had quickly been established in London. On the American West Coast, in San Francisco, a similar listening post was taking shape to cover shortwave broadcasts from Tokyo to Japan's far-flung "Greater East Asia Co-Prosperity Sphere." Washington had just set up an array of powerful antennas in nearby Silver Springs, Maryland, mainly to bring in the multi-language Berlin shortwave service, largely propaganda, beamed overseas.

I was one of the supervising editors assigned to make on-the-spot judgments of the material streaming in; what to discard as irrelevant or repetitious, what to slap onto the continuously running teletype, what to highlight with a bell-ringing bulletin. It was my job to decide regarding a given item whether a summary would be enough, excerpts were warranted, or one of our clients would prefer a full text, sometimes in its original language. I had to alert monitors to subjects of special interest. Around a horseshoe desk I had a staff of a half-dozen editors to whom I allocated the details of preparing copy.

The flood of incoming reports comprised three main categories: hard or spot news, like military communiqués and changes in government; intelligence, and propaganda. Intelligence could be military, economic or diplomatic: the call-up of a reserve class in Rumania, production figures from an oil refinery, the appointment of a new Second Secretary to an obscure outpost. It frequently involved items apparently insignificant in themselves, but meaningful when fitted into a complex, shifting jigsaw.

Propaganda was the most elusive component, riddled with changing themes, significant buzz-words and tricky undercurrents. Hitler and Joseph Goebbels, his propaganda chief, had been exploiting the broadcast medium with cynical savagery, berating the "Zionist-Bolshevik conspiracy" against innocent Germany, confident in the invincibility of the Big Lie. I had to keep a steady handle on the changing enemy motifs, so that everybody could evaluate their implications for Axis morale and tactics, and the Office of War Information in particular could organize effective counterpunches.

Before the struggle for the "hearts and minds of the people" became a tattered political cliché, it was a key part of World War II. The propaganda war was as decisive as, if less bloody than, the war on the battlefield—and FBIS was at the heart of it. In the occupied territories, people gathered around hidden radios to hear BBC broadcasts for which we supplied the raw material. The OWI counted on us for evidence of where their broadsides had struck a nerve. A fistful of government branches—the Office of Naval Intelligence, the Bureau of Economic Warfare—shuffled revealing fragments: a port in Belgium declared out of bounds to civilians; a name suddenly missing from the German hierarchy of steel production.

With twelve to twenty agencies at the other end of our teletype, the triple-jointed assignment was light years away from the never-never land of Hollywood and even from the boisterous camaraderie of the city room. I was glad that in the summer of 1939, between stints at the *Mirror*, I had retreated to that farm in Massachusetts with Donnie Wayne to get Hollywood and its glib evasions out of my system.

It was a shift in perspective that now served me well in gauging the needs of the State Department, the Army's Psychological Warfare Branch, or "Wild Bill" Donovan's Office of Strategic Services, around which legends were already beginning to form. How much of a given broadcast should be reported (we recorded everything on disks) was a relatively routine matter of editorial evaluation; more difficult was the challenge of maintaining a sweeping global perspective.

With the copy handlers around my desk, I tempered my style to match their personalities. I was tough and laconic with worn, hard-bitten Hank Wales, who was making journalistic history when I was in the cradle. Credited with a global scoop on the World War I armistice, Wales had been as enterprising as he was colorful. In 1927, he had filed a stirring story about Lindbergh's arrival at Le Bourget airport before it actually happened, gambling—successfully—on the aviator's precision timing. Obviously once handsome, he still carried a carefully combed sliver of gray thatch.

Soon after he arrived I tossed over the day's French-language communiqué from Paris for editing—a wordless challenge. In thirty seconds I had it back, meticulously edited down to the last accent mark. Hank had mellowed into a quiet, competent desk man, speaking only when he had to, accepting with good grace the supervision of a relative stripling less than half his age. With silver-haired, soft-spoken Guy Phillips, I was careful not to make difficult demands. My most fractious aide, requiring constant attention, was big, shambling Leicester Hemingway; competitive, suspicious, constantly on guard against being overlooked. I couldn't blame him for being peevish; he was the baby brother of the redoubtable Ernest.

For my first few months of duty the news was grim. The Japanese were gobbling up everything in sight from Wake Island to the Java Sea. Nazi armor was driving deep into the Caucasus. The daily war communiqué from Radio Berlin, anxiously awaited in a dozen offices, had to be microscopically edited, with ambiguous phrases transmitted over our teletype in the original German.

Suddenly my name was on the floor of the Senate. Kenneth McKellar of Tennessee voiced the suspicion that the FBIS was up to "spyin'," and demanded to know why this twenty-eight-year-old Berkman was being withheld from Army ranks to further the process.

The agency asked me to submit a statement explaining my role. I flatly refused, saying I would rather be shifted to 1A status than have any such self-serving move on my conscience. The FBIS thereupon picked up the ball, entering a vigorous brief on the importance of my job and my special qualifications for it.

This intervention not only silenced McKellar but had immediate repercussions at FBIS headquarters on K Street. Sub-editors vied for my approval. The huge monitoring staff, many of them college professors and widely-published translators, waited respectfully for instructions as I glanced through their summaries. People were accepting my authority, deferring to my judgment. This was heady stuff.

From Fanny in New York came a request for an appraisal of British broadcasts to the Americas. I fired off a brisk note:

> Good on hard news and exposing Nazi distortions. But BBC commentaries are weak, apologetic, defending past behavior instead of projecting a better future. If your friends at Whitehall have a case for their India policy, they haven't presented it.
>
> They should be telling the world what the RAF is doing to Germany and about the devastating offensive to come in the west—and to hell with British understatement.

My mounting confidence was still coupled, however, with the less flattering conviction that I was essentially unlovable; not the sharp editor of my wistful fancies, but a thick-lipped, near-sighted Jew with a receding hairline. The diffident twelve-year-old dwelling in my head still wrestled with insecurities about appearance, sophistication, manly assertiveness.

What better way to exorcise these specters than to exercise my new status in the direction of sexual conquest? And what better target for my efforts than the most attractive, imperious, undeniably elegant (and unmistakably Gentile) female on the staff?

Sybil Rice breathed a two-foot-thick aura—what the New Age would later call vibes—of hauteur. Boldly handsome, she had high cheekbones dominating a face that might have been carved by Rodin. She conveyed more than a touch of Joan Fontaine in an era when, even more than today, film stars inhabited the undeveloped areas of the American brain. Her carriage was regal, her diction—in English or French—flawless.

Sybil was totally bilingual, an American raised outside London where her father, as chief of European operations for the Remington Corporation had been allocated a lavish apartment for his family in Hampton Court Palace.

At eighteen, weary of quarrels with a mother who disapproved of her desire to paint, she had deserted the luxury of Henry VIII's battlements for a skylight garret in Paris. There she met and soon married a young medical student—Polish, Jewish, decidedly not listed in the Social Register.

By the time the Nazis outflanked the Maginot Line, Sybil was the mother of two small boys. Her husband, who spoke no English, refused to leave the country.

Reluctantly, she took the last train out of Paris with her sons and brought them to Washington, where her brother held a high post with the Securities and Exchange Commission. The boys found temporary shelter on his Virginia estate; Sybil went to work as a waitress in the capital. After several months she had been hired as a French-language monitor by the FBIS.

To my mild surprise—all of this background I learned piecemeal later—she accepted my invitation to a National Symphony Orchestra concert in Rock Creek Park. We discovered a mutual passion for music—her Bach at the piano was better than my Gershwin—a shared penchant for ironic humor, and strong responses to each other physically. Within a week we were lovers. Sex was wonderful, a far cry from the scowling pachyderm in the Ithaca brothel or my few speculative adventures on the *Mirror*. My days of clumsy groping in the bedroom were over.

When Dave Karr moved to greener fields in pursuit of his upward political quest, I inherited our hovel (Dave's term) near Dupont Circle. Sybil and I frequently repaired there at two or three in the morning after working the late night shift. I particularly remember trudging home together, singing, utterly happy, through a warm, misty rain. One weekend I concocted a theme song for us, set to a nursery-simple melody:

> I haven't much gray matter in my cranium,
> I have the brain of an infant geranium
> I'm an idiot, hoo-hoo . . . but I have fun.

Ian Hunter, arriving in Washington to write a special film for the Joint Chiefs of Staff, was frankly envious of my amatory progress. He seemed to feel that in taking up with Sybil I had trespassed on territory that rightfully belonged to him. I rejoiced in his glowering.

Sybil took me to her brother's rambling acres across the Potomac, where a frequent visitor for Friday night poker was Supreme Court Justice William O. Douglas. Bill Douglas, never notably inhibited by matrimonial ties, made no secret of his yen for Sybil. Another of her early admirers was Herblock, the brilliant cartoonist for the Washington *Post*.

I was, literally, feeling no pain. I had absorbing work, with every reason to believe it was making a substantial contribution to the war effort; a beautiful woman; and a burgeoning reputation that was bringing me new friendships.

Reuben Fine, at that time ranked among the three greatest chess players in the world, occupied the office adjoining mine running a secondary FBIS teletype, technically under my supervision. One midnight I invited him home, where I had the temerity to propose a chess game. The boyish, chubby-faced International Grand Master smiled. "Why not?"

I had been a chess buff since high school days, and had rung up a modest success or two against touring chess masters who were taking on a score of other challengers simultaneously, sometimes blindfolded. But it had been years since I maneuvered a knight through its serpentine travels or stared down a frowning opponent.

I drew the first game against Fine—an outcome that would have to be conservatively rated a hundred-to-one shot. Furthermore, in the return contest I held my ground and actually leaped into the lead in the end game, finishing up with king and four pawns to the grand master's three. It was now nearly four a.m. Incredulous, nerves ajangle, I stumbled off to relieve my anxiety in the bathroom.

On my return I fell into an obvious error that cost me a pawn, and within minutes was swept from the board.

I have since been beaten, and roundly, by far less prestigious opponents. But I had, and could forever boast about, my brief span of glory. Late in 1942, against chess immortal Reuben Fine, I drew one and blew one.

Another attachment, treasured then and even more in retrospect, was to Colonel Harry Plotz, the slim, polished brother-in-law of my Wall Street Uncle Jack. Harry, on leave from his post as Chief of Medicine at the Pasteur Institute in Paris, had pioneered the typhus vaccine in World War I; now he was deputy head of the army's preventive inoculation program. I was as awed by Harry's prodigious scientific knowledge as I was attracted to his idealism. Once, visiting him at the Shoreham, I had glanced at a paper he was writing on viruses. The only words I understood were "the" and "and." He had conferred with researchers in Moscow regarding the origins of life; it was his fervent hope that the scientific community would one day lead the world to peace. Harry listened with evident interest to my observations on international affairs. He told Jack that before long my voice would be heard around the world.

Less welcome was an invitation to change jobs. Slowly the tide of war had been turning: at Midway Island in the Pacific, at El Alamein in Egypt. With the burgeoning of optimism in Washington came a flowering of bureaucracy. An early by-product of the FBIS operation had been the channeling of hard news—governmental shake-ups, major military claims—to America's commercial news agencies such as the Associated Press. Suddenly somebody decided this process should be split off and formalized, for which purpose a new bureau would have to be created, complete with its own secretaries and teletypes. In charge would be Matt Gordon of the Office of War Information and Emanuel Friedman, then foreign editor of the New York *Times*; the staff would include Henry Lieberman, who had been a correspondent for the *Times* in the Far East, and Henry Hillman, a classmate of mine at Cornell and later a colleague on the *Mirror*.

Pompous, pin-striped Manny Friedman (a shattering portrait of his self-centered foppery emerges from Harrison Salisbury's *A Journey for Our Times*) phoned me at home. My skillful handling of the FBIS wires had been noted, he said, along with my solid press background. His new bureau would be pleased to engage my services—at a considerable boost in pay—for less strenuous work. I would find the company congenial. And the association, he intimated, would certainly not be harmful to my future career.

I found the notion unappealing, not to say disgusting. The whole setup, in my view, was redundant, unnecessary, a bureaucratic boondoggle designed to fatten the egos and wallets of a smug little clique. I turned the offer down, with a measure of pious indignation probably heightened by growing concerns in another area.

I was having problems with Sybil, or rather with myself over the relationship with Sybil. People were taking us for granted as a couple. Sybil herself made no overt demands; but there were brief, wry references to her status as my *maîtresse à titre*, or official mistress, and to her "two encumbrances," rarely mentioned between us but clearly a greater responsibility than I cared to contemplate.

I had never known a woman of finer character. Her devotion to her two boys—she had taken a menial restaurant job to support them after being raised in silks—was exemplary. She was quick to help less experienced colleagues stumbling over linguistic nuances, and never wavered in her support for Charles de Gaulle when to most of the world he was an obscure, quixotic figure. And she never lost her dry, self-effacing humor.

But the strength I admired in Sybil I also mistrusted. I had had my fill of powerful women with agendas clearer than my own. I was beginning to feel threatened, hemmed in. From there it was a short passage to restless. Scanning a sexual horizon that in wartime Washington was never empty for long, I fell into one brief liaison, then another, climaxed by my arrival home at two a.m. one morning, a transient inamorata on my arm, to find Sybil, decidedly awake, curled up in my bed.

I fumbled through some lame explanation. But things were never the same afterward. It would be years before I began to understand the complex factors involved: my fears of smothering intimacy and of responsibilities beyond my resources, my association of total commitment with hurtful rejection. For the moment all I knew was that I was in over my head, trapped in a situation beyond my resources.

By this time, late in 1943, the German Sixth Army had been forced to surrender at Stalingrad, Guadalcanal wrested back from the Japanese. Soon the Germans were chased out of North Africa, the siege of Leningrad lifted, Italy knocked out of the war.

To cover these wide-ranging developments, the British Broadcasting Corporation in London had greatly expanded its monitoring of medium and long wave transmission directed to home audiences on the Continent, and the token FBIS bureau there was being increased accordingly. Amid gathering rumors of plans for a second European front, a steady trickle of American editors was flowing to the blitz-battered British capital. I let Tom Grandin know I would welcome an assignment to join them.

But when an overseas opportunity opened up a few months later, it was in a quite different direction. The BBC, in order to improve its screening of domestic transmissions in the Nazi-occupied Balkans as well as broadcasts to and from the volatile Middle East, was setting up a new post in Cairo, Egypt, ideally situated for picking up radio material skipping across the Mediterranean (water is radio wave-friendly). Grandin wanted a "tough-minded" editor in Cairo, capable of organizing round-the-clock cable coverage directed to the needs of the FBIS client agencies. Was I interested?

In my state of turmoil I would have packed my bags without a murmur for Iceland or Timbuktu; Cairo sounded relatively exciting, an exotic challenge. Harry Plotz, who had been there, warned me against the perils of microbes in a hot, hygienically backward country. A bedtime nip of Scotch could do no harm, he said, and chocolate bars would provide quick energy. "But don't expect bouquets from the British. They relish our aid more than our presence."

Good-byes in Washington were followed by a brief trip to New York. Among my farewell-to-friends stops there was one at the Imperial Theater, where Danny Kaye, ex-Kominski, was holding forth in *Let's Face It* as Broadway's newest star. Immeasurably aided by Sylvia Fine's brilliant special-material songs and managerial shrewdness, Danny had climbed from summer camp work in the Catskills to a solo act in a major cabaret and then to a featured Broadway role in *Lady in the Dark*; along the way he and Sylvia were married. Although a collaboration for Danny in which Sylvia and I were involved had fizzled, the three of us had remained good friends.

Danny, stripped to the waist in his dressing room, looked rock-hard, all bone and muscle. I had last seen him in the subway, en route to his maiden nightclub appearance. He had seemed modest and quiet then, and now unaffected by stardom. Hollywood would change that.

One more stopover, to see my sister in Nova Scotia, and early in April of 1944 I was enroute to Miami, takeoff point for the transatlantic flight to Africa.

CHAPTER 6

In Egypt Land

At Miami Beach I joined a motley pool of engineers, academics, linguists and information specialists awaiting shipment overseas. Nazi U-boats dictated air travel, some of it over inhospitable territory. C-54 four-engine transport aircraft, adapted for passenger use by strips of bucket seats, did the flying. But there weren't enough of them. With plane space at a premium, priorities were constantly being shuffled and passenger lists revised. Meanwhile we played poker and attended briefing sessions ("If you're forced down over the Brazilian jungle, eat what the monkey eats—then eat the monkey").

After a few days my name went up on the bulletin board for outgoing flight 189 late that afternoon. I said my good-byes and packed for departure. As I was boarding the bus for the airport, the driver waved me back: I had been bumped in favor of a cloak-and-dagger operative from the Office of Strategic Services, bent on a mysterious mission in Turkey. I shrugged and trudged back to camp, estimating gloomily at dinner that the flight I had missed would just about be heading across the south Atlantic.

I was wrong. At breakfast the next morning, we were half-listening to a local news program when a voice broke in over the loudspeaker: "We interrupt the news for a special bulletin. Flight 189, enroute from Miami to São Paolo, lost altitude early this morning and crashed in the Brazilian jungle. There is no indication of survivors."

The huge mess hall fell silent. No survivors. That would include the OSS man who unwittingly chased me from my seat. I imagined his body in the wreckage: silent, crumpled, lifeless. His body, then mine. Monkeys screaming in the mahogany trees above, clambering down to inspect the fallen big bird.

I pushed back my plate of scrambled eggs. Suddenly the war became much more personal.

So much for impatience. Two days later I was strapped into a bucket seat on another C-54 that lurched its way across Brazil and the Atlantic to Dakar. From there we bounced to Khartoum, where in appalling heat we crawled gratefully under mosquito nets before undertaking the final leg to Cairo.

We landed in an eerily blacked-out Egyptian capital. Although the Axis armies had been driven out of Africa nearly a year before, Marshal Erwin Rommel's Afrika Korps had come uncomfortably close to Alexandria in 1942 before the decisive counteroffensive at El Alamein by Marshal Montgomery; the long see-saw struggle in the desert, with the Suez Canal and vital allied communication lines at stake, had left the British uneasy. For a disquieting complication, Egypt's overblown King Farouk had frequently shown signs of being more than willing to change colonial partners; at one point, as a precaution against fifth-column betrayal, tank-supported British Tommies had ringed Farouk's Abdin Palace.

As we rolled into town from the air base near Heliopolis, Cairo lay in ghostly silence beneath a huge magic-lantern silver moon. Pension quarters had been arranged for several of us on the eighth floor of a tall apartment building at Midan Ismailia, from whose balconies the distant pyramids at Gizeh loomed in the night.

Poem, spring of 1944:

EGYPT

Egypt is a tear; a long and hollow wail in the night
And a wailing cry at dawning.
It is clay-faced silent women dressed in mourning black,
Long-striding men in ancient flowing robes,
And Bedouins riding donkeys across the city square.
It is a world dead three thousand years
Yet miraculously preserved in the present.
Egypt is a mummy.

My first letters home sketched the initial period of adjustment:

> One has to exercise reasonable prudence with food here; can't pop into a corner Nedick's for a hot dog and an orangeade. My stomach, after the customary few days of erratic behavior (nothing beyond a mild affinity for the bathroom across the hall), has settled into acceptance.

> We can also get a few American cookies from the army Post Exchange, but the local ants are as fond of cookies as I am. They have no trouble walking upside down and have some secret device for passing the word to all their cousins within minutes.
>
> Another change in routine is the midday nap. Promptly after lunch, your newly-arrived "Américain" feels an irresistible languor creeping over him. He hurriedly peels down to his underwear, lowers the blinds to keep out light and flies, and flops onto the bed, where he spends an hour or so till back at work around 3:30.

I expanded the picture somewhat in a letter to Seymour Berkson, then managing editor of Hearst's International News Service:

> Life here starts at 6:00 a.m., when, having finished work at 0200, one is practically blasted out of bed by a series of blood-curdling screams from the courtyard. These turn out to be merely the warm-up act of an olive oil vendor; advertising is on a primitive level here.
>
> Sleep of course is broken. A bedlam of rug-beating on a dozen balconies, braying donkeys and squawking auto horns makes sure that it stays that way (the natives drive with their horns, using brakes and steering wheels only in extreme emergency).
>
> Promptly at eight my "boy" Abdullah (a fine upstanding lad in his early forties) bangs on the door with breakfast. Abdullah is equally at home in English or French; i.e. he cannot follow simple instructions in either language.

For *Mirror* sports editor Dan Parker, I described the enchanting fragrance of the city's special perfume, "Camel #5."

The Balkan area, the notorious powder keg of World War I, was crucial to allied planning: teeming with ancient dynastic rivalries, ethnic and religious differences, abused minorities and long-standing territorial differences. Overrun for centuries by invading Romans, Goths, Huns, Mongols, Slavs, and Turks, it had a history written in blood, a sorry tale of Machiavellian scheming and ruthless suppression, of transient peace periods stitched together by the great powers through solemn "ententes" which inevitably sowed the seeds for the next round of hostilities.

The Balkan states most recently carved up—Hungary, Rumania and Bulgaria—had joined the Axis chain. We hoped to transform them from enemy assets to liabilities by stirring up latent nationalisms.

Bunched between the Adriatic and Black seas were Yugoslavia, Bulgaria and Greece, with up-for-grabs Macedonia slicing erratically across their common borders. Yugoslavia in particular was an unstable patchwork assembly of Greek Orthodox Serbs, Catholic Croats and Slovenes, and overflow Moslems from tribal Albania, lost in the mountains of the southwest.

Several decisions had to be made: what proportion of material should be speeded to Washington by immediate cable, what could be deferred to airmail, and what would require transmission by code. As a lone operative, I was instructed to function under the administrative procedures—but not the authority—of the U.S. Office of War Information in Cairo. My actual workplace was a block away, in the tawny three-story walk-up occupied by the British Radio Monitoring Service.

Heading up the RMS was one Colonel Fraser: bony, aloof, distinctly cautious about letting an American interloper into his realm. He never met my gaze directly; I felt he was keeping me under constant, faintly disapproving scrutiny. More amiable was his deputy, a husky lean-jawed Scot named Crawford Lochhead who had served as an interrogator of prisoners during the desert campaign; a peacetime executive with J. & P. Coates in Glasgow, Major Lochhead was fluent in German, Italian and French.

Several captains rounded out the brass, among them a drunken, wild-haired Arabic scholar named Williams and bald, gentle Blandy, with a faraway smile and a collection of glass animals à la Tennessee Williams (the RMS, I discovered, was something of a dumping-ground for oddball intellectuals of His Majesty's Forces). Roughly equal in status to Lochhead was a tall, sumptuously mustached Oxonian civilian named Stanley Harrison, recruited from the BBC where he had been a senior news editor.

Beyond these sachems of the RMS stretched in long and ungainly procession the "other ranks" of the staff, privates and corporals and noncoms, distinctly and frequently reminded by signs and regulations of their lower-class status. The rigidity and pomposity of hierarchical arrangements reminded me of Hollywood. Here there were generals instead of studio chiefs, colonels for producers, accommodating secretaries in place of willing starlets.

But of course the British Army, at its games a good deal longer, had been able to develop a more elaborate code of privileges and exclusions. The foot-soldiers, never allowed to forget their lowly estate, passed the snobbery down the line in the form of contemptuous terms for the natives.

Toward me, however, the Tommies to my astonishment directed only a delighted deference. I was "the Yank," a welcome novelty imparting a dash of glamour to their drab routine. At Ivy League Cornell, and in striped-pants Washington, I had always felt vaguely on sufferance, an outsider not quite belonging as a full-fledged equal member . . . a "Jewish boy from Brooklyn." But in colonial Cairo this identity was totally effaced by my credentials as a citizen of the New World colossus coming to the rescue of old Europe. I was still an alien, but now an alien unexpectedly wrapped in the Stars and Stripes, reflecting the dazzle of cloud-piercing skyscrapers, giant steel mills, and bulging bank accounts.

CAIRO SUMMER

The days stalk you endlessly
Burning morn, hot listless afternoon,
Gray and sultry night . . .
High noon in Egypt! Blazing white
Heat that stabs and rays that bite;
People crawling through the city
Dull of eye and lost to pity.
Afternoon . . .
Muffled slam of shutters closing.
The flight begins.

By the start of June I had taken over a fair chunk of editorial responsibilities at RMS, ironed out a communication link with Washington (for the moment, via the local OWI signals section), and generally integrated

American needs into Colonel Fraser's monitoring operation. A second ground front in Europe, repeatedly urged at allied conferences by Marshal Stalin, was clearly on the horizon. Its specific timing was the subject of coded hints from London and Washington, second-guessed by alleged insiders in Cairo. Nothing was going to happen for at least a week, the U.S. Embassy advised; but all hands agreed that once the blow fell, RMS would be swamped day and night with queries and demands. This might be a good time, Colonel Fraser opined, for the service's lone Yank to take a brief break.

I rode a train across the Sinai for a three-day leave in Palestine. Hence, on June 6, I was wandering through the cobbled alleys of Jerusalem's walled Old City, sniffing the exotic spices of a bazaar, when a Bedouin on a donkey came clattering by, bawling the news of the allied landings. The English Channel weather had changed opportunely, and Eisenhower had struck.

Awash in anxiety and embarrassment, I made a beeline for the railroad station. Back in Cairo eighteen hours later, I found that Major Lochhead had covered my absence with brisk dispatch. Fortunately we had laid out our priorities in advance; now, with every transmitter in Europe operating and all our monitoring facilities engaged, we saw no immediate reason to change them.

First on our list was Berlin's Arabic-language service beamed by shortwave to the Middle East. Was it reporting the landings in detail, mentioning them briefly, or omitting any reference to the subject? What claims, if any, were the Nazis floating?

Next in line were the medium-wave government transmitters in the Balkan capitals. How much were they telling their people, and how were they telling it? Wcrc thcy aping thc linc propagated from Berlin, or leaving themselves subtle loopholes? Had any stations vanished temporarily from the air—a sure sign of high-level confusion? And what was the commentary from Moscow in the languages of the Balkans and Middle East?

As the landing forces clinched their footholds and battled their way across France, monitoring emphasis shifted from propaganda analysis to tangible intelligence. The Office of Strategic Services, a major FBIS client, opened the Top Secret files of its Cairo bureau to me, providing invaluable background data and constantly updated details. I scribbled notes, carefully coded, on OSS reports of food shortages in various cities, secret executions, rumored cabinet shake-ups. With allied bombings pulverizing German industrial centers and taking a heavy toll of the Ploesti oil fields in Rumania, every scrap of information on air damage was important. A fragmentarily detected call-up of reserves or cancellation of bridge use might influence the choice of our next bombing target. The maddening—and occasionally heartening—reality about intelligence operations was that an apparently trivial fact, matched up with its proper complement, could alter the entire kaleidoscope.

Major Lochhead had become my on-the-spot ally, juggling staff and schedules while Colonel Fraser contented himself with owlish messages to top brass in London. This instinctive alliance, buttressed by Lochhead delight at my piano pounding of "Alexander's Ragtime Band," led us to take an apartment together in town, combining access to American Post Exchange supplies with those of its British equivalent, the NAAFI, which featured Scotch whiskey and Australian canned beef. We also hired a cook, a grave, round-faced Sudanese who had previously served with a family from Paris. His white trappings—turban and long trailing *galabeah*—were impeccable, his casseroles tasty, his picked-up French fascinating. But neither of us could handle his name—the glottal stop does not come easily to the Western larynx—so with a bow to P.G. Wodehouse we re-christened him Jeeves.

Jeeves did not let down the reputation for ingenuity of his English predecessor. He quickly discovered that the major and I worked different shifts, enabling him to pluck a pound note from Lochhead in the morning and then to repeat the process from me after lunch. When questioned about his expenditures, he protested that he never knew how many people might turn up for dinner. This was true; both his bosses were casual about last-minute invitations.

Mysterious gaps began to appear in our canned goods shelves. One day I ripped the cover off the cart Jeeves frequently trundled to the door after lunch. Our man had excellent taste: Argentine tongue, strawberry jam, Canadian salmon . . .

"Jeeves! *Tu est un voleur* (you're a crook)!"

He met my gaze blandly. "*Tout le monde est un voleur* (everybody is)." It wasn't a defense; just a fact of life as experienced in Cairo, Egypt, 1944.

Another fragment of his philosophy surfaced on the day of an elaborate royal parade, a monumental display of opulence in shrieking contrast to the battered streets and ragged populace of the city. Jeeves, aglow with admiration, leaned perilously over the balcony for a peek at the marchers. Why such worship, I asked, of an indolent and indifferent monarch?

"*Il est notre garçon* (he's our boy)."

There was a sweet, childlike quality about Jeeves, a way of wagging his finger in reproof if I grabbed a nibble before dinner. And there was a certain delicacy in his mild thieveries; he never, for instance, invaded the tins of home-made cookies sent by my mother from New York. Once he came into the dining room as I was writing to her.

"I greet very much your mother," he announced in his fantastic French.

But nothing would induce Jeeves to ration his use of the Klim powdered milk from America. As with his inflated food bills, he would smile genially and change nothing. After a while, the casseroles being persuasive, we gave up.

Jeeves was gracious in victory. He intimated that after the war he would be pleased to continue his association with us. I pointed out that Lochhead and I lived on opposite sides of the Atlantic.

Again the mixture of smiles, customized French and sign language: "I'll cut myself in half."

Only twice did a serious issue develop with Jeeves. The first time came toward the end of summer, when Allied armor was driving toward the Rhine, the Russians were smashing westward, and morale was beginning to buckle in Hitler's satellite states. In the small hours of August 23, Radio Bucharest announced the surrender of Rumania to the Red Army; our flash summary from Cairo "scooped the world," according to a jubilant cable from Washington. For the next several days Major Lochhead and I, totally preoccupied with follow-up monitoring of Hungary and Bulgaria, scarcely saw each other in passing.

The temptation was apparently too much for Jeeves; he stepped up his double-pronged budget raids to outrageous heights. Threatened with dismissal, he was quite abashed, penitent and for a couple of weeks actually frugal.

More than a year later, when Lochhead had departed for Glasgow and been replaced by Stanley Harrison, Harrison brought along his Yugoslav girl friend, one of our monitors. The first female to grace the household on more than an overnight basis, Gina found Jeeves's casual approach to cleaning inadequate. When she picked up a mop to remedy the matter, our dignified butler was appalled. Under Moslem code, women were consigned strictly to the bedroom and kitchen if native, or to the parlor, insulated from labor, if European. Gina's violation of the sexual contract was immoral. Jeeves sulked.

But for the moment our rambling, railroad-style apartment was a welcome counterpoint to the ten-hour days and nights at the office. My ration of prioritizing queries, deciphering multi-lingual translations—our Rumanian and Persian monitors communicated only in French—and filing propaganda summaries in the abbreviated gibberish known as cablese generally ran from 1 to 3 p.m., 5 to 7, then 9 o'clock till 3 the next morning. Thanks to the OWI, I had theoretical access to the Gezira (Westerners only) Sporting Club, but my schedule gave me little opportunity to enjoy it. Gezira's uniformed locker-room crew, immaculate tennis courts and crisp salads by a sun-warmed swimming pool gave me an occasional glimpse of British colonial life. I could see why the British were reluctant to give it up; there was nothing like it in damp, foggy England.

I wrote home that if an earthquake ever struck Cairo, it probably would not be felt at Gezira: "Being an Egyptian quake, it simply would not be permitted in."

Nonetheless, an ardent devotee of the Club was a regular visitor to our household. Lochhead's mistress, Claudia Leeds, was a tall, toothy blonde who would not have attracted a second glance on Piccadilly Circus—but we were a long way from Piccadilly.

I could understand Major Lochhead's hanging on. He had been four years away from home, in the parched, wind-blown desert and now the grinding monotony of Cairo. Many Westerners took refuge in drink: Pim's Number Two on the terrace at Shepheards Hotel for the colonels, beer on sweaty rooftops for Other Ranks.

For the rest of us, the outlet of choice was women. But in a city jammed with troops from every corner of the British Empire as well as Americans and uniformed exiles from the Balkans, there was never enough female company to go around. As I pointed out in a letter to a friend:

> The male-female proportion here is the exact reverse of Washington's, creating a tiny aristocracy of attractive women who can have six dates a day if they want them . . .
>
> European women are either shallow, gaudy Greek Royalists or war-sufferers with complicated neuroses. The American girls are rushed off their feet by a swarm of eager officers from the U.S. Middle East Command almost before they get off the boat. So instead of the anticipated moonlight on the Nile, with night jasmine in the air, I find myself racing up and down office corridors until four a.m., wrangling over untranslatable phrases with temperamental Bulgarians.
>
> But the desert has had its oases . . .

Leni Turner was a German-born beauty attached by some legerdemain of citizenship to the British Army. My psyche, in earlier flight from its sense of ghetto-stained inadequacy, had seen in Sybil Rice among other things, a kind of trophy mistress. With Leni I turned that motif up a notch and added another dimension that would become a hallmark of my emotional gambols: fantasy. To my fevered mind Leni's fair complexion, long golden-wheat tresses and cerulean blue eyes made her a creature from a Heine romance, a blend of Valkyrian goddess and seductive Lorelei transplanted from her Rhine castle to ply her siren wiles on the Nile.

Operations went smoothly enough—a dinner date, a movie, an evening's serenade at the piano—until the night I led her to my bedroom. With the lights delicately dimmed, and the lady responsive, I fumbled for a contraceptive—and the magic link snapped. Evidently, at least in my timing, I had violated some sacred clause of the German Lovers' Handbook. Leni bolted from my bed and headed for the door.

Such petty dramas were a mainstay of Cairo life, the collective refuge of the capital's inmates from its daily toll of heat and sameness. I later discovered that sex in Egypt, especially with British women, was as dry as the dust of the pyramids. It had all the impact of a round of shuffleboard or a browse through a month-old copy of the London *Times*.

There had to be something better. At odd hours snatched from the treadmill, I started looking. For the most bizarre few weeks of my life, every woman I met was a challenge. I discarded my glasses defiantly on dates, risking injury or worse as I stumbled along dimly-lit streets on moonless nights, or leaped recklessly onto a gharry dashboard beside my quarry. Peering in near-sighted helplessness into the jasmine-scented darkness along the banks of the Nile, I was completely at the mercy of my gharry driver, who for all I knew could have delivered my lady and me south to the Sudan or north to Alexandria.

Gradually the fever calmed, partly because there was no time to indulge it. OWI needed ideological fodder for leaflets to be dropped over Germany. OSS, parachuting solo fighters into obscure corners of Yugoslavia, wanted every speck we could dredge up about anti-Nazi guerrillas there. The Office of Naval Intelligence sounded an alert regarding shipping in the Greek port of Pireus.

Also I was becoming more self-sufficient. With a scattering of books, a radio wangled from the RMS, and a rented upright piano of garish red, I had a fair handful of personal resources assembled. And for a time I fell back on the self-preserving technique familiar to overworked hospital interns in crowded emergency rooms; one learned to turn off all sensibilities, go numb. But nothing could shield me indefinitely from the fearful reality of Cairo.

The typical Cairene, barefoot and shabby behind his donkey cart, lived in a world that vanished from western Europe centuries ago. From his medieval stockade, he peered out in uncomprehending wonder at airplanes and medical clinics. These were not for him; by Islamic teaching, nothing changed or was changeable; birth, death and the interlude between were all preordained by Allah. It was pointless, if not sinful, to challenge one's assigned role.

For women, it was even worse. Westerners, cut off by the barrier of language, could only gaze wonderingly down the well, stare at the mute veiled creatures squatting in degradation on the pavement, too caught up in the battle for bread to worry about "women's rights."

A Greek naval officer encountered at Gezira invited me to his farming estate in the nearby fertile, densely populated Nile Valley. I watched Aristide's cotton-picking *fellaheen* or peasants stagger through their paces. Beaten by a merciless sun from dawn to dusk for the princely salary of thirty cents a day, they were landlocked galley slaves.

Aristide took me on a tour of their roofless mud huts—almost as roomy, he pointed out with pride, as the clean wide stalls where he housed his cattle. A *fellah* survived on pita bread, a salted onion or tomato, and vegetable mash. Unable to read, a two-legged beast of burden, he found a hundred-word vocabulary sufficient to convey his needs and interests. Only his wife suffered a worse plight. Assigned to plow his field and warm his bed (perhaps also to share it), she fetched slightly more on the village market than a young donkey, although not as much as a horse.

Urban dwellers could seek sanctuary in Cairo's City of the Dead, an encampment of penniless squatters entrenched in rat-infested, long-abandoned tombs. Walking through it one steamy afternoon, I had to fight back nausea. I wanted to scream my protest—but to whom? King Farouk? The British Foreign Office? Our OWI broadcasts prattled smugly of the "free world" lined up against Hitler. But how free were the starvelings of Cairo?

The saddest man I ever met in the capital was a young, obviously dedicated Egyptian doctor. He told me the average Cairene had some thirty-two known diseases, headed by anemia, hookworm, tuberculosis and trachoma. When American Army doctors brought in a typhus vaccine, he said, it promptly found its way to the black market, where the wealthy set—those least susceptible to the disease—gobbled it up at fabulous prices.

The wealthy had their own problems. Cattaui Pasha, a member of the Senate (and ironically a Jew who would later be driven out by Gamal Abdel Nasser) took me to dinner at a luxurious club whose windows overlooked a teeming square. The Senator wanted my help in getting tires from America for his Packard, "the small car." He gestured toward the square below, where scores of lesser citizens were clinging to the steps and posts of jam-packed trolleys. "After all," he said, "you can't expect me to ride with these wretched vermin."

I wanted to weep for the "vermin." The blindfolded water buffaloes along the Nile, plodding in endless circles under a searing unforgiving sun, were a metaphor for the nation.

In November of 1944, to celebrate the upcoming rainy season (which turned out to be a single afternoon's shower during one of my siestas), I threw a party for the RMS staff. "You Too Can Have a Hangover," trilled the stenciled invitation. "Friends! Are You Cheerful? Brimming with Health and Delighted with Life? Why Stay That Way? Come to Berkman's party!"

The affair apparently went very well. What I didn't mention in a letter reporting on it was a reawakening of the old adolescent feelings of isolation, of the outsider looking in while others, who somehow belonged, paired off in easy bouts of laughter and flirtation.

Even as the final nails were being hammered home against Hitler, new tensions, foreshadowing the Cold War, were rising in the Balkans. In Yugoslavia, ruthlessly fragmented by the Nazis, underground resistance had first been spearheaded by the Royalist Chetniks; communist bands under Josip Broz Tito had increasingly taken over the partisan movement, to the point where our monitoring pick-ups indicated the Chetniks were more bent on beating Tito than on fighting the Nazis. As a result, British support had swung to the Moscow-backed Tito, and the paratroopers dropped by our OSS were taking the same route.

A similar Royalist-leftist antagonism split the Resistance forces in Greece; but there the situation was more complex because Athens had long been a bastion of British power. As the Germans withdrew late in 1944, Tommies landed. But the many-faceted leftist coalition ELAS, firmly backing the minority Communist element in its leadership, flatly rejected British orders to disarm. All-out civil war ensued, with sporadic British intervention on the right-wing side.

RMS had for some time been picking up, on a random basis, clandestine broadcasts from ELAS, apparently emanating from a mobile transmitter in the Greek mountains. The British were attempting by triangulation to pinpoint the transmitter's location, in order to confirm strong suspicions that it was actually in Yugoslavia or Bulgaria, and that they were in fact facing a miniature confrontation with their Russian allies.

But the guerrillas were concerned with other matters than our convenience, and there was no visible pattern to their operation. The transmitter never did yield its secret.

At 4:30 a.m. on a chilly March morning I stumbled through our apartment door to encounter the plaintive strains of a Chopin piano nocturne. It was an Artur Rubinstein recording—his wistful *rubato* was unmistakable—and it shimmered like a diamond on velvet in the eerie stillness of the Egyptian night.

But where was it coming from? Mesmerized, I trailed the sound to the kitchen.

Behind me, embedded in the wall, an ancient dumbwaiter shaft, much like the one remembered from my childhood in Brooklyn, ran its pulleys from the cellar up past our sixth floor flat to the roof. I flung it open.

The melody swelled. Someone in the penthouse two stories above was communing with Chopin.

The nocturne ended. A brief pause, and another began. For twenty minutes I was adrift in Washington, New York, Ithaca, in a web of memories. Then the music stopped. I was in Cairo again, facing a dark empty dumbwaiter shaft. I went to my room and toppled into bed.

A few days later, sunning on the roof, I saw a fair-haired woman of thirty-odd years emerge from the penthouse. I hastened after her into the elevator hall. "That was a lovely concert the other night. The Chopin nocturnes." I explained the dumbwaiter's acoustics.

"You are . . . student of Chopin?"

"I even try to play him. But not like Rubinstein."

She smiled. "No vun is like him." The accent was German. So were the soft round features. But where Leni Turner had been all golds and blues, a canvas in blazing oils, this woman was gentle pastels. We exchanged names. Hesitantly, stepping into the elevator, she invited me to Sunday tea.

The hesitancy, I soon learned, was well grounded. Ruth Kater was a divorcée from Cologne, stranded while vacationing in Egypt six years ago by the outbreak of war. She had long been in semi-hiding, fearful that discovery by some inquisitive Briton would lead to her internment; she might be free to return home if she could stay out of harm's way just a few months more. But my roommate was a British officer . . .

We chatted of Goethe and Beethoven, of Hitler and the Jews, astonished at our harmony of views . . . and at the mutual chemistry. "When you first came into my hall," she confessed later, "I felt an electric chill. I wanted to give you a baby."

But she was fearful of entrapment, of becoming deeply involved with someone who might be snatched away by the war. "How do I know you won't leave tomorrow?" she demanded. "There are three men here who want to marry me, men I feel safe with . . . not rocked by feelings that I thought were dead!"

Ultimately proximity and desire won out. When Ruth yielded herself, it was with a womanly tenderness and concern I had never known before. Soon it was I who was trembling for the future, wondering whether with all my shortcomings I could hold onto this splendid creature . . .

One afternoon I arrived at the penthouse to find Ruth talking with a freshfaced young pilot from New Zealand. She handled the ensuing awkwardness with aplomb, flirting lightly with both of us, dodging my attempts to establish a proprietary intimacy.

I fretted, fumed, and finally exploded in a door-slamming schoolboy exit. The next morning there was a melancholy note in my mailbox: "Experience taught, and teaches me again: all education is superficial glamorwork if there is no natural tact. I would not be able to talk to you as I did before. I lost confidence. I am sorry."

April of 1945 came; Franklin D. Roosevelt died on the verge of victory. There was quiet sorrow in Cairo. I had a profound sense of personal loss. FDR was the lodestar for the liberals and dreamers of my generation. I had seen him once, addressing a joint session of Congress, a towering figure made somehow more powerful by the shriveled legs that never appeared in photographs. Two weeks later, American and Russian troops met at Torgau on the Elbe. Soon Mussolini was hanged, Hitler a suicide, Japan wavering. The founding sessions of the United Nations were already under way in San Francisco.

But in our split-off world of the Middle East, ten thousand miles away, peace was not on the agenda. Not in the mountain passes of Greece, where British troops backing a corrupt Athens regime faced off against guerrilla bands supported by Moscow. And not 800 miles across the Mediterranean, where the spur of Nazi brutality gave sudden urgency to the long-festering issue of Palestine.

CHAPTER 7

Let My People Go

I had many cherished friends in England, but I did not count among them the policy-makers in Whitehall. Britain had been playing a double game in the Middle East. Rulers of the Holy Land under a League of Nations mandate since the end of World War I, the British had in the 1917 Balfour Declaration promised to further the establishment there of a Jewish homeland, so long as the rights of its non-Jewish communities were not violated.

Equally solemn, if more ambiguous promises of independence had been made to Arab leaders by London, and topped in 1939 by issuance of a White Paper restricting Jewish immigration to fifteen hundred a month.

With the liberation of Hitler's concentration camps, a shocked world was recoiling from the horror of gas chambers. Six million European Jews had been exterminated; many people felt the doors of Palestine should be thrown open to the wretched survivors. When no action was taken, a vast underground exodus of Displaced Persons began sweeping across the Continent. From ports in the south of France, the refugees headed east for new lives in Palestine.

The British government promptly dubbed them illegals, and barred them from coming ashore. The Grand Mufti of Jerusalem, long allied with Hitler during the war, leaped into the fray, urging the slaughter of the Zionist invaders. Goebbels was gone, but from the microphones of various Mideast capitals the Grand Mufti thundered on, spewing his message of hate and destruction. I was appalled and frustrated. How many heads did this Hydra monster of bigotry have?

Arab riots broke out against Jewish settlers, marked by British indifference if not support. (In the British view, Arabs knew their place; Jews were inclined to be cheeky.) Angry settlers retaliated by sabotaging British troop movements. The Soviets, eager to gain a foothold in the oil-rich, restless Middle East, sermonized on the evils of capitalist colonialism in their Arabic-language service. Only RMS Cairo, with its large staff and specialized monitoring equipment, could keep up with the barrage inundating the airwaves.

But our staff was being cut: Colonel Fraser long gone, Lochhead and Captain Williams now being shipped in his wake back to England. Administrative as well as editorial responsibilities were falling more and more on my shoulders.

Bone-weary, tired of dust and camels, I yearned for the crisp greenery of a New England orchard, waffles for breakfast, snowflakes on my window, a day without uniforms or PX chits. I settled instead for the company of an engaging young gadfly, John Wellington Donovan, a lieutenant in Balkan intelligence with all the legendary Irish virtues—and all the faults, too. He was puckish, charming, gallant, sentimental and generous. He was also sexually overcharged, a compulsive seducer uninhibited by moral restraints, and a heavy drinker with a tendency in his cups to suicidal belligerence.

His greatest virtue—a passion for honesty, fairness, justice—would in later years lead to his undoing, when his contempt for mindless compliance made him a natural target for a heavy-handed government security apparatus notoriously wary of dissidence.

Good-looking in a virile black-Irish way, John had panache, an extraordinary personal magnetism. Arab *gharry* drivers flowed into his orbit; Greek princesses, Italian night club singers, Bulgarian cabinets-in-exile. Quick to pick up a few phrases in any language, he could stroll into the famous international bar at Shepheards Hotel and collect a bosom-pal crowd, complete with party invitations, in the space of ten minutes.

John became an instant favorite of Ferguson and Jeeves, despite his habit of rarely arriving for dinner alone. He might have in tow Yassin Bey, a local industrialist, or scholarly Kermit (Kim) Roosevelt of TR's Oyster Bay clan.

John delighted in shocking people. "I stand for nothing," he explained. "In this world of groups and labels, this international society of snipers, that's important. I refuse to accept the inviolability of the sacred institutions behind which people take refuge from personal responsibility: church, marriage, Communism. No man-made institution can arrogate to itself all the answers."

At an American women's forces dance in Cairo, his attention was drawn to a gross, heavily-bemedaled figure piloting a statuesque and clearly uncomfortable blonde around the floor. Donovan knifed through the crowd and tapped the fat man briskly on the shoulder. King Farouk of Egypt, bewildered—he had never been cut in on by a prince, much less by a twenty-three-year-old American lieutenant—surrendered his prey, and John marched the grateful lady off.

John was born and raised Catholic. At fifteen, unable to reconcile the rigid formulations of the church with his own perceptions of a world crying for change, he departed the faith. However, he would not make the broad leap to Marxism. That likewise was too doctrinaire for his intensely emotional humanism. I was with him one evening in a New York bar where a religious argument was raging. John turned to the stranger on the adjacent stool. "Tell me," he inquired amiably, "what set of prejudices do you subscribe to?"

His detachment did not sit well with my left-leaning colleague, Stanley Harrison. When Ibrahim, our impecunious handyman at RMS, bewailed his struggles to read (his teacher was his eight-year-old son), Harrison lectured him severely on the evils of capitalism. Donovan gave him a warm Army jacket.

I looked forward to Donovan's unscheduled appearances, his puncturing of the status quo, his fount of amusing one-liners:

"The war is a divine plot to keep us away from women: eight million of us here, eight million of them there." On Russia's declaration of war against Bulgaria: "Now the world community of nations can relax and settle down to an era of universal bloodshed." On the inflexible weathervane atop a suburban villa: "It's a British lion; it doesn't move with the wind." On an Italian countess of unbridled libido: "She's gone to Cyprus—presumably to look for a mountain goat."

In the summer of 1945, a couple of months after the German surrender, Donovan's tour of duty ended. He returned to Cairo in the fall, ostensibly as a business entrepreneur, soon working as network correspondent for the National Broadcasting Company. America was tuning in to the Middle East, particularly to the conflict in the Holy Land.

American air waves, long the province of saccharine soap operas and gimlet-eyed detectives, were coming of age. As a source of information the vocal bulletin was faster than print, with a sharpness and immediacy not available to the composing room. Wartime had seen CBS in particular dispatch correspondents to a number of battlefronts, creating the nucleus for a global network staff. From bomb-shattered London, Edward R. Murrow had pioneered a new kind of reporting: terse, crisp, vivid. In short declarative sentences unencumbered by windy excursions, he brought the scene to the listener and the listener into the scene. Somehow combining rigorous objectivity with personal warmth, he set a standard that in our era of media superstars has rarely been equaled and never surpassed.

By 1946 I too was on the air, for ABC, while waiting for a replacement man from Washington. My shift back to the news had been gradual. With the defeat of Hitler, Britain was relinquishing its senior status in the Atlantic alliance to the younger, wealthier United States. As a tiny ripple in this historic tide, I found myself in charge of the Cairo monitoring operation, elevated in assimilated rank from major to lieutenant colonel, with more than a hundred employees under my direct supervision.

The first thing I did was to wipe out the monstrous inequities in salaries, which had victimized Balkan nationals and all female staff members. This went over big locally—"You like a king!" proclaimed our NAAFI houseboy Sabri after my reorganization speech—but was greeted less warmly at budget-focused FBIS headquarters in Washington.

Weary of bureaucracy, I was also less than enchanted with our military, on whose signals branch I depended to route my monitored reports to Washington. Too many louts in uniform were running free. I had seen a drunken American paratrooper dig his boots into the skinny flank of a local milk-wagon horse, then turn his fists on a gutsy little Tommy who protested. I had been threatened with mayhem myself by a gigantic good-ol'-boy from Louisiana when I complained about the desultory handling of major news bulletins. Most importantly, for more than two years, I had set aside all thought of personal expression. I was starved for a column of print space, the cheerful cacophony of an orchestra pit, an audience. A radio microphone would do very nicely.

As a final prod toward resuming news work, there was the familiar element of the veteran fire horse responding to an alarm bell. Bells were ringing all over the eastern Mediterranean.

Radio correspondence made sense. I knew the political situation on the ground. Through personal contacts I had access to many key players—diplomats, generals, Egyptian Prime Minister Sidky Pasha, Zionist leaders in Palestine, Arab League Secretary General Azzam Pasha. I had been schooled on the *Mirror* in the tight reportage that could pack a strong picture into radio's two-minute time slots. And thanks to training as a singer, I had no problems with voice quality or diction.

The temporary dual role of government employee and broadcaster would be unusual, but my superiors at FBIS, possibly guilty over the delay in sending me the oft-promised replacement, made no objections.

With Donovan back in the States to pursue a hot business lead—as it turned out, only briefly—somebody gave me the name of Bill Brooks at NBC in New York, and late in 1945 a test broadcast was set up. It went swimmingly. A live booking was then arranged for the following week via the Marconi office in Cairo—but nobody there bothered to relay the information to the chief engineer at the radio station, so he in turn couldn't tell me. The worldwide NBC round-up came on the air, the anchor man confidently introduced "Ted Berkman in Cairo," and of course nothing happened. Much gnashing of molars, not least mine.

After a flurry of explanatory cables, I advised Brooks that I was considering resignation from my government post in favor of NBC; I wanted reassurance that he saw the radio spot as one with long-term potential.

His reply was anything but reassuring. He regarded the Middle East as a temporary trouble spot, likely to warrant only occasional fill-in coverage by a part-time stringer. Somebody forgot to tell Arafat and Netanyahu. My ardor cooled. And my disappointment mounted.

Two weeks later Douglas Edwards of CBS arrived in Cairo: a plump, round-faced young man recently promoted from announcing chores in New York to a roving reportorial role, and visibly ill at ease in the Middle East maelstrom. He came to my office with a shopping list of political questions, and a most intriguing piece of information. He had been instructed by Howard K. Smith, then stationed in London as the network's chief European correspondent, to hire me as its man in the Middle East: a full-time staff assignment to an area where CBS expected a lot of news for years to come. I was ecstatic. Deliverance had come to my doorstep. I wanted to lift my roly-poly visitor over my head and dance around the room.

I settled instead for an enormous celebratory dinner. Then I accompanied Edwards to the Cairo radio station, where he was to deliver a two-minute spiel to New York. As we waited in the broadcast booth for his signal to go on, a tall fair-haired man in immaculate khakis strode briskly into the room and stuck out his hand to Edwards. "I'm George Polk."

"Nice to meet you, George. This is Ted Berkman—the new CBS man in the Middle East."

"But I'm the new CBS man!"

As Polk and I stared at each other in consternation, the voice of the station engineer came over the intercom.

"Ten seconds to air time, Mr. Edwards . . . five . . . "

Edwards stepped up to the microphone, took a deep breath, and underwent a transformation that nearly half a century later still dazzles in memory, from a timid tadpole to a booming bullfrog, showering upon America the authoritative lowdown (my lowdown) on the Middle East. It was a virtuoso performance, enough momentarily to distract Polk and me from our personal cliff-hanger.

But not for long. When Doug signed off, the three of us repaired to Shepheards to unscramble our confusions. It developed that, unbeknown to Howard Smith, Edward R. Murrow in New York had several days earlier engaged Polk, then with the New York *Herald-Tribune,* for the Middle East assignment. Not only had the commitment preceded Smith's decision to hire me, but Ed Murrow was undisputed boss of network news operations. An exchange of cables confirmed the regrettable lapse in intra-network communications. There was nothing to do but to swallow this second disappointment and congratulate the winner.

That left a third network still unexplored: ABC. A query to news director Tom Velotta there brought a quick test and an equally quick okay. A host of stories were heating up: the issue of British troop withdrawal from Egypt, the growing strength of the fundamentalist Moslem Brotherhood, overtures to the Islamic world from the Soviet Union (whose Tass correspondent, unlike Western reporters, spoke fluent Arabic). And heading the news agenda in a dozen capitals, the burgeoning crisis in Palestine, where underground Jewish groups were engaged in increasingly ugly confrontation with British authorities.

Bookings of radio circuits, in a feudal world thrust abruptly into twentieth century electronics, were chancy. Nonetheless, on many a midnight I found myself prowling through the dark, lonely streets of the city enroute to a 1:00 a.m. rendezvous with the Taylor Grant show in New York, where Grant did a world news round-up at what for him was 7 p.m. I felt at home in front of a microphone, answerable only to my conscience, in tune with my deepest self. Commanding a regular radio spot, with access to senators, potentates and untold anonymous millions, was like having one's own private newspaper.

Donovan was soon back in NBC harness. With pressure on the Cairo bureau relaxed, we both joined a U.S. correspondents' junket to Greece and Turkey. In Ankara, a stranger sidled up to me. "Would you like to meet an honest newspaperman?"

"Where is he?"

"In jail, naturally."

"Can you get me in?"

"Can you look Turkish?"

Posing as my subject's cousin, I got a scorching jailhouse interview and sold it under a pseudonym to the Overseas News Agency. History changes slowly. Late in 1996 the *New Yorker* reported that Osak Isik Yurctu, former editor of a defunct Turkish daily, was in jail serving a fifteen year sentence for publishing "separatist propaganda."

Control of the FBIS, its reputation now firmly established, was bouncing among various claimants, with rumor giving the final nod to the burgeoning CIA. My nominal superior in Cairo was now the new military attaché there, an ace fighter pilot from Montana named Sandy McNown. Unpretentious and eager to learn the local realities, Colonel McNown was a far cry from his predecessor, who had occupied himself mainly with providing blondes from our Women's Army Corps to King Farouk. McNown asked penetrating questions, made no effort to control my cables, and turned an indulgent eye on my broadcasting for ABC; he even smuggled a tip to me about the secret arrival in Egypt of the rabble-rousing, fiercely anti-Zionist Haj Amin el Husseini, the Grand Mufti of Jerusalem.

By June I was a fixture on the nightly Taylor Grant show, with featured slots three or four times a week. Besides covering Palestine and

Egypt, I did several pieces on the oil-centered government upheavals in Iran. Waiting out the bureaucratic flip-flops at FBIS—my relief man still had not materialized—I also dabbled in the luxury of actually enjoying Cairo.

As FBIS boss, I now had access to a jeep. Between broadcast labors, Donovan and I repaired to a small villa at Gizeh, in the shadow of the Great Pyramids. A hop across the wall took us to the Mena House golf course, where the main hazard was the caddies. As I reported in a letter home, "They have no notion whatsoever of where the ball is traveling, and in fact are generally practicing shots behind a nearby trap while their victim is teeing off." Still, it was fun to swing a midiron under the chipped-off nose of the Sphinx, and of a weekend to savor Donovan's extravagant mix of guests: Egyptian princes, Turkish financiers, an American general, Greek glamour girls—with John in the kitchen exchanging ribald anecdotes with the hired help.

Mena House, where Roosevelt and Churchill had conferred during the war, boasted a couple of nearby riding stables for the convenience of the international polo set. Although Donovan had only been on a horse once, he found the notion of careening across the desert on a fiery Arab steed too much to resist. I had done some riding in newspaper days, and later at Rock Creek Park in Washington, so I agreed to go along. What the stable people neglected to tell us was that our horses had just received inoculation shots guaranteed to put them in a frenzy.

There ensued the maddest gallop across the sands since *The Desert Song*, past the frowning stare of the Sphinx and down the narrow lanes of a Biblical canal, where we scattered several somnolent herds of goats and sheep, Donovan cackling curses and alarms in his fluent street Arabic.

CHAPTER 8

Bombs Bursting in Air

A terrible showdown was brewing in Palestine. From our listening post across the Sinai two hundred miles away, patching together the reports of clashes and ambushes, of ultimatums and defiant counter-threats among Briton, Arab, and the Jewish underground, one could sense an impending cataclysm. Although both Donovan and George Polk were in Athens, preoccupied with the Greek civil war, I felt it was time for an on-the-scene radio report from Jerusalem.

My acquaintance with Zionism was of long standing but shallow. My maternal grandfather, Henry Holtzmann, had been the first correspondent in America for *Die Welt*, the newspaper of Theodor Herzl, founder of the movement. I had dim childhood memories of collection boxes in the kitchen.

After college, with growing political awareness and a global, humanistic orientation, I had frowned upon the notion of still another separate nationalism plaguing a world already over-afflicted with competing societies. That, of course, was before Hitler, before the Holocaust . . . and before seeing Palestine and its incipient Jewish state as a living entity.

On my second visit, in the fall of 1944, I was staggered by the country's Biblical treasures, enthusing in letters home over the half-excavated stones that were Jericho, the breathtaking view from the lofty slopes of the Mount of Olives, the steps of Christ up to Calvary—and was equally impressed by the settler pioneers, especially in the cooperative kibbutzim. Here were young people content with working the earth, literally oblivious to money, enjoying each other and forging a difficult dream.

I was struck also by the pervasiveness of music in the culture. Choral singing, spirited and clear, rang through kibbutz mess halls. Tel Aviv was scarcely more developed than a Nevada mining town, but along every street, pouring out of every window were the sounds of violins and cellos, keyboard clarinets and flutes, as if the little city was a desert Tanglewood.

The girls were tanned and pretty, the men companionable. And the pioneers were refurbishing the squalor of the Middle East. As one of my letters noted, "The new part of Jerusalem was refreshingly clean; had me a fine milk shake ten minutes after I arrived." Perhaps the notion of Jewish nationhood was not so unthinkable, after all.

Lurking behind this change of sentiment, no doubt, were many half-buried relics of anti-Semitic experience, my private archaeology as a Jew: the faint slurs of early school days, the quiet exclusion on unwritten racial grounds from Cornell's Glee Club, and most emphatically, an episode in Nova Scotia where I was taking a brief boarding-house vacation before departing overseas. Coming downstairs to dinner, I had opened the door upon a loud fulmination against Jews, a classic Nazi diatribe, by a French Canadian from Montreal. What was worse, the other guests sat in stony silence. Not a very cheery send-off to the war for democracy.

So I had personal grounds for Zionist sympathies. But two years in the turbulent Arab milieu, coupled with daily exposure to the British colonial scene, had rekindled my initial misgivings. The centuries of Ottoman oppression had left deep and humiliating scars on the Arab psyche.

In June, shortly before returning to Jerusalem as a radio correspondent, I summed up my appraisal of the situation in a letter to my mother:

> I still feel Zionism is an impossible and infinitely tragic dream. The essence of the question remains as it was when I last discussed it with you: the Jews have unfortunately chosen just about the worst, most controversial spot on the face of the globe. The fact that their dream is centuries old, that they have accomplished miracles on the land, that the Arab world is a feudal despotism—none of these changes the character of the movement, which in the eyes of the Arabs is an invasion. The recent Anglo-American Commission report said nothing about European aid for the refugees. It pointed only at Palestine. I am fearful of its consequences.

Over the decades to come, through the Arab *intifadah* revolt and the insistence by Orthodox Jewry on a God-given Greater Israel, through two books dealing with Israel in wartime, I would strive to maintain a balanced view of a complex quarrel in which there were no absolutes, only dubious choices. But those issues were far down the road. In the summer of 1946 it was Jew moving toward showdown against Briton.

Arriving in Jerusalem, I headed for the Pantiles Pension, unofficial headquarters for the foreign press. A dozen print reporters were there. The only other radio correspondent was the BBC's John Nixon, fated to die soon afterward in a plane crash.

Sporadic gunfire crackled around the pension, fading before anybody could check its source: roving Arab bands, jumpy British troops (numbering nearly a hundred thousand), or an element of the splintered Jewish underground? In a desperate attempt to weed out terrorist extremists, the British military were in effect arresting for interrogation the whole city of Tel Aviv. They threw an armed cordon around the city, then narrowed it to smaller rings. Every brigade had its own central cage; each of nineteen battalions its own screening team. Only pregnant women and the certifiably bed-ridden were exempted. Hundreds were thrust behind barbed wire.

On the outskirts of the city, our taxi-load of western correspondents was turned back by a band of sullen club-wielding teenagers, who announced "We make the curfew here; this is a Jewish State." I had a disturbing mix of feelings: compassion for their cause, unease about their tactics.

Clearly an explosion was building up, but it was hard to get news out by radio. The only—and rarely used—circuit for reaching the United States was a telephone line from Jerusalem to Cairo, with radio relay from there to New York. Twice I had tried to arrange such a hook-up; twice it had fallen through.

On Friday, July 19, I made a last stab, and was assured of a definite circuit for the following Monday at 9 p.m. local time.

On Monday morning I was at a local T-nuva dairy, doing something I had been looking forward to for a long time: sinking my teeth into a plate of cheese blintzes swimming in sour cream. Blintzes, a traditional Jewish food, are a tasty blend of eggs, flour, farmer's cheese, butter, salt and jelly. They never appeared on a menu during my long exile from Jewish cuisine in Egypt, where dairy products were suspect.

I tucked in a napkin and attacked my plate, feeling the cheese roll over my tongue with each bite, happily reminded of my mother's cooking and a score of soul-satisfying blintz bashes on the East Coast and in Hollywood. No Chinese emperor swooning over sharks' fins ever enjoyed his delicacy more.

I thought fondly of my colleague Dick Mowrer of the New York *Post*, who had phoned earlier to suggest a noontime drink at the bar of the King David Hotel. I explained that I would like to meet him there a little later, since I had my stomach, if not my heart, set on a late-morning blintz debauch. Dick, a gentle and perceptive friend, was understanding.

As I was wolfing down my last blintz, a blast sounded in the distance. The T-nuva customers exchanged anxious glances, then returned to their snacks. With so much destructive power around, it could be anything.

A siren shrieked. Then another, a long slow wail rising in pitch to a high sustained scream broken by the far-off clamor of ambulance alarms. Something terrible had happened.

A young waiter burst in from the street. "It's the King David. The King David Hotel!"

The King David, housing the offices of the Palestine administration, was a landmark, a major symbol of British authority. I could feel an odd tingling in the back of my neck.

I sprinted, breathless, to mid-town to encounter an appalling scene. The entire southwest wing of the six-story hotel had been sheared off as if by a giant cleaver. Great slabs of concrete sprawled in a hideous tangle of wires and masonry thirty-five feet high; smoke curled up, but no signs of life. On the lawn of the YMCA across King David Street lay two bodies, hurled 100 feet through the air by the blast.

Rescue crews were tumbling out of trucks and ambulances, senior officers barking commands: "Water here . . . somebody get a hacksaw . . . " A stretcher team, carrying a mangled man in Transjordan Police uniform, his right leg blown off, elbowed me aside. Several minutes passed before I announced myself to grimy, silent Tommies in dirt-and-blood-caked uniforms. Revolvers at the ready, they examined my press card carefully.

Through a long afternoon I gathered impressions and casualty statistics (seventy-nine dead, forty-six injured, twenty-six missing), jotting down poignant fragments of conversation: "I suggest you call the guard.

I believe Mrs. Evans is in the morgue." Squads of Royal Engineers, working in four-hour shifts, were digging with derricks, pneumatic drills and pickaxes, listening for faint cries from the rubble. I threaded my way to La Regence, the basement bar, and found it reduced to planks and stones, with great chunks of plaster hanging crazily from the walls.

Finally I assembled official statements: from the aggrieved British, the anti-terrorist Haganah resistance, and Menachem Begin's Irgun Zvei Leumi, which admitted the attack but insisted the British had ignored the Irgun's warnings. While preparing my copy for the evening broadcast, I learned that Dick Mowrer had suffered a broken leg when a stone column in the bar collapsed, pinning him to the ground. Thanks to my passion for blintzes, I had not been sitting beside him.

At eight in the evening I began the half-hour trek to the radio station. The night was inky-black, a tiny slice of moon peering out occasionally from behind low clouds.

Five minutes away from the pension a voice shouted "Halt!", and I heard a rifle bolt click into place. On a stone parapet above me a slim figure loomed, silhouetted against the momentary moon, rifle pointed at my chest. He was young, British and nervous.

"I'm an American correspondent," I protested. "On my way to the radio station." I reached for my credentials.

"Get your 'ands up! Over your 'ead!"

The sentry clambered down. "We'll see 'oo you are!" He prodded me forward with his rifle butt, uninterested in my complaints about a broadcast deadline. We plodded for ten minutes across a rocky field to a base camp where, in the furthermost tent, the major in command sat drinking tea. He listened to the guard's report, then turned to me. "So you're a Yank?"

"Yes, sir." I produced my ABC press credentials.

"Where are you from, Yank?"

"Brooklyn, New York."

"The home of the Statue of Liberty?"

"No, sir. Of the Brooklyn Dodgers."

The major took a final sip of tea. "Let him go, Corporal." The interlude had put me twenty minutes behind schedule.

I panted into the Radio Jerusalem building at two minutes before nine, finding its corridors crammed with Tommies. Learning of my mission, they urged me to tell the world what was going on. That I proceeded to do for ABC, insofar as the intricacies of the situation could be packed into two minutes. When I finished, New York asked Cairo and Jerusalem to keep the circuit open for another minute, so I could ad lib a special bulletin for immediate transmission on the network.

Two days later Golda Meir, in effect foreign minister for the Jewish government-to-be, addressed an overflow press conference. David Ben-Gurion and his moderate Haganah underground detested the Begin extremists, she declared. The Zionists did not believe in terrorist tactics, but did believe in their right to establish a Jewish state, a homeland where the survivors of the Holocaust could live free from further persecution. Toward that end they sought the backing of the international community.

Golda fielded a flood of questions, including this one from me: what role did she see for the Arabs of Palestine in the new nation?

Her reply was short and blunt. They were welcome to stay, she said, and reap what benefits they could.

Did she mean pick up the crumbs from the Jewish table?

Golda shrugged, not disputing this interpretation. Plainly the fate of the Arabs was not her concern.

Her answer troubled me (as my question had apparently troubled her press secretary, who later accused me of being "an anti-Semitic Jew").

After two years among the misery-laden Arab masses, I brought to Golda Meir's press conference dual sympathies: not only for Jews but for Jeeves, for the abandoned as well as the uprooted. I could not simply dismiss Arabs as irrelevant. True, the top layer in Egypt was cynical, corrupt, in league with colonial exploiters; but the crushed pathetic multitudes in the fields and the cities had a claim on humankind's attention. And I had known good and thoughtful people in the small middle class: Yassin Bey, who built a swimming pool for the workers in his glass factory; Mansour Arawi, a dentist who upon learning that my father was a dental surgeon had flatly refused any fee for his services. To my mind the Arabs of Palestine—their frustrations and yearnings, their attachment to the land and to the faith of their fathers, their vulnerability to fanatic and ambitious leaders—were a fact of life, a reality that could not simply be swept aside. Golda was putting a black and white veneer over a decidedly gray picture. Any formula that envisaged for an already beaten, much-exploited people the prospect of unfeeling dismissal, once again imported from the West, seemed to me to hold the seeds of disaster.

Obviously, two sets of legitimate claims were meeting head-on. The need for refuge by Holocaust survivors was undeniable, and all alternative plans for a homeland—in South Africa, in Mexico's Baja California, in the empty acreage of America's Far West—had fallen through. But likewise undeniable was Arab weariness of the foreign yoke, of Englishmen and Frenchmen picking up the riding crop dropped by the Ottoman sultans.

I had keen memories of a conversation in April with the little RMS handyman, Ibrahim. "All people same," he said. "Arabs, Christians, Jews. My uncle works orange place in Palestine. *Keteer felous*—much money. Jews good people."

And a few weeks later: "Jews bad. Want take away Palestine." He seized a chair. "This mine. Man wants take it, I shoot him."

In between, the Grand Mufti of Jerusalem had returned to Middle East microphones from Nazi Germany, whipping up demands for a Holy War. Media can be powerful catalysts.

I saw an outside chance for a peaceful fusion, if each side had the patience and wisdom to step into the other's shoes. There were moderate factions in the Zionist leadership, seeking cooperation with the Arabs; individual communities where the hand of friendship was extended, and Jews and Arabs lived in harmony as neighbors; Bedouin sheiks and settlement mayors who exchanged gifts. The best specific hope, to my mind, lay in the bi-national democratic state proposed by Rabbi Judah Magnes, president of the Hebrew University of Jerusalem. A handful of Palestinian Arab intellectuals, mostly doctors and academicians, shared his vision of a forward-looking society where Jewish skills and experience would spark an Arab reawakening.

But in both camps the voices of hard-liners—Islamic fanatics and messianic zealots—were louder. True, I could not foresee the day, more than four decades down the road, when an orthodox Jewish settler on the West Bank would shriek that only Jewish blood was sacred, while a ruthless Arab dictator would threaten to incinerate the people of Israel. But I could see enough to view the future with foreboding.

Sandy McNown was vexed at my ten-day absence. He reacted like the fighter pilot he was: by commandeering a plane and coming to fetch me back. On the return journey, no doubt to remind me who was in charge, he flew very low over the Suez Canal, buzzing and scattering the crews of half a dozen ships and at one point barely skimming the surface of the water. It was a bravura demonstration, calculated to scare the hell out of me—which it did.

Back among the suffocating dawns and *muezzin* chants of Cairo, I found a cable waiting. My successor would soon be departing from New York. It would be sweet to rest my gaze, without deadlines or responsibilities, upon an elm-dotted landscape.

I would take back imperishable memories from Egypt, the tomb of a few dead pharaohs and millions of the living: the slow, defeated shuffle of women who never smile; the dormant rage of the oppressed, pummeling a sofa outside the British Junior Officer's club as if it were a living thing; the pyramids, impressive from afar, up close, jagged boulders screaming of neglect; the Nile, graceful *feluccas* floating wraithlike in the distance; from its banks, dirty-green and sinister, like some fat, lazy serpent; the colonial Briton, last vestige of a once-mighty empire, dying, not heroically as in battle, but cantankerously, staring at the American in Shepheards Bar with the hatred of a washed-up matinee idol for a rising young star . . .

And England's dubious future. The empire had been arrested by history. Would it go quietly?

Finally, a relic that still sits on my curio shelf, a gift many years ago from John Donovan. He had it as a birthday present from George Polk, whose bitter fate in Salonika Bay still lay ahead. It came to Polk, he told John, from the private collection of King Farouk, who supposedly had exercised his royal prerogative and taken it from the Cairo Museum.

Some twenty-five centuries old, it is a slender horizontal stone carving, presumably once a bottle stopper. On the left is a seated male figure, exquisitely defined, half an inch high. Stretching away from his middle is a gargantuan male organ, swollen to an extravagant inch and three quarter length, more than three times the dimension of its owner's body. Wish fulfillment on the part of the sculptor? Tribute to some once-adored, long forgotten sexual athlete? We shall never know.

In August, the bomb at Hiroshima blasted Japan out of the war and a generation out of its complacency. Sprawled on the lawn of a suburban Cairo villa, I debated with novelist Arthur Koestler, the author of *Darkness at Noon*, the qualifications of American politicians for discharging the awesome responsibilities of the atomic age. He thought Washington was the perfect repository for such unprecedented power; I wasn't so sure.

At long last, FBIS advised that a replacement as monitoring chief was definitely on the way. For my part, he would be none too soon. Although I still got a kick out of hearing my own broadcasts quoted by the BBC and Radio Paris, my body was screaming for a rest. I was ready for the homeward passage on a Liberty ship from Alexandria.

CHAPTER 9

The Appeal of the U.N.

September, 1946. As our converted cargo ship crept into New York harbor, I had my first notice of a changed perspective. Manhattan, the once-glamorous art and commerce center of the universe, shrank before my eyes to a cramped, tiny island swarming with antlike millions, as hopelessly trapped in its stone canyons as the caged lions in its zoo. I blinked in alarm. Could I live again in a crowded American metropolis after exposure to the trackless desert and the wild Judean hills?

ABC had more prosaic questions, to be posed later in the week in a special evening broadcast. Radio had achieved rough parity with the print press as a news source during the war, partly because the rising cost of newsprint and the ferocious competition for advertising had forced a wave of bankruptcies, takeovers and mergers. Cities that had proudly supported a half-dozen dailies were reduced to one or two. A typical masthead trumpeted the *Star-Bugle-Advertiser*.

ABC, split off from NBC by the Federal Communications Commission a year earlier, was headquartered in Radio City. Waiting to go on, I found myself closeted in an anteroom with another prospective interviewee, CIA chief William "Wild Bill" Donovan. I asked General Donovan whether he thought Marshal Tito of Yugoslavia, a member of the Croat minority in a Serb-dominated country, would be able to hang onto power there. Donovan's fumbling reply indicated a less-than-nodding acquaintance with Balkan politics, from which I concluded that other people did the heavy thinking at the CIA, leaving Wild Bill to provide a colorful facade . . . an impression that would be strengthened two years later by his role in the George Polk tragedy.

When my turn came at the microphone, I apparently vexed the network brass by declining to forecast the date of the coming Armageddon in Palestine; they seemed more interested in generating controversy than in communicating facts. Clouding the atmosphere was a vague sense of a hidden agenda, an undefined chill.

Its source became evident when I reported back to Washington for assignment. The Cold War was now on, full blast. Our information-and-propaganda machinery, long trained on Berlin, had shifted focus to Moscow; many in the capital thought—and quite a few appeared to hope—that our guns would not be long in following suit.

At FBIS, now firmly locked into the CIA, I was named Acting Chief of Publications, responsible for the content of three thick daily mimeographs covering broadcasts from Europe, Asia and Latin America. The European Report alone filled two hundred pages.

However, I found my editorial duties constantly interrupted by visits from crewcut young men in Brooks Brothers suits, emissaries of the FBI, bent on probing the political purity of my staff. Did any of my underlings patronize foreign films? Make disparaging remarks about officials of the government? Or read subversive literature, like—gasp—the Communist *Daily Worker*?

Actually, I had seen a copy of the *Worker* in the hands of a sub-editor, a quiet, courtly middle-aged man with a neatly groomed blonde mustache and a name—Wilson Coppock—that would have looked at home among the signatures on the Declaration of Independence. Coppock was not, I was certain, under contract to the Soviet spy network. And in any case, as a supervised pencil-pusher handling only *en clair* uncoded broadcasts, he had no access to classified information. I did not offer him up to J. Edgar Hoover's pillory.

The moving finger of the FBI moved on, and inevitably came to rest on my own file. "Just a routine check"—but was it true that my father had been born in Riga, Latvia, now absorbed into the Soviet Union? Of course it was true; I had volunteered the information years ago.

Two days later, a thin, nervous young man appeared at my office to be instructed in the mysteries of editing radio transmissions. He had little linguistic equipment and less background in foreign affairs, but obviously he was being groomed to replace me. His father had been born in Richmond, Virginia.

Fed up with snoopery, bored with government, I took the hint. My resignation would be effective in two months. There was much that my fellow-Americans, in their comfortable isolation, didn't know about the world.

A fellow-newsman at the *New Republic* magazine, Tristram Coffin, had encouraged me to submit a few short pieces on events in the

Mediterranean. They were accepted without change. The *New Republic*, established in 1914, had a distinguished pedigree. Originally financed by the banker Willard Straight, a "limousine liberal" of Teddy Roosevelt-Progressive leanings, once edited by Walter Lippmann, its stated goal was to "raise small insurrections" in people's minds. Nothing I could quarrel with there. But broadcasting had given me a sense of integration, of a fusion between capacity and purpose, that I had been groping toward since adolescence. Speaking my piece, I could touch the elusive core of self that vibrated to Gershwin and Molière.

Winston Burdett of CBS, with whom I had become friendly overseas, set up an appointment for me with the network's Washington Bureau manager, Eric Sevareid.

Sevareid was a surprise. Icy and remote as a glacier, he made the bookish, reserved Burdett seem fiery by comparison. I had just read, and been enormously impressed by, Sevareid's *Not So Wild A Dream*. The CBS Washington ace was a large man, almost painfully sober. Ill at ease before an idol of my newspaper days, eager to impress, I made a rash overstatement on some minor point; Sevareid's steel-trap mind closed in on my gaffe and the interview was over.

Undismayed, Burdett promised to champion my cause with Ed Murrow. Meanwhile, how would I like to ghost a few speeches for the new, fiercely anti-militaristic junior senator from Idaho, Glen Taylor?

Why not? Learning that Taylor had strummed a guitar as "the crooning cowboy" during his campaign, I suggested that when communicating with me he should identify himself as "Mr. Singer"; the notion of playing harmless cloak-and-dagger under the very nose of the FBI amused me. This brilliant arrangement got off to a comic start the following week when, receiving a phone call from "the secretary to Mr. Singer," I insisted she must have the wrong party. Son of Mata Hari I wasn't; I had simply forgotten.

However, I did supply Taylor/Singer with some thunderous rhetoric. If anti-Communist fervor were to be the sole criterion for evaluating America's allies, I wrote, we could do no better than resurrect Adolf Hitler. In 1948, when Henry Wallace made his unsuccessful third-party bid for the presidency, Taylor became his running mate.

I returned to New York, no longer a bureaucrat. The *New Republic* had been making friendly noises about a staff job, but was still tentative about the post I wanted, foreign news editor.

At that point, former vice-president Henry Wallace was suddenly named to run the magazine, and job discussions slipped off the track. Wallace was preoccupied elsewhere, mainly with lining up backing for a presidential bid in 1948.

Burdett had sent a recording of my ABC broadcasts, along with a strong letter of recommendation, to Ed Murrow. Murrow responded with the observation "those are good words" and an invitation for me to drop in at his corner-view office at 485 Madison Avenue.

Murrow was the most celebrated figure in broadcast journalism, both as vibrant reporter and as architect of an unrivalled news staff. In Europe at first to coordinate international student exchanges and later to aid academic refugees from Hitler, when World War II loomed he was commissioned by CBS to organize a reporting staff operating from various capitals. One night his man in Vienna was unavailable. Murrow stepped in to take over the microphone, his voice resonant and sure, his report arrestingly graphic, and American broadcasting entered a new era.

When Nazi bombers began pounding London, Murrow was on the air every night. From rooftops, street corners and underground shelters he brought into millions of American homes not only his gripping reportage but the shrill sirens and deafening explosions, the horrors and heroics of the Nazi blitz.

When he came home it was as corporate vice-president in charge of news operations, his name a household word. CBS News had many princelings, but only one king.

At six feet two, Murrow was taller than I expected, and more wiry, reflecting his pre-college years in farm work and logging camps. The CBS star was a handsome man: laconic, dry-humored. Dark eyes glowed beneath heavy black brows in a face memorable for its symmetry. Although the home screen was still over the horizon, Murrow might have been destined for television, or television for him.

He favored rakish sports ensembles, a shade bolder than would have been approved at Princeton; I had the feeling he was trying to tailor his way up from his humble beginnings in North Carolina. There was also something forced, nervous in his collegial banter; he never seemed quite comfortable away from his desk.

Remembering my disaster with Sevareid, I let Murrow do most of the talking. He had recently launched in New York Don Hollenbeck's *CBS Views the Press*, whose bold and sometimes cutting commentary on the week's performance by the metropolitan dailies had aroused anxious murmurs among CBS executives. But Murrow, like the Hollywood renegade Bill Howard, was accustomed to swimming in chilly corporate waters.

The series had caught on at once; now the network was thinking of extending it to the main CBS Midwest outlet in Chicago. Would I be interested in writing and recording a test broadcast?

Restraining an impulse to leap onto his desk, I said yes—and on the way home started drafting my script. I turned it in, some seven or eight pages of copy, a few days later; Murrow pronounced it "first class." He was particularly taken with my demolition of Hearst by-liner Karl von Wiegand:

> The *Herald-American* carried little special correspondence last week. But what it did carry was very special. A series from occupied Germany by Karl von Wiegand contained, first, a rebuke to Winston Churchill. Mr. von Wiegand put it this way, and I quote: "Winston Churchill recently called Germany a charnel house. He should know. He helped make it so."
>
> For the downtrodden German aristocracy, Mr. von Wiegand had only pity. Twice he spoke sadly of the former naval officer who, in the correspondent's words, "had to travel thirty hours in a third class train to see me, because Germans are not allowed to use any other class of train." Then there was the "titled German woman"—to use Mr. von Wiegand's phrase—who smiled bravely through her lorgnette and graciously informed him that, quote, "Your colored troops, when not drinking, are kind." Unquote. According to the *Herald-American*, von Wiegand is "Dean of American correspondents." Dean of what school, one might ask?

Murrow also reacted warmly to a segment decrying editorial manipulation of labels:

> During the Spanish Civil War, when the problem was one of cleaning up a disreputable foe of democracy, these dealers in rubber words were

> busy hailing the Falange plotters as "Nationalists" or "Insurgents"—as practically anything, in fact, but Fascists. One conservative London daily referred to Franco's forces simply as the "anti-Reds." Their opponents, of course, were the "Reds," and the Spanish Republic was thus edited out of existence.

I recorded my Chicago script, to general enthusiasm at Madison Avenue, and Murrow sent it winging westward. But the Windy City station didn't bite. "They liked the content," said Murrow, "but they were leery of your Eastern accent."

"I can flatten my accent."

Murrow shook his head. "They'd find another excuse, Ted. The fact is, they don't have the guts to tangle with the McCormicks in their territory." Colonel Robert McCormick was the ultra-conservative wealthy publisher of the Chicago *Tribune*.

I had another thought in reserve. "What about going after the major news magazines? 'The world according to *Time*.' How would you like that?"

"I'd love it. But the corporate boys on the 23rd floor would wet their pants." *Time*, launched in 1922 by two brash young Yalies was the undisputed leader of America's three news weeklies, so far out in front that *Newsweek* and *U.S. News* could barely see its dust. Aimed at supplanting the stodgy *Literary Digest* by giving busy Americans a brief, digestible overview of the world, it pigeonholed the news into 22 departments covered by 100 short articles.

When Briton Hadden, one of its two founders, died in 1929, it became the exclusive property of his staunchly right-wing partner Henry Luce, the China-born son of an American missionary. Luce promptly showered his readers with strong opinions, always his own: on taxes, labor and especially on the Far East, where the corrupt regime of his idol, Chiang Kai Shek, was losing ground steadily to a determined Communist adversary.

Although Luce had a large and competent staff scattered around the globe, *Time* was notorious for its cavalier rearrangement of incoming correspondence. In covering foreign news, a fixed position—Henry Luce's—was established in advance at the home office. Reportage from the field was run more or less verbatim—if it echoed the magazine's party line. If it didn't it was likely to be spiked or, worse, methodically distorted. I remembered the *Time* correspondent in Cairo who, finally getting hold of a copy of the magazine, promptly cabled his resignation; his story had been stood on its head.

Time, later supplemented by *Life* and *Fortune*, has since achieved a measure of balance. But in the 1940s it was an adult nursery book, predigested pap spooned out in a brisk staccato style borrowed from radio newscasts. It also affected an inverted sentence structure, prompting the *New Yorker's* Wolcott Gibbs to snicker, "Where it will all end knows God."

None of this was terra incognita to Ed Murrow. He stared out the window at Madison Avenue, a frown creasing his brow. "Let's get a drink."

We trooped down to the Berkshire Hotel across the street. A good slice of the CBS News staff, including Howard K. Smith, Charles Collingwood and Richard Hottelet, was gathered at the bar. "Brother Ted," Murrow told them, "has been wrestling with the bureaucracy."

"Hear, hear!"

"Haven't we all?"

Collingwood raised his glass. That was my initiation into Murrow's celebrated "band of brothers."

I talked to Murrow several times soon after about Middle East developments. One could almost feel his quick intelligence at the other end of the line, the raised voice in a sharp query, the shrewd summation before he rang off. He spoke familiarly, and with obvious attachment of his wife Janet and his son Casey. But my notion of dismantling *Time* never came off. Although a flutter of interest came from the *New Republic* which contemplated the idea for a weekly column, it didn't follow through.

To cap the bleak picture, my emotional life was at a standstill. I had made great strides in terms of competence and self-confidence, had a steadily growing sense of inner purpose, but relationships remained a puzzlement. Sybil Rice and I had seen each other a good deal in Washington, wandered to the brink of resuming our lovers' status, and wandered back again. Finally, fed up with my wavering, she had snapped: "Be a man!"

Good advice. But I didn't know how. At my old stamping ground, the city room of the *Mirror*, a gaunt high-domed rewrite man named Pete DuBerg opined that my quandaries would benefit from psychotherapy, in which he had lately enrolled himself. He referred me to his practitioner who, overbooked, relayed me to Dr. Stephen Nordlicht, a Freudian psychoanalyst. Reluctantly, despondently, I began sessions.

Toward the end of the war, in which Fanny had fostered a liaison between the State Department and London's Foreign Office, she acquired a new client: Chiang Kai Shek's Republic of China. She had been special counsel to the Chinese delegation at the United Nations charter sessions in San Francisco, and active in the temporary installation of the embryonic U.N. at the former Sperry gyroscope plant in Lake Success, Long Island.

An Englishwoman acquaintance of hers was floundering out of depth there as publicity officer for the just-formed global U.N. Appeal for Children. Unlike the U.N.'s Children Emergency Fund, which was financed by voluntary contributions from member governments, the Appeal was directed at individuals. Its goal was not only immediate relief in devastated and underdeveloped areas, but the fostering of long-range national institutions dedicated to children's needs. Would I be interested in meeting with Norway's Aake Ording, head of the Appeal?

I would have preferred the virtual autonomy of a niche in broadcasting, but it wasn't happening. And if there was any institution on earth that symbolized the future I hoped to help build, it was the newly-formed United Nations.

No longer a humble nephew dazed by auntly eminence, I told Fanny I was familiar with newspapers, magazines, radio, film . . . the media and mechanisms of international publicity. I felt not only qualified but uniquely equipped to handle a worldwide information program.

Aake Ording, after a half-hour interview, agreed. The lady of Fanny's acquaintance was more than willing to be relieved in exchange for transfer to a less exacting position. Within a week I was behind a desk as UNAC Director of Information, responsible for multi-media services to fund-raising campaigns in dozens of countries.

UNAC dovetailed perfectly with a legacy I felt from the war years: since my life had been spared where so many had not, it had to be put to some useful purpose. The U.N. in its infant days was a one-worlder's paradise, a banquet table overflowing with excitement and inspiration. We of its early Secretariat were the happy, lucky vanguard of dreamers, a heady mélange of kindred spirits from Argentina and New Zealand and Turkey, of careerist Parisiennes and pundits from New Delhi. Whether or not the sovereign nations of the globe were ready to renounce a smidgen of their precious separateness, we had already taken the plunge, and loved it. The radical reporter John Reed after his visit to the Soviet Union felt he was looking into a future that worked; we felt we were creating one.

Lunch in the delegates' dining room was a daily adventure in universality, sweeping aside racial barriers, breaking down ethnic stereotypes. The flaxen-haired, sharp-featured Swede at the next table would turn out to be from Athens; the apparent Latino puzzling over the menu, a librarian from the Ukraine. You couldn't tell a Samoan from a South African without a scorecard.

My first task was to assemble the key members of what would be a sizable staff. As my deputy I drafted Pete DuBerg, solid and unflappable; Pete was glad to escape from Hearst to a career that later landed him permanently in Europe. For the print press I hired publicist-musician Leslie Lieber, a versatile idea man, and the novelist Luigi Creatore, destined to win fame as half of the music publishing team of Hugo and Luigi. John Sewall, an experienced commercial artist, took over our visuals, coming up promptly with a warm clasped-hands logo to accompany the UNAC slogan of "Give One Day." We were asking every citizen of the global community to contribute his or her earnings for a single day. Other staffers were responsible for radio and special events; four regional assistants handled liaison duties from London, Prague, Shanghai and Latin America.

My job involved providing a steady flow of publicity material, in the appropriate languages, to some forty-odd countries varying in geography, climate, social structure and resources; evaluating the information tool most effective in a particular area, and matching medium to objective; coordinating the efforts of national committees wherever possible; meeting diverse requests for hard-to-get items; keeping the Lake Success press corps fully abreast of developments; and maintaining contact with related U.N. branches and agencies.

Soon after my arrival the Appeal got an important lift with the appointment of Chester Bowles as chairman of its International Advisory Committee. Bowles was a big, lantern-jawed New Englander with a crinkly smile. It was easy to visualize him in the plain garb of his colonial ancestors; his grandfather had published the widely influential Springfield *Republican*. An ardent New Dealer, he had been a favorite of President Roosevelt, for whom during World War II he ran the controversial Office of Price Administration; earlier he had retired at forty as co-founder of the enormously successful Benton and Bowles advertising agency.

Bowles and I hit it off at once. He was a cogent political analyst, an adept wordsmith and a direct, unpretentious human being whose values I shared. Our association became close over the next two decades and would have been cemented sooner had not Dr. Nordlicht objected to my joining Bowles on a European jaunt; the psychiatrist felt I belonged at the hub of the Appeal in Lake Success.

I was able to whip up considerable fanfare over the news of Bowles's appointment, starting with an evening interview on Ed Murrow's network show. I had stayed in touch with Murrow during this period, sending him occasional quotes from Abe Lincoln or Mark Twain to garnish his nightly newscasts. I had also, at his request, provided my slant on breaking stories in the Middle East. And I dropped in often. Always he greeted me warmly as "Brother Ted." Although never formally affiliated with CBS, I had by royal fiat been welcomed to the ranks of Murrow's fabled "Band of Brothers."

The Band, whose stars included William Shirer, Howard K. Smith and Charles Collingwood, was under constant pressure from the more commercially oriented, ratings-conscious divisions of the network, and Murrow defended it tenaciously. I was in his office one afternoon when a young man wearing a pin-striped suit and an unconvincing smile sauntered in: "Programming would like to make a small loan of your Tuesday evening summary slot."

Murrow shook his head.

"We're just talking about a one-shot feature deal. Early next month."

"No loan, no deal."

The programming man dropped his smile. "Advertising is hot on this, Mr. Murrow. And Sales would appreciate a little gesture of cooperation."

Murrow did not respond. It was obvious that the two had been through this before.

"How about splitting the time, fifty-fifty?"

"No. Not half the time. Not any time. The format stays as it is."

As the staffer stalked out, Murrow turned to me. "Every organization needs a 'heavy,' a bad guy who can say no. Around here, I'm the heavy." He drummed a long nervous finger on his desk. "This news operation is hanging on by its teeth. And the jackals can't wait to move in."

Bowles was no jackal, and Ed promptly scheduled an extended interview on his evening radio show. The two media figures, who had not met before, wrangled politely over Murrow's plan to introduce Bowles with a reference to his guest's argument-riddled past; I pitched in with a compromise to soften the tension. Fifteen years later Bowles and Murrow, in stubborn alliance, would be dissident voices on the left in the Kennedy administration. My chief recollection of their first encounter is Murrow's knees churning furiously beneath the table as he talked, in striking contrast to the calm authority of his voice.

The following week, Tom Velotta at ABC opened up a fifteen-minute prime-time slot for the Appeal; the speech I drafted for delivery by Bowles won a Columbia University award as the best public service address of the year.

We kicked off the Appeal's fund-raising campaign with a multi-network international broadcast, the piercing wail of a hungry infant. Conspicuously foreshadowed in our weekly newsletter, it was a spectacular success, garnering a three-column headline on page one of the New York *Herald-Tribune*.

Unfortunately there was no such display in the *Herald-Trib's* arch rival, the august New York *Times*. The *Times* bureau at the U.N. had simply goofed, letting our detailed advance notice of the upcoming story sail right past their eyes.

James "Scotty" Reston, the bureau chief, cried "Foul!" In his starched collar and prim signature bowtie, looking like a pouter pigeon with ruffled feathers, he screamed his protest at Luigi Creatore—who called for reinforcement. I came down to the press room and told Reston it wasn't our job to force-feed the news; we had our hands full just getting it out. Reston continued his grumbling. But the *Times* made no more such errors.

We soon had an embarrassment of our own to contend with. One of our more colorful publicity people, assigned to beat the drums for the Appeal in eastern Europe and the Middle East, was a White Russian named Serge Fliegers. A chubby little man with deceptively mild blue eyes and a crisp blonde mustache, Serge was a formidable linguist, of mysterious but ample means. He owned a sprawling New York apartment crowded with Pissarros, jeweled Greek Orthodox crucifixes and stray admiring females. Like the novelist Romain Gary, he had been snatched from the path of the Russian revolution by a determined mother who then traipsed across the Continent with him to safety in England. Of his father, no word was ever spoken, although Serge once hinted at "possibly a bit of Jewish blood" in his ancestry. He hobnobbed with social figures like Prince Serge Obolensky and "Bootsie" Hearst, by whose family he was employed as a sometime journalist at the time I engaged him.

By airmail from Cairo, Serge filed a wonderful story. Traveling by car through the rugged Khyber Pass between Pakistan and Afghanistan, along the ancient invasion route to India followed by Alexander the Great and Tamerlane, he had been trapped by a furious squall. Heavy, blinding snows spilled down from the ravines, choking off the highway.

Advancing into the wilderness on foot, he had been encircled and overpowered by a band of wild tribesmen. Even the rich linguistic resources at his command—he spoke all the Romance languages, German, Russian, Polish, English and a spot of Arabic —were useless. Daggers were closing in. Desperate, he pulled from his jacket a photo of U.N. Secretary General Trygve Lie and pantomimed his tale: he was an envoy of this burly chief-among-chiefs of the outside world, eager to bring peace and prosperity to Afghanistan. He emptied his pocket and wallet of coins and bills.

The tribesmen threw the money away, according to Serge, but they were fascinated by the picture of Lie, ponderous and unassailable as the high banks of a Norwegian fjord. They put up his "envoy" in a fur-lined tent and the next day escorted him back to his car.

It was an adventure yarn worthy of Richard Harding Davis. I gave it a big send-off in the press room on a slow Saturday. The New York *Times*, unwilling to be caught napping again by the opposition, spread Serge's saga across the bottom of the front page, where it caught the attention of thousands of readers at Sunday breakfast.

Unhappily for Serge, one of them was a retired British army officer thoroughly familiar with the Khyber Pass. Colonel Peabody sat down and penned a stern letter to the managing editor of the *Times*, pointing out that there was no snow in the pass during the season in question, no tribal dress of the type vividly evoked by Serge, and sundry other details indicating that the author's enthusiasm had exceeded his accuracy. The Appeal—and the nation's premier newspaper—had been had. For several days I walked softly through the news room.

That was Serge: long on chutzpah and invention, short on reliability. It was too late to fire him; his publicity tour had been completed, with otherwise excellent effects. And oddly enough, twenty years later, as a correspondent in the Middle East Six-Day War, he demonstrated that he was capable of genuine heroics before being severely wounded by a Palestinian land mine.

The Appeal rolled on, gathering steam and capital as our weekly newsletter circulated posters, endorsements and ideas among the various national campaigns. My stewardship included meetings with Trygve Lie and with Eleanor Roosevelt, tired and testy but scrupulously faithful to her commitments. I was strangely moved, fifteen years later, to learn that my book *Cast A Giant Shadow* had been among the volumes in her personal library. Screen star Myrna Loy of *Thin Man* fame, a concerned citizen, lent her enchanting presence to a movie short. With a little help from my friends, I did a Spanish-language broadcast to all of Latin America. And from far-off Iceland came the highest per capita response to the Appeal, nearly reaching our target of one day's income.

Less cheering were the performances of the two superpowers. The Soviet Union, touchy and defensive, simply snubbed the Appeal. Despite the widespread suffering among their country's children, the Russians refused to turn to the despised capitalist world for aid; Mother Russia would take care of her own.

The situation was more complex but only marginally better in the United States, where a half-dozen religious factions were in long-standing and intense competition for charity dollars. Although ostensibly working together under the UNAC umbrella, in practice they continued to pursue their separate ways, zealously guarding their traditional sources.

The sole exception was the Quakers, who threw open their considerable files of photographs and tape recordings to the Appeal, and followed its global guidelines unstintingly.

We brought our first year to a climax with a Children's Assembly at Lake Success, peopled mainly with the junior members of delegates' families. Gathered around the big table used for formal meetings by their elders, the youngsters ad libbed their hopes and plans, winding up with a ringing manifesto (discreetly superintended by Pete DuBerg) on children's rights. The press gobbled up the story, together with a picture book round-up documenting the global impact of the Appeal.

The ironic anti-climax came a couple of months later, at a meeting in Paris of the Economic and Social Council to consider extension of the Appeal. The resolution submitted was so cluttered with provisos and double negatives that a third world delegate, misreading it, cast an unwitting negative ballot whose effect was to defeat the proposal by eight votes to seven.

However, when we bowed out soon after, it was not without glory. The Appeal had raised some fifty-one million dollars in difficult economic times. More enduringly, its leaflets, films and broadcasts had ignited consciences globally, prompting the establishment of new children-centered institutions in many lands. Our goals of creating vigorous nutritional and medical programs would be carried forward, with long-term governmental backing, by UNICEF, the Children's Emergency Fund. I left Lake Success with a sense of a major job well done, and something more: an awareness of myself as a world citizen who could never revert to the limited perspectives of Brooklyn, the Ivy League or even Washington. For the first time in many years I felt a curious bonding with my father and the epitaph of universal good will I had inscribed on his tombstone.

As the campaign was winding down my comely assistant, Dolores De Soto, departed to enroll at the Sorbonne in Paris, leaving a train of disappointed admirers including broadcaster-to-be Dan Schorr, then a lowly newspaper stringer. From Lake Success I reported to Dolores on a gala dance for U.N. interns: "Indo-China was represented, and also what you might call Outdo-China. I am constantly being struck by the fragile beauty of Oriental women."

The observation was prescient. A few weeks later, boarding the bus to the train station, I found myself trailing a slim, elegant woman whose silk gown clung to a sinuously curved torso. Her graceful, swaying gait did nothing to diminish the promise of her figure. She sat down, disclosing delicate features under wide crescent-moon brows.

I slipped into the adjoining seat. By the time our Long Island Railroad train rolled into Penn Station, cultural attaché Ma-Than-E of the Burmese delegation and I were tolerably well acquainted. She called me "Ko Ted," meaning "warrior Ted." And she invited me to her home.

As a sexual partner, she was wonderfully knowing, practiced; yet subtly personal. I had no idea of her age—only her hands suggested she was probably closer to forty than to twenty—but she was unmistakably mature, a self-possessed grown woman.

And that, with its implied requirement of reciprocity, was more than I could handle. Her affection enveloped me in a warmth that was intoxicating—and frightening. Although her strength was not the driving, ambition-laden power of my mother or Fanny, it was power nonetheless, making me feel by comparison inept and vulnerable, awakening my old self-doubt. Absurdly, to boot I found myself uncomfortable being seen in a restaurant or a movie house with this ivory-tinted princess; my pretensions to world citizenship could not transcend thirty years of subliminal racist indoctrination.

The warrior "Ko Ted" retreated. Ma-Than-E sensed my backing away; the relationship disintegrated. Not for the first time—or the last—I let a treasure slip through my fingers.

Meanwhile my old base of operations, the Middle East, had taken its troubles to the United Nations. In the spring of 1947, after a tempestuous year of British clampdowns on Jewish immigration, underground smuggling attempts, the King David Hotel bombing and continuing mounting violence as British sailors herded European DPs into new barbed-wire camps on Cyprus, the world body launched hearings on Jewish statehood at its temporary quarters in Flushing Meadow, Long Island. In response to an urgent request from Theodore White at the *New Republic* I worked up a background article.

Attending the sessions just before joining the Appeal, I was struck by the contrast between the Arab world of my experience and the polished façade of its spokesmen. Their star, Fadek Jamil of Iraq, sleek and impressive in his Savile Row pin-stripes, rolled out in a rich and pleasantly accented baritone his concern for freedom and democracy among the region's millions. The Arab masses, his colleagues agreed, were so steeped in the juices of fair play, so warmed by the fires of freedom, that they might in their outraged sense of justice be driven to war.

Amid this deluge of oratory, I had the uneasy impression that something—or someone—was missing. Of course. Nowhere in sight was the common man of the Middle East, the hapless little Mohammed of the city slums and country hovels, who carried the name of the prophet of Islam and little else. The well-tailored, Oxford-accented Arab delegates no more represented him than a Virginia slave-owner could claim to "represent" the slaves on his plantation. I went back to the typewriter and turned out "This Is The Arab."

I placed it with the *American Mercury*, a cantankerous free-wheeling magazine founded in the thirties by Baltimore editor H.L. Mencken and theater critic George Jean Nathan. Mencken's jibes at the credulous "booboisie" made him a darling of the country's intellectuals. After a brief period of stagnation following the deaths of its founders, the magazine had been bought and rejuvenated by Lawrence Spivak, later the moderator of NBC's "Meet The Press."

"This Is The Arab" was in the best Mencken blow-the-lid-off tradition. The *Mercury* gave my 3500 words a cover display and took out large ads in the New York *Times* and other major papers. The article stirred national attention. Gerold Frank, just back from a long tour of reporting in the Middle East but not yet embarked on the female-confessional career that would make him the world's most famous ghost, scribbled a postcard: "Honestly, it's terrific! One of the absolutely best I've ever read on the subject!" And Norman Cousins, whose desk at the *Saturday*

Review of Literature my manuscript had somehow crossed before publication, wrote me a note: "Hope you don't mind my having done a little intermediate eavesdropping. I was impressed with the way you handle the English language. Perhaps some time I might persuade you to write for us."

This was no small tribute. The *Saturday Review*, fashioned in 1924 from the book section of the old New York *Post*, was perhaps the foremost literary magazine in the country. Where popular newsstand magazines were awash in flappers, bootleggers and the booming stock market, the *Saturday Review* rallied to its banner Robert Frost, Willa Cather, Sinclair Lewis, Hemingway and Faulkner. And Cousins was an editor of distinction who did not issue invitations casually.

But for the moment, I was more interested in lending a hand to the motley Zionist delegation—Levantine, South African, Canadian—none of whose experience equipped them to deal with the American media. My misgivings about the site chosen for the Jewish homeland, and the frequently myopic Zionist perception of the Arabs, remained. But it was too late to turn the clock back. Hitler had changed the Middle East equation. The surviving Jews of Europe had been through a hellfire unimagined since Dante. The despairing remnant could not continue to be human shuttlecocks, batted forever to still another camp or back to the nightmare of Germany. They needed some place of refuge and hope, some chance to rebuild a shattered generation. And nothing else was being offered.

True, the proposed Jewish state held little promise for the neglected Arab masses. But as I had just pointed out in the *Mercury*, the heavy foot trampling on the downtrodden fellah was not that of the still-nascent Zionist movement but belonged to his own corrupt, hypocritical leadership.

So, all things considered—and I had considered them long and hard—the Jews had the more pressing case. And at Lake Success they were bucking heavy odds: green amateurs against skilled professional diplomats not attuned by personal history or social training to Jews. The U.S. group, despite President Truman's humanitarian stance, were no exception; a traditionally snobbish State Department indulged everything from the sly machinations of Defense Secretary James Forrestal to the overt anti-Semitism of our U.N. Ambassador, Warren Austin.

The fact that my sympathies sprang from observation on the scene rather than abstract ideology impressed Moshe Sharett, future foreign minister of Israel. At his request I drafted a number of statements for him, then accepted his invitation to sit in on the tactical deliberations of his delegation.

In late November of 1947 a vote in favor of partitioning Palestine squeaked by the General Assembly, thanks in part to my ubiquitous Aunt Fanny who cajoled her Chinese Government client to a benevolent and influential neutrality. The Arabs adamantly rejected partition, and the opposing armies in the Middle East began girding for a military showdown.

John Donovan, still patrolling the area for NBC, kept me up to date with a stream of information too speculative or uninhibited for his evening newscasts. On December 9 he wrote from Jerusalem:

> The story here has been sensationalized and overwritten, but it can and I think will be serious sometime in the future. Of course ninety-six dead and hundreds injured since partition ain't to be sneezed at, but it is all cowboy and Indian stuff right now. Walking around at 2 a.m. ain't a bit healthy either . . . because of the general confusion a bystander can now get knocked off by Arabs, Jews and British. The place is crawling with ammo and nitwits eager to shoot somebody.

Enclosed was a photo of John in his unique all-purpose war correspondent's garb, quickly adaptable to any side: Arab kaffieh headdress, Israeli shorts and sandals, Yankee cigar. His reserve weapon in case of Arab capture, he explained, would be anatomical: an exposure of the uncircumcised penis that had served him so well in more agreeable situations.

Meanwhile his sex life was languishing: "I just don't like very much I see, and what I like will probably get me a few hundred rounds in the back some dark night."

At the Champagne Club in Cairo, he had stunned a posh gathering by dropping his pants. In Capri, he managed to create a stir with his clothes on: "Seems I summed up my opinion on Franco to a whole hill of Spanish Counts and Countesses. Then I drew certain compelling parallels on the organization of the Church as compared to the organization of the USSR and Communism (shades of Bill Howard!)."

By March of 1948 Donovan was back in Jerusalem, where he reported the Arabs massing thousands of guerrillas in the Jenin-Tulkarm-Nablus triangle for heavy thrusts against Haifa and Tel Aviv. The situation of the underarmed, outnumbered Zionists, themselves split between the moderate Haganah underground and right-wing terrorist groups, looked grim to him, with Jerusalem most vulnerable: all transport, water and communications could easily be cut off. Nonetheless, they were undismayed. "The Sternists, Irgun and Haganah talk like a bunch of football players waiting for the Rose Bowl. The Arabs are just as optimistic about their chances in the Jihad Bowl."

From his "Trappist" quarters in the YMCA, John had seen "a few likely lookers" in various underground groups; "but these dames are out blowing up railroad trains or attacking villages almost every night."

A trip to Athens had been enlivened by Donovan's chunky, muscular boxer dog, Timoshenko. Wandering loose at a reception for U.N. dignitaries by Foreign Minister Constantine Tsaldaris, the big dog packed away several pounds of expensive cold cuts, then topped off his depredations by relieving himself on Tsaldaris's desk. Palestine-born Timoshenko, who "spoke" no English, would later become a canine celebrity in placid suburban Huntington, Long Island, trotting down the street trailed by Donovan's stout Irish mother bawling commands in brogue-flavored Hebrew.

In May of 1948 the British pulled out of Palestine, and the world press poured in. On the fourteenth, David Ben-Gurion proclaimed formation of the state of Israel. Six Arab nations promptly invaded.

A month passed before Donovan, on the air every night, had time for a personal letter:

> Izzy (I.F.) Stone is taking our letters home. All these gazebos are now claiming to be first getting through the Jerusalem-Tel Aviv emergency road, so much that we are now introducing new qualifying titles: Izzy Stone, the first hearing-aid correspondent to travel down the road; Jondon, first man and dog correspondent team . . .

John had become chummy with a kindred-spirit, *Life* photographer Robert Capa. "He is good company, and does not dun me, but merely asks me to keep him in cigarettes, beer and shoeshines."

The Israelis, winning in the field, had won over Jondon completely. "Jerusalem under shell fire was quite a show. The people were terrific, and their spirit is so contagious that I started going the other way, making Bartley Crum (the pro-Zionist author of *Behind the Silken Curtain*) sound like a Moslem Brother in comparison. The kids in the Haganah are terrific too. There are a lot of gimmicks in the Jewish side, but what the hell, it's growing pains. I do think that the real problems will crop up in the distant future, but if they get planes and heavy armaments here I think they'll plaster the Arabs all over the map. It's a smelly situation, particularly the British role."

CHAPTER 10

Murder Most Foul

Strangely missing from the press corps at the painful birth of Israel was CBS's indefatigable George Polk. Since our competition-crowded meeting, I had developed increasing respect for George. On May 8, a week before the announcement of Jewish statehood, he had vanished from sight in Salonika, Greece; with a civil war ravaging the land, Polk had been seeking to reach the mountain headquarters of the leftist Greek guerrillas for an interview with their Communist leader, General Markos Vafiades.

On May 16, George's rope-trussed body, a bullet splintering the back of his head, was found floating in Salonika Bay.

The political background of his murder was crucial. Under the Cold War Truman Doctrine of containment, an authoritarian right-wing Greek government, riddled with secret police and death-squad enforcers, was being subsidized by Washington to the tune of a million dollars a day. American reporters on the scene, including Pulitzer Prize winner Homer Bigart of the New York *Herald-Tribune*, were filing copious accounts of governmental corruption, incompetence, and of a ruthless brutality that according to the newsmen was driving apolitical villagers into the arms of guerrilla insurgents.

Prominent among the first whistle-blowers was George Polk, who had referred to some Greek cabinet ministers in a broadcast as semi-fascists. Polk had access not only to the microphones of the CBS network but to the inner sanctum of the redoubtable Ed Murrow. The Greek government, worried, filed a protest in Washington; the State Department chided "uncooperative" correspondents. And phone calls began waking Polk at midnight, threatening his life. Instead of backing away, he stepped up his preparations for going north.

The photo of George's bloated corpse, flashed across America, sickened and outraged me. It could so easily have been me, or a half-dozen other reporters. His murder was an assault against all of us, leaving one voice less to speak out for honesty and humanity. I remembered George well and affectionately. It was hard not to. In his early thirties, George Polk was a foreign correspondent straight out of a Jimmy Stewart movie:

clean-featured, sandy-haired, with a slight Texas drawl and a strong sense of fair play. He was in love with his work, not his by-line; it was a pleasure to share a news tip or a drink with him. In 1946, at the Allenby Bridge in Palestine, he had stiff-armed a British attempt to establish religious criteria for foreign reporters, enabling passage for two Jewish colleagues, Gerold Frank and myself.

The Greek government promptly attributed George's murder to the Communists, charging it was part of a cunning plot to throw suspicion on Athens and thereby discredit the Royalist administration.

This seemed on the face of it far-fetched. The assassination warnings had all come from the Right; the Left stood only to profit from George's digging. Minimally, the case screamed for a tough-minded inquiry.

Within a few days, working with veteran war correspondent Burnet Hershey and several people at the Newspaper Guild of New York, I helped form the Newsmen's Commission to Investigate the Murder of George Polk. Represented besides the Guild were the American War Correspondents Association, the Foreign Press Association and the Standing Committee of United Nations Correspondents. One of our energetic volunteers was Shana Ager, later known to TV viewers as Shana Alexander.

Our plan was to send a three-man team consisting of Overseas News Agency star Constantine Poulos, who spoke fluent Greek; Polk's nineteen-year-old brother Bill, and John Donovan (from John, a brief sorrowful note: "After kicking around with George for a couple of years, I became terrifically fond of him. He was the most sincerely principled guy out here. He had guts and helped everyone he could.").

That same week I was in Washington seeking governmental cooperation. Congressional doors opened quickly. Senators Henry Cabot Lodge, Jr. of Massachusetts and William Langer of North Dakota were particularly receptive. Lodge, a former journalist, was a major voice on the Foreign Relations Committee; Langer was on the Judiciary Committee.

Within forty-eight hours, out of the blue came disconcerting word: another inquiry group had been set up by the Washington-based Overseas Writers Association, with the celebrated sage Walter Lippmann as its chair. Other members included some of the most illustrious names in American journalism: ABC commentator Elmer Davis, Scotty Reston, *Newsweek* Bureau Chief Ernest Lindley, columnist Marquis Childs, and Joseph Harsch of the *Christian Science Monitor*. The Lippmann Committee announced it was sending General William Donovan, of OSS-CIA fame, to Greece as its counsel for the official government inquiry.

Suddenly our Newsmen's Commission of working reporters had lost its clout. What would be the point of a second inquiry body, asked our friends in the Senate? After all, who would challenge Wild Bill Donovan's credentials?

For this job, I would. Apart from his unimpressive display during our ABC encounter, it seemed to me that a man so deeply entwined with the Washington establishment might be a dubious champion for a murdered reporter who had repeatedly nettled that establishment. Accentuating my misgivings was NBC's about-face on John Donovan, who had just been nominated for a distinguished reporting prize by the Overseas Press Club. When John refused to resign from the Newsmen's Commission, he was abruptly dropped by the network "for budgetary reasons."

The working press had been effectively blocked out of the action; by whom and to what purpose would emerge very slowly over the years, and would not be fully explained for more than four decades.

The official investigation in Greece, joined with fanfare by General Donovan, moved ahead murkily. Accompanying the former OSS boss was a crack soldier-linguist, Air Force Lt. Col. James Kellis, who as an OSS operative in World War II had made an enviable reputation with the anti-Nazi resistance in Greece.

At the end of July, Kellis was suddenly and secretly recalled to Washington. Three weeks later the Greek police trumpeted a sensational arrest. They had captured the man responsible for setting up George Polk's execution. Their prisoner had made a full confession.

Gregory Staktopoulos was a newspaper stringer who had worked all sides of the Greek political street: for the pre-war Metaxas dictatorship, the Axis occupying powers, the Communist party, the British Information Service and finally the Special Security Police of Salonika. According to his confession, the actual murder was carried out in the rowboat to which he delivered Polk, by two well-known Communists,

Adam Mouzenides and Evangelos Vasvanas. The story jibed perfectly with the theory previously advanced by the government.

In 1949 a remarkable trial ensued, in which the defense attorney lined up enthusiastically with the prosecution and the judges. All parties agreed that the Communist Party had killed George Polk in order to embarrass their royalist adversaries; the only question at issue was the degree of complicity on the part of Staktopoulos.

Constantine Poulos, covering the proceedings for *The Nation*, detailed a bitter farce of a show trial that would have made Joe Stalin blush. A parade of frightened witnesses, some already in police custody, jumped obligingly through government hoops. One of the alleged triggermen named by Staktopoulos, Adam Mouzenides, had according to the Communist Party been killed by a bomb in a mountain village early in April of 1948. The prosecutor trotted out Mouzenides' brother, who declared he had spoken on the telephone to Adam in mid-April, and then Adam's young sister-in-law, already facing lethal punishment on charges of having harbored Mouzenides in Salonika. She claimed to have overheard the two alleged killers discussing plans for George's execution.

Glaring discrepancies in testimony went unquestioned. The owner of a waterfront cafe, supposedly the locale of a dinner meeting between Staktopoulos and Polk on May 8, told Poulos and Bill Polk privately that neither man was there. He was never called to testify. The government's sole documentary evidence—an envelope purportedly addressed by the defendant's mother—was never examined. Winston Burdett of CBS, seated at the trial beside a beaming General Donovan, noted "a shower of leading questions from the bench" and "no rules of evidence at all."

The trial wound up with a free-for-all assault on the wicked foreign press for daring to impugn the honor of Greece, and an emotional statement by Staktopoulos absolving his "motherland, Greece" of all responsibility.

The defendant was found guilty as an accessory to the murder and sentenced to life imprisonment. General Donovan gave the verdict his hearty blessing. Walter Lippmann in Washington, solemnly echoing his eminent counsel, assured the American public that no innocent man had been framed, and no guilty one whitewashed.

Lippmann's biographer, Ronald Steel, tells a different story.

According to Steel, the famous pundit was quite aware that evidence "pointed damningly toward the Greek government and the CIA," but was unwilling to embarrass his friends in the State Department by saying so.

General Donovan's biographer, Anthony Cave Brown, in the grandiosely titled *The Last Hero* is not nearly so meticulous (he mistakenly says the Lippmann Committee was set up by the Overseas Press Club, which had nothing whatever to do with the investigation) or honest. He squirms through three pages of double-talk: Donovan was "not at all sure" the Greek Communists had killed George, was skeptical of the alleged "confession" by Staktopoulos, but was tied up at the time in "a number of important undertakings."

With no evident sense of irony, Brown runs a picture of Lippmann and General Donovan in jolly colloquy at the first George Polk Memorial Award dinner, instituted with pomp and ceremony by Long Island University to honor conspicuous bravery in reporting. With the single exception of Harrison Salisbury, no award recipient is recorded as having ever urged a fresh, unblinking look at the original murder case. Although the Polk Award has since been multiplied to embrace 19 categories, including best consumer reporting and local TV coverage, the circumstances of George's death are no longer mentioned.

A stubborn handful of news people, led in America by John Donovan, took on the truth-seeking mission of the murder victim and refused to forget. John, an only child, pursued the case with the single-minded passion of a man who has lost a cherished brother. My own involvement was more sporadic. I wrote protests to *Time* and *More* magazines, tried to arouse interest in Hollywood, and buttonholed at random anyone who I thought might be alive to the issue, including Supreme Court Justice William O. Douglas.

Together John and I offered the full Polk story to the cream of the nation's press, including major papers in George's home state of Texas. Nobody would touch it except the St. Petersburg (Florida) *Times*.

True, the Cold War was heating up. Greece was firmly anti-Communist. Beggars seeking allies—so went the argument—couldn't be choosers. So there was "no space" for an exposé that might cast an unflattering light on our Washington Establishment and its corps of renowned by-liners. The once-independent American press, long the envy of less privileged societies, had been decimated by takeovers and realignments, dominated by don't-rock-the-boat chains, till it had shriveled to toothless compliance. The numbers told the story: the total of daily papers was down from 1,911 in the mid-thirties to 1,781 in 1948, many of them satellites of Hearst or Gannett or Scripps-Howard. For the world at large, the waters closed over the memory of George Polk, as they had over his shattered body. Once again as in France's infamous Dreyfus case, truth had been strangled "to protect the national interest." Decades would pass before the ugly truth and our government's connivance in it would blaze through the pages of a book.

Other political battles loomed closer at home. In the fall of 1948, Chester Bowles had made a successful run for the governorship of Connecticut; along with Norman Cousins and Douglas Bennett, I had served as a close adviser. Bowles and I talked often on the phone, and at early breakfast meetings (a predilection he shared with Jerusalem Mayor Teddy Kollek) in New York. I was generally a little dazed at these seances, still fighting off slumber, but Chet was off and running, full throttle. After his election I had a standing invitation to week-end stays in New Haven at what Chet called the local White House—a phrasing that suggested he would not be averse to moving up to the big one.

Knowing that he and Ed Murrow were on the same wave length, I relayed to Murrow the substance of a long account from Bowles of a half-day session in Washington with Secretary of State George Marshall. The ex-general was more critical of Chiang Kai-Shek than of the Chinese Communists; was dubious about encouraging a "third force," shunning the extremes of both right and left, in Europe; and was gradually being edged aside on major decisions by Defense Secretary James Forrestal.

As governor, Bowles faced a host of touchy issues. He was particularly concerned with ending racial discrimination in the Connecticut National Guard—baseball star Jackie Robinson leaped into our corner on that one—and with expanding psychiatric care facilities at Yale, his alma mater, a program regarded with skepticism if not outright hostility by the Catholic Church.

Our weekend policy reviews were often joined by Chet's wife Steb, a large-boned woman not prepossessing by the usual yardsticks of the Madison Avenue where Bowles had made his fortune, but a personality so warm, involved and engaging that within minutes all superficial attributes were obliterated.

One morning in 1949, Bowles came down to breakfast to find me doodling at his Steinway grand, talking to myself through my fingers. For a long moment he stood silent in the doorway, then remarked, "I'd give anything to be able to do that."

As the end of Chet's two-year term approached, our discussions turned to questions of ethics, integrity, personal responsibility. Re-election was clearly in his grasp, if he would bend on a handful of major issues. He had won his point on the National Guard, arguing "public opinion is important, but sometimes it needs a legislative shove;" however, his views on intensifying the state's mental health program did not sit well with the Catholic Establishment.

We chewed over the familiar politician's rationale—"get into office, no matter how—then you can put across your constructive measures"—but Chet refused to buy the "no matter how" part. "I'm not making deals," he insisted.

He lost to John Lodge, a run-of-the-mill Republican of whom nothing was heard before or later, but whose Italian-born wife addressed the Little Italy voters of Bridgeport chummily in their ancestral tongue. It was in this period, during our ruminations on politics, that Bowles made one of the few disparaging comments I ever heard from his lips. Ike Eisenhower, he remarked, nourished a "runaway ego."

In 1951 President Truman, a consistent fan of Bowles, named him Ambassador to India. Chet was an untraditional diplomat, plunging into the spirit and mores of the New Delhi community. He enrolled his children in local schools to which they pedalled on their own bicycles. He met with local workers, teachers and religious leaders.

Chatty stencilled accounts, eight to ten pages long, reported back to a small circle of friends the human adventures rarely entrusted to State Department cables. No slave to diplomatic niceties, Chet had borrowed the Italian Ambassador's cutaway for formal presentation of his credentials. Steb told us of the time when, filling in for Chet at a meeting with

Hindus of the ancient Jainist sect, she was obliged to sit cross-legged for an hour, her face covered with a mask to avoid inhaling innocent insects. She wound up pinned to the ground, unable to move. Being Steb, she made a joke of the incident.

In turn, I encouraged a visit to Chet's embassy by Harry Hussey, the Canadian architect who had built Peking University, learned Chinese, and stayed to become one of the West's few no-nonsense authorities on Asia. Bowles slated Hussey for a fifteen-minute meeting, kept him more than an hour, and later chided me: "Why did you let him introduce himself as a friend of Bill Benton (Bowles's former partner)? If he had mentioned your name, I would have allocated proper time!"

As he later made plain in his book *Ambassador's Report*, Chet was particularly concerned about an issue I had mentioned frequently in my broadcasts from Cairo: the simultaneous presence east of Suez of angry ex-colonial peoples and an aggressive, relentlessly propagandizing Soviet Union.

I tried to fill in the far-off ambassador on the American political scene. On July 11, 1952, in a hopelessly sanguine letter, I asserted that Republican presidential candidate Eisenhower could be taken:

> Not in a personal anti-Ike campaign, which would be disastrous, but by nailing him unmistakably to the wall alongside the bitter reactionaries he represents. He must be forced publicly to embrace—or repudiate—McCarthy, MacArthur and J. Edgar Hoover. The Democrats must make clear where Ike's backing comes from and where his obligations consequently rest: with the Eastern money people who had no great quarrel with Taft's arch-conservatism, but felt Ike would pull more votes. But the Democrats will themselves have to choose an all-out fighter. To nominate a straddler would be fatal; Eisenhower, with his effectively folksy TV manner, could out-straddle anyone foolish enough to oppose him on this level.

My argument had its points; but I completely underestimated, as I would later with Ronald Reagan, the potency of Ike's apple-cheeked grandfatherly appeal.

By 1954 Bowles was back in the States, where a half-dozen candidates were competing for the Democratic presidential nomination two years away. Asked to introduce the field at the annual springtime Jefferson-Jackson Day dinner, he asked me in turn if I could provide some remarks suitable for the occasion.

I obliged with a few pages of notes, opening with the sally that the Democrats were offering the nation a sequel to *Three Men on a Horse*: namely, *Six Men on a Donkey*. This went down very well: partly because, as a Washington columnist pointed out, nobody had expected Chester Bowles to be funny. My draft then enumerated, not too solemnly, the special virtues of each candidate, closing with a reference to Adlai Stevenson as the standard-bearer against whom all others had to be measured. Stevenson eventually got the nod, qualifying him for a second rout by Eisenhower.

Bowles lost no time in acknowledging my help. "I can't tell you how much I appreciated your sending me material," he wrote on May 6. He had made abundant and apparently fruitful use of my "gags and suggestions."

He was uncertain whether "under the best of circumstances" he could be more effective as Governor of Connecticut or in the national arena, but would consider the Governorship only if he had the complete support of all factions, without deals.

As things turned out, he was destined for more crests and dips on the political rollercoaster before landing high in John F. Kennedy's White House, only to run afoul there of the unforgiving hand of the president's brother Bobby when Chet was rash enough to forecast the fiasco at the Bay of Pigs.

His thank-you note in 1954 ended with a written-in greeting from Steb. A final P.S. in Chet's hand near the bottom of the page: "I want to see you soon, Ted."

CHAPTER 11

News About Nellie

In 1949, *Nellie* came banging at my door, never totally to depart. *Nellie* was neither a girl nor a horse, but a musical comedy, the offspring of one of those wild potpourris of clients, friends, relatives and sometimes innocent passersby in which Fanny specialized.

This one started with Edmund Goulding, the bad boy/genius with whom she had first catapulted across the Hollywood scene. Director of Garbo, seducer of everyone in sight (except Fanny whom he feared and adored), London-born Goulding thought there was a great musical in the spicy romance between the street-smart orange girl Nell Gwynn and her indolently lecherous lover, King Charles II. Gertrude Lawrence, Eddie's female counterpart on the Holtzmann office roster, would make a sizzling Nellie.

But Goulding was busy directing Bette Davis. Who could be entrusted with his brainchild? Fanny looked around and her auntly glance fell on not one but two nephews. I had just cleared out of the U.N., was setting up an apartment, seeing my psychiatrist—nothing that couldn't be fitted in with a larger project. When my sister married, Fanny thereby acquired another nephew, Raphael Blau, a successful radio author not yet brought within her orbit. Rafe was a large, formidable-looking man who had practically no small talk—Eddie Goulding nervously dubbed him "the gloomy Dane"—but who when he chose to open his mouth could unloose a devastating dry wit.

Ergo, from two nephews, one writing team. With Gertrude, Eddie and Fanny in our corner, how could we miss?

Oddly enough, it was not the impressive back-up but the potential of the material itself that intrigued us: cheeky, earthy orange girl captivating a dissolute but intelligent monarch in that lustiest of English eras, the Restoration of the crown after the Puritan rule of Oliver Cromwell. Orange girls were robust young ladies who roamed the aisles of post-Elizabethan playhouses, much like the hot dog vendors at modern baseball games, offering citrus refreshment from sunnier climes. The time and place shrieked with possibilities for broad lampooning with twentieth-century overtones: the lowly role of 17th century women if they neglected to keep a dandy handy; the absurd snobbery of hereditary aristocracy; Samuel Pepys, the gossipy diarist who anticipated Walter Winchell by 300 years. It did not escape me that the project also offered possibilities for slipping across the line into song-writing. Although I hesitated to get entangled with Fanny again, I had no such reservations about *Nellie*.

Rafe had gone to prep school in England; I had my impressions of the British from the Korda days and Cairo. Within weeks we had whipped out a thirty-page outline. Although our *News About Nellie* made no allowances for the realities of production, it had undeniable atmosphere.

Playwright George S. Kaufman, decidedly amused, pronounced our treatment "a promising goings-on, and I think you've worked it out well." Cole Porter, who had written one of his most memorable scores for Gertrude Lawrence in *Nymph Errant*, thought *Nellie* was fresh and funny, and told Fanny he would be happy to provide its tunes.

Ecstasy reigned—until an unexpected ship-to-shore telegram from Porter two weeks later. He was taking an indefinite leave of absence in favor of a round-the-world tour with Moss Hart, Kaufman's sometime collaborator.

We were still reeling from our disappointment when it was tempered by a phone call to Fanny from Charles K. Feldman, a lawyer, agent, and most recently producer, a man who knew where all the bodies were buried in the film capital and quite possibly had buried some of them himself. Although he had a law degree, Feldman was famous for Goldwynesque turns of phrase: "I'm telling you Jack Warner is a louse! I ought to know—he's my best friend!" He had read our outline, thought its authors were the hottest discovery since the Marx brothers, and would be happy to lay out $10,000 for its conversion into a screenplay. Floating on Cloud Nine, Rafe and I hardly needed the plane that late in 1948 whisked us out to Hollywood.

Moviedom was no longer the buoyant, confident playground of the thirties. The foundations of The Industry had been rocked in 1948 by the abolition of block booking, a lucrative arrangement that the Supreme Court found illegal. The moguls had from the start controlled film production and distribution, but their stranglehold on exhibition had been hampered by the presence of numerous independent theater owners and small chains. To remedy that oversight, they came up with block booking. A Hollywood henchman would visit each owner and present the mogul menu for the coming year: for instance, two Gables, a Liz Taylor romance, a pair of John Wayne epics and a Bette Davis. Then the beaming exhibitor would discover there was a hitch to this banquet. To get the filet mignon he had to take also the sour apples, all the studio failures and leftovers. The scheme had been applied with virtuous impartiality to movie palaces in New York and converted dance halls in Houston, a cozy arrangement that guaranteed a disaster-proof market for Hollywood and a continued dependence for the hinterland. Now it was gone; in place of untouchable returns, a shaky future.

Furthermore, just around the corner were the gathering clouds of television, not yet directly overhead but clearly on the way. If people could bring Lucille Ball and Sid Caesar into their living rooms at the twist of a dial, why should they take their dollars to the box office?

In this atmosphere of indecision and self-doubt, restaurant tables once reserved for studio chiefs were being invaded by hustling agents. One of the new agent-producers was Charlie Feldman.

Feldman was a big beefy man whose curly black moustache and swaggering air conjured up Rudolph Rassendale, a villain of early twentieth-century melodrama. In March, after we turned in some forty-five pages of full script and a summary of the rest, we were summoned to our first story conference. From an anthill of pills and vitamins on his desk, Feldman kept popping capsules into his mouth as he talked.

His first meanderings, during which he casually re-christened our heroine "Nelly Bly," a globe-trotting woman journalist of the 1880s, made us wonder if he had actually read our pages.

But then he ticked off a lucid list of complaints: our script was overlong, overcautious, had far too many expensive sets, and "needed more boy and girl stuff." Worst of all, it had lost the bounce and sparkle that had first intrigued him.

We turned for counsel to my old chums Ring Lardner, Jr. and Ian Hunter. Ring had kept in sporadic touch with me even before our Hollywood roommate days, chronicling his labors on behalf of the embattled Screen Writers Guild and reporting his coup in devising an ending to Ben Hecht's screen comedy *Nothing Sacred* after a solution had eluded even the redoubtable George S. Kaufman. When my article on the Polish farmer who defied the Public Service Corporation of New Jersey appeared in the *American Spectator*, he had filled two pages with high praises ("you most decidedly have a future"), and concluded with an offer to advance my fortunes at the New York *Herald-Tribune*, where he had managerial contacts; he signed off, "lovingly, Ringgold." Now, however, he nursed his Scotch in bemused silence, apparently numbed by his rigors of the moment in converting the novel *Forever Amber* into a plausible screenplay.

Ian, to my dismay, was openly hostile, his once-disarming, faintly English drawl given way to a brittle cackle. I was no longer an old chum, but another entrant in the fiercely competitive Hollywood writing market. "Who the hell needs you guys here?"

I refused to take offense. "Charlie Feldman, apparently."

Ian flung down his napkin. "Oh, God, a straight man! Now, that's something we can use, eh, Ring?"

Our stage play premise had envisaged a world-weary, sexually sated monarch beguiled by Nell Gwynn's insistence that the last thing he needed was another bedmate; why not substitute levity for lechery, and settle for a companionable sparring partner?

The court need never know, Nell pointed out; gossips would assume the usual hedonistic frolic going on behind the walls of Nell's cottage.

It was a situation ripe for sophisticated by-play, but probably overripe for Dubuque. Now, faced with Feldman's admonition to restore our early bounce while sidestepping the Hays Office moral code, we juggled and twisted scenes, dropped jokes, added characters. The Hays office (prop. Will Hays, a former Postmaster General, with the Catholic Church in the background) prohibited any overt hanky-panky on the screen. Ladies and gentlemen could not occupy the same bed or use loose language. Hays, a self-censoring invention of the moguls, did not care what movie gangsters did in the way of mayhem so long as they kept their clothes on doing it.

Meanwhile, in my rented aerie-cum-piano at the top of Laurel Canyon, I found myself drifting into song numbers. After all, we were writing a musical. And my occasional forays into composition since college had been greeted warmly, not only by Dodger fans but by Gertrude Lawrence, torch singer Libby Holman, the graduate school of music at Columbia and the venerable Dr. Szirmay, resident master of piano arrangements at the publishing house of Chappell and Company.

Prudence, no doubt, would have dictated that Berkman and Blau—not exactly household names in show business—buttress their scriptwriting labors with those of an established songwriting team. But whether greedy for recognition or in irrepressible response to inner need, I plunged ahead and completed several ballads. Rafe threw in a few wry rhymes.

The songs pleased Feldman. So did our various convolutions in the script, to the point where he extended our contract. At long last he pronounced our once-joyful romp a viable property which he would take to Harry Cohn and Columbia as a vehicle for Latin screen siren Rita Hayworth. Price tag: $100,000.

Cohn, no model of virtue in his private life, found the subject matter "too racy." And Sammy Cahn at Warner Brothers, weighing *Nellie* as a project for Virginia Mayo, came up with a more reluctant, regretful "No." Himself an esteemed lyricist, Cahn "liked it all"—book, words and tunes—but felt there was no way of doing it as a picture because the material was "so censorable."

Gradually the key fact became inescapable: we had squashed our feisty Broadway lion into a narrow Hollywood cage. The lion had curled up and died. But ironically there was enough trace left of its original bite to bar it forever from the screen.

A second, more personal West Coast adventure had flourished for a time before ending on an equally inconclusive note: my renewed pursuit of the tantalizing Sheilah Graham.

Sheilah breezed into my life, a tall, leggy blonde, during my closing months at the *Mirror*, where her arrival stirred the usually blasé denizens of the newsroom out of their seats. Fresh from England, a feature writer, she had previously been a dancer with Mr. Cochran's Young Ladies, the

British equivalent of the Ziegfeld Follies; her high-kicking talents had inspired a tribute in verse from the parliamentarian poet A.P. Herbert.

Delicately assembled, nicely rounded, Sheilah would in later years share the back of a book jacket with Marilyn Monroe—and it would not be Monroe who first caught the viewer's eye.

Although there were few kinks in Sheilah's sexual armor, it was her smile, dazzling as blinding headlights on a dark country road, that took no prisoners.

Sheilah was the blonde goddess of my youthful fantasies, the reincarnation of the unattainable campus queen at Cornell, so I pursued her with adolescent longing. She was much impressed with my academic credentials—the first and only practical benefit I ever had from my Phi Beta Kappa key. We drifted together, not on the intimate terms we would one day enjoy but enticingly enough for her to inquire one evening, as we lingered at the door of her Beaux Arts apartment, "What would your mother say if you stayed overnight?"

In 1935 Sheilah had left the *Mirror* for Hearst's New York *Journal-American*, whose dreary columns she promptly enlivened with a series of saucy articles on American sexual behavior. A rival newspaper chain thereupon offered her a movie column in Hollywood.

The film world was foreign territory to Sheilah, but practically a second home to Fanny. Among my aunt's eccentricities was the ability to extend largesse to virtual strangers while fueling savage feuds within the family. Although she had only met Sheilah twice, she fired off a batch of introductory letters that flung open a dozen jealously guarded doors as well as the friendly portals of Frank Scully, the *Variety* columnist who presided over a circle of amusing Bohemians.

Sheilah acclimated fast. A stunner even in the land of starlets, the fetching blonde with the lilting accent and toothpaste-ad smile had quickly captivated F. Scott Fitzgerald. After a tempestuous love affair the novelist had died in her arms in 1940. Two years later she married a prominent English businessman; four years after that she was a divorcée with two small children.

By the time I arrived for our labors with Charlie Feldman, Sheilah was a fixture on the Hollywood journalistic scene, a definite threat to its two entrenched, aging gossip queens, Louella "Lollie" Parsons and the vitriolic Hedda Hopper. But Sheilah herself had faded slightly. Although she still tossed off an occasional high kick, faint bulges marred the London chorus girl calves that had once captivated A.P. Herbert.

Grinding out a daily movie column was an exhausting, nerve-frazzling business: a round of uncheckable rumors and anonymous telephone calls; of dodging libidinous stars like Errol Flynn in their dressing rooms, appeasing outraged moguls, fending off belligerent press agents. The stakes were high, the competition merciless—not only from the two harpies but from radio reporters and the trade journals.

Perhaps I represented to Sheilah a throwback to a less frenetic time. In any event she greeted me warmly and enlisted me at once for a lush, star-bedecked Bel Air cocktail party where I offered a canapé to a startled Charlie Feldman. The next day I brought her flowers with a note:

> Violets are blue, roses are yella;
> Sheilah's got a brand-new fella.

An asterisk next to the "brand-new" amended it to "slightly used." Sheilah laughed and threw her arms around me.

A week later we were in my car, cautiously negotiating the long, steep back road leading to my Laurel Canyon hideaway. Both of us were nervous—I not only about the incipient assignation but about the prospect of later backing down a narrow dirt road—Sheilah about being seen.

"I don't think Hedda is lurking in that tree," I ventured.

"You never know where Hedda is lurking. Do your windows have shades?"

"My shades have shades. It's very private up here."

It was also a disaster—no doubt because I had harbored the fantasy of bedding Sheilah for years. This was to be the glorious turnaround of her teasing indifference from the *Mirror* days, the realization of my endless quest for the perfect blonde goddess. Instead, it was an inglorious flop.

A few days later, at a rendezvous in her neo-Spanish house in the privileged Beverly Hills enclave above Sunset Boulevard, the hurdle was cleared. But our fundamental disparity on the subject of sex would remain a source of mutual frustration. Sheilah saw sex as a smashing of taboos, a wicked indulgence enhanced by "naughty" language. It seemed for her a private release, devoid of feeling, rather than the tender blending I sought; the act appeared more important to Sheilah than the person she shared it with. She liked to schedule sexual encounters almost like a tennis match, and sometimes with less warm-up.

Sheilah and I were together two or three nights a week, usually for quiet dinners before the fire in her huge living room: chicken, peas and mashed potatoes. Sometimes we dropped in at a local restaurant. No charge, of course; they were happy to welcome a popular columnist. As protocol required, I always left a handsome tip. One evening we strolled a block north on Maple Drive to visit Irving Stone, author of *Lust for Life*. On the way back, we were stopped by a Beverly Hills patrolman, suspicious of a couple on foot among the Mercedes-cluttered mansions.

I was touched by Sheilah's children. Wendy, five or six, was slim, dark, shy, and perpetually troubled by some unvoiced anxiety. Robbie, a couple of years younger, was sunny, open, a blonde angel of innocence who clung to me as "my fwend." I played horsie with the kids on the beach at Malibu, Wendy mounted on my back, and worried with Sheilah when Robbie showed signs—fortunately transient—of a polio limp.

I grew to know Sheilah; her conflicts as a career-driven mother; her willingness to strike back in print when she felt mistreated. She was a lonely, frightened woman, for reasons that would not be clear until a decade later. But she radiated a fundamental honesty, a refusal to brook pretense or to take herself or anyone else too seriously.

We went to a number of premières—monstrous affairs with gigantic floodlights sweeping the heavens, prancing stars, and hysterical fans straining at the police lines—and to an Academy Awards ceremony with John Huston and Doris Day. They were a most unlikely couple, clearly pasted together by some beleaguered studio publicity department. Huston was brilliant, acerbic, the quintessential creative rebel bored by Hollywood ritual but fascinated by the possibilities of the screen medium. Day was plump, freckled, inarticulate, a gawky youngster being groomed to exploit her honeyed singing voice . . . and a far, far cry from the svelte, poised star I would encounter at the Paramount writers' table eight years later. In the interim she had been completely redesigned. Like a tenement building converted to an elegant mansion, only the shell remained. Everything that could be changed had been: hair-do, eyebrows, carriage. The paunchy mid-section and overstuffed derrière were gone, streamlined, at heaven knows what cost in money and self-discipline. It was an extraordinary testimonial to Hollywood's skill at fabricating an image.

Sheilah talked a good deal about Scott Fitzgerald, at first tentatively, then with growing freedom. She portrayed a man of devastating charm: quick, light, inventive, brimming over with poetry and whimsy . . . when sober. He had been an earnest follower of global politics and a meticulous teacher, whose carefully tailored program of reading lists and study methods she later outlined in *A College of One*. He even delivered little homilies on such subjects as listening to music in company: "You must never tell someone else what associations come up in your mind. That's an intrusion. People are entitled to form their own impressions."

Scott in his cups was something else; all rages, accusations, ultimatums. She conveyed a vivid picture of the great novelist chasing her around the kitchen of his Malibu Beach cottage, shiny carving knife in hand . . . and of his humble contrition afterward.

Fitzgerald had been a faithful admirer of Ed Murrow, never missing his early broadcasts from blitz-battered London. I relayed this tidbit to Murrow, mentioning as its source "the woman he used to live with."

"And who," Murrow shot back, "is she living with now?"

Together Sheilah and I thumbed through the books Scott had left with her, and read aloud his most cherished poem, Andrew Marvell's "To His Coy Mistress," with its eloquent salute to the joys of the moment:

> Had we but world enough, and time,
> This coyness, lady, were no crime . . .
> But at my back I always hear
> Time's wingèd chariot hurrying near . . .

As a serious author, Fitzgerald was all but forgotten; *Tender Is the Night,* published in 1934, had not repeated the success of *The Great Gatsby*. His reputation for short stories and novels was in limbo; he would be long dead before it was resurrected. Meanwhile, he was little attuned to the harsh commercialism of the studios or the technical demands of screenwriting. His health was shaky. He had financial obligations, including a young daughter at school. And hanging over both him and Sheilah was the shadow of his wife Zelda, the once-merry madcap of his Paris years, now institutionalized in the East . . . a woman he could neither live with, nor abandon to marry Sheilah.

In this maelstrom of conflicts, he turned to the familiar comfort of the bottle. But alcohol was destroying him physically. At long last, with Sheilah's help, he managed to stop drinking, to plunge into work on *The Last Tycoon.*

It was too late. The book that was to be his crowning opus, with Sheilah near its center, never got beyond a draft and copious notes. Fitzgerald's body had become dependent on the stimulation of liquor. Without it, his heart stopped.

Sheilah showed me the poem that at the height of their romance Fitzgerald had written to her, its capricious spelling only enhancing its charm. "Beloved Infidel" expressed not rancor but gratitude to her previous lovers, thanking them for helping to shape and perfect the woman of his heart. It was an extraordinary sentiment, noble in its wisdom and magnanimity, worthy of a tortured genius. To me it epitomized the tenderness and despair of their impossible relationship. Had I had ready access to tears—unfortunately twenty-five years away—I would have shed them. Instead, I told her Scott had made her one further uncharted gift: a title for the memoir she would some day write.

Sheilah gave me a long, unblinking look. "You have a quality," she said softly, "that was one of the things I loved most about Scott. You make allowances for circumstances and limitations. You don't pass judgment on people."

She took to bracketing me with Fitzgerald more often, recounting an incident when they had quarreled and she had stormed out: "I phoned him to apologize—as I would have phoned you if I had run out." Then, after a week-end at Malibu: "I had resigned myself to never knowing a man like Scott again. But you crashed down all the barricades I had put up: success, career, the consolation of my children. You make me want to be a human being again."

Sheilah had by this time been married twice: first as a young London beauty to a much older retired army officer, then to Trevor Westbrook, the right-hand man of England's war production minister, Lord Beaverbrook. She was beginning to drop hints that she might not be averse to a third try. The children needed a father; Robby was quite attached to his "fwend." One day she was more direct: "Would you like to have a son by me? Be a teacher and I'll chuck all this and marry you."

I was flattered but unpersuaded. I had a feeling of something missing, incomplete, in our relationship. Sheilah gave me what she could, but it was not enough. Ill-formed though my needs were, I wanted from a woman a deeper involvement in them. What I craved she had already given Scott; that was a one-time coin, permanently spent. I harbored no envy of Scott Fitzgerald; his road had been hard enough. But I could not feed on the embers of the flame he had shared with Sheilah.

Another disquieting question: would I have been equally attracted to Sheilah if she had been a librarian on Long Island? How much of her appeal for me flowed from the aura of glamour that surrounded her?

During my absence from New York I had sent occasional progress reports to Dr. Nordlicht. Now I appended a footnote about Sheilah and marriage.

By telephone, in a rare intervention, he discouraged any such move. With hindsight, I suspect he was aware that no profound union had been achieved; that I had been intermittently caught up in fantasies of conquest, ready-made fatherhood, instant entree into the most exalted circles of the film world. It was not the right time, he intimated, and probably not the right woman.

I knew he was sound at least on the first point. My purposes and plans, my sense of independent identity, were still cloudy. With mild unease, and no promises, I took leave of Sheilah.

She made no bones about her disappointment. "I'm very much in love with you. Why do I poke at your vulnerable spots? Because you're going—and I want you to stay. This amputation is necessary, I know. But it's painful as hell. Every time something happens, I want to call you. The doorbell rings; Robbie says, 'Is that Ted?' I say no, and feel so lonely."

I winced at Sheilah's distress. We had seen each other through highs and lows together. But for the moment, at least, we had come to the end of a road. And I was beginning to squirm under my old disenchantment with the Hollywood milieu. It was time to move on.

Rafe Blau and I were back in New York with a small backlog of cash, a few songs, and our original nucleus for a stage musical. Gertrude Lawrence was no longer a factor; she would soon be wrapped up in the film version of Tennessee Williams' *The Glass Menagerie.* But Fanny's faith in *Nellie* as a theater piece remained undimmed. She took an option on it herself that financed Rafe and me for a summer of work.

Our creative juices, dammed up in Beverly Hills, ran wild again in rugged Nova Scotia, where Rafe and my sister had rented an old farmhouse. After a splashy opening chorus—"Keep A Dandy Handy"—we segued happily into the king's seductive "Let's Make History," with Nell's cool riposte:

> Good Queen Bess and her friend Essex
> Managed nicely with much less sex . . .

Moving along to "That's Mine," an anthem of free-thinking defiance by a Quaker blacksmith who figured in our secondary story, I felt a gooseflesh crawl of excitement, a surge of certainty. This was strong stuff. It would work.

It did. Our refurbished *Nellie* had an immediate suitor in New York: Ernest H. Martin, fresh from his triumphant launching with Cy Feuer of *Guys and Dolls*. Large and affable, Ernie pronounced *Nellie* unequivocally "one helluva" show. "Who writes the jokes?" he demanded. "You guys are better than Comden and Green!" (Betty Comden and Adolph Green had an impressive string of Broadway book, lyric and sketch credits, including *On The Town*).

Ernie took particular delight in a raunchy bumps-and-grind number, "The Power Behind the Power Behind the Throne," in which one of Nell's hip-swinging rivals for Charles boasts:

> By day he's a rover
> But when the day's over,
> The hand that puts the light out rules
> The king!

Ernie had a question about style: "Are we talking broad farce here? Or is it romantic schmaltz?" But his main concern was the casting of King Charles. "A king has to be polished, regal. You can't put a big cowboy like Ray Middleton up there (Middleton had starred with Ethel Merman in *Annie Get Your Gun*). Alfred Drake could carry it. But he wants to be a director this year. Bring me a King Charles, and we'll go into rehearsal tomorrow!"

Rousing words—but where do you look for an English king?

Obviously, Ernie decided, in England. He penned a confident note to Louis Dreyfus, head of Chappell Music Publishing in London, strongly recommending *Nellie* as a "potential success" if properly cast. If Dreyfus could assemble a West End production, Feuer and Martin would be happy to do the honors in the States.

A second personal note to Dreyfus from Anna Sosenko, manager of the ultra-elegant chanteuse Hildegarde, applauded *Nellie* as a "wonderful play" topped by a "sensational score; the lyrics are dreamy, the melodies lush and memorable." I took off for London.

All hands chose to ignore a quiet warning from the shrewd and knowledgeable John C. Wilson, former "companion" to Noel Coward. Wilson thought our show's "very amusing lyrics and very amusing approach to the subject" gave promise of "a great success on Broadway;" Britishers by contrast would consider it "in the most appalling taste."

Wilson proved to be right—with a single exception. Producer Jack Hylton, a former orchestra leader, tapped his foot to the songs, judged our book to be "beautifully written," and told not only us but the London papers that he was putting *Nellie* on his schedule, with Fernand Gravet as King Charles. He would be talking to Ella Logan, of *Finian's Rainbow* fame, about playing the female lead. Again rejoicing.

And again reversal. Two weeks after I returned to New York an apologetic cable from Hylton advised that at the urging of his business manager, who was worried about *Nellie's* irreverent flavor, he was taking the safer route of reviving *Pal Joey*.

I had had a bellyful of ecstatic takeoffs followed by crash landings. *Nellie* refused either to flame into life or submit to a decent burial. Hilliard Dubrow, later surgeon to Marilyn Monroe, heard two songs and said "Put me down for ten thousand dollars." Saint Subber, producer of

Kiss Me, Kate, was enchanted: "But how can I raise money for an elaborate period production without the insurance of a big name?" I felt like a ping-pong ball being pounded back and forth across the net.

Late in 1952 a new producing team, society figure Courtney Burr and actor Burgess Meredith, materialized on our doorstep, gushing "Where have you guys been?"

According to Meredith, the intense, brooding star of *Winterset* and *Of Mice and Men*, who would later play the fight manager in *Rocky*, on a drive through Westchester County with Alan Jay Lerner at the wheel he had started reading aloud the lyrics of "That's Mine."

Lerner had braked his car and pulled over to listen. He sat in silence till the end of the second chorus:

> Take my pipe of clay, my fields of hay
> I can do without them till another day
> But till hell-fires freeze
> I'll say what I please—
> That's Mine!

The lyricist of *My Fair Lady* and *Gigi* then commented: "That's a stronger cry for freedom of conscience than *The Crucible*. And shorter. I wish I'd written it."

Meredith and Burr wanted more tunes. I enrolled at Stefan Volpe's Contemporary School of Music in Greenwich Village, and the following month wrote two more ballads, "This Is How It Was Meant to Be" and "Pray for Me," that Simon Radie at Decca Records hailed as "definite standards."

Neither ever reached Meredith's ears. By one of those quirks that seemed to plague *Nellie*, Ella Logan had just come back from London to New York, chirping to ship news reporters on her return from London that her next role would be that of the seventeenth century orange girl. She greeted me at her home with a hearty kiss and a stream of suggestions about staging.

Meredith, it turned out, was still nursing his wounds from a stormy love affair with Logan. He was furious at her intervention. We never heard from him again.

This third abandonment was a searing blow. Once again my best work remained hidden from a world whose praises I craved. Where were we going to get a production? In Tibet? On the moon?

Dr. Nordlicht, always sparing of summary judgments, was moved to comment. Lean and balding, he cultivated a detached manner that seemed at odds with the lines of concern in his face. "It is possible," he said in his careful, deliberate way, "that your musical will remain unproduced."

"What?" The idea had never crossed my mind. I would not allow it to.

"The theater is an unpredictable arena. Merit is not necessarily rewarded. Or even recognized."

"But we've come so close!"

His solemn brown eyes fixed on me compassionately. "I'm not suggesting that you give up. Only that you be aware of the realities. This is not the last or only work you will create."

Slowly, painfully, Rafe and I began to turn our attention to other things. There were continuing flickers of interest in *Nellie* from England, where ballet superstar Anton Dolin kept trying to work up a production with Sarah Churchill's husband, Anthony Beauchamp. In 1958 Joe Lilley, head of the music department at Paramount, urged Pat Duggan, a producer at the studio, to do *Nellie* on Broadway: "Two solid standards in the score. Maybe four."

If I were back in New York . . .", sighed Duggan. But he wasn't.

Gradually our much-battered musical slid to a back burner, ostensibly forgotten but a lingering torment till another brush with Feuer and Martin down the road.

CHAPTER 12

Ghost Story

Rafe Blau and I had meanwhile spun out three movie originals. *Blocked Exit*, based on a radio script he had done earlier for the Mollé Mystery Theater, was a tight little melodrama rooted in agoraphobia, the irrational fear of open spaces. It charted the decline of a city political boss, helplessly trapped within a single square block although aware that a vengeful killer is closing in on him. Converted into a screenplay, it was quickly optioned for production by Joyce Selznick, a young cousin of the lordly David.

At our urging Joyce hired Bill Howard, aging and out of favor in Hollywood, to direct. Bill flew in to New York, production offices were set up in an East Side town house—and somewhere along the financial trail the project collapsed. *Blocked Exit* bobbed around in the movie seas for another two decades, attracting the attention among others of Jules Dassin (*Never On Sunday*, *Topkapi*) but never quite making it to shore.

Women for Willoughby was a totally different affair, a lightly satirical comedy lampooning the irresistible public appeal of homecoming war heroes, from Julius Caesar to Dwight Eisenhower. Our genial, fatherly General Willoughby, bitten by the political bug, is challenged for the presidency by the only candidate who shares his famous name: his disenchanted wife. Their house-divided rocks under a tumultuous, sometimes dryly ironic campaign ("The silence you have just heard," intones one of May Willoughby's commercials, "does not necessarily represent the views of this station").

Jules Goldstone, a major Hollywood agent, wired that on the strength of initial responses, he was asking $100,000 for the property and "pitching" it for Clark Gable. Three weeks later came the melancholy sequel: everybody agreed that *Willoughby* was delightful, but no studio chief was willing to risk offending the multitudinous admirers of Douglas MacArthur and smiling Ike. I wanted to tear out what was left of my hair.

Our next offering posed less of a threat to popular icons, if not to grandiose notions about homo sapiens. In the 1930s Robert Yerkes, a professor of psychology at Yale specializing in primates, had done a number of studies comparing the growth processes of baby chimpanzees with those of human infants. Rafe, who had just sold *Mother Is A Freshman* as a solo original to 20th Century-Fox, saw the Yerkes experiments as a springboard for another comedy; but the plot elements weren't quite coming together.

He sent me his draft from Nova Scotia. I eliminated one character, brought in another, and came up with a title. *Bedtime for Bonzo* was born, quickly flowering into an elaborately detailed original story treatment of a hundred-and-twenty pages. It hit pay dirt on its second studio submission, at Universal. However, the star we had hoped for—Cary Grant—would not be part of the package. To our vast disappointment, our staunch academic environmentalist would be played by a decidedly lesser personality, a second-string leading man whose chief distinction was the presidency of the Screen Actors Guild. His career, however, was showing signs of fraying around the edges. His name was Ronald Reagan.

As love interest for Reagan and governess for his primate protégé we would get Diana Lynn. And as the centerpiece of the story everybody would get Bonzo, a five-year-old chimp who had spent the first half of his life in the Liberian jungle and the rest of it in the wilds of Hollywood.

Bonzo, frolicking through his first feature role, was manna for the nation's entertainment pages. From the day shooting started late in 1950, his set became the preferred port of call for movieland visitors, far outdrawing the sound stages where the celebrated profiles of his nearest competitors, Laurence Olivier and Vivien Leigh, were on display. A picture spread in *This Week* showed him in defiant combat with a vacuum cleaner, chalking up a sustained three-minute camera take to break the previous animal-scene mark. The talented chimp, although not a Method actor, could reportedly weep on command or laugh, snarl with hate, smooch affectionately or stand on his head, responding promptly to some five-hundred-and-two instructions—or, as a passing director sourly observed, "about five hundred more than a lot of human actors."

The studio in turn built Bonzo an air-conditioned bungalow-dressing room, its amenities carefully recorded by columnist Sidney Skolsky: bed, dining table, trapeze bar. Bonzo also had his personal dresser, a make-up man ("most concerned about posterior shine") and a stand-in, a stuffed ape whom after one set-up the chimp peremptorily banished from the set.

Reagan and Lynn, reduced to bystander status, could only writhe and stare as their co-star romped off with scene after scene. "At last," quipped a visiting reporter, "the president of the Screen Actors Guild has found an actor he doesn't like."

Reagan later had reason to temper his resentment. *Bedtime For Bonzo*, released in 1951 against such powerhouse opposition as the Tracy-Hepburn *Adam's Rib* and Brando's *Viva Zapata*, soared to the number one or number two spot in box office charts throughout the country, giving a welcome boost to Reagan's flagging professional reputation.

It was also successful enough to engender a sequel—*Bonzo Goes To College*—which opened on a big close-up of hairy anthropoid legs on a registration line at, fittingly enough, Yale. This time Bonzo emerged as an unstoppable Ivy League halfback, scampering under enemy legs and throwing passes with the most formidable right arm since Achilles.

Rafe and I, at the insistence of David Holtzmann, Fanny's younger brother and law partner, had retained commercial rights to the chimpanzee character. David was in the process of drawing up substantial contracts with doll companies and toy manufacturers when an unhappy headline blazoned across the front page of the New York *Herald-Tribune*: a faulty heater had set ablaze the studio Quonset hut where Bonzo, after a triumphant personal appearance tour in the East, was being quartered with several look-alikes. All the animals perished of smoke inhalation. Frank Scully, the columnist for weekly *Variety*, estimated a potential five million in future box-office receipts went up in the smoke.

That the perky little primate would rise from the ashes thirty years later as a popular cartoon figure was as unlikely a prospect as the ascendancy of his former co-star to the White House.

Unfortunately, Bonzo added more to the Universal coffers than to ours. A free-lancer's bills, unlike his earnings, arrive regularly.

Conveniently to the rescue came old chum Gerold Frank, then a senior editor at *Coronet*. A pocket-size offshoot of *Esquire*, *Coronet* had through salty cartoons and muscular prose won a large following during the war. The magazine featured drawings, etchings and color reproductions of famous paintings, along with provocative articles. Gradually switching its portrait subjects from Madonnas to semi-clad models, it rang up a circulation of five million, second only to *Reader's Digest*, before expiring in a circulation war during the 1960s. I did several pieces for Gerry, the first of which, "The Cult of Super-Sex," was reprinted as a prose model by the Columbia University Correspondence School.

Lester Cowan, an independent movie producer of *G.I. Joe* fame, dangled a spot as right-hand man—who would stay at his side and provide the creative spark he himself lacked. The job required a twenty-four-hour presence at the producer's elbow.

It sounded to me like intellectual slavery, hopelessly remote from an increasingly turbulent real world. Hot war had erupted in Korea, soon to pit Douglas MacArthur against Communist China and lead to the general's controversial dismissal by President Harry Truman. Senator Joseph McCarthy continued to fake photographs and hurl reckless charges of treason while Dwight D. Eisenhower, elected to the White House in 1952, sat mute, and even future president John F. Kennedy mused that McCarthy might "have something."

On the entertainment scene, "Red Channels" broke into vindictive print in the early fifties, listing on flimsy evidence allegedly subversive radio and television personalities. The Hollywood Harpies, Louella Parsons and Hedda Hopper—but not Sheilah—were beating the drums for Hearst and the equally suppressive Louis B. Mayer. With a new Senate subcommittee on the inquisitional warpath, America was drifting into witch-hunt complacency.

I sent a supportive note to Ring Lardner, then serving a one-year term in Danbury Prison. It bounced back, along with a form letter in pious government gobbledygook explaining that "as a Federal inmate undergoing rehabilitation" Ring was restricted to a handful of explicitly designated correspondents. Was this my America?

Not coincidentally, television was saturating the American household. Commercials shrieked their wares; Jack Benny's off-tune violin sounded a weekly serenade.

Not everybody was cheering. Tart-tongued Fred Allen forecast a nation "with eyeballs the size of grapefruits," and gray matter reduced to a speck: "Television is a triumph of equipment over people, and the minds that control it are so small that you could put them in the navel of a flea and still have room for a network vice-president's heart."

The Canadian social critic Marshal McLuhan saw couch-potato America on the road to apathy if not somnambulism. Ed Murrow pointed out that television without purpose or conscience was merely "wires in a box;" if the electronic media "are to be used for the entertainment of all of the people all of the time, we have come perilously close to discovering the real opiate of the people."

But the programs multiplied. *Gunsmoke* was riding high, inheriting the movie vogue for romanticizing a West that never was. Soap opera led the way to sitcoms; game shows jousted with quiz shows. A brief "Golden Age" of live experimental drama—Paddy Chayevsky and Rod Serling on *Playhouse 90* and *Studio One*—soon petered out; serious writers could not meet the demands for "product" of the insatiable tube, and were siphoned off to Hollywood. By the end of the decade the national addiction to TV was firm, with the average viewer devoting six hours to the flickering screen seven days a week. *TV Guide*, with eight million readers, was soon challenging the circulations of *Parade*, *Reader's Digest* and *Time*.

Privately, Ed Murrow detested TV: its hot lights, its manipulation by Madison Avenue ad agencies, its accent on pictures over ideas. But the square box was a fact of network life, so he made the most of its dramatic potential. Taking off from *Hear It Now*, a radio feature of historic tapes and recordings he had developed with Fred Friendly, he created *See It Now*, a television series which probed restlessly into some of the less heartwarming aspects of American life. Viewers were taken aboard a bus in the newly integrated, still-smoldering South; gasped for air with coal miners in West Virginia; were drawn into the plight of a Chinese immigrant barred by his neighbors from a chic San Francisco suburb.

Could the show use a creative consultant?

"Brother Ed" was receptive; his producing partner, Fred Friendly, perhaps threatened by the prospect, was not. Huge, tousled, seemingly in a constant state of crisis, Friendly suggested he might open up a reporting spot for me.

I felt that my executive experience and creative background qualified me for something more. Besides, something in Friendly's aggressive, overweening manner put me off. I couldn't imagine being answerable to him.

I went back to Murrow. He bucked me along to his programming colleague Hubbell Robinson, for whom I did a dramatic adaptation stint on *Studio One*.

Later I had occasion to second-guess my decision about Friendly. In 1953 *See It Now* successfully championed the cause of a reserve officer fired by the Air Force because of his family's alleged leftist sympathies. And the following spring, in the most dramatic confrontation of his career, Ed Murrow took on Joe McCarthy himself.

He pinned McCarthy to the wall by the ingenious juxtaposition of the Senator's blatantly self-contradictory statements. McCarthy never recovered. Murrow paid for his courage. Sponsors found him unpleasantly controversial. By the next season his hard-hitting documentaries were driven from prime time, sacrificed to viewers who protested when their entertainment programs were pre-empted by the McCarthy showdown. But what a joy it would have been to share in planning Ed's counterattack against the malevolent monster!

In 1952 I had my own politician, a white-hat good guy, to deal with. Averell Harriman, a veteran New Deal diplomat and trouble-shooter, was running for governor of New York. Tom Wilson, a crony from my Cairo days and a Harriman acolyte, thought I might help the campaign. I cooked up a campaign song, "Win With Harriman," that caught the candidate's fancy and was promptly recorded for radio spots and rallies.

Two days later, an S.O.S. summoned me back from a week-end in Connecticut. The script of a Harriman biography for television, prepared by a major advertising agency, creaked with pompous clichés guaranteed to lull viewers to sleep if not into the opposition camp. Could I hustle down to the agency offices, snatch back the corpse and breathe some life into it?

For the next forty-eight hours I lived on Madison Avenue, juggling film clips and arguing with agency executives. They had a totally different perspective on the world. With Tom Wilson's backing I was able to reshape the biography. But I came away with the conviction that television was an unperceived threat to the future of America, concentrating media power in a way that made the excesses of *Time* magazine and Hollywood seem relatively harmless.

The prospect struck me as so disturbing that I spent two weeks on an application for a Guggenheim Foundation grant. From my years in propaganda analysis, I knew how a population could be manipulated into inert compliance. I argued that the communications conglomerate, spearheaded by all-engulfing television, would if unchecked cripple and perhaps destroy the American capacity for independent thought: in a society ready to reward Sam Levinson with four thousand dollars a week as a stand-up comedian but only valuing his teaching services at the same sum for a year, educators were helpless, hopelessly outgunned.

Ed Murrow, poring over my proposal, registered a quick and hearty "Hallelujah!" So did Carl W. Ackerman, dean of the Columbia Graduate School of Journalism. Edwin Ware Hullinger, deputy director of the FBIS and a former United Press luminary, pronounced my study plan an urgently needed response to the most serious issue facing American society.

The Guggenheim people, presumably preoccupied with such crucial considerations as the development of the intransitive verb in Serbo-Croatian, felt otherwise.

Still on my desk was a sprawl of unfinished projects, including "Shall We Enjoin the Ladies?" an essay on the effusions of some female authors. My favorite was a quote from a story by Adela Rogers St. John in *Cosmopolitan*: "The light caught her dark curls and flung them back so her head looked like a radiator cap."

Since coming back from Hollywood, I had ricocheted through several social circles. I spent some summer weekends at a Deal, New Jersey beach club where the introductions were like a stroll through the Sunday department store ads: "This is Mrs. Saks . . . Mrs. Gimbel . . . Mrs. Bloomingdale," and a longer, more interesting period hobnobbing with the dilettantes of the music world who shuttled between Carnegie Hall and the Russian Tea Room, prattling knowingly of "Lennie" (Leonard Bernstein). I tangled at a party with proletarian playwright Clifford Odets (we both fancied the same divorcée). Since the impasse with Sheilah I had relapsed into teen-age uncertainty about my amatory prowess, foraging in Bohemian quarters among helpless neurotics whose dependent fragility eased my dread of being swallowed up and simultaneously fed my macho longings. I oscillated between the fear that my inamorata wouldn't love me and the equally unnerving fear that she would.

Quite separately, I was engaged in a clandestine quest for the perfect mate. I carried around a prefabricated image of my dream girl, ready to whip out and slap over a new candidate—something like the tailored cut-outs at a Coney Island photo studio with an open space to accommodate the sitter's head.

Beth Moldau violated my usual criteria. She was not a golden blonde. Her appeal was more earthy than ethereal; her slithering sensuous walk could be spotted half a block away. And she was Jewish, a shortcoming I was willing to overlook because she didn't look Jewish.

Beth was exquisitely assembled: long supple lines that flowed like a Picasso sketch, high Mongol/Tartar cheekbones, wide welcoming mouth. With her silky honey-colored hair, she was beautiful enough for a Madison Avenue art gallery to put her portrait on display in its window. She was also sensitive enough to run her fingers through a melting Chopin nocturne, literate enough to write amusing jacket copy for a paperback publishing house—and not quite strong enough to bring her many attributes together. Motherless since infancy, she had been raised by a charming Russian father who looked like Toscanini and gambled like Gaylord Ravenal of *Showboat*: one year a real estate tycoon, the next an improvident borrower.

I impressed Beth, who was accustomed to instant attempts at mauling, by for once having the good sense to soft-pedal sexual demands. We were matched in so many ways—interests, values, aversions—that we both knew physical consummation would come in its own good time. We argued amiably, took turns at the piano, and one evening laughed our way from the kitchen into bed. Here at long last was the complete connection, the happy fusion, that I had been too frightened to enjoy with Sybil Rice and that had been missing with Sheilah.

I took pride in her beauty, experienced an unfamiliar sense of power at a party when David Langdon, a celebrated cartoonist for *Punch* of London, gaped at her with unconcealed longing. I was a happy man, a sailor come to port after a long and wearisome voyage.

But Beth's years of economic tension had left her wary. Marriage to an improvident scribbler, no matter how beloved, was not on her agenda:

"You should have someone who'd build her life around you, devote herself to meeting your needs. I'm just not up to that, Ted."

"Have you ever been so close to anyone?"

"No, but what would we live on? You're the most brilliant, talented schoolboy I've known—but you don't understand the responsibilities of marriage!"

Perhaps she was right. In any event, she was immovable. Ultimately through friends of mine Beth met a young movie producer, heir to a furniture empire, who laid his fortune at her feet. Sobbingly, apologetically, she explained to me her decision to marry him. With the bulwark of his millions, her emotional instability would never again be put under stress; her aging father would be assured of a luxurious retirement.

I was shocked, wounded, deeply hurt, but gradually reconciled to her viewpoint. Her suitor was totally enraptured, literate but limited, unlikely ever to be running off by himself in unexpected directions . . . in short, a dependable lifelong acquisition. I could offer no such insulation against life's future onslaughts.

On borrowed money I fled to a vacation in Mexico. All day, at 8,000 feet above sea level, I leaped across rugged ravines.

Back in Manhattan, I found myself breathless climbing a flight of stairs. Sleep was sweat-soaked, clotted with nightmares. At Mount Sinai Hospital I learned that at thirty-nine I had suffered a heart attack.

Nothing massive, I was told; barely perceptible on the hospital's new vector electrocardiograph machine. A few months of rest and mild medication should repair the damage.

Were the doctors leveling with me, or merely making soothing noises? Clinching my downbeat mood was a letter from John Donovan in Hollywood, who after a Far East tour as Information Officer for various US missions in Asia, had in rapid succession been separated from his second wife, a writing stint for Bing Crosby, and his beloved boxer, Timoshenko.

I had been keeping the landlord at bay with motivational films for industry, winning the best-of-show medal at the Kentuckiana Film Festival for *All I Need Is A Conference*. Things were looking up, at least materially, when Fanny made another of her meteoric entrances into my life. This time it was Fanny herself who needed help.

Gertrude Lawrence had succumbed to hepatitis in September of 1952, after a harrowing summertime ordeal playing the lead in *The King and I*. Fanny, deeply shaken—they were more like sisters than attorney and client—arranged several public tributes, then hatched a brilliant idea: Gertrude's husband, stage producer Richard S. Aldrich, should write a fond account of his whirligig marriage to the bewitching, unpredictable English star.

Dick Aldrich sported a Harvard degree, blueblood social status and a Broadway producing record that included involvement in such major works as *Margin for Error*, *The Moon is Blue*, and *Good-bye, My Fancy*. But the tall, reserved New Englander made no claim to literary prowess.

Fanny was undeterred. He had lived the story, she told Dick; she would put it together, gathering up the necessary research and buttressing it with documentation from her abundant files. Then she would find a professional wordslinger to set it all down. Ghosting was not unheard of, although it had not yet been massively embraced by pop singers, basketball stars, test pilots and other commercially exploitable figures. U.S. Senators, and once even Dan Quayle, had been known to draft their own speeches. Aldrich shrugged; he wouldn't get in the way.

After consulting several editor friends about a ghost, Fanny settled on Dorothy Giles, a large, expansive middle-aged lady who was an experienced practitioner of women's-magazine fiction. Armed with a sheaf of folders from Fanny, Dorothy started churning out pages. Gathering steam, she had half the book drafted by the spring of 1953.

Dorothy's pages had an attractive ebullience, some shrewd insights and a sprinkling of pictorial passages. But there were problems of style. Trained in the gushy mode of housewifely romance, Dorothy could not capture the stoic, understated persona of the man she was simulating (said Gertrude of Richard: "His family landed on Plymouth Rock? He *is* Plymouth Rock!").

Fanny called in Rafe Blau for repairs. He sliced through a good deal of overwriting, trimmed the chapter endings, and added some nice masculine touches. But Fanny soon had to recognize that the trouble went beyond the resources of patch-up and polish. What was needed was a drastic restructuring, with a different, more solid kind of narrative personality shining through. Would I tackle the job?

This would be a new kind of challenge, longer than a magazine article, more wide-ranging than a news broadcast, more personal and probing than a movie script. I didn't know if I could handle it, but in view of Fanny's past exertions on my behalf I felt that I hardly had a choice.

The first task was to rework the sections already drafted, crystallizing the narrator's character. It was not hard to slide into Dick Aldrich's voice, or to evoke Gertrude, either. Although I had been in her company only a few times, her aroma was one not quickly forgotten. Fanny read my rewrite of the opening chapter and handed it back, smiling: "We're on the right track."

Past the half-way mark, I was operating on my own, with only the raw material—memoirs, letters, newspaper clippings—supplied by Fanny. This was unknown territory to me, far beyond any previous adventures in prose. I was writing a book, creating characters and scenes. No director with camera angles to help or hinder me; no actors. Just me and the typewriter and the page.

At my desk I was becoming Dick Aldrich. It was scary, then exhilarating.

At Fanny's urging, my alter ego flipped through a few pages. He began warming up to "his" book. Soon he was browsing frequently in the manuscript, grinning and nodding his head in approval.

One time he ran across a patch of dialogue that stopped him. "I wouldn't say it that way," he told Fanny.

"How would you say it, Dick?"

"I don't know . . . ask Ted."

Fanny was a more exacting taskmaster. As the finish line neared, I turned in what I thought was a moving account of Gertrude's funeral. Fanny shook her head: "You can do better."

She was right. The next time around, I was able to heighten the poignancy. As the old adage insists, "Nothing good is ever written; it's rewritten."

Gertrude Lawrence as *Mrs. A*—the title, Fanny's inspiration, stressed the homemaking role that the actress claimed to like best—was an instant and enormous success: serialized in advance by the *Ladies' Home Journal* and the British magazine *Women*, later condensed by *Reader's Digest*. For its official launching early in 1955, Fanny organized a barrage of publicity, including an Ed Sullivan special on CBS television. Helen Hayes, Judith Anderson and Lili Pons performed in Gertrude's honor. Fanny enlisted Sarah Churchill, Sir Winston's actress daughter, to deliver a tribute on behalf of the British theater, and asked Rafe and me to give the lady a hand.

Red-haired and trim, Sarah had the cool and (to me) unexciting good looks of her fox-hunting forebears, and a brisk manner softened by an undercurrent of melancholy. She read a lot of poetry. We put in several evenings with her at rehearsals, which had a curious aftermath. Scheduled to sing one of Gertrude's favorite tunes, the Gershwin ballad "Someone To Watch Over Me," Sarah decided she could perform it properly only with me at her elbow, providing piano accompaniment. She was adamant and a little mystical on the subject, until reluctantly persuaded that Sullivan's pianist would not let her down.

The book promotion proved almost redundant in the face of the critical notices. John Barkham in the Philadelphia *Bulletin* hailed Aldrich's "glowing, moving personal portrait . . . sensitively written and obviously true to life." "A quality of radiance," echoed Lewis Gannett in the New York *Herald-Tribune*, "told with a mingled wit and pride and a stage director's sense of timing." The New York *Times*, *Christian Science Monitor*, Baltimore *Evening Sun*, and a score of lesser journals varied only in their choice of adjectives: tender, touching, "more than momentous."

Dick Aldrich was deluged with mail—from England, Tanganyika, Buenos Aires as well as every corner of America—and quoted as a sage of connubial understanding, a paragon of marital behavior. Interviewers who hauled him before radio microphones interpreted his halting monosyllabic replies as evidence of commitment to purely literary expression.

The book zoomed to the top of the non-fiction lists, where after a year of exposure it could hardly escape the attention of movie story departments. Paramount entered a sizable bid.

Fanny, who up to that point had paid off her two nephews with a pittance from the English magazine advance coupled with vague assurances of blessings to come, saw a chance for a neat combination. Paramount could have the film rights to *Mrs. A*, she decreed, if they would supplement the cash deal with a screenwriting contract for the team largely responsible for the book, Berkman and Blau.

The Paramount story department, no doubt dazzled as much by her negotiating footwork as by her assurances of our screenwriting talents, agreed: a trial shot for the team, ten weeks at a weekly salary of twelve hundred-and fifty dollars each. They probably felt lucky to be hanging onto the studio.

As a parting salute from the east, Hildegarde sent me from Washington a concert program bearing the imprint of the Eisenhower White House, where she had just performed four choruses of "Take It All In Your Stride," words and music by Ted Berkman:

> When the phone rings at midnight and breaks up your slumber
> And all that they want is a very wrong number . . .
> Take It All In Your Stride.
> When you find that the fabulous Medici Palace
> Is not quite as large as a drug store in Dallas . . .
> Take It All In Your Stride.
> When with infinite care dear Antoine does your hair
> For that heavy date;
> It's the kind of a hair-do that others don't dare do,
> You're feeling great;
> Then there's rain and there's thunder
> And all of those wonder-
> Ful curls go straight . . .
> Take It All in Your Stride!

Two of the other composers on the bill were Cole Porter and Jerome Kern.

CHAPTER 13

Fear Strikes Out

Paramount had a Writer's Building office waiting for us and a Danny Kaye assignment. John Mock, the red-haired, scholarly story editor, personally installed us in ample quarters: two offices separated by a cubicle for our secretary, a motherly, whimsical woman named Ann Wenner.

The Kaye vehicle was a Pagliacci-like tale about "Red" Nichols, a band-leading trumpeter of the 1930s, centered on his laughter-through-tears devotion to a polio-stricken daughter. The story was borderline schmaltz which could easily topple over into soap opera. But the jazz background intrigued me, and Rafe and I saw rich comedic possibilities in Nichols's early struggles.

After several weeks we turned in a forty-page treatment, in which Danny/Nichols pyramided a series of half-promises from better-known performers into a successful Broadway opening, then whirled through a parade of bizarre costumes that exploited his song-and-dance versatility. At a story conference presided over by Don Hartman, a writer who had skyrocketed to the studio's chief of production, we were given an enthusiastic green light to move on into screenplay.

"I'll fight for this!" Hartman shouted after us as we were leaving—a notorious harbinger of doom in movieland.

The doom began two days later, when Sylvia Fine and Danny Kaye made an unannounced appearance in the commissary. Sylvia was little changed from our high-school prom days—still plump, shrewd of glance, mischievously droll. Danny, with a string of box-office bonanzas behind him—*Wonder Man*, *The Secret Life of Walter Mitty*, *The Inspector General*—had acquired golden-blonde locks (a suggestion of Sam Goldwyn's, to give Danny Kominski a more Anglo-Saxon facade) and great self-assurance. Sylvia greeted me effusively and invited me to their table, where she sat through lunch in relative silence, inquiring about my family but leaving the limelight to Danny. No mention was made of the "Red" Nichols project.

That was reserved for the dinner party a week later to which I was invited at the Kayes' Beverly Hills mansion on San Ysidro Drive. Danny was away filming on location. Astutely, Sylvia had not only included on her guest list Jack Benny, George Burns and the lyricist Sammy Cahn, but had also corralled for the occasion the incomparable Cole Porter.

From her perspective of influencing a script writer, this was a brilliant move. Hollywood scenarists were not overwhelmed by mere movie stars; we had seen too many, bereft of bright lights and bright dialogue, flounder like children. A gifted composer-lyricist at the peak of his eminence was something else. This was doubly true for me, given my musical ambitions and my predilection for Porter, whose name I had even used as a pseudonym during college escapades.

Porter, a small man in his sixties, was dressed with a meticulous black-tie formality that reflected his lofty social and financial standing. He had a boyish-old face that must once have been quite handsome; now the smooth even features looked worn. He had an air of great self-containment, with large brown eyes that took in everything but flashed no outgoing signals. He moved slowly; both legs had been broken, everyone knew, in a terrible riding accident. I had an impression of private discomfort rigorously suppressed.

Throughout dinner he wore a tight little smile and said almost nothing, not even joining in the frequent outbursts of laughter that swept the table. That was quite a trick, because the ebullient George Burns (one performer who never needed a writer) was holding forth in splendid form, dousing a wild variety of subjects with irreverent humor.

Over postprandial brandy, Sylvia got down to business. Didn't I think the Nichols story was going in a dangerous direction for Danny? After all, he had made his reputation as a comedian. His fans wanted him to be funny, not a long-faced sufferer. Wouldn't it make sense for everyone to soft-pedal the polio-recovery miracle, and build instead to a comedy climax?

I listened, mellowed by the setting but not hypnotized, and promised to review her argument with my collaborator.

For Sylvia, always the controlling force in Danny's career, that wasn't good enough. She apparently took her case over Don Hartman's head to the ruling brass at Paramount. Two weeks later we heard our script was being reviewed by John Michael Hayes, whose credits included *Rear Window*. According to the secretarial grapevine, Hayes "liked it a lot." Nonetheless the following month, as we were wrapping up the "Red" Nichols screenplay, it was gently taken out of our hands, listed for re-evaluation, and transferred to Mel Shavelson and Jack Rose, a pair of comedy specialists.

Before we could register bewilderment, we were handed a consolation prize: the Jim Piersall autobiography, *Fear Strikes Out*. Piersall, star center fielder of the Boston Red Sox, four years earlier had—after a mounting series of eccentric incidents in ball parks—wound up in a mental institution.

Baseball had been in my bones since early childhood. As I explained many decades later in a column for the *Christian Science Monitor*, I was born "within a strong-armed rightfielder's throw from Prospect Park, which was hardly more than a bunt and a steal from the Dodger playing grounds at Ebbets Field."

But baseball was only the background for the Piersall story. Its essence was the human drama of a healthy athlete driven to the edge of madness, and brought back from the abyss by adroit psychotherapy. And I was fresh from the analytic couch myself.

Unraveling the skeins of the Piersall case we found a frustrated father, denied the diamond-centered dream of his youth, seeking to relive that failed dream through his son—and in the case of John Piersall, who never got beyond semi-pro ball himself, exerting such savage, relentless pressure that the younger man cracked up. I had been spared that nightmare of round-the-clock hounding and its almost inevitable denouement, but the basic situation was all too familiar.

This was a theme—the right of every human being to grow in his or her own direction, untrammeled and unshaped by the leftover needs of others—that I not only understood; I had lived it. I burned to tell it to the world.

So, it turned out, did our twenty-seven-year-old producer, Alan Pakula. An only son, Pakula had originally been groomed to take over his father's prosperous printing business. Granted the benefits of the Yale Drama School, he was then allowed two years of grace to "knock around Hollywood," where he was snatched from experimental theater obscurity by the ever-vigilant Don Hartman.

Tall and slender, Ivy League-polished, Alan was blessed with rosy-cheeked good looks that seemed at odds with his formidable intellectualism; one expected him to prattle of sailboats and polo, not to spout Strindberg and Eisenstein. I was struck by the painstaking focus on detail that would become a hallmark of his productions; his insistence on the precise shade of beige for his apartment curtains was almost feminine.

But Alan was decidedly heterosexual. His early amours included an imported Italian starlet and the songwriter Dory Langdon, who later married André Previn. Alan and our director, Bob Mulligan, were to earn Oscars in tandem for *To Kill A Mockingbird*. Ultimately Alan would make a name for himself as a director, with *All The President's Men* in 1976.

In a 1982 interview with the New York *Times Magazine*, Pakula defined his understanding of the film producer's main role: to provide "the conditions under which people can do their best work." That sensitivity to creative atmosphere was his forte as far back as 1955.

Meeting Anthony Perkins was a jolt. The gangling star of our unwritten picture was stooped, skinny and spectacled, with long dank hair drooping over narrow shoulders. In his early-beatnik outfit of sweatshirt, jeans and scuffed sneakers, he looked like a refugee from a Berkeley commune or a starving poet in Greenwich Village—the last candidate you would choose for a neighborhood punchball team, certainly nobody's idea of a trim professional athlete. To cap his disqualifications, Perkins was left-handed; Jimmy Piersall was famous for the rifle-power and accuracy of his strong right arm.

However, Tony was no intellectual flyweight. He had attended Columbia, played the lead in *Tea and Sympathy*, and would soon be on Broadway again as the tormented Eugene Gant in the adaptation of Thomas Wolfe's *Look Homeward, Angel*.

I had never seen Perkins's much-praised performance as Gary Cooper's son in the Quaker drama, *Friendly Persuasion*. But I had seen John Gielgud—timid, hairless, half-collapsed in a London dressing room—fling himself across the stage twenty minutes later as a reckless and railing Benedick in *Much Ado About Nothing*, so I had some notion of the alchemy at the disposal of a dedicated actor. And Perkins, like Marlon Brando, was an actor who took his craft seriously. His physical transformation, within a few weeks, was relatively easy; contact lenses, a neat haircut and a regime of hard gym training dispelled the sleepy overtone of Ichabod Crane. To correct his lefty stance, he put himself through long, arduous drills in hurling a baseball against a brick wall.

More remarkably, he absorbed and managed to convey the tensions and neurotic instability that had made Piersall such a drawing card on the diamond—and in the end overwhelmed him. Perkins was utterly convincing, at once comic and alarming, in his elaborate charades: dusting off the plate, leading cheers for himself, dancing with an outraged manager. Before the camera he became Jimmy Piersall. When the Red Sox star, back in action with his team, came to the studio to pose with the writers and swap antics with Jerry Lewis, it was hard to tell which was the essential, authentic Jimmy Piersall: the ball player or the actor.

Tony's clean profile and wistful little-boy manner would soon be splashed over billboards from Paris to Hong Kong opposite stars like Sophia Loren. However, the studio had a slight problem: Tony was reported to prefer men, a predilection that could derail Paramount's plans for building him up as a romantic idol. An elaborate publicity program was devised, crowding his social calendar with the most sumptuously endowed starlets the studio could muster. The inconvenient rumors were defused.

Rafe and I concentrated first on laying down a broad story line that would enable us to drive home our theme without ever getting preachy or academic. Then we turned to research, gathering all the raw material possible from Piersall's family, his teammates, Boston sports pages, even the player's psychiatrist, by that time in Mexico. Only then did we get down to planning act structure and scenes.

Screenwriting is a demanding form, partly because the medium offers so many options. The camera can go virtually anywhere your imagination wants to take it. After a number of false starts and detours, we arrived at our step outline, a brief telegraphic blueprint for a shooting script. Proceeding into screenplay, we then divided up the opening scenes, each doing an initial draft and turning it over to the other for revision.

It was twenty-four-hour work, subject to nocturnal prodding from the unconscious. There were days when I left the studio in mid-afternoon, thoroughly drained, to collapse into bed at home.

I remember carrying around snatches of dialogue in my head while driving; sketching a scene in the barber chair, oblivious to the chatter being poured into my ear; then drafting it in longhand by the pool of my Hollywood Boulevard motel. Diving over my shoulder, totally disregarded, was a strapping ex-college jock named Sonny Tufts who was, or aspired to be, one of moviedom's many Tarzans.

This was a new kind of excitement, a new sense of power. My words would propel men to build sets, design lighting, hire extras. My ideas had legs!

Alan Pakula gave us a wide berth and a free hand: no meddlesome demands for pages, no peering over transoms, or snooping for draft carbons from the secretaries. He had chosen his writers; he was willing to live with them.

Gradually we settled into the routine of staff writers at a major studio. The day's activities, we discovered, centered around lunch in the Paramount commissary, and specifically around the august precincts of the writers' table there.

This hallowed rectangle, strategically wedged into a corner enclave separate from the territories of producers, directors and stars, was governed by unwritten but impenetrable rules. Access was by invitation only, not included among the perquisites of stardom. Nor could executives, set designers, or members of the studio's other multitudinous departments sit in. Columnists, talent agents and publicity flacks, accustomed to bullying or buying their way into accommodations at Mike Romanoff's or the "21" club in New York, didn't even try.

Our company included many of America's future rich and famous. Burly Leon Uris, author of the rugged marine novel *Battle Cry*, was sporting a new, cowboy-tinged vocabulary for Hal Wallis's Western epic, *Gunfight at the OK Corral*. Leon took pains to explain to the rest of us that his situation was unique: "I have two careers: in books and pictures." After *Exodus*, published four years later, he needed only one.

The 1955 writers' table also harbored two other fiction writers destined for the top of the best-seller lists: Irving Wallace and Sidney Sheldon. Wallace, cherubic and calm, a Western Buddha whose aromatic pipe seemed a part of his anatomy, regaled the company one day with his plans for *The Chapman Report*, a thinly-veiled novelization of the recently published Kinsey Report on American sexual mores. He would be ladling out a huge ration of uncensored sex, mixing in a dollop of violence and a touch of mystery, then garnishing the pot with just a soupçon of scientific information; nothing too heavy, of course, but enough to round out the percentages of elements required for commercial success.

It sounded like a formula for a soda fountain, but it worked, leading to a string of equally contrived Wallace blockbusters attuned to the headlines of the day—the Nobel Prize, a black president—all as readable of a summer's afternoon as they were forgettable the next morning. Before his death in 1990, Irving had acquired everything he wanted—except the serious consideration he yearned for in the New York *Times Book Review*.

Big, slow-moving Sidney Sheldon shared Wallace's unruffled air. Something of a play doctor, he was called upon for frequent tinkering with scripts passing through the studio mill. During our "Red" Nichols meanderings a screenplay draft by Sheldon for Bing Crosby had somehow strayed across my desk. It was so hackneyed that I felt embarrassed for him, as if I had stumbled on some secret personal peccadillo.

Later I came to realize that audiences might have found much of it acceptable. Sidney had an instinctive pipeline to the American psyche, a firm grasp of the national fantasies, on which he was able to capitalize in amusing television conceits like *Bewitched*, and flamboyant novels like *The Other Side of Midnight*. Whether the studied manipulations of the Sheldon-Wallace-Harold Robbins school and their assiduous female disciples should be called writing seems to me an open question. There ought to be another term for it: verbal collage?

Also in our group, besides Shavelson and Rose, were Jim Poe, a lanky workaholic engaged in two screenplays, and I.A.L. ("Izzie") Diamond, whose conservative business suits camouflaged the brilliant co-author (with director Billy Wilder) of *Love in the Afternoon* and *The Apartment*.

Eminent or not, writers were in front-office eyes somewhat suspicious enigmas, a source of mingled pride and resentment. Y. Frank Freeman, the financial ruler of the studio's inner circle, often roamed the commissary at lunchtime like a ranch boss inspecting his herd. One day he brought his portly Southern-sheriff presence to our corner, beaming and chuckling to himself. Someone asked why he was so pleased.

"Ah was just thinkin'," he confided, "how much earnin' power we have concentrated around this table . . . how much you boys would be worth on the collective hoof."

I joined in the obligatory jolly response to his sally, but I was acutely unamused. The whole episode came back to mind twenty years later in a Bangkok hotel lobby when I ran across a crib of ladies of the evening lined up for scrutiny by Western tourists. Their humiliation and degradation were infinitely greater than ours, but the principle was the same. As Gertrude Stein might have put it, a whore is a whore is a whore.

As an observation post, our table was beyond cavil. Most of the studio's acting luminaries, conscious of the stares that followed them, were on relatively good behavior, soft-spoken and circumspect. Not so Shirley MacLaine, then in her mid-twenties. Her animated conversation and boisterous laughter rang across the commissary from a table fifty feet away. I don't know if MacLaine ever played in Noel Coward's *Blithe Spirit*, but the phrase captures the young Shirley's bubbly personality.

Doris Day was an occasional guest. Bob Hope swaggered by, swapping repartee with all comers. And we had good close-ups of Kirk Douglas and Burt Lancaster, he-men in Western chaps and sombreros, stomping past on boots adroitly designed with lifts to enhance their statures.

And sometimes we spotted Elvis, coming into his own at twenty after a pop-music decade of syrupy crooners. Surlily handsome, ponderously shepherded by his manager, "The Colonel," a wily Dutch immigrant named Tom Parker, the singer looked more like an attentive high school senior being treated to lunch by his principal than like the future king of rock 'n roll.

Conversation at the writers' table tended to be brittle, chaff-ridden, charged with latent hostility. We were a tense, anxious lot, competing for high stakes, feeling vulnerable to sudden disaster. I had been startled by the change in Ian Hunter in 1948; here it was again, the same aggressive jeering on a larger scale.

I had survived the quips and taunts of the city room; I could handle it. But Rafe, the youngest of three sons raised under the intimidating aegis of a famous rabbi, could not. At best uncomfortable among strangers, he found his dry, British-bred wit, so effective behind a typewriter, here shrunken to a pathetic echo.

On my way to the exit one afternoon, I passed Alan Pakula alone at a table. He waved me over to join him in coffee.

For ten minutes, bent on preserving Alan's hands-off-the-writers policy, we chatted about our apartments, cars, the gathering political storms in faraway Vietnam and in Martin Luther King's South. Imperceptibly, the conversation drifted from racism to problems in communication: between countries, social groups, individuals . . . like father and son.

Before we knew it we were embroiled in the hospital scene where Jim Piersall, under the gentle prodding of his psychiatrist, has to at long last acknowledge his hidden rage against his father. Alan, taking on the role of the ball player, launched into a passionate ad lib:

"You don't understand. I love my father. He—he made me what I am today!"

Alan broke off abruptly, absorbing the ironic implications of the speech. "Of course, we can't get away with that," he said. "Too obvious. Heavy."

I wasn't so sure. There was the kernel of a marvelous theatrical climax here, if it could be refined. My mind went back to the spellbinding moment in the production at Cornell of Elmer Rice's *The Adding Machine*, when the harried clerk-hero cried from the heart, "There's some questions you can't answer 'yes or no'!" Something equally electrifying might be within our grasp if the scene was properly laid out and nailed together (Del Andrews, that self-styled "carpenter," really understood film).

Back in my office, I worked over the lines carefully, trying to build up to a hospital outburst that would be not only plausible but natural, preordained, inescapable. These were the closing passages of the draft I turned over, as honed by Rafe:

JIM
I wanted to make good for my father.
Nothing wrong with that, is there? I owe
him something, don't I?

DR. BROWN
You have a little girl, Jim.
Would you like her to grow up feeling
she owed you something?

JIM
Look, I don't know what you're getting at—
but—I love my dad. He's the biggest thing
in my life. He taught me and straightened me out
and kept me in line. Why, if it wasn't for Dad
standing behind me—pushing me—driving me—
cracking the whip—I wouldn't be where I am today!

Tony Perkins played the scene to the hilt, dazed wonderment spreading across his face as he realized the import of what he had said. Audiences shivered; critics spoke of goose-bump chills.

But that was still to come. As our pages piled up into a first draft, Bob Mulligan came aboard to direct, and we moved into a new phase of intensive conferences with him and Alan. Mulligan, earnest and spectacled, only twenty-nine, had been a theology student and a Marine before making a reputation in television for his sensitive handling of *Joey*. He knew his way around in the pacing and tightening of scenes, where his cuts were helpful. He also shared our emphasis on character. The four of us were in synch to a degree I have never experienced before or since.

However, disquieting noises were coming from the front office. Baseball pictures were notorious box-office poison—women generally stayed away—and the box office was already showing signs of anemia, thanks mainly to television. The movies had fought back to stay afloat: a wider screen, stereophonic sound, a spate of "patriotic" drivel to capitalize on anti-Russian sentiment. They unloaded their backlog of features to fend off their upstart rival. And they turned out some remarkable films: in 1954 alone *On The Waterfront*, *Country Girl*, John Huston's *African Queen*.

But Hollywood no longer held all the cards. Not only was television siphoning off ticket buyers, but serious competition was pouring in from film makers overseas: *La Strada*, *The 400 Blows*, Brigitte Bardot. Between 1946 and 1956, attendance dropped from ninety million to forty.

Bob Mulligan had been considered one of the most promising directors picked up in the studio raids on New York talent. But Mulligan's unorthodox tactics—he scheduled long rehearsals with his actors before turning a camera, and was a known believer in the Actors Studio method of emotion-based improvisation—created head-shaking among Paramount executives. The producer and director of the Piersall picture were under thirty. Its writers were suspected of serious literary leanings.

An atmosphere of foreboding began to settle around the project even as revisions sped us toward the "final white" pages of the shooting script. To heighten the gloom, a studio contest in search of an alternative title less specifically pinpointed to baseball yielded nothing. We, and the studio, were stuck with *Fear Strikes Out*.

Meanwhile, a personal storm had been brewing for some time with Fanny. Rafe and I were anxious to put our relationships with the Holtzmann office on a business footing. Fanny never sent us a bill. She preferred to keep things vague and familial, with her beloved nephews dangling from her apron strings.

With our Paramount contract extended to a deal covering options for three years, agents were baying at our heels. We suggested that we pay the Holtzmann office an annual retainer "so that nobody is doing anything for nothing."

Back came a cloud of double-talk. Fanny "never worried" about fees: "You to me are tops and will more than justify our faith in you, so that we will have in you what we have in Eddie Goulding . . . "

Clearly Fanny was bent on superintending our lives, much as she had exercised control over her star clients. But Gertrude Lawrence and Eddie Goulding were spiritual waifs, London street children looking for a warm family—the Holtzmann office—to shelter them. We were at the opposite pole: over-protected Jewish intellectuals trying to shed the strangling ministrations of their elders. At forty-one we were sick of being "the boys." We hated the prospect of a lifetime as beloved (but subtly patronized) nephews.

We decided to make a proposal ourselves, bite the bullet.

We nearly choked on it. Our suggestion of a five percent payment to the Holtzmanns on all future Paramount earnings (admittedly, in retrospect neither over-generous nor discreet) was met with rage, indignation, near-hysterics.

This was the sort of melodrama upon which my mother's family thrived. Suddenly the battle assumed generational outlines. My aunt Stella, attached as an attorney to Fanny's office since her widowhood in

1951, announced she was flying to California to straighten us out. Jack, although pointedly silent, was reported to be "furious."

It was our turn to bridle. Up to our ears in a tough screenplay, we had been trying, "probably in boundless ignorance," we conceded, to resolve an amorphous obligation. We appreciated Fanny's extraordinary services, but were uncomfortable as permanent beneficiaries of family largesse.

The hurricane calmed. Fanny agreed to accept a flat sum for the office's services to date. Her brother David fixed a figure.

During this protracted period of anxiety I had found some relief among a handful of friends. Sheilah Graham, during our seven-year hiatus, had taken a third husband—a huge, roisterous professional football player known as "Bow-Wow"—and shortly before my return, had divorced him. She and her children greeted me warmly, clearly pleased to see me back. Sheilah and I were quickly close again: no longer as lovers, but as tried and trusted comrades.

Sheilah, who revelled in sunshine as much as she wilted under the soggy skies of her native England, had taken a cozy beach house at Malibu. I repaired there often on weekends, usually with Joe Laitin, a veteran foreign correspondent inexplicably turned movie reporter, whom I had known in Washington. Quiet, low-key, reliable, Joe would later become a public affairs cornerstone of the Lyndon Johnson administration and of an astonishing five successor regimes; for the moment he was churning out fan magazine interviews and broadcasts over the ABC network.

Sheilah's Malibu was a comfortable refuge, but not enough.

GET RAINCOAT BIRTH CERTIFICATE FLY SALZBURG MARRY ME. Eight words that said it all. It was a marvelous cable that couldn't be left to languish in an Austrian beerhouse. I dispatched it to Hollywood, eight thousand miles away, thereby lurching into uncertain matrimony. That marvelous cable would cost me $50,000, or $6,250 a word.

It had all begun a few months earlier when Rafe and I were coming down the home stretch on the script of *Fear Strikes Out*.

By May of 1956 the Piersall script had reached its wrap-up phase. Moving into a new apartment on North Hayworth Avenue just below Sunset Boulevard, I had taken old longings with me. At the crowded swimming pool in the back of the building I found a saucy, sexy Australian. For a lunatic week I plied her with jokes and verses until her absent husband, estranged but evidently not quite discarded, drove up from San Diego and spirited her off to Las Vegas.

Undeterred, on an emotional roll, I shifted my attention to the Aussie's buxom woman friend. And let it stay there.

Annahrae White trailed a scent of Old Spain: lacy mantillas, flowered balconies, the stamping feet of flamenco. One of the deities decorating my dormitory wall at college had been Dolores Del Rio; Annahrae was Del Rio with a *Good Housekeeping* seal. She was a Sephardic Jewess; her maiden name, already twice altered in matrimony, was Leon, an ancient city of Asturias in northwest Spain. To me, in constant flight from my Jewish forebears, her soft, well-molded nose suggested that some libidinous Iberian warrior had strayed across her family path.

Annahrae was a sometime poet who earned her bread as a publicist, a profession that assured her literacy but also encouraged some less desirable qualities. Perhaps the best thing about her, from my perspective, was her two teen-age boys.

Steve, a sturdy, handsome seventeen, conveyed a beguiling innocence. Leonard, three years younger but infinitely more sophisticated, crouched warily behind a saturnine mask. But he no less than Steve was quick-witted, ready like their mother for a verbal joust without the sour overtones of the writers' table. Suddenly dinner at Annahrae's across the courtyard became something I looked forward to, a whiff of lively affection mingled with a let-the-hair down intimacy never quite within reach at Sheilah's.

Sex was secondary, almost an afterthought. Our first encounter was less than sensational. Nonetheless the attachment grew. By the time the Piersall script was finished in mid-June, we were seeing each other several times a week.

But the months of concentrated effort had left me tired, brain-weary, eager for another European vacation. In Austria, Salzburg was staging its annual Mozart Festival.

On a misty evening I sat in a Salzburg beer garden, a light rain falling through linden leaves onto my table. Salzburg is a small jewel of a city, spreading its eighteenth century ambiance of narrow streets and broad flowered plazas along both banks of the Salzach River. Above the gentle cloak of rain loomed mountain ridges, capped in the distance by towering Alpine peaks.

My lonely state, and the possibility of ending it through Annahrae, was much on my mind. I had been exploring the existentialist thesis then in vogue among my friends in Paris: God was an archaic fiction; each of us was responsible for his own destiny.

Open before me was a paperback tract by Soren Kierkegaard, the nineteenth-century Danish father of existentialism. As I thumbed through its damp pages I came to a passage underlined by some previous reader, and a chill swept over me that had nothing to do with weather. I could almost hear a sepulchral voice in my ear. The exact words have passed from memory, but the gist echoed the famous Shakespearean warning about timing in *Julius Caesar*:

> There is a tide in the affairs of men, which taken at the flood, leads on to fortune . . .

Berkman, I thought to myself, he's talking to you! Why else would you be running across this particular passage at this moment?

I borrowed a pencil from a passing waiter, and on the back of a menu scribbled my invitation to marriage. For two days the transatlantic wires were humming with acknowledgments and instructions. I was in Munich to pick up a car when a phone call came from my Uncle Jack. He had met my bride-to-be and advanced the requested travel money. Yes, she was a very pleasant lady, but . . .

How well did I know her? Was I prepared for the responsibility of raising two teen-age boys? What was the story of her previous marriages? For nearly an hour, with the sly persuasiveness that had unhinged juries, he harangued me, concluding: "Don't rush into anything, Teddy. Travel around together for a while."

I hung up quite shaken. Hadn't I had enough interference from my mother, Fanny, David? The next afternoon I was at Salzburg airport to meet Annahrae. Another jolt, as I scanned the incoming passengers. That frizzy-haired, bedraggled matron (long plane rides do not beautify) stumbling down to the tarmac—surely she could not be my fiancée? But of course she was. Swallowing my alarm, I advanced to claim my prize.

Back at our hotel, I plunged through a kaleidoscope of sensations, from dismay (Annahrae's birth certificate revealed that she was two years older than previously declared, one year older than I) through panic (what had I done?) to euphoria, trudging down the hall to order our baths (at last I would have someone of my own, like everybody else).

In between there was a moment of blinding clarity: Jack was right. I had not thought this decision through.

Resolutely, I disregarded it. I was forty-two and still alone. What was I waiting for—a bolt of lightning? The following morning we were married, a civil ceremony at City Hall.

For the next four weeks misgivings—apparently felt only by me—were largely drowned in a whirl of travel: Vienna, Hitler's aerie in Berchtesgaden, Venice, then across the Italian and French Rivieras to Barcelona before circling back to Paris.

Just once, at least privately, I dropped the façade of the urbane traveler. On a sleepless night in Venice the panic of our first hours in Salzburg returned. My life was slipping out of control, on a toboggan slide into a bottomless sea. There was still a chance to change course, if I could muster up the courage . . .

I would write Annahrae a fat check that would let her wander around the Continent; at home she could advance the explanation, which I would emphatically confirm, that she was the one who, upon reflection, decided to make the break. I would accept full responsibility for our failure.

In the cold light of day, I couldn't do it. Whatever the scenario for public consumption, the humiliation to Annahrae would be inescapable. Fearful of inflicting hurt, I postponed and thereby aggravated it.

At the American Express office in Paris there was a note from Alan Pakula, relayed from Salzburg. He was happy with the first daily rushes from *Fear Strikes Out*, felt the picture was shaping up as everything we had hoped for, and wanted me to know he had "not forgotten all the work and time and excitement" that Rafe and I had put into it.

Less cheering was a fistful of cables from Hal Landers, our agent at

MCA, who had been tracking me in vain all over Europe to report that Alfred Hitchcock had a possible assignment on hand for Berkman and Blau. Were B and B interested? "Must know by September eighth."

That date had come and gone. My life was indeed in a tailspin. It was time to get back to California, reassess and regroup.

We rented a house on Hollyridge Drive, high in the hills above movieland. The view by night was spectacular, an endless velvet carpet of twinkling lights. Although our own acreage was small, thanks to the lush landscaping of the homes below us there were stunning daytime vistas as well, of sweeping lawns, majestic pines, and rows of what Annahrae aptly called "chorus girl palms."

The studio had a project for us: not on the face of it terribly enticing, and as we later discovered, laden with unlisted political baggage. A.C. Lyles, a lean soft-spoken Georgian who had risen slowly through the Paramount ranks from office boy to front-office factotum, enjoyed the favor of Frank Freeman, a fellow-Southerner. A.C. dearly aspired to be a producer.

Rallying to his side was a major star with whom A.C. had ingratiated himself over the years through a variety of publicity and personal chores, James Cagney. The actor offered to help A.C.'s debut by moving for the first time to the other side of the camera, as director.

To round out the package, the studio had waiting in the wings a slight, smoldering young actor being groomed for possible stardom; some saw in Robert Ivers a potential Brando or James Dean.

John Mock, pushed to comb through his story files, couldn't find a suitable original. But an earlier bantamweight hero had been launched with *This Gun for Hire*. What about a remake of the 1942 Alan Ladd vehicle?

If no wild applause greeted this suggestion, there were apparently no strenuous protests, either. Berkman and Blau were available under their new contract; that closed the circle.

This Gun, based on a novel by Graham Greene, traced the adventures of a ruthless young hit man paid off by his underworld employers in stolen, marked bills which he cannot pass. Determined on vengeance, he takes a detective's fiancée as hostage and snakes though a lonely, desperate flight until police cut him down. It dispensed standard Hollywood morality: the star, assuming he was "cute," could indulge in unspeakable villainies for seven reels as long as he was punished for it in the eighth.

The original screenplay adaptation by W.R. Burnett was taut and well-structured; we saw no reason to tear it apart. However, we were being paid to update the story, not just change a few adjectives. We proposed to give the manhunt topicality and importance by shifting the story's background to the United Nations headquarters in New York.

Production overseer D.A. Doran slammed the door firmly on that one. "It would take us way over budget. We want to do this picture mainly with interiors, preferably with old sets already on the lot. Any locations would have to be in this area." Clearly, part of the political agreement was for a tight rein on spending.

Our next hitch came with Cagney, a self-contained, frequently surprising man likely to turn up on a movie set with a paperback collection of verses jutting out of his hip pocket. And an exemplary parent. Working at his home one evening, a Benedict Canyon mansion with massive iron gates and tree-lined paths that exhaled the fragrance of super-stardom, we were witness to a gently loving but unmistakably firm speech to his teen-age foster son:

"I don't care what your friends say—or their parents, either. I don't want you running around Los Angeles at night looking for a good time. No car tonight. As long as you're my son living in my house, I'll make the rules."

His relationship with writers, however, was cautious, distant, nothing like the open exchanges we had relished with Pakula and Mulligan. Cagney had reservations, Lyles intimated, about the psychological probing in the Piersall picture; the two frequently disappeared for colloquies in Cagney's office from which we were excluded. Cagney seemed bent on turning out a hard-boiled action picture; we kept angling for touches of characterization and intimate detail. Lyles tried to "make nice" with everybody.

Ultimately, as we told an interviewer from *Time*, "not a single line" from the original was kept in our re-christened *Short Cut to Hell*. But the attempt at freshness was a wearisome battle. I began to prowl sound stages restlessly after lunch, feeling like a caged hen ordered to lay eggs on schedule.

The reaction to our labors when the picture opened a year later was therefore a pleasant surprise. *Weekly Variety* found Paramount's "sharp remake" a "crackling melodrama" sparked by a screenplay that never slacked pace. The trade paper *Cinema*, hailing the "polished" screenplay, added: "the script is virile, the dialogue economical and subtle; the plotting ducks the obvious."

Long before that, however, we were basking in a more fervent—and far more consequential—collection of praises.

The first hint of public distinction for *Fear Strikes Out* came at the end of a studio preview. As the crowd was filing out, a husky black-haired man shuffled over to me and extended his hand: "I'm Liam O'Brien," he said. "And I wish I had written that picture."

A fellow-writer—O'Brien was a distinguished one, the scenarist for *Of Mice and Men*, *Chain Lightning* and *The Young at Heart*—can pay no higher tribute.

That was the first trickle in what would become an avalanche. *Daily Variety* in February of 1957 hailed a "highly effective dramatization" built around a "probing screenplay." The *Hollywood Reporter* went further in its analysis of "an absorbing picture" with "a tender and beguiling romance," counterpointed by psychotherapy scenes "accurately and movingly presented":

> The Berkman-Blau screenplay is notable on several counts but it is most remarkable for the freshness of the love scenes, for the authentic dialogue, for the sparing use of actual baseball scenes while impregnating the picture with the baseball spirit, and for creation of Piersall's character as a young man masculine enough to be a big league baseball player and still so sensitive that the mental collapse is sympathetic.

Kudos was shared with Pakula ("a producer of daring and imagination"), Bob Mulligan for his "superior" directing, and the Perkins-Malden combination in the leads ("brooding, brilliant").

The following month Alan went to New York for our Broadway opening, phoning us from Times Square at midnight his time, 9 p.m. ours, with the reviews. The Berkman and Blau families, gathered at Rafe's house in Beverly Hills, held our breaths as Alan, his voice cracking with excitement, rattled off rave after rave, starting with the New

York *Times*. The screenplay "so improved on" the original autobiography, declared Bosley Crowther, as to create "a first-rate psychological film," centered on a relationship "so credibly and sensitively pursued" that the "nerve-wracked observer" had to accept Piersall's breakdown as inevitable.

We fell on each other's necks in an orgy of relief and self-congratulation.

But the topper was still to come. *Time* magazine, in a long and learned critique crediting us with "a solid hit," observed:

> *Fear Strikes Out* is not the history of an illness but the story of a human life; it does not attempt to acquaint the mind with theories but to educate the heart with compassion and understanding. Chief credit goes to the scriptwriters, who have shaped a formless book into tight, dramatic scenes.

More tributes poured in: from Ernie Martin ("Thanks for providing such a thrilling experience"), from the celebrated psychotherapist Franz Alexander ("the most authentic treatment ever of mental illness in film"), and in May from the Christophers in New York, awarding us their bronze plaques for socially constructive work in the visual media.

The most earnest compliment, however, was decidedly backhanded. It came from Cecil B. de Mille who, we later learned from Alan, had intervened with the studio to delay the release of our picture until 1957. His *Ten Commandments* had opened in 1956, and the wily old showman didn't want a possibly stronger Paramount entry competing against him for the Academy Award.

De Mille's maneuver did him no good; *Around the World in 80 Days* took the 1956 Oscar he coveted. But it thoroughly spoiled our prospects. We might have beaten *Around the World*; by the time Academy voting rolled around at the end of 1957, *Bridge on the River Kwai* dominated the field, and rightly. Pictures released early in the year were forgotten.

Well, not quite forgotten. The eminent French director Francois Truffaut, in *The Films of My Life* (Simon and Schuster, 1978), reprinted his twenty-year-old estimate of "one of the year's best American films," praising "the truth of setting and facts" in a "frank, serene, bitter and disillusioned film that doesn't make you want to live in America." A film classics showing in 1985 at the University of California Art Museum in Berkeley emphasized our picture's "frightening probe of a taboo subject," the father-son conflict, as well as its "blow to the success ethic." And the New York *Times* of April 28, 1991, in a long article on the hundred-and-fifty "baseball movies" made since 1902, dismissed most as "sentimental, maudlin or bowdlerized," singling out by contrast the "harrowing" power of *Fear Strikes Out*, "a film whose reputation has grown in recent years."

Regent Jacob L. Holtzmann, Ted's "Wall Street Uncle"

Aunt Fanny Holtzmann, counselor to diplomats and stars

UNLESS OTHERWISE SPECIFIED, PHOTOS ARE FROM THE COLLECTION OF THE AUTHOR

The author's parents: dentist-dreamer Sam Berkman and his suffragette wife, Bertha

Recruit from Brooklyn in the Ivy League: Ted at Cornell U. dorm

City room: the back door to the front page, 1933

Moonlighting Sonata

William K. Howard, Ted's movie mentor. His *Transatlantic* restored the dominance of the camera, 1937

On leave in Cyprus, 1947

On location in England: Robert (Long John Silver) Newton sandwiched between screenwriters Bryan Wallace and Ted

John Wellington Donovan: The lieutenant who cut in on a king . . .

And cut up with a crooner

“Don’t shoot — I’m on your side!” Donovan’s all-purpose combat correspondent’s outfit, for quick change from Arab to Israeli to Briton

Three Who Dared to criticize royalist Greece in 1947. One paid with his life. John Donovan, Homer Bigart, George Polk

Feluccas on the Nile: Timeless ghosts of departed romance, 1946

Jeeves: master cook, gentleman crook, 1944

"Berkman Pasha"

Sheilah Graham, the English beauty who enchanted F. Scott Fitzgerald—and later, the author.

Malibu, 1951: Sheilah's daughter, Wendy and son, Robbie, with Robbie's "fwend"

Thirty-five years down the road: Sheilah at Ojai with her son, Robert Westbrook and Ted.

PHOTOS ON THIS PAGE COURTESY OF WENDY FAIREY

On leave in Tel Aviv, 1944

At work in Manhattan, 1968
(Courtesy of Sam Shaw)

Jimmy Piersall throws a curve or two at the scenarists of *Fear Strikes Out*, Raphael Blau and Ted Berkman, 1956

Emma Marcus, widow of Colonel Mickey Marcus meets Kirk Douglas who plays her husband in *Cast A Giant Shadow*, 1966 *(Courtesy of Paul Schumach)*

The late Yitzchak Rabin and Israeli
President Ezer Weizmann, twin architects
of the Six-Day War

Meyer Levin: alone, he upheld
the integrity of Anne Frank's *Diary*
(Courtesy of Jo Basiste)

General Mordecai "Mota"
Gur, author of children's
tales, philosopher, whose
paratroopers took back the
Old City of Jerusalem

Anne Francis, who welcomed
the author to Santa Barbara

Man about Montecito: the
author with Beverley Jackson,
local society editor

Author, Bonzo and friend: all the chimp ever wanted
was a post in a banana republic

Jam session: "Brother Ted", of Ed Murrow's legendary circle, swings with Murrow biographer Ann Sperber *(Courtesy of Harriet Robbins Ackert)*

The Earl who was king of protest ballads: Earl Robinson, composer of "Joe Hill"

With Artie Shaw: The horn was not his first love

Gurus at the Santa Barbara Writers Conference:
Paul Lazarus, Ted, Ray Bradbury

A local stop on the Orient Express

Across the world from Brooklyn:
The Great Wall of China, 1996

CHAPTER 14

Perlberg's Pearl

The critical acclaim shored up, at least for a time, the shaky timbers of my marriage. There had been one or two moments of total serenity, satisfaction: turning out the lights at bedtime, feeling the exalted responsibility of a certified pater familias.

Meyer Levin, in Hollywood on a lecture tour for his runaway bestseller *Compulsion*, handed down his sour, faintly surprised approval. Gerold Frank, encountered at Arrowhead Springs, seemed almost envious: "Other people have to endure the tribulations of raising children. You fall into a handsome ready-made family!"

But there were alarm signals. When I offered to replace Annahrae's aging Cadillac with a stylish white roadster on sale by my agent, she balked. The roadster was a Ford, beneath her dignity as the wife of a "big" writer.

The flaws were hardly unilateral. I was a restless husband, chafing at the domestic bit, eyeing studio starlets longingly. One afternoon I came home early from the studio as Annahrae was talking on the telephone with a woman friend: "Steve's been having trouble with his teeth for years. Now that there's money in the house I'm going to make sure he's taken care of. Completely."

Our understanding had been that Steve's medical needs would be covered by his father, her second husband.

Matters got worse when Annahrae caught sight of the monthly stipend I was sending to my mother in New York. "That's too much," she protested.

"It's what she needs. And it's just a fraction of my paycheck."

"I don't care," she persisted. "You've got a family to support now." And a dentist, I thought to myself. On the verge of a real explosion, we were pushed back to our corners by another movie project.

Ann Wenner, the gentle mother-hen who did the Berkman-Blau typing, had dropped a significant observation on my head during our struggles with *Short Cut to Hell*. "You have a terrific talent," she declared, "but only on stories you care about. On anything else your talent is crippled, mechanical, only half there. You should be very careful about what you choose to do."

A wise lady, Annie. She had seen many writers wear out their sabers flailing against windmills. Listen to the secretaries.

And beware of agents bearing gifts. In the spring of 1957 Hal Landers of MCA came to us with an opportunity to work for Bill Perlberg and George Seaton, perhaps the most prestigious producing-directing team in Hollywood. Perlberg had produced thirty-five films, many of them directed or written (sometimes both) by his partner. Seaton, the original "Lone Ranger" of radio, broke into screenplay writing in 1940 with the Marx Brothers' *A Day at the Races*; fifteen years later he was elected to the presidency of the Motion Picture Academy. Together the pair had done such hits as *Junior Miss* and *The Song of Bernadette*, but their chief glory rested on two Oscar-winning classics, *Country Girl* and *Miracle on 34th Street*. They also had been responsible for some clinkers, but with such a continuous output nobody was inclined to carp. At the moment they were shooting *Teacher's Pet* with Clark Gable, an MCA client, and Doris Day at Paramount. To be tapped by such a pair was an honor.

There was one small drawback: the story they wanted us to adapt. Perlberg had put a small fortune into the rights for a totally synthetic novel, on a par creatively with the magazine potboiler through which I had met Bill Howard at Wanger's; something about a crooked political boss, his illness-plagued daughter, and a brave young district attorney who got entangled with both.

Rafe and I had identical reactions: appalling junk. What we didn't have was the self-respect that should have been engendered by the Piersall notices, or the self-confidence to say a polite no and walk away. Not even after a sober warning from Jack Rose: "Never take on a story you don't feel good about. It won't work. Wait for something you like." I had forgotten Bill Howard's observation about fear being the hidden monster governing Hollywood, and was kneeling at the monster's throne.

Perlberg took us onto the *Teacher's Pet* set to meet Seaton and Gable. The King was affable and relaxed, clearly a willing player on the P. and S. team. We would be under the same tent as Hollywood's biggest star. Could a fledgling ball player resist an opportunity to be in the same line-up as Babe Ruth?

For two days we did. Then resolution collapsed. During the summer the chance for an association with Hitchcock had slipped through our fingers; did we dare bypass a second summons from the mighty? Hollywood memories were short; how long before the glow of our award-winner would start fading? And what about the families dependent on our earnings? Would employment come knocking soon again?

In short, we were swayed by every consideration except the only one that should have mattered: our loathing for the material.

We read the book again, persuaded ourselves that somewhere in this junk heap there were elements that could be salvaged, and took the job.

The first response to our adaptation outline came from George Seaton, stopping at the writers' table: "I think you're onto something, fellas. Don't know how you did it but it looks like a real story shaping up!" He beamed and slapped Rafe on the back. Looking back, I suspect that Perlberg's pearl was such a non-starter that any changes proposed would have looked like an improvement. Evidently Seaton had shared our apprehensions about his partner buying a corpse.

Perlberg, although more reserved, authorized us to move on into screenplay. There the fundamental shallowness of the story could not be dodged. The characters refused to come to life, hanging limply on the page. As I wrote to Fanny, "Doing a complete original would have been easier. Here we're stuck with justifying Perlberg's expensive purchase of a ridiculous book."

I began looking for diversion on the sound stages, where during the "Red" Nichols filming I had met Louis Armstrong: astonishingly small, diffident, sad. There was a pleading in his eyes, a stain of deep hurt. Didn't he realize he was famous?

Didn't I understand what it was like to grow up as a homeless waif in Storyville, New Orleans?

On one of our prowlings I struck up a flirtation with a long-legged chesty brunette whom I took to be a tourist from New Jersey; she turned out to be Sophia Loren. Another handsome lady aloft in a ship's rigging, exchanging badinage with Anthony Quinn, fended me off amusingly before disappearing into a dressing room marked "Claire Bloom."

Our brief honeymoon with P. and S. ended with a crash. After we had done some forty pages of script, Perlberg summoned us to a meeting. His round, fleshy face was grim. Seaton, tall and raw-boned, sat beside him expressionless.

"We're not going ahead with this," Perlberg intoned (no surprise there—but there was one to come) "because George and I have decided that you had help on *Fear Strikes Out*. You didn't write it yourselves." He looked at us accusingly.

Rafe and I sat stunned, totally taken aback. It was like an ambush from a footpad. A wave of sickness lurched across my stomach; I directed a questioning glance at George Seaton. The Academy president, so free with his early praises, let the hatchet fall uncontested.

My mind raced with protests. Was it inconceivable to Perlberg that he had made a stupid purchase, that no writer or writing team in the world was ever going to redeem his investment?

Before we could find any words, Rafe and I were out in the corridor. Mission aborted.

At a Writers Guild meeting I found myself sitting next to Pat Fielder: slender, snub-nosed, fragile, very young, and in the process of dissolving her marriage. I found Pat silken and appealing, a reprise of the Gentile dream girl who had haunted my college days; she thought I was funny.

We took to meeting for surreptitious lunches. Watching Pat depart from one of these rendezvous, her dainty, desirable little-girl legs twinkling across the sidewalk, I had a deadly premonition: my marriage was over.

Joe Laitin recommended the psychologist he had been seeing, Sidney Prince. Thin, acid and imperturbable, Prince lost no time in pointing out that I had made a fantasy marriage: "You concocted a perfect scenario: tender wife, adoring kids, a sweet little house in the Hollywood hills. Writers do it all the time." This was practically an occupational failing, said Prince: the inability to distinguish between hard reality and the constructs of fertile authorial imaginations. My infatuation with Pat Fielder came under the same heading, he declared.

No surprises there. What the good doctor did not explore was a conclusion I had reluctantly reached about marriage: I didn't like it. Annahrae, Texas-reared and gentle of manner, stirred no harsh echoes of my troubled youth; yet I knew that if she had not been so preoccupied with my bank account, I would have dredged up some other alleged fault. I wanted out, and was looking for a convenient exit.

Many years later Artie Shaw (eight trips to the altar!) laid it all out for me: "Marriage isn't for everybody—and especially not for creative people. Too confining, restricted, monotonous." By 1957 I had already absorbed the point instinctively. Beth Moldau might have proven an exception; there had been enough excitement, variety and shared interests between us to defy the odds. But I doubted that lightning would strike twice.

Like broken bones sticking out through a garment, the jagged edges of my broken marriage were unmistakable. My feisty Aunt Stella, who had sparked my infant adventures at the piano, flew out to handle divorce negotiations.

I trekked east, to spend the bulk of the summer with Meyer Levin and his French wife, Tereska Torres, on Fire Island, until word arrived from Stella that settlement terms had been reached. I was to establish residence in Las Vegas.

I loathed Las Vegas. You'd have to put me in chains to drag me back there. Garish and tasteless, America's desert playground swarmed with people who had given up on trying to manage their lives and were counting on Lady Luck to pull them out of their private morasses. I had written an article for *Coronet* about gambling addicts; now they surrounded me.

Someone in New York had mentioned acquaintance with an interesting maverick, Hank Greenspun, publisher of the Las Vegas *Sun*. Although a small paper with limited news resources, the *Sun* had a wide and influential readership, including many members of Congress. I decided to take a look.

I found myself facing a rumbling human volcano, a big, brawling, blunt-spoken man who chewed fat cigars and spat into a waste basket across the room. Although his manners and associations were questionable—he had briefly done public relations for the Flamingo Hotel and Casino, controlled by the mobster Bugsy Siegel—this was a man who had smuggled arms into beleaguered Israel in 1948 and six years later had been instrumental, even before Ed Murrow, in dethroning Joe McCarthy.

Greenspun was angry, fuming, snarling at the wire service teletype copy flowing across his desk. From where I sat, he was upset about the right things: a crumbling U.S. economy, racial chaos in the South, a militant Soviet Union that was outdistancing us in space with the satellite Sputnik.

I filled him in on my writing background and my divorce. Then, acting on impulse, I added: "How'd you like me to write a piece or two? Your name, not mine." His column, "Where I Stand," was a major feature of the *Sun*.

"What would you write about?"

I shrugged. "Ike, foreign affairs, whatever."

It was his turn to shrug. He wouldn't mind.

Two days later Greenspun came storming into my room at the Bali Hai, hair rumpled, tie askew. "This stuff is terrific," he bellowed, brandishing my pages. "I'm going to lead the paper with it!"

"You want more?"

"You're damn right I want more!"

The piece that had sparked his excitement was a sardonic appraisal of the Eisenhower administration, gone flat and sleepy after five years in office:

> There'll always be a niblick; so who needs Sputnik? It's been a rough month for the U.S.: Federal bayonets unsheathed against American citizens in Arkansas; a Russian satellite cavorting through space; pipsqueak Arab chieftains tugging insolently at Uncle Sam's beard.
>
> But from Washington comes the gladdening news that in these same history-crammed thirty days, the President managed to get in no less than twenty-one exhilarating rounds on the golf course. And it is officially disclosed that on one glorious nine-hole outing Mr. Eisenhower, for the first time in years, shot a 41! To paraphrase Ira Gershwin, "Who cares what banks fail in Yonkers, as long as Ike has a putt that conquers?"

I did another dozen editorials. Several, on the theme of "eggheads vs blockheads," decried the anti-intellectual fever spreading across the country from Washington:

> I can remember a day when a great President deliberately surrounded himself with the most highly trained thinkers he could find, and proudly dubbed them the "Brain Trust." Today intellectuals are busy defend-

> ing themselves in hearing rooms, where little men measure their integrity with yardsticks designed in Fascist Germany.

People were beginning to compliment Greenspan on his newly-acquired literary skills—"didn't know you had it in you, Hank"—and, like Dick Aldrich, he liked it, taking his bows with relative grace.

I was happy behind the typewriter, sounding off after a long silence in Hollywood on issues that mattered to me.

Before leaving Las Vegas early in December I sent several of the pieces to Ed Murrow. Three weeks later Murrow, shepherding eight CBS foreign correspondents through the network's annual end-of-the-year roundup, urged his listeners to remember that in times of crisis, "an egghead is a better investment than a blockhead."

Idling around the pool at the Bali Hai, with time to reflect, I had come to see in my relationships with women a cycle of three phases, all rooted with diminishing intensity in my early sense of inadequacy. First, as with the blonde campus queen, the golden Lorelei in Cairo, and fresh-from-England Sheilah, there was an immersion in fantasy—invariably doomed by the intrusion of reality, yet stubbornly recurring; second, a flight from strong, competent women—Sybil Rice, Ma-Than-E, Sheilah turned powerful columnist—who evoked the meddlesome ghosts of my mother and Fanny; and finally the actual experience of marriage, in which I learned that for all its comforts, its constraints were more burdensome for me than the loneliness of the creative life.

Back on the Hollywood merry-go-round, my next stop was at MGM. Let Sheilah tell you about it. From her "Hollywood Today" column of February 19, 1958: "Debbie Reynolds could be America's secret weapon against the Russians at the Brussels International Fair in the late Spring." According to Sheilah, to counter a flood of headline-making ballerinas from Moscow, MGM would start filming Miss Reynolds in *A Time for Paris* at the Fair. Second lead would be Maurice Chevalier as—what else?—a "fatherly retired Casanova"; script by Ted Berkman.

It wasn't quite that simple. During my domestic unpleasantness Rafe had undertaken an ongoing commitment to Ray Milland. The MGM assignment was a gift horse at a time when my morale needed a gift.

It proved to be one I couldn't ride. MGM was the quintessential movie factory, a huge impersonal lot sprawled over countless acres in Culver City. It nursed a beehive of producers, each no better than his last picture and angling for star-protection on his next one. Vying for the Debbie Reynolds vehicle were Philip Barry, Jr. and Edmund Grainger.

Barry, son of the playwright who wrote *The Philadelphia Story*, had a sensitivity that made me feel we might be able to pull together a picture out of what was essentially a progressionless series of romances. Ed Grainger was an Irish version of Bill Perlberg: bankerish, unbending, immured in clichés about sympathetic heroes and cute box office angles. Naturally, he got the assignment.

For me, the project was doomed from day one. The only thing I liked about Grainger was his secretary, who proved obliging.

Technically, it was MGM that gave me the boot. But the revulsion was mutual. The picture never was made; the Russian ballerinas at the Brussels Fair pirouetted unchallenged.

I began toying with the notion of doing a book. Prose offered a degree of personal expression rarely possible in film, which was essentially a director's medium. On cue, an attractive book opportunity opened up.

Sheilah had been hurt by my sudden plunge into matrimony—"I would have married Ted any time," she told my sister—but had reacted graciously, even gallantly, welcoming Annahrae into her home.

Publishers had been on her trail for some time for her Scott Fitzgerald story; she had finally accepted a bid from Simon and Schuster, but wasn't at all sure she could handle it. Would I like to write the book? She knew all about my involvement with *Mrs. A*.

The problem was, Simon and Schuster didn't. After much deliberation, Sheilah told their editor, Jack Goodman, to make a discreet, highly confidential inquiry of Fanny; Gertrude's lawyer could confirm, off the record, Ted's work on the book.

Goodman, who knew Fanny, called her—and ran into a bland denial. What was he talking about? Nobody but her good client, Richard S. Aldrich, had written a line of the best-seller about his wife.

Stymied, I told Sheilah to get hold of Gerold Frank. She did, and together they wrote *Beloved Infidel*.

A more enduring book project would flicker across my horizon before I left Hollywood. Thumbing through the Sunday magazine section of the Los Angeles *Times*, I ran across an article about a Jewish West Pointer and former New York Corrections official who was a key figure in the creation of the Israeli army and led in the rescue of blockaded Jerusalem. Colonel David "Mickey" Marcus was an intriguing character whose exploits were centered in an area I knew well; I still had folders of unused notes on the Middle East.

But surely, I told myself, a story of such potency, around for ten years, would have found a biographer by now—or else presented unmentioned but insuperable difficulties. Nonetheless, I clipped the article.

Paramount wanted us back: not so much the studio itself, which was sagging though a period of corporate malaise (and fending off the talons of vulturous conglomerates), but two of its brightest lights, Norman Panama and Melvin Frank.

If Shavelson and Rose were the steak-and-potatoes of the Paramount menu—steady, heavy money-makers—Panama and Frank were the pheasant under glass, delicacies for the refined palate. Shavelson and Rose crackled out sharp one-line zingers, easy to grasp, easy to forget; Norm and Mel dealt in sly double entendres, liable to explode again in a viewer's memory three days later. A jolly pair, Norman as thin and underfed-looking as Mel was comfortably corpulent, they alternated as producer and director, usually of their own scripts. Among their credits were *Strictly Dishonorable*, *Mr. Blandings Builds his Dream House*, two Danny Kaye triumphs, *Knock on Wood, The Court Jester* and the Crosby-Hope *Road to Utopia*.

Once in a while they hired other writers; in our case, to develop an original idea of theirs for an "omnibus" multi-episode production to be called *Thirteen Sinners*. It posited a struggle between a peripatetic devil (Rex Harrison) and an equally magic-powered angel (Charles Laughton) over the fate of thirteen passengers on a transatlantic flight. Harrison insists that as unregenerate sinners, all deserve to perish in a crash at sea; Laughton claims to detect hidden virtues in the flock. They agree to review each individual story before reaching a decision, thus providing a springboard for a variety of dramatic and comic explorations of lust, avarice, sloth—the whole gamut of classic transgressions.

Each vignette would be tailored to a major star—Cary Grant, Audrey Hepburn, Sammy Davis Jr., Doris Day, Brando, Crosby—who would make a "cameo" appearance.

It was an engaging premise, and we embraced it heartily. The pages flowed: Davis as an egomaniacal, family-destroying entertainer, Grant running a slippery fake-art ring. There was a holocaust chiller, and a satirical paean to undiluted laziness. Enjoying the sense of common values that we had shared with Alan Pakula, we dug into our own story files and threw everything into the pot.

For our *pièce de resistance* we turned in *The Amorous Clerk*, designed as a quick-switch romp for Alec Guinness, in which a meek-mannered clerk is revealed as an insatiable satyr. Rafe, whose deadpan English humor once earned a salute from Max Beerbohm, had a field day in this slice of sophisticated ribaldry with our send-up of the rigid British social code.

Panama and Frank promptly extended our contract. They were excited by our script; we were excited by their excitement. *Fear Strikes Out* had established us as dramatic writers; *Thirteen Sinners* would confirm our high-comedy talents. The most imaginative production team on the lot was ready to take our brainchild into action.

The studio was not. Norman came back from a front office session in pained disbelief. *Sinners* was being scratched from the Paramount shooting schedule.

Mel was incredulous. Didn't they like the script?

"They loved the script—on paper. They just don't want to see it go before the camera." There had been a vague allusion to heavy costs, expensive cameo appearances.

Mel's jaw tightened. "They knew all that before. This is one for the East Coast to settle." New York, where the bankers held sway and Barney Balaban presided, was the studio's final Court of Appeals. "I'll fly there," Mel promised, "and talk to Balaban myself."

He did—and ran into not only another negative, but this time an explanation of sorts: the winds of audience favor had "changed." According to trend-spotters in touch with these mysteries (Balaban's dentist? A theater owner in Omaha?), fantasy stories were out. Untouchable. In these uncertain times, Paramount was not going to challenge the tide. Our carefully chiseled, lovingly burnished script was destined to remain between covers. Shades of *Women for Willoughby*!

Only later did we learn that Paramount in early 1959 was already disappearing into the vast conglomerate maw of Gulf and Western.

Breezing through Sheilah's doorway one evening I bumped into a lissome smiling blonde on her way out. "Chatting her up," as the British say, I learned that her name was Betsy Drake. Could I call her?

"Why not?" She gave me her number.

When I phoned a couple of days later the voice at the other end was friendly enough, but faltering: "I'm afraid an old love has come back into my life. And he doesn't want me to see other men."

"Who would that be?"

She seemed surprised. "Why, my ex-husband. Cary Grant."

Did I have a wrong number! That's what I got for not keeping up with the gossip columns.

One star-consort down, two to go. At a UCLA Extension anthropology class in Beverly Hills, I found my interest distracted by a slim quiet brunette sitting alone in the back. When the session ended I followed her out to Spalding Drive where she indignantly rebuffed my attentions. Reluctantly, she at last identified herself as Virginia Arness, in the throes of a separation from *Gunsmoke's* television hero, the gigantic Marshal Dillon.

We embarked on a long, histrionic flirtation marked mainly by surreptitious phone calls and harried, guilt-shadowed meetings in such unlikely hideaways as the Farmer's Market in Hollywood. Virginia felt unappreciated as an actress; as a woman, unloved. We created our own little drama of sensitive, star-crossed lovers; I played Tennessee Williams, the misunderstood poet, she the pathetic Blanche Dubois of *A Streetcar Named Desire*. This was strictly a movieland romance, scarcely tainted—or enlivened—by physical exchange.

Which perhaps was just as well. On one of the rare occasions when

I visited her home in Pacific Palisades, a towering silhouette appeared at the door.

"Who's there?"

"Jim."

Six feet seven of scowling husband came through, eyeing me suspiciously. But there was no reason for Marshal Dillon to draw a shootin' iron (not that he would have needed one to dispatch me); Virginia and I were fully dressed, engaged in earnest conversation.

Finally, there was "Toni Olivetti" (offstage, Joan Petrone). I met her on the back lot at Paramount, where she had a minor role in *One-Eyed Jacks*, which Marlon Brando was directing at a leisurely pace that had the front office in tears. The production, hopelessly over budget, was too far along to be scrapped; Brando was too important to the studio to be curbed.

I had met him once, in the corridor outside his office, where he stuck out his hand, flashed a smile of incredible brilliance, and introduced himself. As with Cary Grant, encountered now and then on the stairs, I felt the consciously controlled magnetism; both men conveyed the impression that for the moment at hand, I was the exclusive focus of their burning attention. John Donovan had the same animal vitality; Brando made a high art of it.

He was shorter than I expected, about my own five feet eight or nine; wide sloping shoulders, powerful chest and narrow waist made him look bigger.

Brando had a penchant for dark, small-boned girls, delicately assembled but amply bosomed. Toni personified the type. She had been a Broadway "gypsy," part of Manhattan's pool of musical-comedy dancers; Brando had snatched her from the chorus line of *Guys and Dolls* to join his mini-harem in New York, then brought her out to the coast.

After a couple of obligatory lunches, Toni invited me to dinner at her apartment where I made the obligatory pass. She kicked and squirmed, sank her teeth into my arm.

And I—in retrospect it's hard to believe this—I dropped my grip and retreated from the fray.

"What are you doing?" she demanded. For Toni, a spot of struggle was *de rigueur*, part of the mating ritual.

"Sexual brutality was the norm in my family," she later explained. "I resent your gentleness; it shows you're superior to me."

The resentment faded. And one evening she announced her independence from Marlon Brando: "He called me at 3:00 a.m. this morning and told me to hop over. I told him to forget it; I had found a man who didn't have to push me around in order to prop up his own ego. He was furious." She smiled gaily.

But Toni and I could not resolve our own differences of temperament and sexual conditioning; I was back in New York before we could explore fully the possibilities of our relationship.

Production at Paramount had ground to a virtual standstill. In 1956 Ned Brown, the natty little man who superintended MCA's writer clients, had chirped to Fanny about his enthusiasm at landing Berkman and Blau:

> The more I see of them, the more I am certain we have two of the most potentially finest (sic) writers, not only in pictures, but in all fields.

(Hollywood mores did not demand that the head of an agency literary department be literate.)

Thirty months later Brown was throwing up his hands. There was nothing more he could do with us or for us. He had not, of course, read the script of *Thirteen Sinners*.

I hated to give up the certified glamour of Hollywood, the respectful wave of the security guard as I strutted through the Paramount gate, the strolls among the starlets. Yet part of me remained unfulfilled, the part that still reverberated to Steinbeck, Faulkner, and Sholokov's *Quiet Flows the Don*.

Television? A communications resource that could bring light to the Dark Continent was pimping for beer and deodorants. Screenwriting? Technical skills were outweighed at the studios by the jockeying for power, spy networks, agency deals. Berkman and Blau would always be alien fish in the Hollywood pond.

I began to take long solitary walks, up the two steep blocks from my West Hollywood cottage to Sunset Boulevard, then roundabout returns past quiet blocks of silent houses, peering into lighted windows: a metaphor, I felt, for my outsider's life. I dabbled in the classic texts of Buddism, and against the materialism of twentieth century America found them strangely soothing.

A note to John Donovan in New York prompted a typical response:

> The false values the U.S. has worshipped for so many generations—our materialism and indifference to corruption, mediocrity and stupidity—have put us in a very vulnerable position. These idiot government spokesmen tell us there's nothing to worry about. Sons-of-bitches never read the last chapters of Gibbon, and think Athens and Sparta are Greek restaurants.

To Ed Murrow I sent a note applauding his "Small World," an interview show in which he bracketed unlikely partners—for instance the Bohemian poet Robert Graves, the stodgy historian Arnold Toynbee, and novelist Philip Wylie—with Ed presiding as a contemplative gadfly. Murrow was having his own troubles with the medium that had made him a wealthy celebrity, and that was now being embarrassed by his outspoken criticism. In a Chicago speech before the Radio and Television News Directors Association, he had declared of television:

> This instrument can teach, it can illuminate, it can even inspire. But it can do so only to the extent that humans are determined to use it to those ends. Otherwise it is merely lights and wires in a box . . .

I reported to Ed that Hal Humphrey, the Los Angeles *Times* television columnist, had run his full text: "The snarls from the direction of Henry Lucifer were confirmation of your bull's eye."

I concluded with a program idea that had been percolating in my mind:

> Pity that Mark Twain, who has some trenchant and previously unpublished observations in the December *Harper's*, isn't available to join the (Small World) jousting. Or could he be? Mayhap we could have a word or two on that, if I ever really desert these pallid vineyards—or do you perchance have a West Coast visit coming up?

Murrow had no plans for California; but he was "eager to talk" with me about possibly reviving some of the conversations of the ancients. When was I coming east?

Early in 1959, I advised that I expected to finish up Hollywood labors in a few months: "Leave us have a whack at putting the ancient sages into modern focus."

What I did not know was that Murrow was suffering from bronchitis and pulmonary emphysema, and was under terrible pressure at CBS where many forces were combining to squeeze him out. A few weeks later, physically battered and emotionally drained, he asked for a year's sabbatical to commence on July 1.

By the time I returned to New York in the summer of 1959, Murrow was away on a round-the-world trip. He would not be back until May of 1960. His days at CBS were clearly numbered; Fred Friendly, once his junior partner, was at the documentary helm.

Nonetheless he was quick to return my June phone call. "You'll have to come up to the farm for a long weekend, Ted." His Glen Arden farm at Pawling, New York was Murrow's cherished sanctuary. "We'll be able to sit down and kick around some ideas, starting with your colloquy among the ancients."

"Great. I've got a few thoughts on that."

"I'm sure you have. And on other things."

"When shall we do it?"

"Let's shoot for . . . how about a week from tomorrow? Thursday the seventeenth?"

"Can do."

But the "week from tomorrow" never came. Three times we set up dates, three times Murrow had his plans disrupted: by an out-of-town reporting assignment, a bronchitis attack, a long conference with CBS executives at 485 Madison Avenue. The network's controversial star, the object of more public admiration than any other figure in broadcasting—and more corporate sponsor antagonism—was undergoing a slow crucifixion. It would be more than two years before I saw Ed Murrow again, in his Washington office as Director for President Kennedy of the United States Information Agency.

On January 15, 1977, Steve Allen launched over the Public Broadcasting System a television program called "Meeting of the Minds," described in the press as "a show where actors portrayed famous people gathered for a round table chat," with Allen as host of their "imagined discussions." The program ran for two-and-a-half years.

I had better luck with music. Soon after our arrival at Paramount I sent Hildegarde the words and music of a new specialty song, hardly calculated to stir huzzahs in the feminist age, but in its own less-enlightened era very well received. Envisaged as a divorcée's lament, it counseled tolerance for male failings:

> Let him have that eighth martini,
> Catch him when he starts to sway;
> When he's had a tankful
> Just take the man home and be thankful, but
> Don't Let Him Get Away!
> Let him have his polo—
> As long as you're not sleeping solo . . . just
> Don't Let Him Get Away!

In 1958, coming out of Ed Grainger's office at MGM, I had run into Ernie Martin in the producer's waiting room. He grabbed my hand, and for a long moment stared. "I just had an idea," he said. "A helluvan idea. Can you come to my place tomorrow night?"

At dinner Ernie unveiled his idea: *Nellie* was the ideal musical for a TV spectacular. "It's better than anything that's ever been done on the tube. And it's a complete package, book and score ready to go, a rare find for the producer.

"As a matter of fact," he went on, "Sy and I might be able to do it ourselves. We have a commitment to produce a musical for CBS. I went over your score with Sy this morning, and he liked it, number after number. Our main question now is timing."

There was a potential conflict, he explained, with a show they had slated for Broadway, book by Sy and himself—their maiden effort at playwriting—score by one Moose Charlap. Called *Stay Away, Joe* (an inviting target, I ventured, for unsympathetic reviewers), it celebrated the romance on an Indian reservation between a barmaid and a barfly. Would I like to hear the score? He put a record on the turntable.

Charlap's tunes struck me as familiar, his lyrics awkward, the combination flat and forgettable, a long, long way from the songs in *Guys and Dolls* or *Silk Stockings*. To voice praise would be an act of bootlicking hypocrisy. But a negative judgment could be seen as the jealous back-biting of a rival songwriter. I managed a few non-committal adjectives . . . "lively" . . . "interesting." Ernie wasn't listening; he had enough enthusiasm for both of us.

And he was getting more optimistic about the possibility of doing *Nellie* at CBS. "After all, the whole thing is there." He walked with me to my car. "Tell CBS you want fifty thousand," he shouted after me as I roared off.

I drove home in a daze, Euphoria Unlimited. A production at last! Once we had national exposure, theater stagings would follow. Vindication of our faith would be sweeter for the long delay.

That was Tuesday. Friday evening, again at Ernie's house, the retreat began. He and Sy had spent the entire day going over their production schedule, trying to work in the CBS-*Nellie* project. They had come up empty. "It wasn't just a matter of timing," said Ernie. "That was tough enough. But when we got into the politics at the network . . ." He shook his head.

On the other hand, he assured me, there was good news. Feuer and Martin had at long last solved the question of how to present *Nellie* on Broadway: as a tongue-in-cheek satirical take-off on Jeanette MacDonald-Nelson Eddy operettas, much as their hit *The Boy Friend* had made merry with the musical comedy conventions of the 1920s.

He and Sy were chary of doing the show straight: "Only Dick (Rodgers) and Oscar (Hammerstein II) can get away with that kind of stuff." But the amiable burlesque would give us the best of both worlds. "The jokes and comic songs like 'Let's Make History' and 'Old Oliver' will play perfectly. The melodic ballads will be milked two ways, like 'Wunderbar' in *Kiss me Kate*: poking fun at the high notes held forever, yet giving the audience a catchy tune to carry away."

For King Charles they would cast an actor named John Carroll, who had a native pomposity, was "a genuine damned fool," and would therefore be twice as funny in a solemn portrayal of the king. "We'll have a ball. And we'll have a hit, too."

All this, of course, would have to wait upon their production of their own baby, *Stay Away, Joe*.

Late in 1958 *Stay Away*, re-christened *Whoop-Up*, opened on Broadway to dismal notices and a brief run. Its epitaph, registered in

Gerald Boardman's "American Musical Comedy Theater," concludes: "Moose Charlap's music is as undistinguished as the book."

The author-producers, much chastened, retired from the scene for several years. *Nellie*, inured to gaudy promises, went back to sleep.

An intervention from the divinities of drama came in the unlikely person of Max Rosenberg, a wild-haired City College intellectual turned film producer. As the mogul world was losing its grip, independent producers were leaping into the breech; with studio contracts receding, agents were making their stars available. Rosenberg had acquired movie rights to *The Call Girl*, a collection of real-life sex-for-sale case histories by the psychologist Harold Greenwald. Anne Francis would star, supported by John Kerr (of *Tea and Sympathy* fame) and the veteran character actor Lloyd Nolan. Would Berkman and Blau, after their success with Jim Piersall, like to come to New York to weave a feature picture out of Greenwald's rugged raw material?

The subject and cast sounded interesting. But after Perlberg's pearl, never again would we take on a story with our eyes tightly closed. Separately, in Hollywood and Nova Scotia, we studied Greenwald's book; it was indeed absorbing.

CHAPTER 15

The Call Girl

Max Rosenberg stuck a hundred-dollar bill into my hand. "This picture is about call girls," he said. "I like my movies to be authentic." An intense little man half-hidden behind huge tortoise-shell glasses and a tumbleweed nest of hair, Max bounced around the floor of his mid-Manhattan office, briefing Rafe and me.

"We'll have something to say about sex, money, the dirty underside of American life. But"—Max held up a warning hand—"we don't want to sacrifice our dramatic values: the sadism, the kinky aberrations. Those are the grabbers for our audience."

This was our first clue that our producer, who had filmed Harold Pinter's enigmatic *The Birthday Party* in England, was driven by two precariously balanced principles. Big studios wanted big profits. Idealistic young filmmakers craved recognition. Max wanted both. As we soon discovered, he could start in one direction and meet himself coming down the other side of the street.

The Call Girl centered on the high-priced "aristocrats of prostitution" dotting the canyons of New York's upper East Side: the pimps and "Johns" with whom they were entangled, the emptiness and confusion and self-contempt that often stalked their lives. Our main job was to forge from these elements a believable, sympathetic central character.

Anne Francis, tall, blonde and beautiful, with full lips, uptilted nose and succulent curves, brought to the role the sensuous allure it demanded, and something more: a quick, subtle intelligence that augured well for our film. She startled me, not unpleasantly, by planting a kiss on my mouth as I got out of her cab after our first meeting.

There were less spontaneous kisses to come as I began my personal research into the call girl scene. Max's hundred-dollar bill was in those pre-inflationary days at the top of the price scale for luxury-class ladies of the evening. Joe Cates, plucked from television by Max to be his director, set up the prescribed "recommendation" from a trusted client of my prospective partner, and within the week I was ushered into her tastefully appointed apartment on Central Park South, making mental notes on the décor and the conversational patter.

The lady took my Stetson and threw me a curve. "Is Warren back yet?" Warren was our supposed mutual chum, a v.p. at NBC. Joe Cates had seen him the week before, so I figured he had to be back from wherever away was.

"Oh, yes," I said. "He's back."

"How is he feeling?"

"Feeling? He's feeling great."

"Even after the operation?"

This was getting sticky. I hadn't been briefed about any operation. I groped for a catch-all response that would cover all bases. "Well, you know Warren. He's a tough cookie."

"That he is."

She smiled. I had struck the right note. Ultimately we arrived together at the downy sheets. The ensuing contact was like a set of tennis with the club professional: smooth, efficient, expertly performed but passionless. For all the badinage later surrounding the encounter, it was a learning experience not available in any classroom.

As our screenplay began taking shape, Rafe and I were alternately buoyed by our producer's enthusiasms and baffled by his gyrations. Superintending the script, Max was like a man trying to direct traffic from a swaying suspension bridge. His perspective changed constantly, one minute focused on a meaningful theme, the next on a provocative, audience-baiting bit of business.

At long last we turned in our final draft. Max pronounced himself content. Rafe headed back to Nova Scotia.

A week later I learned from Joe Cates that Max, apparently overtaken by panic, had turned over the script to one of his production assistants for revisions. The changes she made were character-eroding and blatantly sensational, to the point where Cates felt obliged to intervene.

Max, thus confronted, shifted course again. Yes, he had gone astray. He telephoned me; would I kindly return to the Rosenberg payroll and repair the damage, line by line?

Clearly I would have to settle in for the long haul: forage for an apartment and pick up the tattered strands of my Manhattan social life.

Karen Meyers was a wealthy arts buff with whom I had been briefly involved at the time of the New York auditions for *Nellie*. During my

Hollywood interlude with Sheilah, Karen had written regularly, intimating strongly that although her interest remained more than casual, if I had no further intentions she would succumb to the entreaties of a devoted young surgeon.

I hadn't; so she did. Now, ensconced with her husband in a plush East Sixties town house, she took pleasure in dinner parties where she mixed political leaders like Senator Jacob Javits with theater and media personalities; Alistair Cooke, jazz pianist as well as commentator, was one of her favorites.

As a certified screen writer and former broadcaster, reasonably presentable and unattached, I met her casting requirements. Her surgeon husband had double grounds for cordiality; he was an ardent admirer of my cousin Harry Plotz, who had briefed him for overseas duty in World War II, and equally of Bonzo.

On my first visit Karen had a playmate picked out for me, a wispy divorcée in her twenties. Instead I gravitated to a woman twice the divorcée's age and infinitely more worldly, the widow of a New York University history professor. Although still supple, Marcia was slightly faded, somewhat jaded, with deep-set brown eyes and a mocking wit.

I took her back to her apartment in Greenwich Village, and stayed the night; Marcia was not given to poses or subterfuge. For two weeks I reveled in steak dinners and lusty embraces.

One afternoon the doorbell rang. Marcia, busy in the kitchen, asked me to answer it. I opened the door and faced Danny Kaye.

I don't know which of us was more surprised. I fell back a step. "Hi, Danny."

"Hello to you, my friend".

"I didn't know you were in town."

"I wasn't, until a few minutes ago. Just landed my little plane at La Guardia."

"Are you here to dazzle the masses?"

"Only a handful. I'm cooking a Chinese dinner tonight for Marcia and her guests."

Whether Marcia knew of my previous connection with Danny, and mischievously planned to startle me, I never found out. Nor do I know whether she had tipped off Danny to my presence. He skipped gaily into the living room, and flung his overnight bag into a closet; clearly he was at home in the apartment, and on intimate terms with Marcia. How intimate, I wondered? And for how long?

As they chatted about his flight, I found myself vaguely irritated—as much on Sylvia's behalf as on my own. I was hardly in a position to moralize, and there was no clear evidence of a physical liaison between Danny and Marcia, but I felt a curious loyalty to Sylvia, despite her meddling on the "Red" Nichols picture. She had given me encouragement on my music when I needed it, had taken pride in my first compositions; we had worked together on an early radio show for Danny, whose title, "Full House," blossomed decades later on television. I knew how much she had contributed to Danny's success, if not actually created it; and how unhappy her parents had been at the thought of their talented daughter marrying an actor. What right did he have to play the strutting, bachelorish man-about-town with his wife three thousand miles away?

Duly garbed that evening in splendid white apron and chef's cap, Danny served up his Oriental specialties for nearly two hours. Marcia's eight or nine guests oohed and aahed their way through soups and salads, dumplings and duckling, ostentatiously proclaiming their ravenous desire for seconds. Danny, preening in the doorway, graciously bestowed his favors.

Although I yielded to no one in my admiration for Danny's acting skills, I cannot say the same for his culinary gifts. I have had better meals on Mott Street. I therefore did not join in the otherwise unanimous plea for seconds—not even when the chef fixed a disapproving eye on me and hovered over me with full platter. I shook my head. Danny stared a moment in disbelief, then moved haughtily on.

The next day he was on his way back to California. Marcia and I resumed our affair. But not for long. By the time Karen's next invitation rolled around, my claustrophobic don't-pin-me-down complex had reasserted itself; I turned up at her soirée alone. A few nights later, Marcia and I were abed when she learned of my defection. "You broke our contract. You can't take emotional responsibility!" She tossed my trousers in my lap. I never saw her again.

❀ ❀ ❀

The script revisions for Max were finished. The only further agonizing was over the title: should it be *Girl in the Night* (the authors' preference) or the more sexually overt *Girl of the Night* (Max's)?

That was the title under which our picture opened around the nation in October of 1960. New York critical reaction was varied, with the more socially oriented viewers providing the warmest response. "A film that holds your interest consistently, touches the heart and gradually persuades you to take sides," trilled the *Post's* Archer Winsten, second in influence only to Bosley Crowther of the *Times*. "A good picture which improves everything it touches."

Newsday praised "an understanding, penetrating portrait" highlighted by Anne Francis's "electrifying" performance. Although Bosley Crowther conceded only a "fairly fascinating" drama, there was enough media applause to gratify Max Rosenberg's most altruistic impulses. And in the early box-office returns, enough to satisfy his commercial side. Business was "torrid" in Detroit, "lusty" in Louisville.

It was a marking time period for movies. Although John Garfield (ex-Julius Garfinkel of the Group Theater), walking with me in Central Park, deplored the shortage of "real reality" in The Industry, it had not yet succumbed totally to the conglomerate accountants. And bald, brawny Otto Preminger had broken through the Hays Office barrier in directing *The Moon Is Blue*, defiantly using the word "virgin" (previously verboten, along with "sex" and "damn").

Radio got a lift with the introduction of the transistor, which made receivers small and portable. But the odds-on media leader was television, wallowing in soap operas by day, quiz shows and Ed Sullivan vaudeville in the evening, Jack Paar and Johnny Carson at night. The decade ahead would see America rocked by sit-ins and urban riots, chilling assassinations, Tim Leary's LSD and rebellious "flower children;" television would roll on serenely with the Beatles and Hollywood Squares.

In 1961, after scandals erupted over the blatant fixing of quiz shows, FCC Chairman Newton Minow excoriated television as a "vast wasteland." The riposte of the networks was to update the gladiatorial spectacles of Rome by hiring mighty-muscled professional wrestlers to engage in the fake heroics of slamming each other around.

And yet a complacent public was turning increasingly to the tube for information. A survey by Elmo Roper in 1963 reported that the "most used and most believed" source of America's news was television, dominated by the well-staged star turns of figures like Walter Cronkite. Daily papers and weekly magazines were retreating from hard news to features and "think-pieces."

In one respect television news served the country well. Its vivid on-the-scene battle footage from Vietnam cut through Pentagon mumbo-jumbo of "body counts." Murrow was right. The tube had enormous unexplored potential.

CHAPTER 16

Cast A Giant Shadow

In the fall of 1960, other things were on my mind. John F. Kennedy had just been elected to the presidency, precipitating one of those exhilarating moments which, like the 1933 victory in New York of the reformist Mayor Fiorello La Guardia, the launching twelve years later of the United Nations, and in 1991 the triumph of the resurgent Russian soul over the coup-mongers, restore one's faith in the instinctive wisdom of humanity. Kennedy meant the Peace Corps, progress, a return to the egalitarian goals of FDR. Artists, said the new leader, would be accorded "full recognition . . . I see little of more importance to the future of our country."

High in the oligarchy of Kennedy's New Frontier would be my two political lodestars, Chester Bowles and Ed Murrow; Chet had been instrumental in bringing Murrow aboard. During my long Hollywood exile I had kept in touch with Bowles, noting wistfully in a letter that I "would probably be happier writing educational films for some Asiatic country struggling toward a more rational future." Stranded in the East in the fall of 1957, I had tried in vain to catch him at Essex.

He and Steb were "terribly disappointed" that they were away from Essex when I came through, he wrote back in December. He would appreciate advance notice of my next trip East; there seemed to be "more than the usual amount" of items for discussion. A handwritten postscript said he was considering a run for the Senate; he hoped he could "borrow" some of my time.

The time Chet wanted was pre-empted by Paramount. And his 1958 bid for the Democratic U.S. Senate nomination went awry. He laid out the melancholy details in a long single-space letter. Bill Benton, his former ad agency partner, had charged into a race where Chet held a substantial lead over Thomas J. Dodd. Benton's bid split the liberal vote.

Chet had later accepted the consolation prize of a House nomination, won without any trouble, and risen rapidly to the chairmanship of the Democratic Platform Committee.

In the spring of 1960, breakfasting with him at a New York hotel shortly before the party's national convention in Los Angeles, I was mildly surprised at his firm advocacy of "Jack Kennedy," then a relatively obscure figure outside of the Belt Parkway. After Kennedy's election, and his designation of Bowles as his future Undersecretary of State, Bowles promptly set about recruiting Ed Murrow for government service.

Both were men of unchallengeable principle in a world crawling with charlatans. Bowles and Murrow had first met a dozen years earlier when I brought Chet to Murrow's broadcast booth on behalf of the U.N. Appeal. Both were concerned about the lure of communism for the newly liberated populations of Asia, and favored countering Soviet influence by extending democracy rather than falling back on repressive regimes. And the reporter shared the fears of the politician about unmet domestic needs, ignored by a media-drenched public.

But Murrow's pre-convention impressions of "that boy" Kennedy, as recounted in Ann Sperber's excellent Murrow biography, were decidedly negative: a rich kid, careless about Joe McCarthy, burdened by a poor attendance record. Once in Washington, exposed to the new president's agile, well-stocked mind, Murrow would temper this view; but for the moment it was up to Bowles to bridge the gap. He assured Murrow of a seat in the inner councils of the Administration; "you can make an enormous contribution to foreign policy."

The sheer credibility of his proselytizer, "so seemingly close" to Jack Kennedy, drew a wavering Murrow onto the team a week after the inaugural, to take over a staff of 2,400 people at the U.S. Information Agency.

A few weeks later I had a breezy note from Murrow: He and Bowles—by this time "Brother Chet"—were on occasion "stirring up the animals," and he was enjoying it. When was I next coming down?

On March 8, 1961, I got off a long letter to him urging development of an "electronic university" which would bring the blessings of American education to the Third World:

> Am glancing Washingtonward with mingled envy and delight as the new Frontiersmen start putting democracy back to work. History, which does not always show consideration in these matters, seems to have timed things perfectly for you . . .

> In 1946 I pontificated that the big fact of international life was the simultaneous existence of a triumphant Soviet Union and the awakening nationalisms of the East. Today I am struck by a polarity with a similar dynamic potential: i.e., the fierce hunger for learning in the new democracies, and the huge American warehouse of systematized information plus communication facilities.
>
> We are in a position to offer genuine invitations to learning, scaled to the needs of different countries. Visual instruction, with a minimal teaching force, can make real inroads on illiteracy and poor sanitation, before going on to vocational and academic training . . .
>
> I feel an itch to get into the game. But shrink not in alarm. This is no bid for a return to the bureaucratic bosom, no matter how alluring its current décolletage. I'm deeply involved in a biography for Doubleday of Colonel Mickey Marcus, the West Point boxing champ, Pentagon egghead, paratrooper etc. who shaped Israel's Haganah into a modern army and then outgeneralled Brigadier Glubb in the battle for Jerusalem.

Murrow's reply was prompt and unequivocal. He would follow through on my suggestions. And he was steamed up about the book on Mickey Marcus: "What a subject he should be, and you are the boy to do it."

That had been my own conclusion, after a year of meandering since stumbling across the Marcus story in the Los Angeles *Times*. Books had integrity. And staying power. It was time to take the leap. From Ann Wenner, our faithful secretary at Paramount, a drumfire of letters had been scolding me for letting my gifts shrivel in a "self-made smog":

> Your real happiness will always be in writing, and you have plenty of talent. Even on Golden Journey your first draft was terrific before Mr. Perlberg got his heavy and experienced hand in there. Forget Hollywood ever happened . . . You can be brilliant, but not when you try to write down.
>
> No good writer ever got there without a period of being lost. Find a subject that engages your deepest feelings—maybe something involving a cause or a movement.

That was practically a prescription for the saga of tough, chunky Mickey Marcus: dreamer, fighter, an authentic hero in a hero-starved world . . . the first General of Israel in two thousand years, and something more: in the quiet phrase inscribed on his tombstone at West Point, a Soldier for All Humanity. The background of the tale was at my fingertips: Brooklyn, wartime Washington, the maelstrom of the Middle East.

Preliminary inquiry indicated that rights to the Marcus story were in the hands of a Hollywood cinematographer named Lee Garmes. Several seasoned writers, including Lowell Limpus of the New York *Daily News* and best-selling author Jim Bishop (once my fellow-rewrite man on the *Mirror*) had reportedly started on the project and abandoned it, unable to fuse the seemingly contradictory elements of a complex character. The cooperation of the Israeli government and army would be necessary, especially concerning the cloudy circumstances surrounding Marcus's death.

The key to all these matters was clearly the colonel's widow, still living at their modest house in Flatbush. I found Emma Marcus a gentle, unpretentious woman, her attractiveness preserved in her fifties, with a direct but pleasant manner that must have served her well as a grade school teacher. She set me straight at once about access to the story: Lee Garmes's option had lapsed, so it was available. But why should she let me do it?

I handed her a copy of *Mrs. A*. Three days later she invited me back. Spread out on her dining room table were clippings, photos and scrapbooks, a file of letters from her husband, the unfinished biography manuscript by Lowell Limpus and a report commissioned by the Israeli Defense Forces on Mickey's activities there. Boxing medals from West Point mingled with tapes of speeches in Mickey's high-pitched impatient tenor made when he was running New York's Department of Corrections.

I rattled off a five-page outline and brought it to Le Baron R. Barker, Jr. at Doubleday. Sharp and spare, aristocratic of mien (he had captained Yale's track team in the 1920's), Lee Barker had risen from the sales side of the old publishing house to the post of executive editor. As an insider in the clannish world of publishing, Barker knew of my labors on the Gertrude Lawrence book, and thought my new project was worth a five thousand dollar gamble.

I began my research in the Brooklyn semi-ghetto of Mickey's boyhood, then moved on to West Point and the labyrinthine corridors of the Pentagon. The generals in Mickey's service life remembered him well: MacArthur, who was superintendent at West Point when Mickey won the intercollegiate welterweight title there, and who recalled him "as a cadet under me . . . a good cadet;" Maxwell Taylor, who drew me a longhand sketch of the landings at Normandy, where Mickey made an unauthorized parachute jump; John Hilldring, to whom Mickey was answerable at the General Staff in Washington; Lucius Clay, the colonel's boss during the four-power occupation of Berlin. Clay, lean and lemony, laid down strict orders: "What drove Mickey Marcus was a passion for justice. If you can't get that across, don't bother with the book."

Not everyone thrilled to my new undertaking. Ernie Martin scoffed at the notion of a reading public panting for word about a "Yiddish general." And Henry Strauss thought I would do better to put off the book and pick up a juicy fee for a documentary commissioned by IBM.

But Ed Murrow's enthusiasm remained undimmed. And so did my own. The day I managed a firm "No, thanks" to Henry Strauss marked a turning point in my growth.

Although Mickey's feisty little sponsor in city politics, former Mayor Fiorello La Guardia, was gone, there was no dearth of New Yorkers eager to reminisce about Mickey's early years, among them Jules "Indian" Yablok, a backfield All-American at Colgate University before sharing a law office with Marcus. The more I learned, peering into remote corners of my subject's life, the more I had to like a man who would spend his first big fee on a grand piano for his music-loving wife; who accepted the foibles of his friends: "That's the way Harry is, Emma; don't look for what he can't give," and who refused to press a delinquent debtor: "If he can't pay, he's in worse trouble than I am." I liked, too, his brand of religiosity, focused less on ritual than on ethics.

Mickey's rendezvous with history, of course, lay 8,000 miles away, in the land whose stubborn struggle for survival had inspired him, and whose citizen-soldiers he in turn inspired. For my return to the Middle East after fifteen years, Emma Marcus invoked the high-level contacts she had maintained there since Mickey's death. A few days before I left New York in 1961, there was a momentary flurry of confusion when a nervy American newspaperwoman turned up in Tel Aviv, claiming she had exclusive authorization from the colonel's widow to write his story; Emma lost no time in shooting the pretender down.

I found the nascent Jewish state of my Cairo years transformed into a bustling, dynamic nation, confident almost to the point of cockiness but still grateful to the American officer whom David Ben-Gurion had saluted as "the best man we had." Gershon Rivlin, a thin, brooding poet once active in the Haganah underground, now doubling as a lieutenant colonel (shades of Rupert Brooke, England's soldier-bard of World War I), was assigned by the Israel Defense Forces to line up my interviews and field trips.

Mickey's erstwhile protégés were quick to cooperate. A brief circuitous drive from my hotel in Tel Aviv deposited me on a barren strip where Yitzchak Rabin, the number two man in the army and future Prime Minister of Israel was waiting. Raw-boned and freckled, with meaty forearms and thick, competent farmer's fingers, Rabin had in 1948 been Chief of Operations for the night-raiding elite Palmach.

His khakis were clean but casual, with no hint of the spit-and-polish dear to more conventional services. Rabin's distaste for public display was legendary. During his marriage a decade earlier, when the rabbi began booming a hearty prayer, Rabin begged him to lower his voice: people were looking. Likewise legendary was his boldness both in combat and command. Late in the Six-Day War it would be Chief of Staff Rabin, not a hesitant Defense Minister Moshe Dayan who would launch the successful invasion of Syria. Dayan was brilliant, a gleaming sword blade; Rabin a blunt mailed fist.

Like Douglas MacArthur at West Point, Rabin in secondary school broke all academic records and won a scholarship to the University of California at Berkeley. He was prevented from accepting it by the outbreak of World War II, which he spent disrupting communications behind the Vichy French lines in Syria.

None of this derring-do was evident in the quiet man before me, taking a swig from a bottle of orange soda pop. He motioned me toward a nearby helicopter, a pilot at its controls. A tiny two-seater, it looked about as formidable as a mountain bike.

As we climbed aboard, Rabin reached out for a rifle from one of his aides and tucked it under his arm. "We'll be flying along the Jordanian border," he explained. "Sometimes they shoot."

We took off and were soon at a couple of thousand feet. Without the enclosure of an airplane cabin I felt as if I were astride Pegasus in mid-air, a speck in the wind, strangely vulnerable. Gradually the terrain below was changing from gentle foothills to wild, craggy slopes. Giant rocks mingled with clumps of thick-based eucalyptus trees and the ruins of ancient fortresses. Between steep, stony walls, a narrow road slithered snakelike eastward toward Jerusalem.

Rabin leaned forward. "Until Mickey broke the Arab blockade, this was the road to Jerusalem—more often the burial ground—for our convoys. Perfect ambush country. Snipers on both sides, under total cover from trees and boulders. It was a hell." He pointed down at the battered shell of an armored car. "A lot of them"—for the first time his voice softened—"a lot of them didn't make it." Later I would hear from his soldiers that Rabin agonized over every casualty—and not only on the Israeli side.

A few days later, I got a ground-level view of Latrun, the complex of Arab Legion strongpoints—police station, monastery, artillery ridges—that had throttled the original road to Jerusalem, cutting off a hundred thousand Jews in the capital. Chaim Laskov, husky and plain-spoken, who had commanded a tank battalion under Marcus and would soon become Israeli Chief of Staff, drove me through scrubby foothill country to the staging area that had served for repeated unsuccessful Israeli assaults. He pulled up on the barbed-wire edge of no-man's-land.

As we scrambled down a weed-smothered incline, he turned casually. "I'm not sure we ever cleared our mine fields here. Nobody comes this way any more."

My toe hit something hard—the stake of a Hebrew-language sign slanting up from the brush. This was not a neighborhood for no-parking signs. Laskov glanced backward at the mine warning. "Guess we didn't," he grunted. And marched on. His intrepid guest swallowed—and followed.

For the antidote to Latrun, the Middle East "Burma Road" carved out of mountainside under cover of night by Mickey's forces and civilian volunteers, my guide was Amos Chorev, the Palmach scout who had blueprinted the daring by-pass. A round, bubbly engineering genius—he was to sprint through an M.I.T. scholarship in two years—Chorev piloted our armed jeep up an abandoned donkey trail, then hurtled at a forty-five-degree angle upward through scrub trees, over slabs of slippery limestone, and finally down along the rim of four-hundred-foot cliffs. Enlivening our journey was a withering *khamseen*, the oven-hot desert wind from the east. Chorev took the jaunt blithely; I gorged my weary body on a quart of ice cream.

Yigael Yadin, archaeologist and military planner, led me over the detail maps he had used to brief Mickey Marcus on operations. A gaunt, spidery man with humorous eyes in a sensitive face, he was a model of patience and understanding.

Less forthcoming was another archaeologist-general, the legendary Moshe Dayan. Dayan's special bailiwick had been the Galilee in the north where, he intimated, the American colonel had been less active than on the central front or in the Negev desert. I found Dayan mysteriously withdrawn on the subject of Mickey, non-committal to the point where I wondered if the two had had any differences. No one would say.

A bulwark throughout my visit was the bluff, calm presence of Teddy Kollek, not yet mayor of Jerusalem but close to Prime Minister Ben-Gurion and respected everywhere. Keen and pragmatic under his Viennese *gemütlichkeit*, Kollek quickly arranged a mutually agreeable payment to the ex-sergeant who had assembled the IDF data on Mickey, which included some flavorsome dialogue. He checked out my draft of the opening chapter with the prime minister, and returned it with B.G.'s blessing and his own comment: "This is really fine writing. Thanks." Most importantly, when the film rights were being negotiated, it was Kollek who broke up the log-jam on personal releases from recalcitrant military figures.

Keeping a jaded eye on my personal life was my avuncular friend Meyer Levin, short and compact as a snub-nosed bullet. Meyer spent a good deal of time in Israel, a frequent background for his novels, and was building a villa at Herzlia, outside of Tel Aviv. He ferreted out a comfortable, modestly-priced pension for me in Tel Aviv and, ever-solicitous of my less prosaic needs, introduced me to a striking Rumanian divorcée.

The pension developed considerable traffic after an article appeared in the Jerusalem *Post* urging ex-soldiers who recalled Mickey's cheery presence to drop in and tell me about it. From one of his drivers I learned that the paperback left in Mickey's tent on the night that he died was *Human Destiny*, by Le Comte de Nouy.

My notes piled up. And so did the strain of questioning, searching, exploring in the relentless heat of an Israeli summer. For the climax of my trip I had been promised a private meeting with David Ben-Gurion. But as I climbed the stairs of a Tel Aviv apartment building for a lesser interview on a stifling July evening, the protests from lung and muscle were overwhelming. I had had enough. Much as I longed to chat with a maker of history, to linger further would be to invite disaster. I booked a return flight via Paris.

My hunch was vindicated. A few hours after arriving at Le Bourget, sitting with a friend from the U.N. at the Cafe de la Paix, I felt an unfamiliar flushing sensation that swept through my body. Breathing came in short bursts. "Julian," I gasped, "I think I'm dying."

"No, you're not. You're just very, very tired. Nervous exhaustion. It happened to one of our people last week, just back from Africa."

Julian tracked down a doctor, who diagnosed my symptoms as a panic attack caused by stress, and gave me some pills. My breath would come back, he assured me; "*Ça vient, ça vient. Il faût vous reposer.*"

For three days I holed up in a hotel room, nibbling at an Agatha Christie paperback I found there. Normally I loathe mysteries, but this was no time to quibble. Normally I am also not given to prayer, but I remember thinking, "Just let me finish the book, God. Please."

Gradually peace and breath came back. On the fourth day I was able to return to New York.

I had found a new apartment in Manhattan's Upper Bohemia, a strange little single-block enclave running along East 95th Street between Park and Lexington Avenues. There, with painter Mark Rothko on one side of me and novelist Ann Roiphe (*Up The Sandbox*) on the other, I settled in with a Weber baby grand, my typewriter, my notes and my deadline.

The street was also known as Shubert Alley North. It housed musical comedy star Alfred Drake, Broadway cartoonist Al Hirschfeld, restaurateur Vincent Sardi, and playwrights Betty Comden and Franklin

Lacey (*The Music Man*). I had a little trouble adjusting to Drake; it was hard to reconcile the slight, retiring figure shuffling past my kitchen window with the dashing bucko of *Oklahoma* and *Kiss Me, Kate*. Drake, in contrast to American opera singers who adopted Italian names, and ballerinas from Grand Rapids who became fashionably Russian, had anglicized his Italian family name to court the favor of Middle America.

For extra glamour, our block boasted Marlene Dietrich and June Havoc as absentee landlords. My own landlord, very much present, was Louis Kronenberger, the acerbically witty drama critic for *Time* magazine. To accommodate his late mother, Kronenberger had carefully remodeled the basement of his three-story town house into a cozy if unconventional retreat: ample kitchen, long corridor leading into a spacious living room with fireplace, bay window looking out on paved courtyard, and sleeping quarters just big enough to accommodate a double bed.

One block to the north, separated by one of New York's invisible boundary lines, began the time-worn tenements of East Harlem; three blocks to the south rose the poetry halls and abundant gymnasium facilities of the 92nd St. YMCA.

I buckled down to a steady routine of morning and afternoon labors, broken up by swimming sessions at the Y. For weekends through September I frequently escaped to Fire Island, the city's nose-thumbing response to the summer playgrounds of Europe. A friendly little speck off Bay Shore on the southern flank of Long Island, Fire Island was reachable on the last lap only by ferry, after a longish railroad or auto trip from New York. But the noisy little ferry was itself a romp, the start of the holiday experience; ties were loosened, shoes kicked off, baggage tossed into racks below, while male and female passengers assembled in rows on the deck, hair flying in the breeze, to inhale the refreshing salt spray. For me the trip offered the major pleasures of sailing, without the attendant discomforts (I have been miserable aboard the Queen Mary, and known to get mildly seasick in a rowboat).

I turned in my first three chapters to Lee Barker on a Monday. On Friday his appraisal was in my mailbox: "This has all the earmarks of a splendid biography . . . " I danced down the hall in delight, exulting in a sense of rightness, arrival. Books were a personal statement; editors deferred to authors in a manner unimaginable in Hollywood. At long last I was on my way, making real strides in the journey to myself.

Lee's note was enough to fuel me to the end of the book. Another boost came in June of 1962 from Meyer Levin, ploughing through my galley proofs in Israel.

"You have done a helluva fine job," Meyer wrote, "with a very difficult piece of organization. The research work is great. Had I had a real inkling of the material, I'd have done it myself, but I don't think I could have done it better."

"A wonderful book," echoed a letter from Leon Uris a few weeks later. And from ever-responsive Sheilah in London, "Absolutely fascinating, and beautifully written."

The first public notice came from Robert Kirsch in the Los Angeles *Times*. It was read over the phone by an excited book dealer to Lee Barker, who relayed it to me: "A remarkable and moving biography which illuminates not only the man but the times in which he lived." Although two decades later, in Santa Barbara, Bob Kirsch and I would become good friends, in the 1960s I knew him only by his reputation, which was considerable: no other critic west of Chicago had as much prestige. My morale shot up.

And for quite a while stayed there, as other reviewers chimed in: from the St. Louis *Post Dispatch* ("Heart-warming and often thrilling"); from Lewiston, Maine ("A spell-binding, inspiring story").

Of the fifty-odd reviews pouring in, only two were dimly negative, questioning my abundance of "reconstructed dialogue"—much of which had actually been gathered by the Israeli army in 1948 from the parties concerned.

New York's dailies had not eluded the mergers which elsewhere had left many cities with a single paper; the *Sun* was gone, the *Mirror* tottering on its last legs. But the *World-Telegram*, one of the city's surviving papers, elected to serialize *Cast A Giant Shadow* in twelve daily installments, launching its widely publicized series with a picture spread covering half the front page.

What was still missing, unfortunately, was any mention in the sacrosanct columns of the New York *Times*. Without coverage in the nationally respected *Sunday Times Book Review*, for many sellers and librarians a new work was in effect invisible.

An occasional contributor to the *Book Review* was Hal Lehrman, the debonair president of the Overseas Press Club, a man who groomed his words as carefully as his crisp gray mustache. His prize-winning foreign correspondence had included several years in the Middle East. I knew Lehrman slightly through Gerold Frank, and in the summer of 1962 had told him of my upcoming opus. He indicated then that he might talk to the *Times* about covering it.

Now, months later, I had a guarded phone call from Lehrman, seeking clarification on some details of Mickey's life. Then, silence.

Was a review coming up? I dashed out at midnight Saturday to pick up the Sunday paper at Times Square. Nothing. Again the next week, and the next. Every book, it seemed, but mine.

The New York *Herald-Tribune*, arch-rival of the *Times*, lumbered into print: "A rattling good yarn, presented with skill in a clear, free-wheeling style." But still nothing from the one paper that counted. Discreet inquiry there by Doubleday elicited the information that indeed the book had been assigned, but nobody guaranteed that every review submitted would see the light of day.

As the weeks passed, gloom deepened to despair. And then, of course, on November 25, the review appeared, three fat columns under the by-line of Hal Lehrman.

Lehrman swept off his hat before a "fascinating" story "of awesome dimensions," told with an expertise that made it "wholly believable—and unforgettable."

Cast A Giant Shadow soared into four printings. In several cities it made the best-seller lists, despite what Doubleday pointed out as the notorious manipulation of sales figures by book dealers overstocked with heavily promoted titles. A children's edition that I assembled for the Jewish Publication Society with Chaim Potok, later famous for *The Chosen* and other novels, ran into three more printings. Later, Pocket Books blanketed the country with paperbacks.

For one *Times* reader, Lehrman's report was unpalatable. Amitai Etzioni, an Israeli sociologist at Columbia, complained that Mickey Marcus was merely a high-ranking "staff adviser," never a military commander. Further, he compared the failure of Mickey's amateur forces to overrun the impregnable fortress at Latrun with the American disaster at Pearl Harbor, a parallel that was bizarre if not obscene.

Emma let that one fall of its own weight. But she did pen a note to the *Times* referring the presumably literate sociologist to the document from David Ben-Gurion appointing Mickey chief of the Central Front command, and to several field orders issued by "Brigadier Stone," Mickey's pseudonym.

To me, the colonel's widow sent one of his gold boxing medals from West Point, with the book's title embossed on the back.

I went on the road to speak, in Philadelphia, Cincinnati, Louisville, Miami and Los Angeles, mostly before Jewish groups like the Zionist women's Hadassah. Authors who didn't freeze before a microphone were apparently a welcome anomaly; I shared a platform at the Plaza Hotel with novelist Rona Jaffe, Moshe Dayan's daughter Yael, and nutritionist Gaylord Hauser; addressed a private dinner on Park Avenue with Peter Ustinov and Eli Wallach; followed Norman Cousins in an upstate lecture series, and was headlined at the White Mountains Festival of the Seven Arts in Pike, New Hampshire.

My talks ranged beyond the immediate subject of Mickey Marcus. I told a Los Angeles audience:

> We shower our young people with imposing evidence of our "know-how," but little sense of "know-what" or "know-why." We worship the winner, regardless of the game. And we wonder why they flee to passive conformity or beatnik withdrawal.

I reveled in the increasingly strong audience responses. Broadcasting had been fun; the intoxication of commanding a live microphone was not unlike that described by airplane pilots reaching for an obedient throttle. But in radio, even if an occasional observation was picked up by a news agency or a foreign government, one never knew how much of the network was really listening. As Winston Burdett constantly pointed out, "You might be talking to yourself."

Here I could see my audience, sweep my eyes over them, fix my gaze on someone in the front row and feel the locked-in eye contact. People were smiling with me, sharing my anger and concern, reacting visibly and sometimes vocally to my every word. The discovery that I could sway an audience brought back childhood memories of my mother, at a

Brooklyn political rally, haranguing a dazzled assemblage of Republican faithful.

Occasionally I ran into grumblers and nay-sayers who, evidently finding Mickey's stature a rebuke to their own petty perspectives, would come slinking to the podium, demanding the "real lowdown" on Mickey Marcus. Why did he go to Israel? For money? Glory? Girls? Dedication to principle was more than they could stomach.

I noticed a quiet change in Fanny. No longer my self-appointed mentor, she began submitting draft letters to her overseas clients to me for approval or revision.

As a low-grade celebrity, I landed in a column by Walter Winchell (for whom I had been a captive audience in 1933), exchanged quips with Johnny Carson, then hosting something called "Who Do You Trust?", and acquired a measure of international standing: a Paris quiz show asked contestants to name the American author connected with both *Fear Strikes Out* and *Cast A Giant Shadow*.

I was away on a speaking engagement when my Uncle Jack succumbed to leukemia. I had a mixed reaction. Jack had taken me to Ebbets Field, financed me through Cornell, opened the doors to my newspaper career. He had also saddled me with his immigrant anxieties ("Fix your tie!") and pushed me relentlessly to academic honors. He had been conspicuously unkind to his gentle, whimsical younger brother, leaving David to the benefactions—and torments—of a junior partnership with Fanny. And I had a vague sense of letdown about his own career. Yes, he had conquered Wall Street corporate law, and as a State Regent had pioneered educational television, there granting me the role of his conscience; but I clung to the adolescent fantasy that with his extraordinary gifts he should have settled for nothing less than a seat on the U.S. Supreme Court. He had not fulfilled an admonition of Thomas Wolfe's that haunted me: make the most of your capacities.

Cast A Giant Shadow slithered its way to the screen, but not without a struggle. There was immediate resistance to the subject in Hollywood's largely Jewish imperial quarters, always skittish about any hint of appearing to favor their fellow-religionists. As one studio tycoon put it, "I give to my temple. On the screen I'm a hundred percent American."

Nonetheless a bold producer at MGM, Robert Weitman, persuaded his West Coast bosses to plunk down ten thousand dollars in option money. A cloudy silence ensued, reportedly involving difficulties in getting the necessary personal releases from various prominent Israelis; privately I was informed that a storm of opposition had broken out at the MGM front office in New York, and the picture would never be made. The Egyptian government had threatened to expropriate everything MGM owned (theaters), or distributed (films), or in any way touched in the Middle East.

As predicted, the Culver City colossus buckled. The only consequence of its brief proprietorship was a change from the book's projected title of *Decision at Jerusalem* to *Cast A Giant Shadow*.

In his *Variety* column, Frank Scully fumed at the MGM retreat: "Under an earlier Warner-Zanuck regime this magnificent opus, so beautifully told, would have been in production three days after the Marcus funeral . . . and nuts to the Arab market!"

At the suggestion of George Litto, my aggressive little Sicilian agent, I made an exploratory trip to the Coast, where I had an enthusiastic call from George Seaton: "I see big possibilities in your book. Not only visual values, but epic scale. You don't want to lose that."

Alan Pakula was equally excited, but more direct. He and Bob Mulligan had both read my book, liked it a lot, and had already discussed several approaches to a film version. Could I meet them for lunch in half an hour at the Beverly Hills Hotel?

Once again I shudder to record the incredible fact. I stalled, sloughing off an invitation to talk about my book with the most talented young production team in America, if not the world. Why? Because Alan's call reached me in the kitchen of my cousin, Bernice Sheinart, where I was about to sit down to a home-cooked repast of borscht, latkes, kasha, and—need I say it? Blintzes. I suggested to Alan that we meet the following day; I would phone him at his office in the morning.

I never did catch up with him. Alan, in the throes of a turbulent divorce from Hope Lange, was constantly on the run, leaving a trail of baffling messages. To my everlasting regret, I never found out how he and Bob Mulligan contemplated handling Mickey's story.

Another ex-Paramount colleague moved into the vacuum. Mel Shavelson, professing a distant kinship with Mickey and a determination to see the picture made, put down a substantial payment for the film rights.

But Mel's credentials, however imposing, were as a funnyman, not in international drama. All the specialists in that genre whom he approached were suddenly preoccupied with earlier commitments; and no production company would even take a look at his project without a screenplay. So, as Mel recounted it later, he reluctantly withdrew to his own typewriter, dashed off thirty pages of script, and sent them out: not to Sam Goldwyn or Harry Cohn, but to John Wayne, star-spangled superpatriot and number one box-office draw in the world. Would "Duke" come into the game, not of course as fortyish Mickey Marcus but as one of Mickey's superiors in the Pentagon, an amalgam of brass hats?

"Hell, yes!" was the ducal response—but on one condition. Only if Mel himself would write the rest of the screenplay.

Mel had the big-name breakthrough he needed. United Artists, not vulnerable to Arab appropriation of its theaters because it didn't own any, agreed to finance his production, which Mel would direct. Yul Brynner joined the cast, then Angie Dickinson as Emma, and Frank Sinatra in a daredevil pilot role. As I wrote to David Holtzmann in 1964:

> The Marcus-movie project lurches forward, stumbles, picks up, reels sideways . . . seems on the whole to be in fairly promising shape. The Israeli Army has been lined up—unless the Syrians claim a higher priority on their attention. But the title role has not yet been cast. Burt Lancaster, whom UA and everybody else wanted, decided that audiences might not accept him as a Jew.

Ironically, decades later Lancaster would portray Leon Klinghoffer, the elderly wheelchair-bound Jew murdered and thrown overboard in 1985 by the Arab terrorist hijackers of the cruise ship Achille Lauro.

My own preference was for William Holden or Marlon Brando. Ultimately, for a pittance of a cool million, the producers landed Kirk Douglas.

Mel went ahead with his script. No doubt under pressure from his money people, he introduced one significant departure from the Marcus story. My book had mentioned a very attractive Hungarian aide assigned to Mickey for driving and secretarial chores. In Mel's adaptation, she became a provocative temptress with whom a more breezy, wise-cracking American colonel fell into a sustained affair before going back to his wife.

From an advance reading of the screenplay, I was troubled: not only on Emma's behalf (she had been promised "tasteful" handling of Mickey's private life), but about the entire shift in emphasis that the change portended. It seemed to me likely to diminish not only Mickey's achievements but his motives and personal stature. I was afraid that between Mel's snappy one-liners and the exigencies of the star system, Mickey Marcus was getting lost. I conveyed my misgivings to Mel, along with a half-dozen suggested cuts to restore what I considered a proper balance. He chose not to make any changes.

When the picture opened with tremendous fanfare at the De Mille theater on Broadway in the spring of 1966, critical reaction confirmed my fears. The New York *Times* scolded Mel for creating "a contrived hero . . . more concerned with romances than with his stake in the future of Israel." *Time* magazine complained of the "smokescreens dreamed up" by the writer-director: "any resemblance to persons living or dead is sacrificed to make elbowroom for hero Kirk Douglas." *Newsweek* snorted at Shavelson's "kibbutz Casanova;" the *New Yorker* at "a screenplay of flawless vulgarity."

In spite of these tirades, Mel's script was consistently entertaining, if salted with dialogue more attuned to Bob Hope than to Mickey Marcus. And as Arthur Knight noted in the *Saturday Review*, Mel's battle scenes had sweep and authority. If, as the critic conceded, the film's epic flavor was diluted by a routine movieland romance, "Without this compromise, the picture would probably never have been made;" and that, Knight felt, would have been a distinct public loss.

Mel took the notices with good grace, and five years later converted his disappointment into *How To Make A Jewish Movie*, a hilarious and often touching prose account of his adventures on location in Israel.

Although a public school in Flatbush was named in honor of Colonel Marcus in 1976, for his widow there was only more travail: a brain tumor that led to blindness and then to her death in 1982. She is buried beside Mickey at West Point.

As a phrase, "Cast A Giant Shadow" has turned up in a 1967

Philadelphia *Inquirer* article on advertising, a 1970 New York *Times* sports essay on Mohammed Ali, and various columns in the *Christian Science Monitor*, New York *Post* and Los Angeles *Times* between 1976 and 1989, apparently in the language to stay.

And in David Ben-Gurion's former home in the Negev desert, now a national museum, the book that gazes down most prominently on the departing visitor from its central position on a shelf above the exit portal is *Cast A Giant Shadow*.

CHAPTER 17

Trolling With Truman

"I like Ike," Irving Berlin chirped to America at the start of the Eisenhower boom. Personally, I have always preferred Harry.

I admired Harry Truman because after inheriting the most awesome job in the world he stood up to two imperious challengers, Joe Stalin and Douglas MacArthur; because he came through unequivocally for Israel when the new Jewish state needed a friend; because he took responsibility for his actions ("the buck stops here"); and not least because he lambasted a music critic who found fault with his daughter's singing. I thought he was an original: refreshingly honest, engagingly human. So when the opportunity came to work with Truman head to head, man to man, I jumped at it.

In the early 1960s the ex-president, ten years out of office, had at long last consented to appear in a twenty-six-part television documentary series, *Decision*, that would recount his handling of major crises. As a successful biographer I was one of a handful of writers selected to collaborate with him. I would not only be scripting an episode on Russia's belated entry into our war against Japan, but would write the two-installment opening segment on Truman's dismissal of General MacArthur.

The scribblers were a hand-picked team: my former partner, Raphael Blau; documentary prize-winner Ernest Kinoy; a couple of novelists, a historian and myself. The pay was good but I'd have taken the assignment for nothing. How many writers through the ages had been privileged to sit face to face with a maker of history, and help him frame for posterity a documentary record of his crucial decisions? What would our libraries give to have such a personal account from Talleyrand or Peter the Great? Historians could pontificate, commentators comment down the ages. But this would be a reminiscence every child could see and hear for himself or herself. I had missed my chance to go one on one with David Ben-Gurion. I wasn't going to miss this one.

We were flown to Independence, Missouri, where the former president was waiting, forthright and feisty, to greet each visitor with a hearty handshake and guide us around his home, a rambling old structure with spacious rooms and a broad wooden porch, as unpretentiously Middle American as the man himself.

Our host's flat nasal twang was standard Missouri, but his piercing blue-eyed glance was pure Truman. He moved in quick, short steps, always a few feet ahead of his interlocutors.

From the living room, I caught a glimpse of an ebony grand across the foyer. "That looks like a Steinway."

Truman grinned. "Sounds like one, too. Do you play?"

"Somewhat."

"Come along." I followed him to the Steinway, where he sat on the long bench and motioned me to join him. "What's your speed?"

I assumed he was not talking Duke Ellington. "Beethoven," I mumbled. "A little Chopin."

"You take the left hand." He plunged into the "Moonlight Sonata." His hands were surprisingly small, with long slender fingers.

I went along for some eight bars before he stopped. "Not bad, Mr. President. Who's your agent?" Our brief duet, I discovered later, put me in the company of Eugene List, Victor Borge and Jack Benny.

One of the novelists was at Truman's elbow. "Could I trouble you for a photograph, Mr. President?"

"No trouble at all." The rest of us tagged along to the book-crammed presidential study, where we lined up like schoolboys for personally inscribed head close-ups of the seventy-nine-year-old former Chief Executive; the portrait studies—square-jawed, resolute, statesmanlike, in contrast to our host's affable accessibility—were the nearest intimations of vanity I could detect in Truman.

Next we were whisked a few blocks to the Truman Museum, its lobby graced by an eloquent 32-foot mural, "Independence and the Opening of the West," by Missouri-born Thomas Hart Benton. Darting among the documents, photographs, replicas and other memorabilia of the presidency, Truman rattled off typically pungent commentaries:

"One thing we're trying to do here is to make Americans more aware of their history. If you don't know history, you don't know anything."

Before a huge display of weaponry: "Governments change, styles change. But you can't change human nature."

Under a photo of the famous premature Chicago *Daily Tribune* headline, DEWEY DEFEATS TRUMAN:

"Every editor in America thought he knew more about running the country than I did."

Truman had never quite captivated the press—or manipulated it—like his predecessor. But his blunt honesty was respected. Eisenhower would be remembered in the press room as the great delegator, Nixon for his blatant hostility (heartily reciprocated), Kennedy for his charm, Lyndon Johnson for his brutal domineering. Gerry Ford would register as an amiable passerby, Jimmy Carter as a fanatic for details, and Ronald Reagan as a man in perpetual retreat from confrontation.

Truman made it plain that he harbored no rancor. Editors were only human; honest men doing a tough job.

Then it was time for business. Truman talked the way he walked: with a brisk no-nonsense self-assurance that never crossed the line into arrogance. He was a willing, interested listener. The goal of the TV series was not merely to create a documentary record of historical events, but to illuminate the internal conflicts of the national leader at the center of each storm, the personal values that shaped his decisions. The format would lean heavily on straight-from-the-shoulder, undiluted Truman, framed and balanced by careful background narration.

For the MacArthur segment, I had already read everything the producers could get their hands on about Truman's attitudes concerning the presidency, the military, obedience and constitutional precedents; pursuing those issues with the man himself, I asked a lot of questions. Truman didn't hedge on the answers. Less bombastic than many a Hollywood tycoon, he made it clear that he had fired MacArthur in 1951 for repeatedly defying the instructions of the general's commander-in-chief, thereby risking a third world war: "The sonofabitch thought he was bigger than the republic!"

Next I plotted a story structure that would build suspense from the unique perspective of the Oval Office. For visual variety I used maps and stock footage, supplemented by offbeat touches like a ceramic caricature of General MacArthur.

Last came the words. Each episode had to be fully scripted, in language that would be comfortable for Truman if he cared to use it, and still leave him elbow room to expand. Unlike some successors who could scarcely recite their names without a cue card, Truman was an instinctive ad libber, an independent spirit who didn't really care for scripts. But he was speaking for history, about complex events; he had to be kept reasonably on track. The idea was to give him enough printed text to keep him from going off course, without undermining his wonderful spontaneity. Wherever possible, I tried to preserve his peppery idiom.

My second show, *Reluctant Ally*, invoked the *pas de deux* between Truman and Josef Stalin over the long-stalled Russian invasion of Manchuria. The American president needed the attack to save American lives; but he didn't want to precipitate "another Berlin" over the post-war occupation of Tokyo. Coming to grips on the issue with the Soviet dictator at Potsdam, he told me, was "like wrestling with an octopus." Who could improve upon that?

A few months later shooting on the series began, and Truman commuted regularly to New York, going before the camera for three hours in the morning and a couple more in the afternoon. As anticipated, like a Method actor he improvised in places, trimming or embellishing the script. But nobody tried to pin him down to slavish accuracy. This wasn't Marlon Brando or Tony Perkins taking occasional liberties; it was the thirty-third president of the United States.

The loose collaboration worked, beyond expectations. The New York *Post*, reviewing the MacArthur opener, hailed Truman's "pungent, forthright, highly personalized" approach; the *Daily News*, no friend of New Dealers, declared that regardless of a viewer's political leanings, the program could "only be applauded as a rich, human slice of history . . . a memorable half-hour." This was not the mindless television I had inveighed against ten years earlier; it was television in the Murrow manner. The series was still being cited in 1995 in a revisionist appraisal of Hiroshima.

Murrow—or rather our mutual regard for him—had been a factor smoothing my path with Truman. During the Hollywood dickerings for *Cast A Giant Shadow*, Murrow had been constantly supportive. I sensed a certain deference on his part to my years of experience in print journalism; even at the height of his fame, Murrow was self-conscious about his own headlong leap from an educational foundation into broadcasting. Keenly interested in the movie adaption of *Cast A Giant Shadow*, upon learning of the early MGM plans he had volunteered his intervention to "shorten the lead time." Later, when Mel Shavelson announced his acquisition of the book, Ed warned that the transfer to the screen would require a very sensitive director. His next comment was wry and not a little prophetic: "The Hollywood boys will probably foul it up; but that after all is their habit."

Before undertaking the Truman assignment, acting on word from Murrow that he would "welcome a visit," I dropped in at his USIA office in Washington.

No novice in propaganda, Murrow had taken the post with the express understanding that he would be included in all major decisions, underlining a reality that he and I had often discussed: the unwillingness or inability of politicians to realize that the content of a policy, especially in a democracy, was more important than its verbal costume. Brave words could never save an untenable action.

Murrow was at his desk in the middle of a cavernous room. Surrounded by bustling messengers, he looked a little peaked, the aftermath of a bout of pleurisy. But his eyes were bright and his manner chipper. The most visible change was in his dress. The natty, immaculately tailored sports jacket, once the trademark of the ex-country boy from Washington State, had given way to the anonymous dark blue uniform of bureaucracy.

I looked around. "This is quite a set-up."

"As desk jobs go, it's a beaut."

"But you miss getting out in the field?"

A wry smile. "Don't we all?" He turned to face me. "What's going on with Mickey Marcus?"

"Agents, lawyers, stars. The only firm cast we have is the Israeli army."

"Unless the Arabs attack." He gestured toward a wall map across the room. "See peace breaking out anywhere?"

"What do you know about Vietnam?" I asked. The United States had just expanded its ground forces in Indo-China.

"Not much. And what I do know I don't like."

"Bowles has been flashing a red light there for years."

"Brother Chet's been sent on a long flight to Africa. He's in mid-air and a lot of hawks on the Hill would like him to stay there."

"Do you think we're headed for trouble?"

"No." He picked up a sheaf of teletypes. "We're *in* trouble. Up to our asses in French commitments."

I mentioned my upcoming series with Truman, to whom he had gone for advice in the late 1950s when urged by New York State Democrats and the city's Liberal Party to run for the U.S. Senate. Truman had discouraged the move, saying Ed would be "more useful on camera, than in camera."

Murrow leaned back nostalgically. "A helluva guy, little Harry. We could use him around here now."

We chatted for a while about mutual friends and the New York theater—Murrow had been a promising college actor—until a red-headed secretary appeared. "They're waiting for you upstairs, Mr. Murrow."

Murrow walked with me to the door. "Have a good summer, Brother Ted. And a good movie!"

In the fall of 1963 Murrow was once again hospitalized, this time more ominously, for removal of his left lung. From New York, where the Truman-MacArthur segment was being filmed, I sent Ed this report on his good friend "little Harry":

> I find Truman pretty irresistible. He cannot conceal his loathing for MacArthur, and tends to wind up each take with a muttered, "I should have fired the sonofabitch then and there!"
>
> Today on the set he was regaling me with broad winks and asides. He displayed no temperament whatever—rather a humility that would bar him from any consideration for the Screen Actors Guild.
>
> He opined that Ed Murrow is a "grand fella" who "better get well fast—we need him." Amen.

Murrow, seriously ill but stubbornly droll, replied in a few weeks that he had just thanked Harry Truman for a letter sent to him in the hospital: "This shows I did not discriminate against you by getting these words off so late."

A month later, in January of 1964, Murrow resigned from the government, the decline in his health matched by that in his political fortunes. He had never been granted the inside track to Kennedy that had been promised. Ever since the Bay of Pigs landing by Cuban exiles in April, 1961, which he and Bowles had strenuously opposed, his star had been on the wane. He had been much disturbed by press developments in Vietnam that had eerie overtones of the George Polk case. Homer Bigart, who had been one of George's outspoken comrades in Athens, joined David Halberstam in charging manipulation of the news by the American military.

In his last letter to me, from his farm in Pawling where he was battling the aftermaths of skull surgery and radiation treatment, he let a glimmer of reality slip past the gallant façade. The "mending" was slow. He not only had no immediate plans for going to New York but "would be happy" if he could limit future trips to one or two a year.

That was on August 18, 1964. In mid-September, at Madrid airport on a European vacation, I ran into a long-faced Charles Collingwood. "Brother Ed is very low," he said. The following spring, Ed Murrow was dead.

By that time Chet Bowles was back at his old embassy post in New Delhi, after undergoing a protracted siege at the hub of power. He had joined the Kennedy camp as chief foreign affairs adviser nearly a year before the 1960 nominating convention; as he explained to me in New York, he had preferred Hubert Humphrey but didn't think Humphrey could win. The country was at a crucial crossroads; Kennedy was young, articulate and courageous, with a strong potential for growing.

After Kennedy's election, Chet was the logical choice for Secretary of State, except for the familiar bugaboo: he was controversial, the bête noire of powerful forces in Congress and industry. So he quietly accepted the role of Senior Undersecretary, deliberately bowing out of the limelight.

But it soon became obvious that his differences with the staid, methodical Secretary were not only deep but irreconcilable. Dean Rusk took an almost reverential view of the State Department as a sacred institution not subject to tampering; for Bowles it was simply an instrument of policy, grown rusty through isolation and misuse.

The friction between the two came to a head over the Bay of Pigs fiasco, a CIA stratagem inherited from the Eisenhower administration. Although Bowles and Murrow were both left out of the planning "loop," they were alerted by newspaper leaks to what Bowles called the upcoming "Cuban adventure," and both registered strong protests. Bowles submitted a memo denouncing the maneuver on both moral and practical grounds, arguing that it would break our non-violence commitment to the Organization of American States, and had no better than a one in three chance of military success. Rusk never relayed the memo to the White House.

The failure to dislodge Fidel Castro was a humiliation for the Administration, and it brought the military solution advocates, notably Bobby Kennedy and Vice-president Lyndon Johnson, into the lists against Bowles, who had committed the crime of being right. Pressure piled up for his resignation; but despite a conspicuous lack of backing from the president, Bowles refused to disappear.

During this trying period I had several letters from him. They made no mention of the internal wrangling at State, but focused mainly on the quicksand he felt was engulfing us in southeast Asia.

Meanwhile, I had a sharp reminder of Chet's earlier influence on his home terrain. Jackie Robinson, the baseball star, had been active in the Bowles push for civil rights in Connecticut, which embraced not only integration of the National Guard but legislation assuring every citizen the right to buy a house, eat in a restaurant, or have an equal opportunity for a job anywhere in the state.

In the fall of 1962, Robinson was called to appear at a televised session of a House committee investigating race relations. To the dismay of several members, he refused to take persistent hints that he should melt in gratitude at his own success, or to dismiss the evidence of continuing blatant discrimination. The fact that he had managed, in one limited area, to surmount racial barriers, did not mean the barriers weren't still there holding back millions of others.

He declined also to condemn the apostasy of Paul Robeson, who had declared a preference for the Soviet Union. Although he disagreed with Robeson's position, he made it plain that in his eyes the treatment to which the great singer had been subjected in the United States had been cruel and crippling enough to explain almost any degree of reaction. Throughout the questioning Robinson maintained a calm dignity, neither obsequious nor truculent.

I found myself strangely moved, replaying in my mind the whole kaleidoscope of my own oscillating responses to color differences: the first awareness, dating back to school days, of the disparaging Yiddish epithet "schwartze," referring to blacks; the shock of my first visit to Harlem, its high-rent hovels and angry roving gangs; my rage in the 1930s at Al Jolson, the erstwhile blackface minstrel singer, for trying to keep blacks out of his precious San Fernando Valley; my own flashes of home-bred intolerance in Egypt, among dark-skinned neighbors; my scribbled notebook memo about the appeal of a sleeping black child on a Madison Avenue bus: "Why do we find him so cute as a baby, and deny him our warmth as he grows up?" I thought of the black women I had bedded, not always nobly, sometimes exploiting their economic disadvantage, and of the bigots I had known: the nurse I was dating from Texas who staged a minor riot at New York's Café Society when the manager had the temerity to seat a black party between us and the stage; the WASP movie writer who in 1958 hissed his rejection of the up-and-coming novelist James Baldwin—"a Negro homosexual!"—as though no lower category of human being could be imagined.

If mine was a muddy, inconsistent record, at least I had the sense to recognize a clear one. I went to my typewriter and sent Robinson a brief appreciation of his stand.

His reply gave me a terrific charge. He did not know, Robinson wrote, when a letter had made him "feel as good." He was glad to count me among the "many decent people" who, sharing his grave concerns on the subject, had reinforced his confidence before the congressional committee on race relations. Although a role in politics was not on his personal agenda, he had total faith in Chet Bowles.

Before the end of 1962 Bowles accepted a shift—a demotion, really—to the role of Kennedy's "special adviser for Asia, Africa and Latin America." He logged 80,000 miles in missions to twenty-nine countries—and returned to find his thoughtful recommendations shelved. At long last he opted to return to India, where instead of playing a lonely King Canute trying to hold back global tides, he could at least confine his efforts to familiar shores.

Once retired in the 1970s, Chet resumed regular touch with me from Essex. Actually getting together was another matter. As veteran sailing buffs he and Steb made long and frequent cruises on their seventy-two-foot schooner, and I had as little taste for sea travel as they did for New York.

Then Chet's robust frame fell victim to Parkinson's disease. After that, communication from Connecticut dwindled to an annual Christmas card, always an intimate photo with the patriarch surrounded by a swarm of children (five) and grandchildren (eleven). The last word I had from Essex was relayed by Ann Sperber, Ed Murrow's biographer. Seeking an interview with Bowles for her book in 1982, Ann was regretfully informed by Steb that Chet's ailment had afflicted and virtually throttled his vocal cords; but she and Chet would appreciate it if Ann would convey to me their "very warm regards."

When Chet died a few years later, I was in far-off Santa Barbara. I felt a profound sense of loss, for the nation as well as for myself, much as I had at Ed Murrow's passing. Both men had gravitated hopefully to the Kennedy White House; both committed the lover's fallacy, so familiar to me, of pinning an idealized image onto a flawed human being. Murrow, the veteran reporter, always took the Camelot myth with a grain of salt; Bowles was the more disillusioned because he had harbored more illusions.

With characteristic generosity, Bowles argues in his memoir *Promises to Keep* that Jack Kennedy was growing steadily and that if he had lived he would probably have pulled back from Vietnam and become an outstanding president. We'll never know. What seems more certain, however, is that Bowles himself, had we had the wisdom to follow Harry Truman's advice and elect him president, would have steered us—and probably the world—in a very different direction. But in 1960 the American public, its mental processes half-paralyzed by a long decade of television, was already drifting into an era of image-making, shallow rhetoric, and a penchant for shadow over substance.

My second trip to Spain, in the fall of 1964, was pure delight. Andalusia in the south, where Christian, Moorish and Jewish strains mingled in exuberant union, overflowed with the most spontaneous music-making I have ever experienced. In the heart of Cordoba, at a tiny tavern no bigger than a Nedick's orange stand in New York, I had my first taste of flamenco: no trumpets, no castanets, only the wild piercing cries and stamping feet of a half-dozen male patrons, hurling themselves across the floor with passionate intensity, fingers snapping, heels clacking out the rhythm. Without a single instrument, they whipped up the emotional storm of a Brahms symphony.

Beckoned into their circle, I stayed for a long afternoon with my two hosts, local university professors. They taught me the lyrics of their flamenco ode on the death of the beloved matador Manolete. I still have our supper menu from El Caballo Rojo, and their souvenir postcards extravagantly inscribed in Spanish to "the most simpatico of North Americans, with admiration and respect."

Waiting back home was a letter from Sam Boal, an old *Mirror* buddy who had won a wide readership during World War II as the London-based columnist for the New York *Post*, chronicling the impressions of a mythical charwoman. Sam's proudest possession was a letter from Ernest Hemingway saying "I wish I could write letters like you." From Edmonton, Alaska, where he was doing a piece for *Playboy*, Sam sent me this one:

> There are no girls in Alberta. They are shipped South in mid-November. Seems they freeze anyway, like exposed water pipes, and eat up what tiny scraps of pemmican, blubber and ptarmigan we can flush from the "bush."
>
> However, the fellows in the barber shop were talking with great ribaldry of an Eskimo village to the north. I may mush on up and whistle at the girls outside the corner Walgreen igloo. I have bought some glass beads and bright pieces of calico, and I may make a score.

Sam, a nonstop smoker, was suffocated in 1964 when he fell asleep on a sofa with a cigarette in his hand.

Another chum cruising into view was Gerold Frank, a large-scale will-o'-the-wisp who since Middle East days had been dipping in and out of my life as a fellow-correspondent, *Coronet* editor, and replacement on Sheilah's *Beloved Infidel*. Gerry's talent for creeping into the psyches of his female subjects, including Zsa Zsa Gabor, had won him a huge close-up on the cover of *Life*. I had elicited, for some editorial suggestions the flyleaf inscription "To Ted, the best friend a ghost ever had."

Gerry was a shy, elusive man with an indecisive manner so pervasive that it created for me the assumption of a flabby physical presence; I was astonished, when we swam at the pool of a mutual friend in Westchester, to see him clip through the water powerfully, with a big well-muscled body.

Gerry's prose was fluid, graceful, smooth as instant-shaving cream. Unlike Meyer Levin, whose faith in his own gifts was exhilarating, Gerry seemed always to be trembling on the brink of self-abandonment. In the 1970s he dismissed a huge advance to write his autobiography: "I can't remember anything—and I don't like the guy!"

For many years, Gerry lived on the upper West Side—and in a constant quandary. His friends could count on plaintive phone calls during which he would read aloud an opening paragraph—then two or three alternatives. And what about this new idea he had for an ending? Too short? Not strong enough? Whatever the answer, it was subject to further change on his galley proofs, to which he clung desperately before surrendering them to the finality of the printer.

Indecision was a way of life for Gerry. He once submitted for my scrutiny the new letterhead on his personal stationery—too large? immodest?—correctly surmising that I would some day cite this rather endearing eccentricity in my memoirs.

After *Beloved Infidel*, Gerry sought my counsel. He had written a dozen books, seven of which had made the best-seller lists. Yet his "soul" cried out to do the unwritten book that was "in him."

I knew what story was gyrating in the back of Gerry Frank's mind, and so did he: the 1944 assassination in Cairo of Lord Moyne, the British Minister of State in the Middle East, by two young Jewish terrorists, members of the extremist Stern Gang. It was undeniably murder, yet murder by a pair of genuine idealists, desperate to call the world's attention to the suffering of their people . . . an intricate many-sided drama loaded with moral contradictions. Could Gerry—or anybody—bring it off, make the killers understandable if not sympathetic?

He could, I assured Gerry. And he had to—whether or not his previous readers approved, because clearly the story was burning a hole in his gut.

Gerry skipped into his familiar ballet: yes, no, maybe, but, if . . . A few others, notably Meyer Levin, added their urging, and Gerry finally took the plunge. He emerged with *The Deed*, his most powerful, riveting work, soberly appraised by the *New Yorker* as "sad, sanguinary and touching."

For a new friend I had Hal Lehrman, who presided over a country hideaway in Brewster, New York that was the ideal week-end retreat for me and my ladies of the moment. At this point, with most of my friends married and bachelorhood growing tedious, I had decided it was time to take another look at more enduring arrangements. But I took the precaution of confining my search to women in whom, whatever their allure and accomplishments, I could sense a reassuring turbulence underneath. The unconscious is a powerful tenant.

CHAPTER 18

Sabra

My return to the Middle East for *Cast A Giant Shadow* had signaled, appropriately enough, an end to a long period of Mosaic wanderings. Once escaped from the anonymous money mill of Hollywood to the self-sufficient individualism of the publishing world, I did not intend to slide back. But Mickey Marcus was the quintessential tough act to follow; and I was a stranger on literary terrain.

Max Rosenberg, brandishing vague promises, lured me into a couple of speculative film treatments: a World War II spy story, the Henry James novel *Portrait of a Lady*. He then squared accounts somewhat by a paid assignment on *Sex and the Teenager*, a typical Rosenberg blend of "sociological statement" and titillating box-office; despite tie-ins with several prominent European directors, it never got to the starting gate.

Turning to music, I proposed a television special, "Orpheus in America," celebrating the remarkable tour of the United States in 1877 by Jacques Offenbach, for which I would create new English lyrics set to the French composer's bouncy operetta tunes. Joe Cates read a couple of samples, gushed his admiration—and two days later sent the whole package back: "Too highbrow for the boob tube."

I had dinner in Greenwich Village with a pale, solemn Japanese woman named Yoko Ono. Not yet associated with John Lennon, she took me to her loft in Chambers Street, where she played several records of her own compositions: melodically limp, lyrically insipid. She then led me to a concept-art "happening," in which a stack of papers were set ablaze onstage. The audience applauded wildly. (In 1991 Yoko returned to "performance art," hammering a cloth-covered vase to smithereens at the Whitney Museum).

Would my epitaph be that of a restless dabbler, the best lyricist among foreign correspondents, the best jazzman in the Screen Writers Guild? To my agent, who sent me a list of television-series producers hungry for writers, I replied in a note:

> If, at this stage, the best I can do with the accumulated years of insight and craftsmanship is bondage to the electric monster, I should go back

> to policy-level government work, where I could take some active part in the world rather than join in lulling it to sleep.

My next stop, however, was a kind of delaying action with a giant of the corporate circuit, International Telephone and Telegraph. A veteran movie-maker of my acquaintance had a contract with ITT to produce a global film embracing its philosophy, structure and multitudinous subsidiaries. I would have access to key executives, staff meetings and plants, as well as employees in a half-dozen European capitals.

The proposal offered a rare chance to penetrate the inner workings of the corporate world—as remote to me then as an alien planet—and also the miniature electronic universe being created by microchip technology.

Although little equipped to appreciate it, I had a preview of the upcoming communications revolution and the changes that led up to the Internet: improved sensitivity in electronic components; space vehicle transponders capable of handling 1200 simultaneous telephone connections; complete electronic circuits embedded in hundreds of tiny chips broken down from silicon wafers.

Easier for me to grasp in the months of travel was the subtle, serpentine exercise of corporate power, how the alleged meddling of ITT in Chilean internal politics could become the subject of an investigation by the House Foreign Affairs Committee.

What made ITT run was not so much ruthlessness as total detachment; it lived in an environment of bottom-line figures, not people. The blessings it delivered were real, but incidental; sales called the tune. I have never been able to understand why a senior vice-president who markets his mind to a boss he despises is hailed at testimonial dinners, while a woman who does the same thing with her body (perhaps at the behest of said vice-president) is condemned as a social outcast.

ITT president Harold Geneen, an expressionless ex-accountant, ruled his cowed cohorts with all the charm and consideration of a medieval caliph. I saw Geneen several times, in his office and in solitary repose on the beach at Cape Cod, a strange, lonely man, a chilling symbol of life at the top in corporate America.

Somewhere around this time I at last had, or thought I had, a worthy biographical subject: Judy Holliday.

Dazzling was the word for Judy. The night I first met her at a small gathering on New York's West Side she overwhelmed the room, a tall commanding presence striding across the floor in spiked heels, her crown of blonde hair swept dramatically back. That was in the late 1940s, a couple of years after she had crashed through the Broadway barriers as Billie Dawn in *Born Yesterday*.

More than a decade later, with star billing behind Judy in the musical *Bells are Ringing*, we were both guests at a splashy party on Long Island given by Joe Levine, a prosperous film distributor and friend of Max Rosenberg. Perhaps both put off by the setting—overdressed producers, underdressed screen hopefuls, noisy agents—we exchanged friendly knowing smiles. Judy had an affinity for musicians; she had been married to a clarinetist, and long involved with Gerry Mulligan, the baritone sax master. When I drifted over to the piano and started doodling, she came to sit beside me. We chatted, a pair of political lefties momentarily stranded in Republican territory. By the end of the evening I had her phone number, and an invitation to call her at the cavernous old Dakota Apartments on Central Park West.

I didn't know quite what to do with it. If I was impressed by Judy's golden aura, I was absolutely stunned by her talents. She could do things with a song that other performers never even conceived of. Betty Comden and Adolph Green, to whom Ernie Martin had compared Rafe and me, had showered her with lush material in *Bells*; she had enriched it immeasurably by her impeccable phrasing, satiric nuances, and lightning shifts of mood. Judy could belt out a knock-'em-dead chorus that ended in a timid, catch-in-the-throat whisper. Her merry laughter trembled on the brink of a tear; she had the hint of vulnerability within strength that some saw as the key to John Wayne's appeal. There were echoes of Chaplin's genius in Judy, and of Edith Piaf's street-waif heartbreak.

Cautiously, I called. At dinner with Judy in Greenwich Village I felt like a jumpy teenager, acutely conscious of the stares following us. Who was I to be squiring this queen of Broadway—who had also, it turned out, just written the book and lyrics for a musical? "That," said Judy, "was the easy part."

"What's the hard part?"

"Showing it. Doing the songs for an audition."

I reared back. "But you've had so much experience, Judy! You're the luckiest thing that ever happened to a song!"

"I throw up a lot before going onstage. And that's with other people's stuff."

"And with your own?"

"I'm twice as nervous." She stared up gloomily at the ceiling. "Why can't I be like Jule Styne? (Styne had done the music for *Bells*.) Nothing bothers the man. When he sits down at the piano to show off his stuff, he positively revels in it. So he's half-way home with an audience before he starts."

"He's a little guy with a nothing voice. What's he got that you haven't?"

"Confidence." She picked up a menu. "Let's eat."

More dinners followed, and an occasional visit to the theater; shy of public recognition, Judy preferred out-of-the-way places. I played the studiously circumspect suitor, the formal gentleman-caller out of Tennessee Williams's *Glass Menagerie*. I could rail and sneer at the star system like any other social critic, but getting its impact out of my own gut after decades of worshipful absorption was another matter. Once I was subjected to cautious inspection by Judy's mother: "Show him your mink," she commanded. Judy obliged with a dutiful twirl.

Actually our whole relationship was a stately minuet, the distance accentuated on my side by my adulatory posture and on hers, I suspect, by awareness of her deteriorating health. According to the biography of Judy pieced together in 1982 by Gary Carey, she had suffered a throat tumor in the early 1960s, followed by a mastectomy and then throat cancer. None of this ever entered her conversation, other than a rare impatient reference to her doctor's "double-talk."

The subtle, unspoken element that sparked our meetings was a mutual sense of frustration. Each glimpsed in the other a kindred spirit who, despite acknowledged attainments, was starved for recognition in other areas privately considered of more importance. We were both bursting to show off our songs—mine from *Nellie*, hers from the musical in progress—but fearful of a negative response. Despite Judy's constant encouragement—"You play better than he does," she would assure me as we listened to a Village cocktail pianist—when at long last I was persuaded to run through "Let's Make History" at her home, I stumbled over the chords, stammered the lyrics, and thoroughly ruined the piece. She in turn several times seemed tempted to share her creations, but always at the last moment pulled back.

Gradually changes crept into Judy's appearance: pallor, puffy cheeks, added weight. The weekend came when she had to cancel a date, then the day when the phone was answered by her mother; Judy was in the hospital "for tests." From the tone of the older woman's voice, I knew her daughter was seriously ill. I knew also that a door was being firmly closed; further communication would not be welcome.

At 3 a.m. on June 7, 1965, Milton Rosenstock, who had been the orchestra conductor on *Bells are Ringing* and was one of Judy's closest confidantes, awoke in terrible pain. It was the hour of her passing at the age of forty-three. Rosenstock was one of a half-dozen people I spoke to in seeking clues to Judy's life. I felt that the world had lost a woman of value, who like Sylvia Fine Kaye long afterward, had died with her deepest potential unrealized.

I took my notes to Lee Barker at Doubleday. He shook his head. Judy was too special a subject, he intimated; not a fan-magazine goddess, a national icon.

Nearly two decades later the biography by Carey appeared. I learned that Judy had rung up an IQ of a staggering 172; also that she and her mother had been deserted by her father when she was quite small.

But Carey's book was sadly superficial, largely a rewrite of published interviews. It had little original source material and less insight into Judy's complex personality.

I still think Lee Barker was wrong. No doubt I was motivated in part by a strong personal identification with Judy's sense of gifts unappreciated. But her story, like her talent, was unique; it deserved to be told.

"What about Oscar Wilde?" The suggestion came from Meyer Levin's novelist wife, Tereska Torres. Raised in France, Tereska had a birdlike charm, a mischievous smile and a taste for sexual improvisation. "Fascinating character, intriguing background."

"Everybody's done the guy," I objected. But I agreed to take a look.

I looked at Wilde, and what I found was his sometime verbal sparring partner, James McNeill Whistler: Bohemian painter, pocket Casanova, expelled from West Point and expatriate from America, a waspish, unpredictable rebel among rebels. It was Whistler, I recalled, who with a careless bon mot had drawn from Wilde the envious comment "I wish I'd said that!"—and who had promptly nailed the plagiary-prone poet with the crusher, "You will, Oscar, you will!"

Other than that, I was familiar only with Whistler's celebrated portrait of his mother, a staple of sentimental greeting cards. Surely a man of such fiery wit would also have put his studio to less conventional use?

He certainly had. A few museum visits and some reconnoitering of library shelves revealed a wide range of drawings, etchings and oils, among which I was particularly struck by Whistler's delicate, faintly Oriental "Twilights" of the Thames.

His feuds alone, punctuating his history, confirmed my hunch of an irresistible subject. This was a man whose tempestuous life, with its defiant arrogance on behalf of artistic integrity, would stretch any writer's capacities. But because of Whistler's deliberate theatricality, his grandiose poses, the book would have to be written from the inside. Only a biographical novel, with authorial freedom to range through the byways of thought processes, could illuminate such a character.

I took my theory, and a brief outline, to Doubleday. This time Barker was willin'.

We had barely signed contracts in June of 1967 when, 8,000 miles away, Gamal Abdel Nasser of Egypt closed the strait of Tiran at the southeast tip of the Sinai Desert, choking off Israeli access to the Red Sea, and moved nearly 100,000 troops across the sand toward the border of the Jewish state.

Israel hit back, with a devastating preemptive air attack. Six days later Nasser and his Arab allies writhed in defeat: burned-out Egyptian tanks strewn across the dunes, Syrian snipers blasted from their strongholds on the Golan Heights, the West Bank of the Jordan overrun by Zionist forces, the Old City of Jerusalem wrested back from the crack professionals of Jordan's Arab Legion. The Israelis had learned well from Mickey Marcus: outnumbered and outgunned, they had gambled everything on leadership and morale, superbly coordinated in a swift pulverizing blow.

A jaded world gasped at the miracle. How could a relative handful of amateur fighters bring off such a coup?

And how, incoming voices on my telephone demanded, could the biographer of Colonel Marcus fail to explore these questions and report his findings? The query was thrust at me in a dozen calls from friends, relatives, readers.

I had a prior commitment, I explained. Still, willy-nilly, a format for a second Israeli book began to suggest itself. *Cast A Giant Shadow* had been the biography of one extraordinary man; this was an opportunity to do the biography of a whole nation, to convey its essence through portraits of sharply defined individuals, from ambulance drivers to generals, caught under the microscopic lens of war.

David Holtzmann's son Eddie, a lawyer with Harper and Row, mentioned my notion to his boss, Harriet Pilpel. Pilpel invited me in for a chat, then set up a meeting with Harper editorial chief Evan Thomas, son of the veteran socialist leader Norman Thomas. Evan read my three-page outline and nodded. When could I start?

As I pointed out to Lee Barker, Whistler had already waited sixty-odd years for the resurrection I planned; another few months would not make much difference. Lee had no objection to extending my deadline. Within the week I was installed at the Tel Aviv Hilton, armed with a tape recorder, an old address book, and high hopes.

This was a more demanding research project than *Cast A Giant Shadow*. Surely there was no dearth of stories here—but how to unearth them? With swarms of other writers from many nations mining the same hills, taxing the resources of a government press office understandably more concerned with security than with processing information, I would be thrown back on reportorial skills long grown rusty.

Most of the people involved with my previous Marcus labors greeted me like an old friend. Ex-tank commander Chaim Laskov did not. "Talk to Dayan," he said brusquely. Had he lost close comrades in the fighting? Did he regard me as an interloper, a vulture feasting on the sorrows of others? Was I in fact exploiting the sacrifices of better men?

I brooded, but only briefly, on these issues. I was a writer, in Israel to develop a concept which, if brought to proper fruition, might advance the world's understanding and acceptance of the Jewish state.

However, even the most obliging of my army sources were of little immediate help. Freewheeling improvisers in battle, they floundered in the bureaucratic puddles of peacetime.

So I buttonholed taxi drivers, secretaries, hotel porters, looking for leads, grasping at straws. My lucky straw turned out to be a hospital orderly who knew Lt. Karni Bilu, the twenty-one-year-old personal aide to Mota Gur, paratroop conqueror of Jerusalem's Old City. Karni was plump, vivacious and immensely bright, the daughter of two 1948 underground fighters. She led me not only to the colorful Colonel Gur but to David "Dudu" Sela, a paratrooper-concert cellist who refused to give up after a shell from an Egyptian tank ripped his body apart and reduced both hands to lumps of twisted flesh. Thanks to a team of five surgeons—and his own indomitable spirit—Dudu would be touring the United States with a chamber ensemble in 1969.

I soon stumbled into a brief Berkman-as-Dayan period. In the crowded alleyways of Jerusalem's Old City I acquired an eye infection, and after its treatment a black eye patch of the kind romanticized by the swashbuckling Israeli general. For several days, despite my protestations I basked in the sympathetic glances and attentive courtesies accorded a war hero.

Gradually I pieced together a network of tipsters, and began lining up candidates for interviews: a typical tank crew, all in their early twenties, mingling lean "Orientals" of Yemenite descent with "Mayflower family" kibbutzniks; a skinny bespectacled Orthodox youth credited with capturing a Syrian command post; a tiny volunteer nurse, savior of a score of wounded men at Jerusalem's Ammunition Hill, who as a child had seen both parents executed by German occupiers in Italy; an idealistic economics professor, survivor of the Warsaw ghetto, who although physically ineligible for military service had chosen to defend his family and, untrained in the ways of war, had fallen prey at a border lookout post to a Jordanian sharpshooter.

For paradox it was hard to top Mota Gur. His impetuous foray into the Old City had restored Solomon's Western Wall to Jewry. Yet the rugged paratroop commander was a sometime teacher whose chief delight was to spin Snoopy-like tales for playground children, an existentialist philosopher who forbade his troops to speak disparagingly of the Arab people. A week after his victory, with his name still ringing in the air, a shirt-sleeved Gur stood patiently in line with me outside a popular Tel Aviv restaurant, unwilling to claim special attention. I tried to imagine De Gaulle, after the liberation of Paris, hanging back from the maître d' at Maxim's.

To complete my coverage, I ferreted out a wife's eye view of Yitzchak Rabin. My one-time helicopter guide over the Tel Aviv-Jerusalem highway had by 1967 become Israeli Chief of Staff, with an eye cocked on political ascendancy. My own choice for national leadership would have been the more flexible, imaginative Gur or Ezer Weizmann, the British-born architect of the audacious air attack. Mota did become top man in the army, and like Weizmann was later elected to the Knesset or Parliament, where both opposed the militance of the expansionist "Greater Israel" factions. But although Weizmann ultimately won the ceremonial post of president, as a die-hard individualist neither could make the compromises or the calculated maneuvers that build political machines.

Unknown to me at the time, a press hero of the Six-Day War had been the erratic and peripatetic Serge Fliegers. I had last seen Serge during my ITT research in Paris, where I watched him rattling coconut shells to mimic horses' hooves as he delivered a stirring "on-the-scene" broadcast account of a military parade. A year later he lay in a Tel Aviv hospital, battered survivor of an Arab ambush that killed two fellow-newsmen.

I came away from Israel with a renewed sense of respect for a remarkable people, stirred to the point where I wondered whether, in failing to follow my impulse to join a kibbutz in 1945, I had not made a mistake. The young field workers I had encountered then on a visit from Cairo were traveling by bus for their vacation in a neighboring settlement, no coins jangling in their pockets but a lusty song on their lips. They had seemed the personification of happiness, molders of a society where, without the taint or pressure of money, true brotherhood might be possible. I suspect that this sense of a vision betrayed spurred my later bitterness when the drumbeaters of the extreme right came into power in Israel, hawking their message of Biblical redemption.

I had had some contact with the less frenetic Orthodox citizenry, a number of whom distinguished themselves in fighting for Jerusalum. They differed from their more secular compatriots in their somber dress, their highly concentrated family life, and their devotion to the Talmud, the only source they would consider for the education of their children. Many of them had a serenity and apparent contentment that struck me as enviable. But although I was aware of occasional fierce outbursts of religious dogma from fringe groups, in 1967 I heard no serious claim that the Orthodox and they alone held the only keys to truth, that God had committed exclusively to their custody large slices of real estate now occupied by other people, or that any deviation from their path would be denounced as treason to the entire Jewish people.

Returning to New York, I ran into an upheaval common in the publishing industry. Evan Thomas had departed from Harper to take over the reins at a rival house.

Incoming chiefs were notoriously hostile to commitments made by their predecessors. As I entered the office of the new managing editor, he sat scowling at a map of the Middle East. "Just where," he wanted to know, "is Jordan?" It was not a promising augury. Nor was I reassured by his judgment on my opening chapters: "No problem with the writing. But interest in the subject is fading." He would ponder publication.

The young editor originally assigned to shepherd my manuscript came up with an idea. Suppose, suggested Judy Sklar Raminsky, I reorganized my episodes and character vignettes around the framework of the war's six days, a chapter for each day, starting with the aerial blitz on Day One?

It was a classically simple, abundantly fertile notion, needing only some jigsaw-puzzle shuffling to make it work. I sketched a new outline, opening on a supersonic pilot skimming in a dawn run over the Mediterranean on June 5, and closing with an emotional scene at the Temple Mount in Jerusalem, where Mota Gur's paratroopers reassembled, gaping holes in their ranks, for a reunion, in Karni Bilu's words, of "the entire brigade, the living and the dead."

The managing editor swallowed, cleared his throat, and withdrew his objections.

I called my book *Sabra*, the Hebrew term for the native-born Israeli, who, like the local sabra cactus, is said to conceal beneath a prickly exterior a tender succulent core. Introducing "a new breed of Jew, hardened by border clashes, educated to a different understanding of his people's history and his role in the world," it was well received, *Publishers Weekly* sounding the keynote: "An affecting, sometimes too painful look at the ordinary Israeli whom love of country has made larger than life. Berkman has a flair for the fast, vivid vignette." Max Lerner, resident sage at the New York *Post*, endorsed it in his syndicated column as "history come alive, told with both strength and compassion."

The book went into paperback reprint. Overseas, a British edition was followed by translations into Dutch, German, Hebrew and French. A friend in Paris reported an impressive *Sabra* display in a Champs Elysées bookstore.

Making the usual media and lecture appearances, I found myself bucking unexpected headwinds. Israel, from the sheer bravura of its military performance, had in the eyes of many Americans been transformed overnight from its customary role of plucky underdog to that of swaggering aggressor. Arab propagandists, busily portraying Rabin's troops as the new bullies of the Middle East, picked up support in the New York *Times*, where Cyrus Sulzberger was writing warmly of Jordan's "courageous little king" and the "interesting" assassins of the PLO; Drew Middleton, decrying an Israeli reprisal raid against Suez, had described a bomb-ravaged church with the splintered Christ figure hanging by one arm from the cross . . . as I commented, "another crucifixion by the dirty Jews." And the Arab capitals were openly abetted by a small coterie of Jewish intellectuals, led by I.F. Stone and Noam Chomsky, apparently eager to establish their credentials as New Left global revolutionaries. In *Ramparts* magazine, the spiky "alternative" predecessor to *Rolling Stone* and *Mother Jones*, Stone railed against an Israeli "little Prussia" being unkind to Egyptian dictator Gamal Abdel Nasser, "the first ruler to give Egypt's downtrodden *fellaheen* a break." *Ramparts* gave a prominent display to my rejoinder:

> This is a strange way to characterize the wanton sacrifice of thousands of peasants' sons, forced into Army service, to Nasser's dreams of a 20th century caliphate. Who does Mr. Stone think did the dying

> in the Sinai desert? Not Nasser and his tennis-club, swagger-stick generals.

Sabra and its offshoots were winding down. There was a flicker of interest in a screen version from John Cassavetes, perhaps the most underrated of American filmmakers; but Cassavetes was having his usual desperate struggle getting release financing for his latest feature, *Husbands*, and the project lapsed.

However, I found compensation in a belated letter to Harper from an official of the Miami Public Library. Although Helga Mason, head of Community Relations, would "never forget the scene of Mickey Marcus's death," she considered *Sabra* "even more inspiring than *Cast A Giant Shadow*, and better written."

CHAPTER 19

In Search of Whistler

The Whistler book was beckoning, a charge into the unknown that demanded a level of concentration beyond anything I had yet experienced. How else to create the atmosphere and realistic detail of a bygone century, deal with the intricacies of an art form I had scarcely peered at, evoke famous personalities, and invent supporting players only dimly documented by history but nonetheless vital to my story? And weave these elements into the portrait of a controversial, not always lovable central character frequently at odds with the world and to some extent with himself? All this within the framework of a compelling narrative faithful to many inescapable facts, yet plausibly bridging strange gaps in the record?

The genre I had chosen, welding history, anecdote, interior thought processes and dialogue, had tripped up many and been mastered by few, notably Lion Feuchtwanger and Mary Renault. And in Whistler's case, thanks to his "Mother" portrait and public linkage with Wilde, the popular perception of my central character veered toward sentimentality and perhaps homosexuality—two inferences with which he would have been vastly annoyed.

It was a fools-rush-in situation. Had I paused to consider the scope of the task, I would probably have been frozen to inaction. But *Sabra* had emboldened me. Instead of backing off I boarded a plane for London, where Whistler had dwelt along the Thames, immortalizing on canvas its foggy banks while he bandied challenges, seduced models and in the picturesque company of Dante Gabriel Rossetti and Algernon Swinburne carried on his acrimonious feuds with critics, art dealers and patrons. Through my old crony, Donald Wayne who had quit as managing editor of *Parade*, joined his family in London and established himself in British literary circles, I obtained a "bedroom-sitter" at the far end of King's Road in non-conformist Chelsea. Whistler's first house was around the corner, Thomas Carlyle's austere graystone a few blocks away. I could gaze down on the Rossetti mansion, from which George Meredith and Charles Dodgson (Lewis Carroll) would let scrawny little Swinburne loose for a bibulous evening on the town, a return address pinned on his lapel for the guidance of coachmen.

Except for minor remodeling, the area was remarkably intact. By night, in the ghostly silence that followed the closing of the last pub doors, one could summon up the Victorian clatter of hoofs along the pavement. It was here that Whistler, as the most experimental member of Rossetti's irreverent circle, got caught up in the Oriental-collecting vogue of the 1870s. It began with blue porcelain plates imported from China, then shifted to Japanese woodblocks of the capital's brothel district, stumbled upon by the painter's impressionist friends in Paris. Richly colored, exquisite in line, they charmed Monet and captivated Whistler, to the point where he assembled lanky English models on a balcony and draped them in vivid flowing kimonos for a group portrait. Some elements of the Japanese compositional style—bold foreground figures, eloquent spaces and deft balance—became fixtures of his technique, and the weightless transparency of the East suffuses his "Twilights."

Whistler's travels were many. During two long years of research, I tried to walk in his footsteps. I went back to West Point, where like Mickey Marcus he had made a lasting impression—but for very different reasons. As a dubious military theorist and breaker of the Academy record for piling up demerits, he was personally booted out by Colonel Robert E. Lee.

In historic Hastings, site of his mother's cottage and her grave, I wandered the chalk cliffs, then crossed the channel to study her portrait and ferret out other Whistleriana along the winding corridors and musty storage racks of the Louvre.

Also in Paris I tracked down the haunts on the left bank where Whistler anticipated by fifty years the American expatriate colony of the Jazz Age, and trailed him to Trouville on the Normandy coast, where he and the earthy realist Gustave Courbet turned out remarkably contrasting studies of Whistler's red-haired Irish mistress, Jo Heffernan. In Scotland, I thumbed through previously unreported correspondence bequeathed by his heirs to the University of Glasgow; in Washington, D.C. I checked out the papers collected at the Library of Congress, and the breathtaking panels of Whistler's Peacock Room at the Freer Gallery.

Today, when a hundred-mile trip from Santa Barbara to Los Angeles gives me pause, I am staggered by my Whistler journeys: to museums in Spain (Velasquez was one of his favorites) and Holland (Frans Hals was another), to newspaper archives of the British Museum at Collindale outside London, to the crumbling palaces of Venice, unforgettably preserved in Whistler's etchings. My ignorance was an asset; it prompted me to more painstaking inquiry than an expert in the field might have felt necessary. I started, like the readers I hoped to reach, from scratch; what puzzled or intrigued me, I assumed, would likely do the same to them.

Toward the end of my travels, a disconcerting note began to crop up. Before leaving for England, I had been hearing vague party talk in New York about a similar Whistler project being contemplated by Leonard Levinson, a staff writer with weekly *Variety*. Suddenly in Glasgow, then in Paris, the vague warning became a reality; another American—tall, florid, spectacled (all of which fit Levinson)—had been canvassing the same trail, poking into the same corners. Nobody seemed to know how far along the other author was in his research, or whether he had a publisher. Still, it was not a comforting development.

Back in New York with a suitcase full of notes, I felt the need for a more interior, centered approach to my subject; I wanted to experience the feel of brushes, the smell of pigment, the whole perspective of the visual artist. So I enrolled in painting classes under my artist cousin Aaron Berkman. Aaron, a wiry, elegant man with a rakish black mustache, had been the original art critic for H.L. Mencken's *American Mercury*. A wisp of Montparnasse clung to him, a relic of student days in Paris. Aaron was dubious about my plan to novelize Whistler, mistrusting of the literary genre, but willing to help.

To model for his life-study class, Aaron had recruited a slim Japanese dancer. I was struck by her quiet dignity, the cheetah-like fluidity of her movements; here was the evanescent Eastern fragrance that had entranced Whistler. It entranced me, too. Unfortunately I displayed my ardor in full view of the class. With grave courtesy, the lady informed me that although she found me intelligent and attractive, she could not as the sometime mistress of a globe-trotting banker risk being detected in an outside affair. I lacked the discretion essential to her life.

Dismissed, I retreated. But I was hooked, reminded of my Burmese enchantress of the U.N. days, drenched again in the seductive scents of the Orient.

I began unconsciously scrutinizing passersby from the East. They touched some atavistic chord deep within me, stirring me in a way that females from the West did not. I liked their fragile loveliness: high cheekbones, delicate ear lobes, glossy manes of jet black hair, the small flat noses so different from the fleshy protuberance of the "Jewish nose." Exotic, forbidden, they were super-shiksas trained, as old Asia hands reported, to build their lives around pleasing men. They seemed less threatening than their aggressive occidental counterparts, less demanding, more overtly appreciative. Their oblique but persistent message was "I need protection. You won't be sorry."

The trans-Pacific vision for whom I had been scanning the horizon materialized in the delegates' lounge of the United Nations, where I was joining my novelist friend Meyer Levin for a drink with an Israeli press officer. The lady, obviously Asiatic, sat at the bar surrounded by a horde of drooling newsmen, a striking figure in a clinging silver *changsam*, a close-fitting silk gown provocatively slit along the thigh. Meyer, ever alert to matchmaking possibilities, cut through the crowd and introduced me to Li Ping, a best-selling novelist in Asia, former publisher of a leading Shanghai magazine, and—obviously—an international beauty. She had the dramatic facial structure, glittering eye and regal manner of the Dragon Lady in the adventure-comic strip "Terry and the Pirates," matched to an incredible figure: breasts that swelled to a surfer's wave, tapering to a schoolgirl waist. With a saucy Basque beret perched on her head, Li Ping was a synthesis of ancient charms and modern promise that would have stopped traffic on an MGM set.

Hal made small talk, inquiring about a mutual friend known to have stalked the lady for years. Li Ping wrinkled her flawless nose in dismissal. "Dan is not *lomantic*," she declared.

For some reason, Ted was. Within two weeks we were together constantly, roaming through Central Park, at restaurants and movies, in my apartment or hers. Her phone rang constantly with calls from less privileged admirers: people prominent in the newspaper world, law, and politics, reaching up to exalted levels in Washington.

A wealthy woman with American stocks and Asian real estate, she told me that as a popular literary figure in China she was on excellent terms with both the palace guard of the exiled Chiang Kai Shek and their

Communist successors in Peking. Curious about these claims, I took her to meet Fanny, who had been counselor to the Chinese at the founding of the United Nations. Fanny chatted with her briefly, and called me into the kitchen: "Your friend definitely has connections. At the top, on both sides . . ."

Apparently comfortable in any setting, Li Ping had one mortal enemy: the Japanese. "What they did in Nanking and Shanghai, you here will never know—and we will never forget."

What she wanted most from me was acceptance in America as an author. She in turn educated me in Chinese ways, such as the medieval custom of binding women's feet to accentuate their frailty and dependence. But the tiny mincing steps and coquettish air she sometimes affected were less a bow before the genteel Confucian tradition than a mockery of it.

She bestowed on me a remote romantic dream that by its very character seemed unlikely ever to make a real demand for intimacy. In time, it acquired jarring dissonances. Passing a stately town house, I remarked on its superb friezes. Li Ping squinted briefly: "I could have had it for a hundred and twenty five thousand." Status was important to her, the only reason she clung to her dark, crowded apartment in the East Eighties: "Everybody, all over the world, has heard of Park Avenue."

And she nursed a tireless ambition. Although she deplored American brashness, she craved American applause. It was only a question, she insisted, of establishing which of her many novels were most suitable for translation or adaptation.

I tried, very hard. As far as I could tell, her work was in the sentimental vein popularized by Fannie Hurst in the 1930s, like *Imitation of Life*. It had wit and observation. But the language, values, and especially the slow, winding pace, were born of a different culture.

Li Ping changed tack. "All right. I have material for a new book, a modern story that nobody else could write. We will go together to Hong Kong to finish the research, then write it together." She flashed her devastating smile.

I mumbled a protest: "I have a long way to go on Whistler." What bothered me was not the proposal itself so much as the unspoken word I sensed behind it: marriage. I still felt temperamentally at odds with the institution; and even if I hadn't been, Li Ping and I had different goals, conflicting values; she wanted to conquer the world, I to change it. She looked up at business, down at blacks. In music she knew the names of composers but didn't seem to hear what they were conveying. And we were too much alike in our needs—both outsiders, neurotically self-absorbed, desperate for support—to make a balanced team over the long haul.

I indicated marriage was not in my plans. The following week she became accessible to other men. But I was Asia-snared, for decades to come a frequent traveler on the Orient Express.

I labored steadily on the Whistler novel. As my focus on the book intensified, I found myself funneling every new experience—the faces observed on a bus, the nuances of a relationship—into the work at hand; what didn't connect I automatically discarded. I reached back into memory, distilling from a long-gone Irish sweetheart and Beth Moldau's wild early beauty the essence of Whistler's longtime mistress, Jo.

Finally, the awful midnight known to every author arrived: the moment when all the raw material has been assembled, the themes underlined, plots and counterplots sketched—and none of it makes any sense. Total chaos without an escape hatch in sight.

Except that this time around there was the MacDowell Colony, planted among the pine groves of Peterborough, New Hampshire by the widow of the American composer Edward MacDowell. Thanks either to my writing record or the intervention of various friends—I'll never know which—I had been approved for a month's stay in the summer of 1969.

MacDowell, open to a relative handful of composers, authors, painters, sculptors and filmmakers, was a creative artist's heaven. I was assigned a quiet cabin in the woods, with a comfortable bed, work desk and chair, fireplace and piano. Lunch of my choosing was brought to my doorstep. I was required only to turn up in the main hall for breakfast and dinner, and to respect the privacy of my colleagues; uninvited drop-ins were verboten. The company was congenial, frequently amusing, and non-competitive, a far cry from the jungle atmosphere of Hollywood; colonists were pitted only against themselves.

In this blessed setting—one of the previous occupants of my cabin, according to a name-carved plaque above the fireplace, was Leonard

Bernstein—it was not hard to lay out related segments of my story as on a palette, then dig into them one by one, trusting for guidance to instinct and the mysterious powers of the unconscious.

Back on 75th St., the chapters started rolling. The following summer I returned to MacDowell to wrap up my first draft and go through the entire manuscript for revisions. When *To Seize the Passing Dream* landed on Lee Barker's desk—the title had popped into my head during a subway ride to the New York Public Library—four years of work lay behind it.

Barker, never celebrated for rash enthusiasms, opined we just might have something special. He invited me to a private dinner with him and his wife on the roof garden of their East Side apartment—a ceremonial, Doubleday underlings confided, reserved for projects considered of major potential. There Barker read aloud a letter from Irving Stone, to whom he had sent galley proofs of my book. According to Lee, Stone was usually not eager to share his special turf. Yet here was his unreserved praise for "a biographical novel in the finest tradition, fastidiously researched yet springing to life with verve and gusto." Barker declared that as Doubleday's executive editor, he was prepared to throw his considerable weight behind a "respectable" advertising campaign. I was stunned, delighted, not quite sure the whole episode wasn't a mirage.

Literary man-about-town Cleveland Amory, on the Barry Farber radio show, pronounced the book witty and artful, "a story that will haunt you, about a man you will not forget." "A remarkable book," chimed in Meyer Levin, "to be savored, and to be kept." On February 27, 1972, Doubleday took out a full-page ad for my novel in the Sunday Book section of the New York *Times*.

For a crowning touch, my publisher joined Simon and Schuster in sponsoring a four-way party at Meyer Levin's home to celebrate publication of Meyer's *The Settlers*, by S. and S., and three Doubleday books: *Seize*, Gerold Frank's *An American Death*, about the killing of Martin Luther King, and Gerald Green's *Blockbuster*.

The bash was duly ballyhooed in such quarters as the Leonard Lyons column in the New York *Post*, and attended by the usual swarm of editors, agents, booksellers, pretty publicity women and people to whom the authors felt obligations. I was home free and in good company, with reviews to gather, book clubs to court, and no further problem with the long-whispered but never-materialized rival enterprise of Leonard Levinson.

Not with Levinson, no; but incredibly, up from the woodwork crept still another Whistler novel, previously unheralded, published the same week by none other than Simon and Schuster.

I, James McNeill Whistler—a title borrowed unblushingly from Robert Graves's *I, Claudius*—was the work of Lawrence Williams, an author of little previous reputation, dismissed impatiently by Lee Barker as an "established hack." But the book was brisk, once-over-lightly fare that on its own terms was quite successful. Treating Whistler less as a serious artist than as an engaging personality, making no attempt to explore the painter's milieu in depth and no corresponding demand on the reader's attention, it offered an afternoon's diversion and had already been bought for serialization by *McCall's* magazine.

More importantly, it posed an immediate threat to *Seize* in the scramble for the Literary Guild Book Club, whose judges had been eyeing my book benignly. Doubleday owned the Guild. That, as Lee explained, put them in an awkward position; if the club chose my book it could be accused of favoritism.

By a 3 to 2 margin, the judging committee chose to play it safe and gave the nod to Williams. Book critics later came down overwhelmingly in my favor, but on the Literary Guild issue the damage was done, some twenty-five thousand dollars of it.

A half-dozen reviewers covered the two books together. The best Williams could claim was a draw in two cases. Typifying the majority opinion was Harold Haydon, art critic of the Chicago *Sun-Times*, who found *Seize* "infinitely superior" in its "richness of detail, preference for fact over fancy, sympathy for his protagonist and solid information . . . Whistler emerges, heroic and pathetic, in a portrait more fully rounded than those he painted."

Of my solo reviews, twenty ranged from good to rhapsodic, five were negative and two mixed. "It all comes back to life," wrote Frank Getlein in the Washington *Star*. "The places, the people, Whistler's painstaking and at times very uncertain creation. We end up with a full understanding of his work and a deep sympathy for the man, a rare combination for anyone to have for Whistler."

Some of the hostile minority made up in venom for what they lacked in numbers. Stomping across my pages in hobnailed boots was Donald Demarest of the Minneapolis *Tribune*, described as a novelist, former art critic and "amateur painter." Opening with a blast at the entire biographical-fiction genre—"presumptuous as turning the Bible into a comic strip"—Demarest laced into me as a "sly pornographer" whose "many failures" included a muddied, heavy-handed portrait of my subject. Demarest had no qualms about distorting facts to suit his convenience. In my last chapter I described Whistler on his death-bed, recalling the evening he first saw Jo Heffernan whirling across a tavern dance floor; in the reviewer's inflamed version, "As Whistler lies dying, all his great models and landscapes float before him."

But what strikes me most forcibly in retrospect is the incredible contradictions in the reviews. How could the same book be called "a masterpiece, very hard to surpass" (the Camden, N.J. *Courier-Post*) and "a pretentious big book about a pretentious little man" (the Vancouver, B.C. *Sun*)?

One of the aims set forth in my preface was to create dialogue that would blend indistinguishably with Whistler's celebrated bon mots. "Fond hope," snorted Donald Demarest. Yet John Yeomans of the Whistler Society in Chelsea thought I had brought it off and so, apparently, did Noel Coward. A letter to Fanny from Coward's secretary in Montreux, Switzerland reported that the Master "had read the book with great enjoyment and admiration; please be sure and tell Mr. Berkman this."

In a perfect world, critical columns would be reserved for seasoned observers, of demonstrated achievement in the field under consideration. Minimally, I submit, it would be salutary for publications to indicate the credentials of their reviewers.

To Seize the Passing Dream went into a paperback reprint, and a separate English edition. Negotiations for a Japanese-language version, at first animated, disintegrated under what appeared to be mutually indecipherable correspondence. Early in 1973 Evelyn Oppenheimer, book critic for a major chain of radio stations in the West, awarded me her "Oppie" for the best book of 1972 in the biographical novel category.

Oddly enough, I took more cheer from the uniformly appreciative response of working painters, among them my once-skeptic cousin Aaron Berkman. From Yarmouth, Nova Scotia, landscape veteran Alex Gigeroff wrote: "I'm enthralled, captured utterly . . . your reconstruction of the inner thought-processes of a painter is to my mind *sans pareil* (though Joyce Cary's *The Horse's Mouth* pops up in memory)." No negligible association!

CHAPTER 20

Anne Frank Betrayed

"Your Whistler book screams for a movie adaptation!" Meyer Levin was at my door, rumpled and resolute. "Shot in the original locations, in England and France. I'm sketching an outline—no charge—'faithful mistress battles implacable mother for painter's soul!'"

Meyer stomped away. Two days later he sent his treatment to Vanessa Redgrave, who agreed that Jo Heffernan would be a fascinating role. But who, she wanted to know, would be capable of mounting this kind of elaborate production—the period interiors, the paintings?

Only when Meyer confronted the unpleasant reality—there were no Kordas left in London—did he back off from his campaign.

Meyer's tenacity underlined his unswerving loyalty and single-minded resolve. Once he took a position, nothing could sway him from it. Like George Polk, Meyer paid a high price for his refusal to be accommodating. Although the two never met, they spoke the same language of fair play. The bland indifference of the State Department to George's murder was a testament to official Washington hypocrisy; the systematic denigration of Meyer in connection with the Anne Frank Diary spoke with equal eloquence of cynicism in American literary circles.

Of Meyer's talent and achievement, there is little serious dispute. His first major book, *The Old Bunch*, was hailed by the New York *Times* as a "landmark in the development of the realistic novel." *The Settlers* evoked comparisons with Tolstoi.

Robert Kirsch, the widely respected critic of the Los Angeles *Times*, called him "the most significant American Jewish writer of the twentieth century."

Yet you will not find him even mentioned among the seventy-eight authors in the New American Library's 1977 *Anthology of Jewish American Literature*. Somehow, as a literary entity Bob Kirsch's "most significant" figure has been wiped out, like the non-persons in Soviet political history.

The object of unparalleled personal abuse, he has been caricatured in the New York *Times* as a money-grubbing hysteric, "possibly paranoid, definitely trouble-making, constantly complaining," whose "deranged fury" and legalistic "excesses" alienated even his closest friends.

Why this astonishing chasm between appreciators and detractors? And why did I feel his anguish so deeply?

Out of a simple passion for justice—and something more. Eight years my senior, Meyer had over the course of a three-decade relationship become the encouraging Dad I had sought and been denied in adolescence, as earnest and principled as the original but much more accessible. I found him a stimulating and supportive presence, never intrusive but always available. His homes had been open to me, and mine to him, wherever our paths crossed—in Israel before and after statehood, in Hollywood, Fire Island, Paris, New York.

There were even physical resemblances to my gymnast father. Like Sam Berkman, Meyer was stockily built, muscular, with bold craggy features seemingly designed to peer out of the back of a book jacket. Again like Sam, he was a creature of sudden moods; flashes of Puckish humor struggled against an ancient anger in his eyes. Nearing seventy when *The Settlers* was published, he no longer pounded up the steep trail to the fortress of Masada in the Sinai; but there was still force in his deep-chested body, still determination in his step. He waved aside the discount-for-elders fare offered by New York busses; he was Meyer Levin, independent author—not some enfeebled senior citizen.

Eager to promote my love life, he peppered me with promising phone numbers and introductions to poets, heiresses, singers, a psychiatrist; he had more tips than an enterprising stock broker. One of his candidates was Adele Morales Mailer, Norman's fourth wife and the target of his famous knife attack. Adele, a Peruvian painter, had a smoky south-of-the-border appeal and clearly reciprocated my interest, but for some reason the affair never caught on. I suspect my perception of Adele was murky, enveloped in the scowling image of the enfant terrible who fathered her children.

Meyer moved around like a migratory bird, shuttling from New York to a Tel Aviv suburb in winter, stopping off for a few months in Paris, never quite unpacked. His life, like his crisp book titles, was pared down to essentials: his family, a few close friends, Chinese restaurants and his

IBM Selectric. He was totally indifferent to fashion. "Formal dress in Israel," he told me, "is wearing socks with your sandals." All he needed was a telephone-free haven in which to work: in New York, a cabin above the Hudson at Nyack; in Israel, an abandoned British sentry post a few miles down the beach from his villa at Herzlia.

In 1967, while occupying my New York apartment, he wrote *Gore and Igor*, chronicling the bawdy, hilarious collision in Israel between a war-protesting American folk singer like Bob Dylan and a swinging proletarian poet (Yevtushenko?) from the Soviet Union, satirizing among others a blonde Lorelei bent on bedding every stalwart kibbutznik in sight. "I am a German," she declaims. "I want to atone." Meyer inscribed its first copy, "For Ted, in whose bed some of this was conceived."

By the mid-1970s, Meyer was the casual patriarch of a movable salon. Writers as disparate as Mailer, Joseph Stein (*Fiddler on the Roof*), Herbert Gold, the poet Sandra Hochman, Joseph Heller (*Catch-22*) and Fredric Morton (*The Rothschilds*) sought his counsel. At long last solvent thanks to *Compulsion* and *The Settlers*, he had a loving family, a comfortable home, and devoted listeners. He also had a twenty-year ache in his heart.

On one of the Levins' jaunts to Paris in 1950, Tereska picked up a French-language translation of *The Diary of a Young Girl*, originally written by Anne Frank in Dutch. She recommended it to her husband.

Meyer was overwhelmed. This was the "voice from the mass grave" he had been searching for, ever since as a correspondent with advance Allied troops in World War II he had burst into the horror wards of the Holocaust. He wrote to Anne's father, Otto Frank, offering his services in helping to arrange American publication. When Doubleday agreed to do the book, Meyer poured his admiration into a long, stirring Sunday *Times* review that pitched it overnight onto the best-seller lists.

All he wanted by way of acknowledgment, Meyer told Otto Frank, was first crack at a stage adaptation. He would turn over to charity any royalties beyond compensation for his time.

Frank cabled Doubleday that he was appointing Meyer "to guarantee" preservation of the Diary's authenticity. Meyer drafted his play script, sending a copy to Cheryl Crawford, prestige-laden producer of *Porgy and Bess*, and another to Otto Frank. Crawford registered her approval—"promising, good enough to proceed." Frank complimented Meyer on his fidelity to Anne's text, but said he would leave final word on a production to "the professionals."

Enter, *misteriosamente,* Lillian Hellman, prize-winning playwright, long-time mistress of Dashiell Hammett, and long-time apologist for Josef Stalin. A phone call summoned Meyer to Crawford's office, where the producer told him a "night's discussion" with Hellman had persuaded her to withdraw from a draft that was "unstageworthy" and "unactable." Both ladies advised Otto Frank that prose authors were incapable of writing for the theater, conveniently ignoring Chekhov, Camus and Steinbeck.

Within days Meyer had the backing of Herman Shumlin, the veteran producer who had brought to Broadway *The Children's Hour* and *Grand Hotel*. "No good," decreed Miss Hellman. "Herman is no longer capable of producing a hit" (Shumlin soon after presented *Inherit the Wind*, and in 1964 won a Tony for *The Deputy*). Three other established producers offered to do Meyer's script and were turned down.

By this time Hellman had enlisted her own choice—her friend Kermit Bloomgarden—and Otto Frank had come to New York. What was really needed now, Hellman told him, was a big, world-famous playwriting name that would draw proper attention to the Diary and ensure its box-office success. Frank relayed this to Meyer. Meyer, confronted with the prospect of an Arthur Miller waiting in the wings, or Hellman herself, felt he had no choice. He bowed out; whereupon Hellman snapped her fingers and pulled from a hat the Hollywood writing team of Albert Hackett and his wife, Francis Goodrich.

I knew of the Hacketts from my studio days. They had three minor Broadway credits, the last of them in 1942. Although their movie credentials were far more impressive—five Writers Guild awards—every screenplay was a comedy. The Hacketts had made a career of whipping up amusing froth, thereby apparently qualifying, in Hellman's judgment, to write a harrowing drama of the holocaust.

But Hellman did take the precaution, it developed later, of "supervising" their efforts. An entry in Frances Goodrich's diary for September 5, 1954 reports "amazing" and "brilliant" advice from Hellman on construction. The Broadway term is "play doctor."

The Bloomgarden production was a smashing success, winning both a Pulitzer and the Drama Critics Prize. Unfortunately for its authors, it exhibited parallels with the Levin draft in structure, staging, key scenes and even invented incidents. A plagiarism jury in New York State Supreme Court found the playwrights guilty of "appropriation of ideas," and awarded Meyer half of their royalties, or an estimated fifty thousand dollars.

Still more serious, in Meyer's eyes, was the Hellman-Hackett distortion of the Diary. A long, eloquent passage by Anne Frank had dwelt on the uniqueness of Judaism and the inspiring particularity of the Jewish fate. In the Hackett version, this underwent a 180-degree change: "We're not the only people that've had to suffer. There have always been people . . . sometimes one race . . . sometimes another."

Suddenly a new trial was ordered on the technical grounds that the plagiarism jury had failed to specify the exact amount of damages due to Meyer. Meyer could not summon up the resources, financial or emotional, for a second trial. Despairingly, he rested on his moral victory and a fifteen thousand dollar settlement to cover his legal costs.

Only upon fine-combing the arbitrated settlement did Meyer learn that an ambiguous clause left future "proper use" of his play adaptation to the discretion of Otto Frank—whose lawyers promptly clamped it in an iron hand. Public performance was permanently banned.

But the Soldiers Theater staged a bootleg production in Israel, where leading reviewers hailed it as "infinitely superior," "more honest" and more dramatic. Albert Camus, Elie Wiesel, and I.B. Singer joined Arthur Miller and Norman Mailer in urging that the ban be lifted. They urged in vain.

Meyer pressed his case in two books, *The Fanatic* and *The Obsession* and countless private declamations. He had been pushed aside, he insisted, by a Stalinist literary cabal which had never forgiven him for refusing to be seduced in the 1930s by the "universalist" trappings of Communism. I never told Meyer so, but I found his argument roundabout, cloudy, farfetched.

Until, very gradually, the invisible web woven around him began to unravel. In 1963 Saul Bellow, in a preface to a collection of American-Jewish short stories, scolded Meyer acrimoniously for an aesthetic argument Meyer had never made. Bellow's publisher, embarrassed, hastily rushed into print with a correction.

But why such a vicious thrust by a future Nobel laureate?

The answer came four years later in *Making It*, Norman Podhoretz's breezy, candid account of his rise in the literary world. The editor of *Commentary* revealed the existence of what he affectionately called "the family," a tight circle of brilliant intellectuals, fiercely Marxist in their allegiance, clustered around the influential *Partisan Review*.

Although buttressed by Dwight MacDonald and Mary McCarthy, the family as described by Podhoretz was predominantly Jewish: Irving Howe, Hannah Arendt, Delmore Schwartz, Sidney Hook. The head man, number one on the Podhoretz list? Saul Bellow.

According to *Making It*, the Jews of the family were united by a strong sense of alienation from the American mainstream. "Universalists" all, they regarded Zionism as yet another form of bourgeois nationalism, and they looked forward with equanimity to the disappearance under socialism of the Jewish people, seeing no point in their survival. Meyer Levin had not only made no secret of his Zionist convictions; he had risked his life to underline them in 1947 by filming *The Illegals*, a journey on foot across the Alps by holocaust survivors.

Did Lillian Hellman share the universalist creed of "the family"? In her 1974 memoir *Pentimiento* she told of "Julia," a purported friend who, smuggling a substantial sum into Hitler's Germany, told her "about half" would be used to help Jews: "Jews are not the only people who have suffered here." This is almost a verbatim reprise of the Hellman/Hackett alteration of Anne Frank's Diary. Later, in *Scoundrel Time*, Hellman boasted of refusing before the House Un-American activities Committee to "cut her conscience" to suit the prevailing fashion; she had no such qualms about re-tailoring the Diary.

The Hellman façade began to crack. Martha Gellhorn, a highly regarded foreign correspondent and former wife of Hemingway, accused her of nine documented lies about Spain. Sam McCracken of Boston University charged in *Commentary* that Hellman's so-called "reminiscence" of Julia was a wholesale fabrication.

To cap the demythicizing barrage, Paul Johnson in *Intellectuals* depicted Hellman as a devious, unscrupulous behind-the-scenes manipulator who dispensed falsehoods like mail-order flyers; the "queen of radical chic," powerful enough to arrange suppression of a book that would have referred to her in unfriendly terms; and author of a "cunning, mendacious" letter to the House committee.

Johnson's caustic sketch dovetails all too well with my own impressions of Popular Front tactics in Hollywood. Not everybody in the Malibu outposts of the *Daily Worker* could claim the philosophic orientation or benign character of Ring Lardner Jr. The leftist camp was idealistic in its hopes for a better world, puerile in its bragging about affiliates under its control—and on occasion ruthless in trampling opposition. The Party faithful too had flaws.

Hellman died in 1984, but the vendetta against Meyer Levin persisted, even after he was eight years in his grave. In 1989 he was pilloried in the *New Yorker*, in an article by one Judith Thurman, as "hapless and demonic," a crackpot "vandal".

In 1995 Lawrence Graver, a professor at Williams College, published *An Obsession with Anne Frank: Meyer Levin and the Diary*. Graver confirmed Hellman's "decisive influence" in the ethnic cleansing of the Diary, and concluded that the Levin script was indeed better, "more accurate, more faithful to the original."

Two years later Frank Rich, re-examining the whole bitter controversy in the New York *Times*, judged that Meyer had been shabbily treated, and paid tribute to his lonely "crusade." Who then were the real vandals? The single stubborn defender of the Diary or its cynical exploiters?

CHAPTER 21

Learning To Teach

Among my consultants on *Seize* had been Reuben Fine, long since transformed from chess grand master of the 1930s to national sachemhood in psychoanalysis. Reuben had undergone analysis, in exchange for chess lessons, from Dr. Ben Weininger of Harry Stack Sullivan's Washington School, had obtained his doctorate as a therapist, and had risen in that field as rapidly as at the chess board, churning out books on Freud, developing a staff of disciples at his own Institute, and winning the presidency of the American Psychological Association, an acknowledged expert on every aspect of human relations except his own private life, which was in a constant state of turmoil. Scattering wives in his wake, he had swept through a half-dozen marriages, constantly expressing surprise at the female neuroses unearthed during intimacy. Through all these excursions he retained an air of bland serenity, a round-faced, squirrel-cheeked oracle sporting a jaunty Basque beret (a longtime affectation of my own). Although Reuben no longer competed at chess, he wrote books on its psychological symbolism and was much in demand as a commentator on world championship contests. He also held an annual New Year's Eve party which was the Manhattan equivalent of Mel Shavelson's January 1 gatherings for prominent screen writers; attendance at Reuben's bash was confined to leading psychoanalysts, subjecting the occasional outsider like myself to a dizzying evening of exchanges in the lofty patois of the trade.

Reuben was delighted with the reception of my Whistler novel, acclaimed its "felicitous" title, and asked me to join him in a lecture on creativity at Marymount Manhattan College, a Catholic women's school in the East Seventies. The dean then invited me to introduce a course of my own devising there.

I opted for The Artist in Society. Although W. Somerset Maugham's plea for "pity" for "those who carry the burden of talent," voiced from a palatial retreat in Switzerland, seemed to me somewhat overblown, the artist does stand apart. The sensitivity that informs an artist's work also makes him or her vulnerable to the harshness of everyday living. Thus

Laurence Housman declares himself "a stranger and afraid, in a world I never made." Lawrence Durrell tells us that underneath all the "chattering forebrain" of the novelist is, "quite simply, a man tortured beyond endurance by the lack of tenderness in the world."

More often than not, in my observation, art is something that talent carves out of loneliness and despair. Facing an intolerable daily reality, the creative person seeks to reshape it into a privately designed world; in the words of Robert Frost, opposing "black and utter chaos" with a "small man-made figure of order and concentration."

In the process, the artist may feel swept aside by an unseen power that virtually takes over, reducing him momentarily to the role of agent or channel. "Sometimes what comes out of that piano frightens me," said George Gershwin. My friend Don Wayne spoke of a supernatural presence that joined him at the typewriter and "fled when a stranger entered the room."

For myself, I shall never forget the excitement of composing "That's Mine" in Nova Scotia forty years ago, the words and music arriving together out of nowhere, as if they had been waiting to be summoned.

But the Muse is a demanding mistress. I have found myself summoned to attention while walking in the woods, driving on a dangerous freeway, swimming in a pool; when suddenly the groped-for phrase or concept appears, all that matters is getting to the piano or typewriter and giving it expression before it escapes, perhaps never to be trapped again.

Artists feel "meaningless and unacceptable," observes psychiatrist Arnold Hutschnecker, "without the passport of their creative production." I had experienced, in *Nellie's* shifting fortunes, the hazards of putting all my emotional eggs in one exceedingly fragile basket. To the sensitive creative spirit, everything short of total embrace is a rebuke. When Bizet's *Carmen* was ridiculed and flung aside, he died a few months later at forty-seven.

The artist is a dubious candidate for emotional involvement. As a perfectionist he sets standards of beauty and behavior beyond any mortal fulfillment. As a sensualist he demands constant change and new stimulation; not only to smell the roses, but to be greeted by a fresh one on the table every morning. In my case, feeling myself unstable, a giant one moment and a pygmy the next, I am as likely to slide into a funk as to dance on the ceiling. Finally, in my heart I suspect I am committed elsewhere, to the Muse-mistress whose delights, unlike those of passing flesh, defy time and change.

Leave it to Voltaire to sum up the hazards of the creative life. "If your talents are unfortunately mediocre," he wrote to a young author, "your regrets will last all your life; if you succeed you will have enemies. You are walking at the edge of the abyss, between contempt and hatred."

Gifted women face all of the above plus gender bias, sexual intimidation and nest-making expectations.

My first brush with teaching came in 1968, when for reasons beyond present recall I persuaded the dean of the New School for Social Research that he should entrust to me a course on Alienation. The New School, a Greenwich Village institution, enjoyed a national reputation for innovative courses and distinguished faculty.

My arrival was noted in a substantial ad in the New York *Times*. Unfortunately only a handful of students registered for the class, and by the third session these had dwindled to one, the mother of Herb Gardner, playwright of *A Thousand Clowns*. Nonetheless I decided to risk Marymount, on the premise that this time my subject would be less austere and my connection with it far more personal.

Facing a sea of poised pencils and expectant faces, many of them belonging to nurses pursuing graduate degrees, I suddenly yearned for the undemanding company of my typewriter. Somehow I stumbled through the hour. The next session was a little less painful—to my mild surprise, all of the enrollees returned—and as our mutual shyness gradually wore off, I realized I was actually enjoying myself.

Without any formal courses in education, I knew that its object was to inspire rather than command; "educare" means to lead out, encourage inherent possibilities. It's a kind of matchmaking; you bring student and subject together—then get out of the way. Most of the faculty handed out B-plusses and A's to anyone who showed up regularly and stayed awake. I preferred to stress personal growth.

No self-respecting lecher could be blind to the possibilities presented by a nubile student body, but I was relishing my professional role too much to imperil it. I did get briefly involved with a Sister on the art faculty. She gave me an astonishing glimpse of the private world behind nunnery walls: severe emotional conflict and depression, bouts of heavy drinking, whiskey bottles crashing down into the courtyard . . .

When Marymount arranged a faculty exchange with the nearby Mannes School of Music, I acquired a whole new set of students for whom my subject had more immediacy. Some were only months away from symphony auditions and jazz club employment—or unemployment. Since they were extremely varied in age and background, I assigned individual biographical studies calculated to pique curiosity and perhaps provide role models, thereby giving some of my charges the pleasant surprise of finding they were bonded to a long-established fraternity.

Like hundreds of other lonely Manhattanites, I had been drifting into the "singles" activity proliferating in the city. Cocktail-hour gatherings, often in mid-town hotels, brought together swarms of hopeful strangers, willing to gamble a couple of hours and a few dollars on the chance of striking up rapport with a kindred spirit. Populated mainly by leftovers from the matrimonial scramble—women running out of biological time for motherhood, men marked as oddballs or social failures—these rallies were haunted by an air of desperation, a flavor of losers anonymous.

I came to roost at the Universalist Unitarian church building a block below the Museum of Natural History on Central Park West, whose vast spaces attracted a weekly throng of every conceivable type. Nobody was obliged to check fantasies or eccentricities at the door, so the milling mob was a melting pot of neuroses, and the proceedings were the sexual equivalent of a California swap meet: catch-as-catch-can, make your own deal.

A polite veneer of discussion groups, with an assigned topic of the evening, broke up the crowd into manageable units. If your group offered lean pickings, a concluding mass coffee hour enabled you to explore the field. Over the course of a few months I had brief entanglements with an erotically ravenous school administrator, a black nurse, a Korean bank clerk and a back-packing nature lover who introduced me to the Bronx Zoo.

My come-uppance came up in a phone call to a prospective quarry. She had given me her phone number but—first point of dismay—couldn't seem to remember me. Then she did—and that was worse. "Oh, yes!" she cried cheerfully. "The old guy!"

I realized that I was indeed nearly sixty. I cocked a brotherly eye toward a carved wooden mask brought back from Michoacan, Mexico in 1953. It depicted a toothless grinning libertine who, stirred by the stamping feet and swirling skirts of the village maidens snaps out of his lethargy long enough to lead them in a wild, terpsichorean fling, then lapses back into his usual torpor. I had a certain fond identification with the old satyr—but was it time to look for another role?

I had acquired a firm grasp of external facts enabling me at one level to become the confidant of great men. But in the corner staked out by emotion lurked the unhappy little boy, prompting me to soar one moment, crash the next, at the promising rustle of a skirt. I could not shake loose from little "Teddy," encircled by doting, demanding aunts, in search of a father always disappearing around the bend, combing the woods for a mother who would not embrace me tenderly one moment and shrug me aside the next.

A neighboring couple steered me into Primal Scream therapy, which contended that early traumas could be released only by re-experiencing them, and unloading one's torment in an agonized howl. It didn't work for me, until I switched to an offshoot group that put more emphasis on encounter.

On my very first evening Marco, the leader, guided me gently into a reminiscence of my fruitless struggle to make contact with my inaccessible father.

"How does that leave you feeling?" he asked softly.

"Needy . . . I'm angry—but mostly I need."

"Louder."

I felt a stirring in my gut, a mixture of loneliness and fury that exploded in an incoherent wail across the room.

Marco gestured toward the young man sitting next to me. "Tell Bruce about it."

I turned to meet a sympathetic brown-eyed gaze. "I need, Bruce."

He nodded. "I know." He placed a hand on my shoulder.

Suddenly I was bawling, blubbering like a baby—and feeling a release I had not known in years, if ever. It was as if an iron bar had been lifted from my chest. At Marco's suggestion I got to my feet and circled the group, embraced in turn by each friend in what moments ago had been a roomful of strangers.

"How do you feel now?" Marco wanted to know.

"As if I could dance all night."

Although such epiphanies were rare, through succeeding sessions the sense of growth continued. For all the bumps and detours, I could see positive changes in myself: a willingness to trust others, to topple backwards in a free fall confident that strong arms would catch me. I no longer held back anger, or buried assertive impulses. I retreated from my concern with image. And after screaming out before the group my resentment of my mother's early demands, I was able to come to terms with her in private: "I know you meant well. You did the best you could, given the conditions of your time and place."

The crowning gift of the encounter sessions was a measure of self-acceptance. For several years I had been announcing my unworthiness, my not-good-enough rejection of myself, by covering my thinning pate with a lustrous hairpiece. I had worn it, sometimes awry, always self-consciously, during my research trips abroad for *Sabra* and *Seize*; had impressed Li Ping with my "beautiful head of hair," and discounted female assurances that I looked better without it.

One afternoon in the middle of a therapy session I took off the rug and tossed it on the floor. I didn't need it. I enjoyed the congratulations that followed, but I didn't need them, either. I was at home with myself, or at least with my physical presence.

CHAPTER 22

Fabulous Fanny

Two book projects were at hand: one dimly formulated and remote, the other ripe for execution. A third option—an offer from England for a biography of Marlon Brando—simply left me cold. This was terrain too heavily trampled, the domain of the fast-food authors, whose formulized output was to literature what MacDonald's is to Maxim's of Paris.

My nebulous project had its roots in several trips to Spain in the early 1970s, their precise itineraries vexingly beyond recall (the State Department's Passport Office, when asked for aid in establishing dates, reacted with haughty suspicion, demanding my purposes, birth certificate, notarized signature—everything but my grandfather's driving license). I know there was a longish stay in Madrid, an Atlantic stopover in the Canary islands, and a pleasant meandering through Majorca on the other side of the peninsula in the Mediterranean, where I fingered Chopin's piano in a sodden monastery and spent an hour with fellow Doubleday author Robert Graves. The octogenarian poet, huge and amiable, sipped straight brandy for breakfast in a neo-Athenian setting of dancing blue waves and lush olive groves.

But the focus of my travels was Seville, whose medieval Jewish quarter of Santa Cruz I had first glimpsed in 1964, and been haunted by ever since. Surrounded by landmarks of old Seville—soaring cathedral towers, Moorish gardens, Inquisitorial burning grounds—the original ghetto gate and five-hundred-year-old street plan of the *barrio judío* remained virtually intact. Where else on the globe could one find the Street of Kisses, a passageway so narrow that a couple in opposite top-floor balconies could embrace?

Here, in the winding alleys and forgotten plazas of the *barrio* was a microcosm of the Jewish experience in Spain, its transcendent glories and its ultimate tragedy. Behind these flower-hung balconies and massive iron gates, somewhere among the Moorish arches and gushing courtyard fountains, there were stories to be told. In the summer of 1970 I had written to Dolores Palà, née De Soto, of a "book idea rattling about" that would be centered on a Jewish family in Spain, "some members of which convert to Catholicism in the time of the Inquisition and Columbus."

Back in Seville a year or two later, I had passed up its midtown residential splendors in favor of a modest hostelry inside the *barrio*. From there I roamed the streets, gobbled up tourist leaflets and local lore. Within three days I had my story.

On January 6, 1481, Don Diego de Suson, the wealthiest merchant of Seville and the chess companion of princes, was burned at the stake. His crime? The secret practice of Judaism while posing as a "New Christian" convert to the one True Faith. His accuser? His own daughter, famous throughout Andalusia as La Hermosa Hembra (The Beautiful Woman), who afterward plunged into a life of debauchery and prostitution; at her deathbed request her skull was nailed over the portal of her father's house, as "an example and punishment" for her sins. A century later the Suson mansion was torn down, but its locale in the shadow of the Alcazar fortress is still marked by the chilling street name, *La Calle de la Muerte* . . . the Street of Death.

All this was recorded in the city annals of Seville, and embellished by a monk's abbey chronicle of the period, according to which Don Diego's daughter had been entangled in a love affair with an Old Christian knight; the two lovers, on their way to a clandestine meeting, had reportedly stumbled across an equally surreptitious Passover ceremony presided over by Don Diego.

The operatic dimensions of the material were matched by its abundance of themes still relevant in the twentieth century: filial loyalty versus sexual bonds, human rights in a monolithic society, the moral dilemmas posed by religious conversion. Should life, at any price, always be chosen over death? How far can men compromise without losing their singular identities? What are the prospects of a strong-willed girl in a macho culture?

All this against a background of greedy kings, swashbuckling adventurers, and a see-saw Spanish struggle against Moorish invaders from which the Moors wound up virtually blanketing the country, only to be driven back to a sliver of Andalusia and finally forced out in 1492. An Arab legacy of architecture, mathematics and medicine would be carried forward by Jews: philosophers, doctors, astronomers; merchants and bankers and artisans; Jewish stewards administering the estates of untutored Castilian warriors . . . until the Inquisition. There was also the extraordinary but little-noted intersection of the Old World and the New: in the very year when the Catholic Monarchs, Ferdinand and Isabella, issued their ultimatum to Jewry—convert, go into exile, or die—Columbus set out on his historic voyage, financed largely by Jewish florins.

I thought of my movie mentor, Bill Howard, and his insistence that stories had to be "about something." Well, this was about practically everything . . . perhaps more than I could handle, but definitely more than I could pass up. What had Browning said? "A man's reach should exceed his grasp—or what's a heaven for?"

This would be no light assignment to be dashed off in a Fire Island summer. The Whistler book had dealt with a period only a hundred years removed; here the challenge would be to enter the skulls of men and women inhabiting virtually another planet, where the Catholic Church and its warnings of hell-fire shadowed the dreams of the serf in his hut, the weaver at his work-bench, and the duke under his damask bedcover. Meyer Levin, I knew, had nurtured *Compulsion* for decades; how long I would need was anybody's guess.

Meanwhile, another intriguing subject was on my doorstep—or, to be precise, occupying a high-rise condominium in my mother's apartment building. My Aunt Fanny's phenomenal career had already inspired a two-installment profile in the *New Yorker*; besieged for a follow-up by book publishers, she had airily waved them aside. But Fanny was at long last slowing down.

She had revolutionized copyright law with her "impossible" victory over MGM in the Rasputin libel case, in which she represented members of the Russian royal family; the subsequent disclaimer in thousands of books and films—"any resemblance to living persons is unintentional"—was a direct consequence. She was a shaper of formidable entertainment careers. An intimate of Eleanor Roosevelt and Adlai Stevenson, she had joined the Churchills at Chartwell for Sir Winston's eightieth birthday party. On the eve of World War II she conspired with young John Kennedy (and against his father) to smuggle Jewish refugees out of Hitler's Europe. As special counsel to the delegation of China at the

United Nations she had swung precious votes toward the creation of Israel.

No less intriguing than her achievements were the paradoxes of her character. Fanny could be at once maddening and amusing, self-obsessed and generous; unforgivable in the cruelest of her rages (Alexander Korda once ran in terror), unforgettable in the magnanimity of her impulsive gifts (a brand new mink at a Hadassah rally). She could switch from the patois of Damon Runyon's Broadway to the dulcet accents of Mayfair, and was as comfortable trading genial insults with George Bernard Shaw as in discussing the Talmud with her revered grandfather.

Although she never married, her dark-eyed intensity attracted admirers ranging from penniless novelists to King George IV of Greece. Yet for all of the paths she blazed, she remained at the core a little girl consumed by a hunger for love and attention, who ultimately channeled that need into a flood of painting and sculpture.

A biography of Fanny would enable a plunge into my own roots; perhaps in defining her I could make another step toward defining myself.

Under Fanny's alternating benefactions and demands, I had shifted gradually from worshipful nephew to respected adviser. Since my emergence with *Cast A Giant Shadow*, there had been a tacit acceptance of my separateness, and even a kind of role reversal: she would begin phone calls like a cub newswoman addressing the city desk: "Fanny reporting . . ."

Fanny's first reaction to a biography was equivocal. She curled up for three days with *To Seize the Passing Dream* and changed her mind: "If you can do for me what you did for Whistler . . ."

I made it plain that I would have to have a clear hand: my project, my own agent to handle the business side; she agreed. I put together a five-page outline, the William Morris agency (to whom I had been recommended by Gerold Frank) conducted an auction, and it ended in a contract from Little, Brown.

I began taping sessions with Fanny in her apartment three or four evenings a week. Rather than trying to impose a particular structure, I let Fanny follow impulse with her reminiscences.

We were well on our way when a crisis of sorts intervened. A London publisher cabled an offer for the British publishing rights to

Seize. Happy news—except that the publisher had recently been embroiled in a bitter dispute with Fanny. "You can't possibly sign with him," she insisted. "It's a matter of family loyalty."

"An English edition could make a difference in a movie sale," I pointed out. "And it's the only offer from London I've got." She made a sulky retreat.

Another brief distraction came via Gerold Frank. Gerry had been approached to do a book on Edward Weston, the eminent California photographer. He bucked the sponsors of the project along to me, and for twenty-four hours I was tempted. Then an image popped into my head: John Donovan rallying with me on the other side of a tennis net in Cairo, lunging after two tennis balls at once—and missing both. I decided to concentrate on Fanny.

We piled up some fifty-odd tapes. Follow-up research had its own charms. Gloria Swanson, at first suspicious and aloof on the telephone, gradually let her guard down and became unstoppable in her recollections of Edmund Goulding, Fanny's first important client and first love. Goulding had directed Swanson in *The Trespasser*. "He was Chaplin's only rival as an improviser," she declared. "Give Eddie a cue—on any subject—and he'd work it up to an epic."

On a single weekend I learned about Chiang Kai Shek's Jewish general, Moshe Cohen, and interviewed a leftover Romanoff prince as well as composer Jay Gorney ("Brother, Can You Spare A Dime"), and a spirited black man who with a boost from Fanny had parlayed a job as chauffeur to Gertrude Lawrence into a Harlem limousine fleet. I bounced from the Hallmark greeting card company, whose Christmas ads had featured a Fanny Holtzmann winter skating scene between canvases by El Greco and Matisse, to my aunt's lively correspondence with George Bernard Shaw, to Rose Halprin of Hadassah, who described Fanny's "incredible tenacity" on behalf of Israel at the U.N..

But there was certain ground where I walked lightly, unwilling to stir acute discomfort: Fanny's repeated frustrations in love, and especially matrimony. I let her tiptoe around the edges of these matters, pursuing them with her sisters, her secretaries, and letters from her motherly confidante, the Duchess of Rutland.

Another sensitive issue was the pattern of tantrums that were an inescapable part of life with Fanny, directed mostly at her one unmarried sister. I reiterated my intention to record such outbursts.

Fanny shrugged: "It's your book." Later she went further: "I don't even want to see your manuscript. You can say in your preface, 'Unread by Fanny, uncensored.'"

But when the galleys came up, she revised her position. Emphatically. From the first dozen pages, she "hated" the book. As she read on she found it cautiously acceptable . . . if I would make a few changes.

The few became so many—and to my mind so arbitrary—that I could see three years of labor going up in smoke. I asked Roger Donald, my editor at Little, Brown, to come down from Boston and mediate. He did, most skillfully; enough was cut out to mollify Fanny, and enough left in to satisfy me. Mostly intact, the galleys went to the printer.

A major source of information about my subject's early years had been my mother, who as deputy ruler of the Holtzmann household had virtually raised Fanny. Since her eightieth birthday eight years before, Bertha's health had been in decline, with emphysema complicating long-standing heart problems. She still held court for an occasional visitor to her small ground floor apartment on East 64th Street, but ventured out less often.

It was her custom every fall, as the evening weather got cooler, to bring hot coffee or a cup of soup to the doormen and elevator men in the building; they in turn looked in on her from time to time. One Saturday night in September of 1974, however, with a large party upstairs creating a stream of elevator traffic, nobody made the usual check-up stop at my mother's 1-C.

That was the night my mother, climbing a stepladder in her kitchenette, lost her footing and fell to the floor. Her hip broken, unable to move, she lay sprawled through the night until a delivery man found her there in the morning.

At Lenox Hill Hospital, my doctor friend Harvey Mandell was grim. "She's too frail for surgery, Ted. Her heart couldn't take it."

For several days relatives trailed in. Silent, inert, surrounded by life-support gadgetry, "Bertha darling" followed their movements with lusterless eyes. Occasionally she murmured a half-audible name in recognition. Finally, clinging to my hand, she was reduced to a wordless clasp.

I turned to my sister. "This isn't living . . . not Bertha-style."

"What does Dr. Mandell say?"

"It's not likely to change. I think we should let her go." Helen nodded.

At six the next morning, Harvey called to report that my mother had died during the night.

A few hours later I was at the hospital; there were documents to sign. As I stood in the lobby, an elevator door opened and an attendant wheeled out a gurney, its white sheet covering a small shapeless mass. I knew instinctively that this sodden lump was my mother, or the flesh that had been my mother. I was shocked at its pathetic size, its utter helplessness. Was this all that remained of a once-vibrant woman, the final outcome of a lifetime's dreams and labors?

It was a moment too bleak, too desperate for tears.

I didn't want to look at my mother in the coffin; I had memories enough. Of the funeral, I recall only two things: the dentist mourner who came to the services in a rumpled sweater (unthinkable!), and the eulogy, ribald but tender, by John Donovan.

Gradually the sense of loss gave way to the realization of a burden removed, a responsibility that had haunted me for decades. No longer constantly tuned in to my mother's medical reports, I was free! Free to pick up and go, live where I pleased, wander the world . . .

I opted for the Far East, and one of the truly intoxicating voyages of my life. This was indeed the other side of the world, light years away from the America of Watergate and the dreary, hackneyed presidency of Gerald Ford.

In Tokyo I gawked at temples and shrines, the bustling throngs along the Ginza, and the brilliant neon signs blazing across the night sky: commercial messages for the natives, dazzling abstractions to the untutored Western eye. These terse geometric slashes, distilled from more elaborate Chinese ideograms, were for me a gigantic outdoor art gallery.

From Japanese inamoratas, I had gained a glimpse of an enormously complex, group-oriented culture that placed loyalty above other virtues, devalued women, and was so enmeshed in ritual that it could devote three years to the proper procedure for peeling an orange.

But I was unprepared for the sheer physical beauty of Japan: the snow banks melting into clouds above Mount Fuji, the exquisite fifteenth century costumes of Noh music drama, the parapeted Golden Pavilion, once the palace of a medieval shogun, at Kyoto, where I also picked up a superb Hiroshige woodblock. "Sudden Rainstorm at Atake" is a study in melancholy: huddled figures battling winds and sheets of rain as they struggle across a curved wooden bridge, while in the background a lone fisherman in a long slender craft poles his way through the water.

I flew on to Taiwan—gourmet delicacies on every street corner, a formidable art museum with treasures snatched away from the Communist-ruled mainland—and then to the rocky bastion of Hong Kong, twenty-nine square miles of pure capitalism fronting on a vast landlocked harbor: rugged peaks, bulging warehouses, sleek modern skyscrapers frowning down on scruffy sampans plowing through the water.

Where efficiency in Japan co-existed with mystic ritual, Hong Kong was unadulterated commerce. From the high rise splendor of the Hong Kong Hilton I had a clear view of the Bank of China, the colony's Supreme Court, the grounds of the Hong Kong Cricket Club and a public park where every dawn hundreds of local citizens fortified themselves for the competitive rigors of the day ahead by performing the solemn exercises of *tai chi chuan*, a series of deliberate slow-motion movements based on martial arts. Ten years later, in Santa Barbara, I would become a practitioner of *tai chi*.

The last leg of my trip—and what a closing act it made!—was Thailand. Here the visual opulence of the Orient ran wild: tier upon tier of elaborately sculptured stone, glittering spires thrust to the heavens, fanciful mythological animals, slender jade Buddhas that seemed to mock the complacent butterballs of Japan. The hundred-and-ten-foot Temple of the Dawn, sparkling in the sun like a golden layer cake, vied for attention against the royal palace complex across the Chao Phaya river, a fairyland of gabled roofs, marble columns, rainbow tiles and altars of almost suffocating grandeur.

But even the humble dwellings along the *klongs*, the man-made canals spiraling between villages, had their quirky charms: intricate lattice work, odd-shaped windows. In a delirium of pleasure, instant Kodak in hand, I ricocheted from floating markets to classic dance performances. For virtually pennies I acquired a half-dozen rice paper rubbings from temple bas-reliefs of lute-strumming musicians; I wish I had bought out the shop.

Thai women were comely, gentle—and abundantly available. The ground floor of my hotel offered among its lobby shopping attractions a criblike cubicle where ladies of various types, in circumspect everyday dress, were on display, chatting and sewing. Guests were free to survey the assemblage, make a note of their choices and phone in their requests for service in their rooms.

I did just that, after fixing on a round-faced sprite of trim proportions. For a brief time I waited; then, impatient, I stepped out into the hall just as a heavy-set woman left the elevator and came shuffling in my direction. Her gait and manner were unfamiliar. The hotel clerk had sent up the wrong person.

I would be pleased to report that I gallantly overlooked the gaffe and graciously welcomed the substitute. The fact is that I sent her back. To the humiliating grind of prostitution I added that of rejection. We all live closer to the barbarous edge than we like to think.

The Lady and the Law, my biography of Fanny, came off the presses to virtually unanimous hosannas, the best notices I had yet received. The St. Louis *Post-Dispatch* welcomed a "remarkable" biography, "coherent, compassionate and penetrating." Norman Nadel, theater critic of the New York *World-Telegram*, pronounced Fanny "a joy to know," and thanked me for so "enchantingly" sharing her story.

A handful of complaints, not unexpected, questioned my cautious, kid-gloves treatment of Fanny's emotional life. But majority opinion was typified by the trade monthly *Best Sellers*: "An absorbing and inspiring portrait . . .Ted Berkman writes superbly, with an exquisite sense of timing, humor, and wit." To which the Mark Twain Society added an honorary membership.

More heartwarming still was the flood of letters from readers, most of them seemingly dashed off by hand in the afterglow of setting the book down. They were from housewives and rabbis and college students, from a psychiatrist in Detroit, an atomic physicist in San Diego, a retired diplomat in the Bahamas. Their common theme was gratitude for what an eighty-two-year-old accountant in Chicago called the most arresting biography among the "thousands of books" he and his wife had read. I rejoiced at the "magnificent, a great achievement" from ballet immortal Anton Dolin and even more at a note on the letterhead of the law school at my alma mater, Cornell:

"What a splendid book," wrote Professor Irving Younger. "I had my copy with me last week in Boulder, Colorado. There I sat, the Rockies over my shoulder and the world of the *shtetl* eight thousand miles away. I read about Angela and Tante Frimme and cried from beginning to end. My hat is off to you."

Yet the many forecasts of best-sellerdom were not being realized. Part of the problem, once again, was the indifference of the commercially crucial New York *Times*. Although Howard Thompson of the *Times* entertainment section turned out to be a fan of mine who went into raptures over a borrowed copy of *Lady*, the paper's literary columns had not carried a line.

At Thompson's request I sent him two review copies, one of which he promised to thrust under the nose of his office neighbor John Leonard, the former editor of Sunday Books. At long last coverage was then assigned. However, it went not to show business-wise Thompson but to an obscure law courts reporter who turned out a dry, juridically-oriented review.

There were difficulties of distribution. Tillie Pekelner, a lecturer to women's groups in Florida, wrote to Roger Donald: "This book has had the warmest audience response of any book I have used in my decades in this field. People deluge me with phone calls. But they have a hard time finding a copy."

A note from Roger Donald advised that my book had been chosen as an alternate selection by the Movie Book Club. Television, in the person of producer Roger Corman, came up with a movie-for-TV offer which neither William Morris nor Fanny considered adequate. For the next decade and more, dramatization projects of one kind or another would continue to spawn option money, excitement—and letdowns.

Had the book been worth doing? Sixteen years later, in the summer of 1992, a friend in Scottsdale, Arizona reported an elaborate four-book display in the lobby of the handsome public library there. Featured were new biographies of James Joyce, Indira Gandhi and Japanese Emperor Hirohito . . . and, as the "unmistakable centerpiece" of the group, *The Lady and the Law*.

CHAPTER 23

Patty Hearst

With *Lady* launched, I went back to my novel of the Inquisition, making a second application for a Guggenheim grant, this time with the hearty endorsement of Hal Lehrman, a Guggenheim Fellow. I spent long hours in research, burrowing deep into every aspect of medieval Spanish society, from royal successions to the pattern of tiles in a courtyard fountain.

In March of 1977, Guggenheim said no. Its published list of grants indicated a preference for more academic proposals, more narrowly focused.

I was tired of gnawing on the Big Apple. For all its lingering treasures—Lincoln Center, the Stage Delicatessen, the winking lights of the George Washington bridge—the city had become too laced with memories. And New Yorkers paid extravagant rents for filthy air, crowded buses, the privilege of being mugged. Central Park had become a wilderness, the Times Square theater district a scabrous mess. And every year the sharp raw blasts of winter put a more stifling clamp on my breath, snapped more at my aging bones. It was time to move on.

But where? From one of my peripatetic literary agents, previously distinguished only for launching wild goose chases, came a possible clue.

Patty Hearst had been in the headlines ever since she was snatched from her apartment on the hippie campus at Berkeley in February of 1974. As a member—whether by choice or compulsion—of the underground "Symbionese Liberation Army," nineteen-year-old Patty had provided covering fire during a Los Angeles store robbery, and brandished a menacing carbine rifle during a bank hold-up. Captured by the FBI in September of 1975, she had been brought to trial the following February for armed bank robbery and possession of a firearm during a felony.

According to Patty, she had been blindfolded, starved and tormented by her kidnappers, then slammed into a tiny closet where two SLA members repeatedly raped her; so she performed the bandit role for fear of her life. According to the government, she was a reckless thrill-seeking rebel enjoying a wild fling with her terrorist lovers. In March she had been found guilty; six months later, with the trial judge dead, she had been sentenced to a seven-year term, and was at the moment out on $1.2 million bail.

Shepherding Patty through her fourteen-month legal battle had been a bronze-skinned, dramatically attractive Mexican-American named Janey Jimenez, one of the few female deputies in the U.S. Marshals Service. A year older than her prisoner, and like Patty one of a five-sister family, the Chicana working girl from the Los Angeles ghetto had become the intimate and confidante of the beleaguered heiress.

Their economic and social backgrounds could not have contrasted more. Patty was the granddaughter of the legendary newspaper tycoon William Randolph Hearst, whose father had pioneered the Homestake gold fortune; Jane's grandmother had been a penniless immigrant, hitchhiking a thousand miles from central Mexico in flight from Pancho Villa's guerrillas. While Patty was dawdling through private schools and debutante dances, Janey from the age of eight was mowing lawns and scrubbing floors. Fatherless at thirteen, Janey fed her fantasies with clippings about the awesome Hearst Castle at San Simeon. Patty didn't need clippings; she was one of the castle's living princesses.

Janey's unsought assignment had catapulted her from obscurity to national prominence, with the relationship between the two girls becoming as much a press and TV lure as the court testimony. News people, legal commentators and psychiatric analysts jousted for seats. In *Time* and *People*, sharing the top of the magazine heap, readers gaped at photos of the robust Mexican-American, with her boldly sculptured features, propelling her fragile charge through a cordon of heavily armed guards.

After Patty's trial, *Playboy* was eager to display Janey as a centerfold nude. She turned that down, but settled for an elaborate contract with a Chicago merchandise-licensing corporation under which they would guarantee her education through law school. Her sponsors then made publication arrangements with a midwest firm controlled by the Universal Press Syndicate.

The publishers, however, insisted on having an experienced hand put the book together—at which point my ever-vigilant agent got into the picture. Would I be interested in being Janey's mouthpiece? There would be joint credit on authorship, and a fairly good advance against royalties.

Two factors distinguished this from a routine, dismissable ghosting offer. Apart from its biographical promise as a close-up of an enigmatic, controversial young woman, the story had mythic overtones as a microcosm of an America bristling with student rebellion, anarchic violence, generational conflict and swaggering attorneys, capped by the irony of a sensation-mongering press largely inspired by the example of Patty's reckless, circulation-hungry grandfather.

Equally important, this chore would give me a chance to make a first-hand check on the irresistibly quaint neo-Spanish hamlet of Santa Barbara, where my roommate Ring Lardner, Jr. had hopped out of his car and into the Pacific on a balmy New Year's Day in the 1930s. Its location on the California central coast was not beyond reach from San Diego, where Janey Jimenez lived. Between research visits, I could sandwich in a trip or two north.

Flying out to San Diego, I found Janey sweeter and more shy than her press coverage suggested. She had no great literary ambitions, and was clearly relieved at the prospect of professional assistance. But she seemed uneasy about disclosing her innermost feelings to a total stranger; my first task was to win her trust.

By the end of the first day, meandering through notes and photographs and press clippings together, we had established a comfortable relationship. I discovered that Janey had enlisted in law enforcement to give Mexican-Americans a different voice in a prison system that had become all too familiar to one of her uncles.

She had spent some 350 hours with Patty Hearst, in jail cells, courtrooms, hospitals, security-packed convoys; in the glare of photographers' flash bulbs and the privacy of women's rest rooms. She had seen her prisoner in every conceivable mood: panic and anger and rare moments of lightness . . . a Patty not on guard in any sense, away from the lunatic threats of the SLA's bomb-throwers and the careful coaching of her lawyers. The two had talked about all the things important to girls of their era, from college courses to earrings, and had speculated on the charms of males in passing cars.

I taped all our discussions, for guidance in setting everything down in her language rather than mine. So long as the phrasing was plausible for a twenty-two-year-old girl, a touch of self-deprecating humor wouldn't hurt: "If Patty was America's most wanted criminal, I was its least qualified marshal."

To buttress my research, I traveled to all the key locations involved—incarceration centers, the San Francisco Federal courthouse, the bullet-pocked doorway of Patty's Berkeley apartment—and slogged through the 1,250,000 words of the trial transcript.

Janey, conscious of the spotlight on her as a young minority female, had initially been determined not to "get involved" with her prisoner. That resolution wavered when Patty, subjected to an examination for vaginal bleeding, cringed in terror, screamed "Oh, my God," and collapsed weeping in the deputy's arms. Patty's reaction spoke to Janey more eloquently than any testimony in the courtroom.

Humor drew the two girls together. Patty, badgered on the witness stand about her diminished bowel activity while locked in an eight-foot closet, whispered to Janey as she returned to her seat: "I should have told him I was scared shitless." They also discovered parallel views on such subjects as sex (sensual pleasure wasn't enough) and feminism (a fair shot in the marketplace, yes; militant anti-male crusading, no). The Patty who gradually emerged before Janey's eyes was sensitive, curious, naively impressionable; willful, sometimes inconsiderate but always open to logical argument; defiant on the surface, courageous at the core and in between pathetically vulnerable.

That was not the girl the jury saw. To counter the outlaw-tainted image created by Patty's months with the SLA, her high-priced, high-profile lawyers, headed by F. Lee Bailey, completely rearranged her appearance, contriving a grave, unsmiling robot.

As a result the jurors, most of them in their forties and mistrustful of Patty's generation, found her an enigma. Heightening their confusion was a mountain of conflicting psychiatric testimony, most of it in weighty technical jargon. Arbitrarily withheld by the trial judge was a relatively straightforward summation by a court-appointed, nationally famous mental health expert. Louis J. West, chairman of the psychiatry department at UCLA, characterized Patty as a "crushed, battered child" whose pulse shot up to 140 at every mention of her ordeal, and whose fragmented memory patterns mimicked the "survival syndrome" of tortured war prisoners.

The jury brought in a verdict of guilty. The foreman announcing it promptly threw up; several others soon experienced health or marital problems. Plagued by doubts, the jurors continued to meet as an informal support group for a year, by which time they were virtually unanimous in telling Janey they had originally reached the wrong decision.

A torrent of mail, mostly sympathetic, poured in to both Patty and Janey. In September, with the trial judge dead and a clamor for law-and-order coming from the political right, a new judge handed down a seven year sentence. By that time, after reviewing the entire trial transcript and the many peculiar intangibles permeating the case, I had arrived at my own conclusion: Patty Hearst was the target figure in a complex circus of media excitement, limelight-seeking lawyers, and schizophrenic revolutionaries. If her name had been Patty Jones, she would never have been convicted.

In the closing pages of the book, I had taken off the wraps and expressed some opinions that I knew Janey fully endorsed.

> I think the Hearst case has some unpleasant things to tell us about present-day America: our rejection of human values in favor of televised sensation; our galloping mistrust (the jurors didn't believe Patty partly because after Vietnam and Watergate and the nursing home scandals we have stopped believing very much in anything or each other); and above all, our unwillingness to look at the nasty cracks in our society: our seething prisons, drugs, unemployment, a crazy slate of priorities that makes millionaires of ball players but keeps cutting the budget for schools. We'd rather deal in platitudes than tackle our real problems. It's easier to comfort ourselves by "upholding the law" with a Patty Hearst while disregarding the message about the evil beneath the story, the festering despair that throws up, like mud from a geyser, a murderous "Cinque." But poverty and illness and a criminal response to hopelessness won't go away. America is a single community, whether we acknowledge it or not.

Our publishers, although nervous about what they perceived as a public climate increasingly hostile to Patty, let my comments stand. However, they decided to modify our title. I had fixed on *My Prisoner, My Friend*; to Janey's visible dismay, they lopped off the *My Friend*.

The next—and final—word would come from the critics.

Meanwhile, my Santa Barbara inspection scheme had worked out well. Twice, between work sessions with Janey, I had managed instructive jaunts northward.

From my first sniff of the breezes at the Santa Barbara airport, my spirits soared. Nothing so balmy had come my way in many years; it was like a gentle caress after the harsh December winds of New York.

Friendly company was waiting on the runway. Sybil Rice, my old flame from Washington, had moved to Santa Barbara with her husband, a Greek diplomat-poet, around 1970. They whisked me along the town's main arteries: U.S. Highway 101, a twentieth century expansion of the old *camino real* or royal road of Spanish days; Milpas Street, and Cabrillo Boulevard, lined with lofty palms stretching along the coast.

Just before the boulevard curved northward, tucked away in a sheltered pocket stood Kingswood Village, later re-named El Escorial, a four-building apartment complex snuggled around a capacious swimming pool. This had everything I was looking for: clean ocean air, stunning vistas, good walking terrain and a year-around heated pool. The only thing it didn't have was an available apartment.

I stayed overnight with my obliging hosts, but on my second trip roamed solo, taking taxis and buses to savor the local atmosphere and check out alternative housing possibilities. I found nothing to compare with Kingswood, so spent several hours chatting with its residents. This led to a sub-let arrangement that gave me a chance to spend a couple of experimental months there. I returned to New York with a full set of complex blueprints and high hopes of landing an apartment, just as *My Prisoner* was reaching the book stores.

Reviewers greeted the book with gratifying warmth. "The portrait of Patty that emerges is likable and believable," declared the advance notice in *Publishers Weekly*. "Few readers will remain unmoved." The Atlanta *Journal and Constitution* called it "a moving story that I couldn't put down," about "two unforgettable characters." New York *Post* by-liner Harriet van Horne devoted her entire column to a sympathetic account of this "sad little book" with its "small endearing views of Patty."

But the most extravagant appraisal came in the Chicago *Tribune* from Andrew Greeley. Totally won over by a "transparently sincere" and "heartrending" book, Greeley concluded that Patty Hearst was "an innocent woman badly traumatized twice, once by her insane kidnappers and once by the government of the United States." President Jimmy Carter, declared the columnist, "ought to read the book. If he does, as a Christian gentleman committed to compassion, he would have to issue a presidential pardon."

That was in October of 1977. In mid-May of the following year, Jimmy Carter ended Patty's long ordeal by commuting her sentence to the twenty-two months she had already served.

That same week, I was moving my piano into Kingswood Village. Any lingering reluctance about leaving New York had been dispelled the previous month when an uninvited visitor burst into my 75th St. apartment, missing my return by a matter of minutes. The intruder had torn my heavy steel-shielded apartment door off its hinges, scooped up valuable statuary and ripped open my strongbox. He had helped himself to my gold Phi Beta Kappa key, which I never wore; and, far more grievously, to the gold boxing medal won by Mickey Marcus at West Point and passed on to me by his appreciative widow.

When the phone call came in early May from Kingswood Village, confirming the availability of a mountain-view one bedroom apartment, I was more than ready.

CHAPTER 24

High Society

My life in Santa Barbara has been largely a procession, not always orderly, of vivid personalities, most of them human: Robert Kirsch, Jonathan Winters, Anne Francis, Artie Shaw, Ray Bradbury, composers Elmer Bernstein and Earl Robinson, author-painter-bullfighter Barnaby Conrad, and Bonzo.

Thanks to Bob Kirsch, I was nibbling caviar with the likes of Robert Mitchum before I had memorized my new telephone number. Kirsch was the literary critic of the powerful Los Angeles *Times*, bearded, plump and erudite, a jolly Rabelaisian monk transported to the twentieth century, and arguably the most widely quoted reviewer west of the Hudson. Rumpled and cheerful, he frequently looked as if he had just shaken loose from his bed, or had dressed while taking a shower. Every time he dismounted from his ancient Volvo, a pile of books spilled out in his wake.

But he had done the first public critique of *Cast A Giant Shadow*, a warmly flattering one that I still carried in my wallet. He was a friend and admirer of my crony Meyer Levin. And he had dispatched his children to dreamland for years with the cry, "Bedtime for Bonzo!" Enduring relationships have been built on less sturdy foundations.

Although Bob's contract allowed him to ply his wares from anywhere in the world, his home base was Santa Barbara. He knew the town, its social groupings and its history. The site was first spotted by a Portuguese explorer in 1542, five decades after Columbus. Spanish conquistadores who came ashore two centuries later found a flourishing culture of peaceable fishermen and traders, the Chumash Indians, who created the plank canoe and lived in attentive harmony with their environment.

Spanish guns and crucifixes put an end to that. The emissaries of European civilization seduced the most attractive Chumash and enslaved the rest to build their local Mission. To the "benighted savages" of California the enlightened intruders brought Christianity, diphtheria and venereal disease. The religion endured; most of the Chumash did not.

The Spaniards were driven out in 1822 by Mexican forces, who were themselves supplanted in 1846 by United States cavalry; four years later statehood came to cattle-rich California.

After the Civil War, fortunes accumulated elsewhere brought spa-seekers to balmy Santa Barbara. With the establishment of a rail link, palatial estates sprang up in the hilly enclave of Montecito, where the Fleischmann yeast family and their peers put down roots, hiring the Chicano descendants of the vanquished Mexicans to serve their wines and tend their gardens.

The town itself remained nondescript until 1925, when a devastating earthquake flattened much of it. A small clique of reformers seized the opportunity to create a new Santa Barbara refashioned to their own elegant tastes. They would build a dream city of white adobe, red tiles and wrought-iron balconies, meticulously faithful to neo-colonial architecture, more Spanish than Seville. And they did, right down to a luxuriously landscaped courthouse sheltering the most beautiful jail in America.

A few decades later the unique setting of the town, cradled between rugged mountains and the sea, drew the emissaries of the New Age—hippies, gurus, transcendental meditators—to sprawl in jacuzzis and "go with the flow."

Bob Kirsch and I shared many enthusiasms: jazz, Mexican restaurants, pretty girls (his appeal to women, despite pot belly, baggy trousers and general indifference to style was baffling but undeniable). Himself the quintessential man-about-town, he decided my social life needed a fillip.

He whisked me first to the home of a Montecito hostess, blonde, soft-spoken Leinie Schilling, whose family's spices occupied whole sections at the local markets. Next stop was a quasi-literary cocktail party, where I found an eager listener in Jacques La Tourette, thirty-odd, almost unreasonably handsome, and visibly fascinated by my tales of the Mideast.

Bob Kirsch filled me in. Jacques boasted direct descent from the Count de La Tourette, a French Huguenot who fled his homeland in the late seventeenth century after revocation of the Edict of Nantes, which had guaranteed religious freedom to French Protestants. The count had settled in the Blue Ridge foothills of Virginia, and intermarried with the colony's first families. Today, the La Tourettes hobnobbed with Arab oil emirs and lived in an imposing anachronistic chateau overlooking an estate that looked to me like Central Park: twenty Montecito acres of oaks and eucalyptus.

La Tourette's stamp of approval won me a lunch invitation from Elmer Bernstein, whose movie scores embellished the sound tracks of half the films coming out of Hollywood. A fey, wary-eyed little man with a leprechaun air, famous for his *Man With The Golden Arm* theme, Elmer presided over a richly appointed Montecito mansion complete with riding trails for his two young daughters..

Elmer was, like Irving Wallace on the literary front, awash in dollars but pining for serious professional recognition. Movie music, by its auxiliary nature, raised aesthetic questions. Elmer had the further misfortune of sharing the family name of the charismatic "Lennie," to whom he was not related, and of inevitably being eclipsed by him.

Over a lunch of sliced bread and cold cuts, almost comically spartan in the cost-be-damned setting, he lectured me earnestly on the artistic legitimacy of movie scores and plied me with supporting pamphlets. Evidently he hoped, while cementing his social standing, to recruit me for his crusade. His declamation fell flat.

A week later my Mustang nestled among the Bentleys at the most elaborate party I had ever seen: scores of guests swarming over the parapets and stone balconies of the La Tourette chateau, flowing across the capacious lawn; incredible giant strawberries, each as large as an ordinary grocery basketful.

Jacques' mother, predictably beautiful in the Zsa Zsa Gabor mode, decided a few days later that an authentic Middle East banquet honoring her Lebanese heritage would stand the town on its ear. Under a twenty-foot ancient Moroccan tent, diners assembled on cushions around a long table lighted only by thick glowing candles. The hand-picked guest list included three presidents of major companies and their wives, a hotel-magnate couple visiting from St. Moritz, two corporate attorneys, and the bubbly little society editor of the local *News-Press*, Beverley Jackson. Plus one added starter: Jacques' new chum, Ted Berkman.

Regional costume being obligatory, caftans and turbans from *The*

Arabian Nights were on display, along with harem veils and generous expanses of female midriffs. I kicked in with a dazzling multi-colored robe acquired in the walled Old City of Jerusalem. The props and décor of the setting alone would have financed a homeless shelter for weeks, but I was too caught up in my social coup to be thinking in such terms. From Brooklyn to Babylon! If this wasn't heaven, it had to be in the neighborhood.

Mme. La Tourette's prodigal spree won an entire column from Beverley Jackson, who not only paid tribute to my colorful garb but added that Ted Berkman "later in the evening proved to be a great jazz pianist."

In succeeding issues, *News-Press* readers were apprised by Beverley of my every move, learning that I exchanged movie talk with Bob Mitchum and Stuart Whitman at a book-launching party for Anne Francis, and "played wonderful after dinner piano music" at a Newcomers Club reception graced by Jonathan Winters. For her culminating flattery, Beverley cited her own opening-night query to the proprietor of a new Mexican restaurant in Montecito: "Isn't that Jane Russell Peoples standing in line waiting for a table behind Ted Berkman?"

Jane Russell! I was not only in America's Paradise, but coupled with one of its ranking angels. After equal billing with a busty legend of Hollywood history, what else could there be?

Easy. A full-scale interview in the *News-Press*. On November 20, 1980, two fat columns of type clustered around a four-column photo of author-at-typewriter on the balcony of my "inspirational mountain view" apartment. Headlined "Award for Piersall Film," the story traced my long trail from Cornell to the "amenities of Santa Barbara." What prompted this lavish attention was the resurgence of Bonzo, an unexpectedly born-again chimpanzee.

CHAPTER 25

Born Again Bonzo

Americans like a spot of color in their politics, a whiff or two of comic relief; we have an endemic reluctance to take professional windbags too seriously.

The national tickets for 1980 were not exactly loaded with fun and fireworks. In fact, they offered the dullest White House pairing since a century earlier, when James Garfield waltzed to the polls against Winfield Hancock. The toothy smile and doleful "malaise" of the incumbent, Jimmy Carter, were all too familiar; and to much of the country his Republican adversary, Ronald Reagan, looked like a movie-actor cowboy in a starched shirt, striking presidential poses. Neither man had the cheery insouciance of Jack Kennedy, the flamboyance of Lyndon Johnson, or the feisty directness of Harry Truman.

Newsmen, poking through the Reagan files in search of a promising angle, stumbled across Bonzo. The chimp had been Reagan's co-star in *Bedtime for Bonzo*, a light satirical comedy that Rafe Blau and I had written thirty years earlier, in which Reagan as a brilliant college professor (admittedly something of a stretch) had demonstrated the transcendence of environment over heredity by bringing up a frolicsome simian like a human child. The chimp had never quite faded from public memory, thanks to a cultish passion for *Bedtime* screenings on certain campuses, and even more to the attentions of Johnny Carson, the popular host of the *Tonight* show. Carson's producer, Frederick de Cordova, had been the director of *Bedtime*, and Carson, a merciless tease, never let him forget it.

First to explore Bonzo's news potential was a reporter for the Canadian Broadcasting Company who referred airily—and inaccurately—to Reagan's sharing the spotlight with the chimp in *Bonzo Goes to College*. Rafe Blau, happening to hear the broadcast at his home in Nova Scotia, penned a polite note to the CBC pointing out that Reagan was present for *Bedtime*, but either dropped out or was flunked out of College.

CBC promptly fired back an invitation to fly up to Toronto and enlighten all of Canada, coast to coast. Rafe was on the air for seven minutes; when he came off a call was waiting from Rudy Maxa, a syndicated columnist for the Washington *Post* with four-hundred newspaper outlets around the world. Maxa did a piece that in turn elicited for Rafe a long live telephone interview with a radio station in Sacramento, California and a request for a thousand-word feature for the op-ed page of the Baltimore *Sun*. Obviously, Bonzo answered an appetite.

Picking up the cue, I floated a mock rumor that the chimp was still alive, if exceedingly venerable, and living in quiet retirement on the balcony of my Santa Barbara apartment. I then invited two local women writers—Bert Fields of the Scripps League Newspapers and Ann van der Veer of the *News and Review*—to conspire with me in arranging a tongue-in-cheek interview in which I would act as spokesman/interpreter for the animal star.

The whimsy worked, garnering astonishing space from Oregon to Iowa. Bonzo was an ardent Californian, I revealed, conforming strictly to the Golden State life style: "He practices meditation, jogs—partly on his hands, of course—and subsists on a health food diet of soy milk and trail mix."

What did he think of his former co-star? "Very sure-footed. Able to move quickly—especially to the right." Was Reagan honest? "He never stole a scene from me!"

Bonzo was described as being "somewhat miffed" at Ronnie choosing George Bush over him for the vice-presidency, but "willing to consider an ambassadorship to a banana republic." The ladies reported that he was intrigued by the space program—"several of his cousins are astronauts"—and was dabbling with a play script, testing the psychological theory that if a monkey hammered long enough on a Remington, he would eventually come up with *Macbeth*.

Reporter: What about the rumor that he is planning a run of his own for the White House?

Berkman: No! I deny that. But of course I can't speak for Bonzo. He stands on his own feet—or hands, as the case may be. But he's his own chimp, and I might not be able to keep him from accepting a mandate.

The local university paper blazoned its cover with photos of the two *Bedtime* stars and me; inside was a long interview and more photos, including me at the piano playing the title song I had written for the picture. Even the dignified *Christian Science Monitor* leaped aboard, requesting an exclusive slice of anthropoid briefing. I obliged with an update, including a tidbit about the chimp's football-passing exploits in *Bonzo Goes To College*: "Bonzo was credited at the time with having the intelligence of an eight-year-old human, which presumably qualified him for the Yale backfield."

Rafe, meanwhile, was having a belated look at our *Bedtime* contract with Universal. Commercial rights to the chimp character, he concluded, remained in our hands. In a few days we were the bewildered proprietors of Bonzo Enterprises and the possessors of another contract, this one with the International Licensing Associates, whose roster of clients included Gloria Vanderbilt Jeans and the Newport Jazz Festival. ILA promptly put together a huge star-spangled color poster from Western Graphics—first printing, 100,000—showing Bonzo with a friendly arm draped around the ex-Governor of California, and the scribbled inscription: "To Ronnie, Good luck always. Love, Bonzo." The country's largest T-shirt manufacturer signed up with ILA and went into instant production. Negotiations were under way for slumber bags, a Bonzo doll, various clothing items and novelty giftware. The agency assured us we were sitting on a gold mine.

We hired a media specialist. Bonzo landed on the cover of the stately leftist *New Republic* and in the columns of its rightist intellectual rival, William F. Buckley's *National Review*. The gossip-peddling *National Enquirer* hustled into the act. The *Wall Street Journal* observed learnedly that Bonzo's appeal flourished across the board: nostalgia for oldsters, fun for collegians, a pet for tots.

And Rafe and I were bombarded with calls. Between close-ups for a photographer from Tokyo and a telephone interview with the London *Telegraph*, I did a live broadcast over Australian National Radio. A big spread in Lisbon's *Correio de Manha* introduced Bonzo to Portugal. A Labor paper in Israel opposed to Prime Minister Menachem Begin bawled the optimistic headline, "Bedtime for Begin." And the Paris *Herald* reported that "*l'heure du dodo de Bonzo*" reigned unopposed on French television screens.

Reagan's election in November prompted us to bring back his co-star alive. The original Bonzo, of course, had gone up in the smoke of the Universal compound fire. After surveying the chimp scene, we engaged a talented young anthropoid (from Tarzana, naturally) to play Bonzo III. The new chimp replicated the rare white face and floppy white ear of the original; there was a strong possibility, I confided to the press, that he was a grandnephew of the original. "It's hard to authenticate," I admitted, "but the first Bonzo was something of a sexpot. Presumably he had his flings like any other star."

People magazine rose cheerfully to the bait, sending a small squad to Kingswood Village. *People*, a cocky little rag founded by *Time* in 1974, had parlayed a Winchellian nose for celebrity gossip and a flare for offbeat photo features into competitive standing with *Reader's Digest*, *Parade* and *Modern Maturity*, if not quite with *TV Guide*. Bonzo III as my guest rode a tricycle around the pool, took a dip in the jacuzzi (the manager was furious), and snuggled contentedly in my arms for the journal's photographer. *People* gave us two full pages of words and pictures, marred only by the fact that a reporter with either a tin ear or a hangover mangled my name. Bonzo lost no time in registering a mild reproach:

> A carload of coconuts to you for bringing me back alive so vividly, but in the process you annihilated one of my co-creators, Ted Berkman. Your story refers to "Ed Brickman," a name which will ring no bells for admirers of Ted Berkman's book *Cast A Giant Shadow*, his award-winning film *Fear Strikes Out* or his Harry Truman memoirs on television. Boo-boos are supposedly for chimps, not PEOPLE. For the future, I am available for proofreading most evenings—until Bedtime.
>
> Bonzo (that's B-O-N-Z-O)
> San Simian, Calif.

Television was equally on our heels, thanks to a change in network news budgets. After years of accepting newscasts as a pay-back for free use of the public airwaves, and subsidizing them with the profits from programs like "Gunsmoke," the networks had saddled their news departments with financial self-sufficiency. The result was semi-invented "news magazines" and the dressed-up controversy of shows like *Sixty*

Minutes, until the lines between news and entertainment blurred into their bastard offspring of "infotainment." The new format enhanced the status of preening reporter-performers like Sam Donaldson, who started out as a disc jockey. And it was made to order for our sprightly little chimp.

With Bonzo III in tow we traveled to New York and a Christmas Eve appearance on the NBC television network. Our protégé came through nicely, cavorting with children in the audience. He sneered at the host of the show, Tom Snyder, but refrained from the nasty biting to which his predecessors had sometimes been inclined. I explained our disappointment at failing to snare Cary Grant as our star: "Of course, if we had we wouldn't be here. Then again—Cary Grant might be president."

Headlines kept piling up. But licensing agreements, oddly enough, were not. Bulletins from ILA continued to intimate that new contracts were being "ironed out" or "wrapped up" with a small army of manufacturers. Comic page artists Mell Lazarus ("Momma") and Bill Rechin ("Crock") were turning out sketches for a Bonzo doll. Waiting in the wings were a children's book, and a cartoon panel which would feature Bonzo as a wisdom-dispensing elder stateschimp, something of a cross between Will Rogers and Henry Kissinger. Meanwhile actual advances, lost in a labyrinth of documents, were paltry.

During this lull in our fortunes, a pair of inventive students at the Harvard Business School came up with an alternative poster. Colorful and witty, "Bedtime for Brezhnev" displayed a grim, resolute cowboy Reagan collaring a sheepish Brezhnev in ranch attire. Backing the white-hatted hero were a stalwart trio in Stetsons: George Bush, Alexander Haig, and "Henry Kissinger as Doc." Also in the cast were Fidel Castro, "courtesy of Bolshoi Films," and "Jerry Brown as the Preacher." The poster sold eight thousand copies and financed its authors' second year at Harvard.

At long last, in the middle of 1981, Bill Rechin's sketches for a bean-bag doll were approved, and substantial advance payments materialized from Knickerbocker Toys. Their Bonzo doll grinned from both front and back covers of their color catalog for Spring, giving us a presumably important bellwether for the February, 1982 Toy Fair in New York.

Gradually the cheery scenario began to disintegrate. Licensees were not following through with their commitments. In the late spring of 1982 Knickerbocker suddenly changed course, relinquishing its option to develop additional products.

Very reluctantly, we had to face the disagreeable truth: manufacturers were fearful of offending Reaganite millions for whom the former movie hero had become an untouchable idol, now shrouded in the mystique of the presidency. It would be blasphemous, or *lèse majesté*—the outlines of an imperial Reagan were already on the horizon—to poke fun at Ronald Righteous. Once again—in 1952 I had told my Republican uncle that nobody I knew would vote for Eisenhower—I had misgauged the gullibility of the American public.

Ironically, Reagan himself had shrewdly embraced the Bonzo motif during his campaign, realizing that it softened the image of a man who had welcomed California student protesters to a "blood bath." The candidate clowned with a stuffed chimp on his campaign plane, and joked about the alleged gender ambiguities of his co-star.

His followers, manufacturers felt, would brook no such lowly associations. A buckle-and-suspender novelty tycoon, stomping out of a meeting, summed the matter up crisply: "You don't wanna kid no public icon."

Columnists and cartoonists were less timid. For more than two years Art Buchwald all but adopted Bonzo. He devoted a long and hilarious column to the disclosure that Bonzo was secretly ensconced in the White House, cuddling regularly in the Chief Executive's lap, lunching on bananas and Democrats, and on one occasion wandering into the Communications Room, where he amused himself batting out teletype messages that inadvertently demolished the welfare system and insulted the entire Soviet leadership.

A savagely mocking essay by the Canadian commentator Wayne Howell suggested that Bonzo's alleged vocabulary of three-hundred-odd words would easily match that of the notoriously incoherent Secretary of State Alexander Haig, and that the chimp would fit nicely in a political establishment widely characterized as Neanderthal.

Editorial page cartoonists welcomed Bonzo like a long-lost relative, which he possibly was. Paul Conrad's stiletto thrusts in the Los Angeles *Times* included a sketch of the chimp at a Senate confirmation hearing: "Other than your friendship with the President, Mr. Bonzo, what qualifies you for this Cabinet position?" Another Pulitzer Prize winner, Patrick Oliphant, drew Bonzo lolling among starlets at a Hollywood pool, while a haughty butler tells a telephone caller that "Mr. Bonzo has no comment on" a foreign policy crisis. After the decimation of the Reagan Cabinet in 1987 by firings and resignations, Florida's Orlando *Sentinel* showed a hapless president facing the chimp across a conference table; an aide murmurs, "He's the only one left, sir!" The cartoon deluge spread to the comic strips ("Which one is Bonzo, Dad?", demanded Dennis the Menace before a television set), to the other side of the Atlantic in London's *Independent*, and across the Pacific to *Asahi* of Tokyo.

Bonzo lingered in the public prints for a long time. In April of 1989 the historian Arthur Schlesinger declared, "Reaganland is finished, bankrupt; at last it is truly bedtime for Bonzo." A year later, the "adorable ape" was cited, along with *My Fair Lady*, *The Wizard of Oz* and *The Ten Commandments* in a *People* salute to films best reflecting American mores over the past six decades. Soon after, Rafe and I had to blow the whistle on an animal trainer trying to palm off his pet Cheetah as the original Bonzo; a cute fiction, we noted, "smelling only slightly of press-agentry or senility, to both of which Cheetah at fifty-six is entitled." And when Kitty Kelly published her unauthorized biography of Nancy Reagan, including libidinous accounts of the president's alleged adventures between the sheets as a Hollywood Lothario, the New York *Daily News* trumpeted the headline, "Bedtime for Ronzo."

Gradually, Bonzo faded from the national scene. Reagan unfortunately did not.

CHAPTER 26

Regretfully, Reagan

It took me a long time to acknowledge in my heart the fact of the Reagan presidency. The notion that an affable, garrulous movie actor now occupied the seat once ennobled by Washington, Jefferson and Lincoln was simply too much for me to absorb. I recall waking up on several mornings with a sense of relief, convinced that the election of Reagan was nothing more than a bad dream from which a return to consciousness had rescued me. It was more than disconcerting to realize after a few minutes that I had the matter backward: sanity was the dream, Reagan the incredible reality. That owlish pundits would one day analyze Reagan's "achievements" in office, while worshipful admirers urged addition of his profile to the great figures adorning Mount Rushmore would seem on the face of it unthinkable.

Yet to anyone steeped as I had been, in propaganda analysis on one hand and the shaping of character by words and pictures on the other, Reagan's election was not only plausible but inevitable. What made this second-string utility actor emerge as a Colossus on the global political scene was an extraordinary confluence of public susceptibility, fortuitous casting, and adroit manipulation by "handlers" who knew how to rub the Aladdin's lamp of television.

A populace pounded into passivity by a decades-long barrage of media hokum and hype, an onslaught in which the line between information and entertainment had become hopelessly blurred, provided the Republican candidate with a ready-made audience conditioned in advance to the star system. In my mid-century Guggenheim grant proposal I had predicted a time when Americans, drowned in the words, pictures and canned laughter of a televised fantasy world would surrender their intellectual autonomy, and the shallow shibboleths of Madison Avenue would lead to the mindless enshrinement of manufactured "celebrities." That time came in the 1980s.

The approaching Reagan era had been glimpsed far down the tracks. In 1959 Ed Murrow had warned a London audience that a television-soaked public might vote "for profile rather than principle: an unruly lock of hair may be more effective than a disciplined mind."

The new medium would not have taken kindly to George Washington's clumsy, speech-mangling wooden dentures. Nor would it have welcomed Lincoln's worn, creviced features or Franklin Roosevelt's polio-ravaged legs. Ronald Reagan, on the other hand, was "clean-cut," the boy next door: friendly, gregarious, breathing the political virtue of mediocrity and the well-rehearsed pitchman's aura of sincerity.

Camera-schooled, Reagan was able to draw upon a copious bag of tricks. Yet he was not "difficult"; he learned and performed the lines handed to him. In fact, he was totally helpless without them. Ralph Nelson, the distinguished film director of *Requiem for a Heavyweight* and *Lilies of the Field*, had unflattering recollections of steering Reagan through a television drama. "I never knew an actor so dependent on the script," Nelson told me. "He had less gift for invention than Bonzo."

As president of the Screen Actors Guild, Reagan made it possible for his own agent, MCA, to by-pass usual union rules and double as a television producer. When MCA in 1952 launched its General Electric Theater, its host for the new show was its loyal client, Ronald Reagan. GE sent him out on its banquet circuit, bestowing his ghosted anti-government gospel on a quarter of a million enthusiastic listeners.

In 1964 he delivered a television broadside for Barry Goldwater. Movie heroes were no novelty in California. An ex-hero with puppet possibilities was something else.

Sheilah Graham, keen of eye under her Hollywood flimflam, in an August, 1981 article for the New York *Times,* listed department store magnate Alfred Bloomingdale and Armand Deutsch, inheritor of the Sears-Roebuck fortune among the puppeteers.

Sheilah recalled Reagan as an unstoppable talkative interviewee when he was a two-hundred-dollar-a-week B-picture staple at Warner Brothers in 1937: "a nice, not too bright, amiable young man." He later became smarter, she observed, "smart enough to allow the men behind him to pull the strings for the attractive mouthpiece they promoted" to the governorship.

In 1980, Governor Reagan's handlers took their act to the White House. Its essentials were simple: keep the front man dancing out front, while policy decisions were made backstage. When the script was ready, and production details had been orchestrated by skilled professionals under the baton of veteran public relations man Michael Deaver, call in the mouthpiece to deliver the message.

From there on it was simply a matter of adapting the star system, as memorably sketched for me by Arthur Ripley, to the political arena. Just as at Paramount, a cast of thousands was assembled: script writers, scene designers, lighting experts, sound men, make-up people, still photographers, continuity assistants, press spokesmen, supporting character actors, bit players and extras. Every scene was carefully laid out, and if possible rehearsed. Nothing, from a "photo opportunity" of the hero riding into the sunset to a summit dialog with Gorbachev was left to chance. President Reagan (Mike Deaver referred to him as "the talent") was a p.r. confection, a Mike Deaver production.

Studio mores required that a star image be not only created but sustained. Thus, it would not do for Anthony Perkins, playing a virile ballplayer to be revealed as a homosexual. On the same principle, Ronald Reagan's contentious first marriage and his difficulties with his children were swept out of sight. Mike Deaver put his "talent" on display only against traditional, easy-to-grasp backgrounds: riding a horse, chopping wood . . . the same settings that had worked for John Wayne and Henry Fonda. Reagan's political poses were chosen with equal care. On my wall a huge banner headline from the local *News-Press* bears the firm, uncompromising message, "Reagan praises American motherhood."

Between camera "takes," Reagan was assiduously shielded from contact with the press, lest one of his facetious ad libs ("We begin bombing Russia in five minutes.") send the damage-control staff into overtime. He spent more time sawing wood on his ranch than Nero spent sawing on his fiddle. But Reagan had a larger staff than the Roman emperor, and one of their prime functions was to see that no nosy reporters bothered the boss.

Now and then the White House felt obliged to hold an actual news conference. Reagan feared and hated the ordeal. Robert Donovan and Ray Scherer, in their *Unsilent Revolution*, capture the moments before gladiator Reagan went out to meet his could-be executioners: the fervent hand-holding, whispered encouragement and farewell kisses from Mommy Nancy, the last-minute notes pressed into his hand to "bring him up" by master handler Deaver. At one conference he barely managed to stumble and fumble his way through queries on Salt II negotiations and affirmative action.

But there was no way totally to ward off his outlandish responses. Although Reagan's World War II service was confined to California, he was caught faking a melodramatic account of taking photographs at a Nazi death camp.

The task of guarding the presidential image was entrusted mainly to White House spokesman Larry Speakes, whom I watched in action when the Washington press corps came to Santa Barbara.

I looked on, disbelieving, as he led the historic watchdogs of the Republic through his hoops, compliant as well-trained Airedales.

The economy? "Stimulants" were under consideration. The missile vote? No comment. Ditto on Iran-Contra. But the president had pancakes for breakfast, and there would be a photo opportunity, Reagan trimming a tree, at two o'clock. Class dismissed.

Would the electorate have been dismayed to learn that a San Francisco astrologer was dictating the sites and dates of Reagan's meetings with Gorbachev? Probably not. The myth had been established of the lonely cowboy riding above the fray.

In September of 1985, I underscored the point in a letter to the *News-Press*.

> With Ronald Reagan at the national helm, John Gavin running our embassy in Mexico City, and Fess Parker poised to offer his services as U.S. Senator (if Charlton Heston doesn't crowd him off the G.O.P. screen), perhaps it is time to reconsider our constitutional qualifications for high political office, and give proper weight to the public predilection for glamorized media figures. How about sitcom stardom as a prerequisite for state office, feature-picture billing as the credential for a federal post, and for the plum role of the Oval Office, confining future eligibility to those who are clearly the divinities of popular choice, our rock 'n roll idols?
>
> Madonna for president, anyone?

This was one of a dozen effusions—including an exchange with the resident of the White House—to which I was driven during the Reagan era. In a letter to the *News and Review* I proposed the creation of a double presidency: one man to discharge the serious responsibilities of the office, the other to fulfill the ceremonial duties of modern monarchs. This national m.c. "could be decked out with a splendid wardrobe, perhaps even a set of Kabuki-type masks appropriate for addressing particular audiences: firmly grim for the Moral Majority, infectiously jolly for the Bartenders' Union."

I was amused several years later when former House Speaker Tip O'Neill conceded in his memoirs that for all of Reagan's deficiencies as a chief executive, "he would have made a hell of a king." And I had a royal reward much sooner, on January 9, 1984, in the form of a greeting on my seventieth birthday, bearing the presidential seal and signed (or stamped) Nancy Reagan and Ronald Reagan, both "proud to share this memorable occasion." A neighbor in Kingswood Village had apparently notified Reagan of my upcoming natal day.

Flattered and touched in spite of myself—did they fire off these things by the truckload?—I dispatched a hearty thanks, and added "a point of curiosity: was I being honored because of, in spite of, or irrespective of my connection with *Bedtime for Bonzo*?"

Back came a letter on White House stationery, with the chummy salutation "Dear Ted":

> After seeing some of what passes for "entertainment" on the screen today, I think we can look back with pride on "Bonzo." I'd be very proud for my grandchildren to see "Bedtime for Bonzo," but I wonder how many of today's movie stars will be able to say the same thing? Nancy joins me in sending our warmest wishes for a happy and healthy New Year.

Yes, my response agreed, *Bonzo* by today's lights "assumed heroic proportions." And so would he, if he balanced our enhanced military posture with a flight to Moscow "in a determined effort to set humanity free from the nuclear nightmare."

End of correspondence. Joe Laitin, then ombudsman of the Washington *Post*, did a wry column reporting the exchange, but nothing further arrived from Reagan.

A few months later, after warm tributes to Francisco Franco and Philippine dictator Ferdinand Marcos, Reagan rounded out his slate by hailing the mercenary "contras" of Nicaragua as "freedom fighters" emulating the heroes of the American Revolution. He proposed to honor them with special "identity cards," a notion I compared editorially with "pinning Boy Scout medals on a squad of Mafia hit men: sad, ludicrous and ultimately obscene."

Instant-history has been incredibly kind to Ronald Reagan, crediting him with ending the Cold War by outspending a Soviet Union that was already moribund. Reagan's America was a great place to be if you were an arms merchant, a banker, or an oil lobbyist. It was less endearing for inner-city adolescents, underpaid single mothers or an underfed child dependent on the Administration's "let 'em eat ketchup" approach to school lunches.

Richard Nixon was dreadful, but relatively visible beneath the nervous facade; Reagan was all mirrors and shadows, a movie trick, a puff of smoke. He was a personified TV commercial who mouthed empty slogans while presiding over the atrophy of the American heart, and preserved the American dream by putting at risk American reality. We were lucky to survive him—if we do.

CHAPTER 27

At Home in the Monitor

In the early 1980s I resumed my writing career with a review in the Los Angeles *Times* of a tediously erotic novel. The *Times*, having survived the cannibalism devouring the nation's press, had swollen to telephone-book dimensions. One of its weekend features was a Book Review section headed by my chum Bob Kirsch. Bob invited me aboard.

The first book that landed in my lap was a dreary, unbroken recital of orgies and seductions that after thirty pages had me nodding. As I observed in my critique,"Its people exist almost entirely in their pelvic manifestations. We are stuck with a literary pilot who sees by the fly of his pants."

My next salvo was my last. Reviewing a book on the nuclear submarine rivalry of the Cold War, I pronounced it an exercise in swaggering infantilism, "closer to the gung-ho heroics of a television series than to the sober realities of the atomic age." I deplored the frequent salaams of its Annapolis-trained author before an arms establishment that he himself accused of outright lies, his collegiate comparison of the big power confrontation to a Superbowl football game, and his insistence that America "could no longer afford the indulgence of a disloyal and dissenting minority."

The aggrieved author complained that as a "Hollywood hack" who held the "wartime rank of sergeant in the Signal Corps," I was unqualified to review his masterpiece. I bridled at the demotion. In Cairo I had the assimilated rank of lieutenant colonel.

With Bob Kirsch out of the country, his deputy wanted to run the navy man's letter. "No problem," I told him, "as long as you follow the New York *Times* practice of also running my reply."

"Well, we don't usually do that . . . "

"This isn't usually. This is a matter of fair play!" I was astonished at the intensity of my feeling. Before I could stop myself, I had gone further: "If you help him float that canard, I'll be obliged to sue!"

Sulkily, the deputy decided to spike the letter. But the flow of books to me stopped.

By that time, however, I had secured a toehold on several other literary trapezes. The first was *Santa Barbara* magazine, a beautifully produced glossy-paper publication distinguished for its handsome photography. I sent them a trial piece; they came back with a request for a monthly column. My "Snapshots" began with a sketch of the local Royal Presidio of the 1780's, built when the sleepy pueblo of Los Angeles to the south was guarded by four men under a sergeant.

The town's "alternative weekly," the tousled, irreverent, vaguely leftist *News and Review*, now rechristened the *Independent*, asked me to take over its theater criticism. I found the post a convenient platform for exposing meretricious claptrap like *Evita*, which sentimentalized a woman who at great personal profit give sanctuary to scores of Nazi criminals. I was able also, with an appreciative notice, to help a struggling dance company obtain several substantial grants.

But by far my most rewarding labors were for the *Christian Science Monitor*, ranked among America's great newspapers, to which I had been recommended by a long-time *Monitor* contributor. The *Monitor* was and is one of our last citadels of press independence, no flunky kneeling at the feet of some chain czar, no tool of admen or pressure groups. Its religious content, despite its name, is minimal. My special stamping ground was the Home Forum, a gathering place for random reminiscence, philosophy, nature studies and poetry. I began with a tribute to the charms of Santa Barbara, hailing the "helicopter dance" of the hummingbirds among the potted marigolds on my balcony, the tang of the rugged coastline below:

> Quite suddenly I am in the shadow of towering cliffs that overlook a secluded cove. Waves wash quietly over sentinel stones at the water's edge. I inhale the silence of centuries and the aura of trees; a fallen trunk, bleached naked on the sand, another split by a lightning streak. A lone, distant runner imparts to the shadowed beach the chilled, eerie quality of a Dali landscape.

Soon I was a regular contributor, delivering articles on travel, ethics, the decline of language, John Donovan's fiery indignation, and the lovable incompetence of the old Brooklyn Dodgers. Melvin Maddocks, the paper's ace columnist, put in an encouraging word: "It's an act of integrity in journalism today to have *any* theme, and you have the best. Keep on being gadfly to everybody's conscience." I felt at home in the *Monitor*, my inner man thoroughly appeased as it had been sometimes before a microphone but rarely in Hollywood. Having space available to me in one of the world's most respected journals was pure joy; I felt like the muralist in Joyce Cary's *The Horse's Mouth* stumbling upon acres of blank wall.

With my fellow-Americans, in their passion for quick fixes turning to radio therapists as the antidote to despair, one of my *Monitor* columns, on the folly of "Wanting It All," was quoted at length over the NBC network by Toni Grant, a popular lady guru. The last line of another—"Words are as beautiful as wild horses, and sometimes as difficult to corral"—landed among the Quotable Quotes in the *Reader's Digest*.

But the essay that for me had the most staying power was "The Seeds of Love." It rejected equally the blissful chirping of Voltaire's naive Candide, and the doleful forecasts of an imminent replay of the fall of Rome:

> Rather I sense, vibrating all around me, a tremendous ongoing struggle between the fading society of old values and an emerging community of brotherhood . . . For every dismaying factor there is a counterforce straining into existence or peering over the horizon.
>
> Must we still confront one another with the terror-inspired ethic of the cave-man, merely replacing the battle-ax with the supersonic bomber? I cannot accept that.
>
> What we face is a peak moment in the perennial human condition of simultaneous growth and decay, advance and retreat. The clash of opposing forces is thunderous. We can concede the field to them—or we can recognize that we too are here; that our compassion, our acceptance or denial of responsibility, are part of what is happening. Do we have the spiritual resources to ride with the winds of change, and nurture the seeds of love?

Among those deeply affected by the piece was Robert Marquand, then a college journalism student, who read it "with open mouth," unable to believe that "anyone could so beautifully verbalize what I was feeling myself."

Three years later, risen to the Home Forum staff, Marquand wrote to me to express appreciation for a message that he frequently quoted as his personal credo. And in 1993 I was pleased to see his by-line on crisp, authoritative accounts of the festering crisis in the former Yugoslavia. He gave a full airing to dissident newsmen in Belgrade, men much like the defiant editor I had interviewed half a century earlier in an Ankara jail. I felt a thrill of avuncular pride; despite all the glitz and shallowness of the electronic media, the spirit of crusading journalism I had first encountered in the grimy environs of Hearst's *Mirror* was still alive.

My Spanish novel, *Don Diego's Daughter*, had been on my desk for months. It was time to get it into my typewriter. I was wary and weary of big book projects. With Whistler I had been working from a base of reality; here I would have to create characters from scratch, and evoke a long-vanished scene. But the ancient tale haunted me, finally beyond resistance.

My story would be related by a Jewish physician of the period, intimately acquainted with both Don Diego and his daughter. For greater accessibility to American readers, I made my narrator a member of Columbus's crew, his Jewish identity hidden under the garb of a Christian apothecary. He began his prologue in July of 1492, when the Catholic Monarchs, having driven out the Moors, were completing their ethnic sanitization of Spain by expelling its entire three-hundred-thousand-strong population of Jews:

> A brilliant fool, this Columbus; his grasp of medicine is primitive, and his attempts at astronomical calculation ludicrous. Yet he has an instinct for fundamental relationships in nature, and a tenacity generally encountered only in madhouses. He is tyrannical, unyielding—in short, the kind of man who leaves his mark on history . . .

When I had drafted some seventy pages and an outline of the rest, I shipped them off to a handful of trusted advisers.

Bob Kirsch called me at midnight: "It's tremendous, Ted. Beautifully written, very readable. You might want to draft another twenty-five pages or so, turn the next corner, before sending it out. But what you have right now is publishable. And strong enough to command a decent advance. Maybe thirty-five to sixty thousand."

After he rang off, I sat for a long moment, phone in hand. Bob Kirsch, hailed by the historian Will Durant as "beyond question the best book critic in all America," had put his imprimatur firmly behind *Don Diego*. I didn't sleep much that night.

An agent, recommended to me by a novelist at MacDowell, was more cautious. Although she found "much to admire" in the writing and atmosphere, she felt that the story's appeal wavered between "two non-overlapping types of audiences: the Knopf-type hard cover reader and the reader of paperback originals."

"Commercial stereotyping," snapped Bob. "These people can't handle a book unless it fits into a familiar slot." He sent me to another agency which shared his enthusiasm and quickly rounded up publishers' responses. There were tributes to "the fine quality of the writing" and "grand evocative backdrop," but some misgivings about the setting. One major house conceded *Don Diego* was "obviously publishable," but they would have to sell 15,000 copies to cover costs, and "in the present shaky market" that was not assured.

Baffled, I turned to Meyer Levin. Meyer suggested that I focus on the fast-action, high-romance aspects of my story, with minimal detours for history.

Solid advice, no doubt. But I didn't want to settle for a bodice-ripper. Yet I had to face the fact: although I had achieved some memorable passages, like splendid patches of sleeve and hand in an otherwise flawed portrait, I had not been able to bring off the complex novel I had intended. I had made an honorable try at a difficult subject; I would have to accept the disappointment.

A larger loss was at hand. Bob Kirsch was suddenly gone, victim of a liver cancer as abrupt and unpredictable as the man himself.

Bob had always been an enigma. His widow insisted I was the only close male friend he ever had, yet I never felt that I knew him. He would pop up in my life without explanation, and disappear without warning. A postcard would arrive from London, then another from the Midwest, deploring the poverty of the region's dinner menus. From a lecture jaunt to Rumania, he turned up at my apartment with a hand-crafted leather belt.

Although technically a married man with a sizable domestic menage, Bob was for all of his pear-shaped corpulence as tireless an amatory adventurer as he was a traveler. From my first luncheon at his home, it was obvious that he and his wife agreed on practically nothing, and took pleasure in correcting each other; neither protested my description of them as eminently "combatable." For two years I listened to his accounts of mysterious liaisons in faraway Paris and nearby Morro Bay; occasionally I caught glimpses of his mistresses. He never volunteered any clues to his erotic prowling, and I had too many quirks of my own in that department to encourage questions.

Early in 1980, Bob suggested that I join him in buying a weekend villa on the pine-clad shoreline of Cambria, north of San Luis Obispo: "Just a comfortable little place built for relaxing around the fire, listening to music, walking the beach—and entertaining. Don't worry about the down payment; I generate a lot of income."

And he did. Not only as a critic, racing through a dozen books a week, turning out some nine thousand columns for the *Times*, but as a teacher, lecturer and editor. A maverick publisher paid him well to complete an unfinished manuscript left by Dalton Trumbo, perhaps the most brilliant of the Hollywood Ten. And—somewhere in the dead of night?—he was an active author. After writing several novels under other names, he crawled out from behind his pseudonyms to publish *Casino*, a skillfully-constructed piece of fiction a la *Grand Hotel*, centered on the gambling scene at Las Vegas.

I was looking forward to lively conversations at Cambria. Bob's learning was formidable—he could shift from an essay on Chinese architecture to a witty parody of John Lennon—and his curiosity unquenchable.

In mid-May, he remarked casually that he was going down to Los Angeles for "a couple of days of hospital tests."

I was surprised. As something of a New Age health buff, Bob

chewed ginseng and usually scoffed at the orthodox medical establishment.

"Anything serious?"

"Nah. Probably some kind of hangover from a fall when I was a kid. But they want to make sure."

When I saw Bob at lunch a week later, I had to cover up my shock. The color had drained from his cheeks, suddenly plaster-white against his dark beard. A pouch of skin sagged below his jaw. And in mid-June, when he addressed the Writers' Conference, my misgivings grew. Bob had never been a fashion plate, but he had not been a scarecrow, either; I was alarmed at the way his jacket flopped around his shoulders.

He came for an afternoon's swim to my complex, and I was truly appalled. Great slabs of homeless flesh dangled from his once-ample middle.

The call to his daughter the next day was a formality; I knew. "What's going on with your Dad?"

Her voice was bleak, distant. "It's . . . not good, Mr. Berkman."

"Is it—?"

"Yes. Cancer of the liver. Inoperable."

I felt a rush of tears, a surge of helpless protest. Bob Kirsch was fifty-seven.

Once the diagnosis was in, Bob took it with Socratic calm. He had no interest in prolonging mere physical existence by mechanical means. "I will not go through chemotherapy or other medical indignities," he told me. "I didn't come into the world with an intravenous tube and I don't intend to go out with one."

After a brief stay at Cottage Hospital, Bob was transferred to a small rented house near the ocean. Here, guided by his "combatable" wife of twenty-odd years—they had divorced a few months earlier and almost instantly remarried—he said his good-byes. He never relinquished his comic sense. Confined in his last days to a liquid diet, he was unable one evening to find the necessary straw. "This must be the most penurious death," he observed to his wife, "since Edward the Confessor."

On my farewell visit I found him stretched out on a bed, quiet and contemplative, fully clothed. Toward the end his appearance took on a beautiful, distilled quality. His face, thinning and pale, had the patriarchal nobility of a carved Byzantine Jesus. He had arrived at a kind of serenity, a place where there were no deadlines, no obligations; where, as he said, "all the ego stuff has been burned out."

He raised his eyes and spoke softly. "This is like a departure from Southampton," he told me. "The ship sails at midnight, and it's now five to twelve. You're well aware of the departure hour, and that the ship will leave on schedule. So you say your farewells to the people closest to you, on the dock; and when it's time you go aboard peacefully. Even happily."

I spoke at memorial services for Bob in Shoreline Park overlooking the Pacific, and at his widow's request penned a column of tribute to him in the *News-Press*:

> Robert Kirsch carried high the banners
> of courage, integrity and kindness.
> To the vast reservoir of world literature,
> and the still broader pool of man's brotherhood,
> he made gifts beyond measure.

CHAPTER 28

Last Hoorah

Other friends were slipping away: Hal Lehrman in New York, Meyer Levin in Israel, Beth Moldau from her mansions in Europe and North Carolina, Sheilah Graham and John Donovan in Florida, Sylvia Fine Kaye in Hollywood, then a steady drumbeat of grim announcements: chess wizard Reuben Fine, Ian McLellan Hunter, and my feisty ninety-two-year-old Aunt Stella, last of my mother's generation.

Sheilah had been a fixture in my life for more than fifty years. Bored with retirement, she had gone back to turning out Hollywood memorabilia; I could count on the occasional call from London or Palm Beach—always warm, breathless, urgent, spiked with mystery—tracking down some obscure tidbit of information.

Her failing eyesight had been brushed off in an amusing 1986 column for the New York *Times*, where she told of marching down Park Avenue flanked by a pair of total strangers, convinced they had been her companions at lunch.

A heart attack two years later could not be disposed of so easily. Only then, from a long obituary column in the *Times*, did I learn that Sheilah was and always had been an incredible ten years my senior. She had been born Lily Sheil, a Jewess, and raised in a London orphanage. According to her daughter Wendy, she kept her comic spirit to the end.

Unlike Sheilah, John Donovan did not exit laughing. A letter in 1986 from John, his once-rugged body racked by an aortic aneurysm, diabetes and peripheral neuropathy sketched a "vision of dying" where he was reunited with his beloved boxer Timoshenko:

> I walk toward a clearing. In the distance I see a large dog happily bounding over the terrain. I run towards him calling his name. He stops and barks in recognition and is off at a gallop heading my way. The vision fades before I can cradle him in my arms.

Two years later, a long rambling letter from John's wife Vita reported that he had suffered two strokes, blinding one eye and paralyzing his vocal cords. A film-making crew from Greece, after subjecting him to four hours of unremunerated taping on the Polk murder, had run off with his files on the case. She thought a phone call from me might cheer him up; she enclosed their unlisted number.

I followed through, and ran into the most painful "conversation" of my life: a long monologue from my end, punctuated by a kind of eerie keening from John. He could not formulate words. Fearful of silence, I rattled on about our days in Egypt: our gallop past the Sphinx, the night he cut in on King Farouk. Vita came on the phone; John was scribbling something, she said, on a pad in his lap. I waited. Finally she deciphered my old friend's message: "Thanks for the memories." I dropped the phone, devastated.

My next letter came back undelivered. The Donovans had vanished, leaving no forwarding address.

In the fall of 1990, at long last a definitive book on the Polk case appeared, authored by Kati Marton, a former ABC television reporter and ex-wife of anchorman Peter Jennings. *The Polk Conspiracy: Murder and Cover-up in the Case of Correspondent George Polk*, although it slighted John's labors in keeping the issue alive (while making liberal use of information from him), did expose beyond argument the hypocritical role played by Walter Lippmann. Marton confirmed the revelation by the pundit's biographer, Ronald Steel that Lippmann, once cited by the historian Henry Steele Commager as a moral giant worthy of appointment to the U.S. Supreme Court, had turned a craven, unseeing eye on the State Department's whitewash of Polk's killer.

As the only still-active contemporary of Polk, I was interviewed for half an hour by Canadian National Television, and quoted in the *Monitor* to the effect that Marton's research substantiated "what a handful of Mr. Polk's colleagues have been shouting into the wind for decades."

A few months later I learned from Elias Vlanton, a newsman still bird-dogging the forty-three-year-old Polk scandal, that John had died in Florida in the spring of 1989, five weeks after losing his wife. It would have been comforting to think of John strolling through the Elysian Fields with George Polk, blasting away at official malfeasance while eyeing some well-rounded sprite; but I didn't believe it. John was gone, leaving a gap in my life that yawned beyond filling.

Age was settling in: no longer a visitor but a full-time presence. On after-dark roads, approaching headlights stabbed into my eyes; in the theater, I leaned forward in vain to pick up dialogue.

Aging is when you begin to see the tunnel at the end of the light. The burgeoning belly strains against your trouser buttons. The body that has given you so much pleasure puts in a bill for past sins, and will henceforth require constant negotiation. "Looking at my contemporaries," I wrote to Don Wayne, "is a painful reminder of what I am. Looking at the sprightly young, of what I am not and shall never be again."

Cicero, one of the first great persuaders, discourses at length in *De Senectute* on the blessings of old age—the condition, he points out, that all men aspire to and, once attaining, grouse about. One is released from the bonds of sensual passion, "a fruitful source of treason," and set free to teach the young. Avarice recedes; "is there anything more absurd than to seek more journey-money, the less there remains of the journey?" Death would be a "coming to port at last after a long voyage." Cicero intended to "quit life as I would an inn, not a home. For nature has given us a place of entertainment, not a residence."

Noble words. But Cicero was a clever lawyer who could have made Nero look like a sensitive music lover. The fact is that although seasoned judgment can make up somewhat for departed muscle—in baseball parlance, you develop better control as you lose the zip on your fast ball—aging stinks. Where there should be patriarchal glory, tempered wisdom, a guns-saluting, flag-waving climax . . . only this creeping decline.

The worst thing about aging is the sense of a foreclosed future, the sure knowledge that whatever tomorrow holds, it will probably be less enjoyable than today. How ill-tempered of nature! Why couldn't we start out old and ailing and blossom steadily into carefree youth? That would be a utopia worth struggling for! Or was nature being infinitely shrewd, making the whole affair increasingly less desirable so we would welcome death as a deliverance?

I felt a terror not of death but of dying alone, incomplete, unmourned, like Harry Plotz in Washington. I longed to be ushered out gently, like Meyer Levin with his family gathered at the patriarchal bedside, surrounded by love and warmth. I didn't so much mind leaving the party—its pleasures were wearing thin—as the thought of leaving it alone, without send-offs or good-byes.

I had been vaguely aware of a half-dozen retirement communities around town, places to which older people disappeared to pursue mysterious rites I had always considered irrelevant to my interests. Some offered lifetime care, dribbled out in stages based on declining degrees of self-sufficiency.

I found an array of buildings in a green, sheltered valley which had a swimming pool and a fair complement of retired professionals. It also had a fortress ambiance that after a few visits I found unnerving; no interplay with youth, little involvement with the outside world, only swarms of inmates in docile assemblage outside the dining hall waiting for the dinner gong. Seals lined up for feeding at the Central Park zoo? Tuskless has-beens parading to an elephant burial ground?

Most dismaying of all were the semi-hospital quarters where residents reduced to dependency were tucked discreetly out of sight. I winced at the blur of narrow cubicles, bustling nurses and blank gaping faces . . . my preview of the delights of nursing homes. I scrutinized the pathetic little announcements of diversions: bingo, setting-up exercises. I peered into narrow strips of garden where wheel-chair dwellers convened to devour a brief patch of sunlight, and tried to imagine myself as one of the throng: helpless, hopeless, quietly vegetating into nothingness.

In a kind of masochistic compulsion, I trekked around to several unadorned free-standing "convalescent centers," frankly designed as waiting rooms for the mortuary. I was appalled: at the stench, the catatonic unseeing stares, the blatant teasing of the powerless by underpaid attendants.

This was the way the richest nation on earth disposed of its leftover elders, the unmentioned nightmare of the American Dream: not the dignity and respect of senescence on the Continent, not the honors of the Orient, but a waste-basket dismissal of discards from the poker deck, reflecting the youth worship of a society that concentrated mind and muscle on the productive career-success years. I was reminded of the Northern Ojibwa Indians, who regularly staged ceremonial dances in which their elders were brained with tomahawks. Their method had at least the virtue of swiftness.

My next New Year's greeting wrapped the situation up:

I sing to thee, for '93
Man's less than perfect destiny:
From dainty maid
To hearing aid.

Unlike Cicero, I saw no grounds for self-congratulation in my dwindling sex life. Although the mountains above Santa Barbara were dotted with religious retreats, I had not upon moving west opted for monkhood. I found sex in the new ambiance more casual, open, almost an indoor adjunct to the jogging and surfing. However, my amatory excursions got off to a less than blazing start.

Soon after arriving from New York, I had put in a call to Anne Francis. Once groomed as a rival to Marilyn Monroe, still blonde and beautiful, Anne lived in a French provincial manor on a Montecito hilltop, where she headed a foundation engaged in spiritual pursuits. No dilettante, Anne produced and narrated a number of films featuring distinguished scholars, including a world-famous authority on Aramaic, the tongue of Jesus.

The one-time Hollywood sex kitten had matured into a regal lioness, full-figured and trim. We had quickly renewed our mutual fondness from *Girl of the Night* days; when Anne started drafting her sensitive, reflective memoir, *Inner Space*, I threw in a number of suggestions. As with Judy Holliday, I was somewhat inhibited, not to say intimidated, by Anne's Hollywood sheen. But we were frequent companions at parties, movies, New Age gatherings.

Could we have been something more? On our first date in California, as we emerged from a downtown restaurant into a driving rain, Anne glanced up at a hotel sign flickering across the street: "Suites." She looked over at me, a smile playing across her lovely face. "Shall we go there?"

Was she serious? Teasing? A little of each? I didn't have the presence of mind to find out.

I soon embarked on other, less decorous adventures, essentially reruns of earlier affairs; Santa Barbara had no shortage of restless divorcees, casualties of the domestic upheavals in which California led the nation. I had by this time, like my much-married friend Artie Shaw, a well-developed knack of attaching myself to someone I knew was fundamentally a poor long-run prospect but who would play out my little comedy-drama of flirtation, mutual oaths of devotion, growing ambivalence on my part and finally rejection, in which my beloved would ultimately fail my repeated tests of trust, thereby confirming my hidden agenda of female unreliability and my own inability to cope with it. Just once, my safety net nearly proved porous.

In my concocting of fantasy romances I had not up to this point, despite my affection for Molière, Voltaire, and bookstalls along the Seine, enlisted any partners of French background, perhaps chastened by two experiences. In 1981, at the recommendation of the ebullient Jacques La Tourette, I had invested in two real estate ventures, one in Santa Barbara and the other in the Caribbean. Both had gone emphatically awry.

Later, I had extended substantial aid to a Niçoise model in New York while she waited for the auction market to turn around on her Louis Napoleon Sèvres vases. It never did.

But I was still wide open for that special Gallic élan, and Elyot had it.

I first saw Elyot McNeil on the waterfront, propped up against the base of a pinwheel palm, reading, a tall, leggy redhead who might have doubled for Diane Keaton (she had doubled in French films, it turned out, but only as a singer dubbing English-language sound tracks for tiny Edith Piaf). Her book was a volume of essays by the existentialist philosopher Jean-Paul Sartre; the lady herself was a French-Irish Parisienne, a lyricist-performer on the loose in America, with green eyes, saucy upturned nose and a spectacular figure. She was temporarily quartered with a woman friend in town, after an unproductive exploration of the recording scene in Los Angeles.

Chatting animatedly about books and music—Elyot was bi-lingual—we walked back together to my apartment, where she showed me some of her lyrics. They were not for hard rock, a genre I despised, but somewhere in the avant garde terrain mined by the Beatles in "Sergeant Pepper," tinged with melancholy humor and wild beauty. The lady could write. To my delight, she also could sing; we coasted through a couple of American ballads with me at the piano. Then Elyot looked over my refrigerator and announced she would cook dinner. She lingered to stay the night. The next day we went in my Mustang to fetch her belongings, and she moved in.

Elyot was a sensation at the pool. For sheer corporeal splendor—although obviously with significant differences—I had seen nothing like her body since Johnny Weismuller. As a subtle fillip, Elyot sported a reckless Bohemian air that intimated I would not be held to a long-term commitment.

Elyot, eager to rescue a daughter marooned in Chicago with Elyot's Archie Bunker of a father, had held high hopes for the music scene in Los Angeles. They were quickly shattered. "The atmosphere was unbelievable. At every audition, they handed out marijuana at the door . . . cocaine, if you had the money, upon request. Everybody was stoned, perpetually. One of the so-called recording executives moaned to me, 'I am surrounded by mediocracies.' Then he made his automatic pass. I don't think he would have restrained himself with my eight-year-old daughter. How could I bring up Jennifer in a scene like that?"

In Santa Barbara, Elyot mused, there was a composer who might respond to her work, Barry DeVorzon. Although the name meant nothing to me, a few phone calls landed us in DeVorzon's lush Montecito mansion. The composer was young, slight, unassuming. He took a thick sheaf of papers from Elyot and promised to "get at them pretty quickly."

We settled in to wait. Elyot was a breath of Montparnasse. For a couple of weeks we dined by candlelight, frolicked in bed. She left me tender little notes: "*Je t'aime*," and "Cold chicken in fridge. *Je t'embrasse*." I reveled in the affection of a beautiful talented woman exactly half my age.

Gradually the telephone, eloquently silent, became a presence. Coming through the door, Elyot would head for the answering machine. "Any calls?" I shook my head. Again and again.

"He probably hated my songs. You'd think he'd at least send my things back . . . "

A few mornings later she announced America just wasn't "going to happen." Would I like to live in Dordogne, in the southwest of France? Before I could resolve the matter, Elyot altered it. "Tahiti! It's a part of French Oceania. As a bilingual French citizen I could teach there. Jennifer would like that."

Tahiti! Gauguin, quiet lagoons, the very essence of imagined paradise. All that, plus a little family of my own . . .

In the blackness of the night, a jangling telephone. "Overseas operator for Miss McNeil." I handed the receiver to Elyot, heard a man's voice at the other end, high-pitched, angry. When she hung up, "That was my ex-husband. He's having trouble with my other child, my son."

She flung herself out of bed, stumbled across the room, suddenly dissolved in tears. "I'm a fraud," she sobbed. "I'm neither a functioning artist nor a responsible mother. I'm glib, clever—and that's it. Strictly façade."

"Nonsense," I protested. "You're a creative woman, Elyot!"

"Elyot," she snorted. "even the name I use is phony. My name is Maureen Ellis. You're living with a charlatan, Ted."

"Hey, wait a minute. I've seen your lyrics—"

"And where did they get me? What have they done for my daughter, living with her troglodyte grandfather in Chicago? I'm bad news, Ted."

The next morning I sat down with Elyot and figured out the costs of a pilgrimage to Tahiti by her and her daughter. I drew up a brief loan agreement, payment to be cancelled in the event of my death. If things went well, we agreed, I might join her.

A few afternoons later we went downtown to wrap everything up: currency exchange, travelers checks, plane tickets. That was on a Thursday.

Friday at 9:00 a.m. the telephone rang: Barry DeVorzon. Trembling, Elyot picked up the receiver. Listened. "You what?"

A torrent of words from the other end. She stood transfixed, threw back her head, took a deep breath. "Really? *Vraiment*?" She was laughing, crying, mascara streaming down her cheeks. "I'm thrilled, Barry. Of course. But I had given up hope . . . let me call you back. By this evening, yes."

She hung up. "He wants to make an album with me, Ted. Just the two of us, using more than half of my songs. He thinks the lyrics are moving, modern. 'Fabulous,' he says. He's ready to talk to my agent—which I don't have." She took a long swig of coffee. "What do I do, Ted?"

Jennifer had her heart set on Tahiti, she pointed out. On the other hand—Elyot's eyes locked into mine. A word from me, I knew, and she would elect to stay.

I didn't utter it; she opted for Tahiti. I felt a strange mixture of loss and relief.

I had a cable when she arrived, a letter a few weeks later, a postcard the following month, then nothing. "Elyot" and my loan vanished into the mists of Polynesia.

Nor did I ever see Barry DeVorzon again. Sometimes I wonder how my life might have been changed if he had read those "fabulous" lyrics the day he received them, and picked up the phone sooner.

As the years advanced and opportunities for liaisons retreated, I had to face certain disagreeable facts. My female contemporaries simply turned me off. If, like some couples I knew, I had married early and kept pace with my bride in acquiring wrinkles, the adjustment would be easier. But I hadn't. The opposite prospect was just as bleak. What delicious creature at the peak of her charms, unless she was, like Elyot, somehow skewed, would hand over her life to an ancient quirky writer of modest means? Yet somewhere in my cluttered psyche lurked a resistance to being bounced from the sexual carousel to the limbo of harmless grandfathers, a longing for one more fling with a young Oriental beauty, an erotic last hoorah.

A half-dozen Japanese females, summer students at UCSB, were staying in my apartment complex, enjoying tennis and other games with a group of lusty young exchange collegians from Spain. For days I hung on the edge of their gathering, an old goat trying to crash a forbidden pasture. My pawing at the ground went unnoticed.

Then on a sultry afternoon lightning struck. I literally ran into one of their compatriot visitors, an enchanting wisp of a twenty-one-year-old airing a small dog. The proper blandishments came easily, and soon Nana was cradled in my arms, floating around my apartment to a Kern ballad.

I suggested a weekend rendezvous; Nana was willing. But like most female foreign students she was quartered with an American "host family" living near the university; their watchful eye could be eluded, but it took careful planning. Patience was the word.

Patience was the last thing my Oriental Lolita inspired. After waiting a few days, I got into my car and drove out to the private home where she was staying.

A peremptory knock brought to the door a chubby housewife in curlers. She was astonished to confront a bearded, beret-clad Bohemian; then appalled to discover that the aged satyr was in pursuit of her presumably innocent ward.

No, she snapped, Nana was not available. Nor would she be, it was obvious from her guardian's manner. The lady fixed on me an expression of distaste that would have won her a scholarship from the Actors Studio.

Suddenly I saw myself as I must have appeared to her: a sinister character out of the Left Bank, Haight-Ashbury or worse. I burst out laughing.

For me the chase was over. No longer would I dance to the rattling of old chains. When Nana's protector slammed the door, it was not only on me but on my last hoorah.

That left still another whole gender to draw upon for companionship, including two giants of the music world whom I had held in extravagant esteem over the years.

CHAPTER 29

Music, Maestros, Please

If before leaving New York I had been asked to name the five living American musicians I most admired, two of them would have been Earl Robinson, the composer of "Ballad for Americans," and clarinet virtuoso Artie Shaw. Never in my remotest musings did it occur to me that either would cross my path in California. Both became integral parts of my life.

Robinson, my lunch companion for years, held a singular place on the American musical scene. Folk composer and balladeer, veteran of the Old Left with Woody Guthrie and Pete Seeger, he created melodies irresistible not only to audiences but to his fellow performers, from Frank Sinatra to Paul Robeson. Like his favorite composer, Bela Bartok, Earl frequently drew upon folk song motifs, subtly reharmonized. But his supreme gift was for melody, for the quick, catchy phrase that goes straight to the listener's heart—and stays there.

Earl first made his musical mark in the 1930s with the labor anthem "Joe Hill." Hill was a union organizer and songwriter (father of the sardonic phrase "pie in the sky") executed for murder in Utah in 1915 on dubious circumstantial evidence. Earl's tune, based on a poem by Alfred Hayes, leaped back into the limelight forty years later when it was performed at Woodstock by Joan Baez, and became a rallying cry, translated into fifteen languages, for workers around the globe. It was a lifelong favorite of Ed Murrow, who never forgot the union struggles of his logging-camp days.

Earl's "Ballad for Americans," sung over the CBS network by the great bass Paul Robeson in the fall of 1939, was a milestone in radio history and an epiphany for me: a stirring celebration of America's melting pot heritage, with lyrics by the young Richmond poet John La Touche.

Eager to hear more Robinson, before going overseas I tracked down "Abe Lincoln," a vivid portrait of our sixteenth president, and "Lonesome Train," a cantata evoking Lincoln's burial train. Earl had an uncanny ability to capture the cadences and flavor of a particular setting: the quiet, hymnlike dedication of "Joe Hill," the sensuous Caribbean beat of "Hurry Sundown," the powerful minor progressions in "Abe Lincoln" that evoked the majesty of their subject. Earl hit pay dirt in 1945 with "The House I Live In," a salute to democracy promptly adopted by Frank Sinatra, who kept it alive for four decades and featured it as the centerpiece of the 1986 centennial celebration of the Statue of Liberty.

But there were long, politically shadowed dry spells in between. Despite—or perhaps because of—Earl's close friendships with Eleanor Roosevelt and Supreme Court Justice William O. Douglas, he ran afoul of Senator Joseph McCarthy. Like many young idealists in the 1930s, Earl had been attracted to the official Communist agenda of peace, social justice and racial harmony. Disabused over time of these pretensions, he nonetheless landed in the McCarthy dragnet and was for several years blacklisted.

I met Earl at a casual dinner party, a smiling pixie in his mid-seventies. His smooth, even features reminded me of Cole Porter. Robinson radiated the good health of a man who began each day with a round of yoga and an icy dip in the Pacific. Behind light-rimmed glasses his brown eyes glowed with an electric intensity.

Soon after our meeting he invited me to a party at the foothill hideaway where he lived and worked in a kind of rustic, rundown comfort, playing Bach tapes in the living room, composing at the piano in a barn-studio.

The party turned out to be a seance. Earl was an ardent devotee of channeling, in which mediums transmit messages presumably voiced by enlightened souls long departed. Something of the earnest naiveté that had once led Earl to embrace the panacea peddlers of Marxism now convinced him that one "Dr. Peebles," a visiting "entity" from the nineteenth century, would guide him to nirvana.

I listened to the channel, heard the entreaties of his transfixed followers for advice on the stock market, and told Earl he had fallen into quackery.

To my mild surprise, he forgave me. In fact, he was soon confiding problems he had previously entrusted only to "Dr. Peebles." Earl's career was on a bumpy road. A symphonic pageant slated for Lincoln Center, "Earl Robinson's America," had been washed out by New York City's budget crisis. A similar proposal was languishing at public television headquarters in Los Angeles. His application for a grant had been turned down by the National Endowment for the Humanities.

And the great issues of his youth had been resolved or mitigated. Unions were an accepted, often conservative, fact of life; civil rights had advanced to the front burner. Creatively, he was adrift in a drug-soaked new world reigned over by Madonna and three-chord heavy metal groups.

Yet he kept stubbornly at his craft, landing an occasional concert out of town or a spot in a new LP anthology. I tried to aid his projects, pointing out his achievements to local producers. When he needed volunteer singers to tape a new cantata on St. Francis of Assisi, I rounded up tenors and sopranos and found a private home where they could rehearse.

The acknowledgments came streaming from his typewriter: "I really appreciate you, man. Thanks so much for your encouragement and I will continue to reciprocate, any and all ways." Seeking permission to use my name on a local concert program, he added: "Take good care, sir. You are needed, a valuable resource."

Earl's home town, Seattle, had been making overtures to him to return, with promises of statewide honors from the governor and legislature. On the eve of his departure from Santa Barbara, he made a last and most appreciated gesture. He knew of my profound admiration for Paul Robeson, whom I had met backstage just before going overseas in World War II. I marveled at Robeson's rapid rise from football star to lawyer to concert singer to internationally acclaimed actor. I understood why, refused service in a San Francisco restaurant, obliged to use a freight elevator in his New York hotel after his return from a standing ovation at Carnegie Hall, he had sought sanctuary in the Soviet Union. And I was impressed when, in defiance of a Stalinist ban on Jewish music, he thundered a half-hour of Hebrew and Yiddish songs in Warsaw.

Earl knew also of my particular admiration for the "Ballad." Without fanfare, he brought to my apartment a Vanguard LP featuring the Robeson recording, autographed by the singer. Sprawled above Robeson's signature was Earl's penned inscription: "For my friend Ted Berkman, who knows and appreciates whither, and wherefore, and why. Earl Robinson."

A few months later he was dead, victim of an auto accident outside

Seattle. At memorial services in New York's Greenwich Village, among those paying homage were Harry Belafonte, Pete Seeger and Oscar Brand.

Earl had provided me with an example to follow in growing old, an example of unbroken spirit. In a memorial tribute to him, published in the *Independent*, I said:

> Earl Robinson—my friend, Everyman's friend, is gone . . . Earl was a lifelong and unquenchable fighter for the causes he believed in . . . What made him unique and irreplaceable as a composer was his ability to distill his rich technical background into simple, expressive melodies . . . Earl Robinson was an ornament—some would say a monument—of the American musical scene.

"Dance music? Who needs it? You can dance to a windshield wiper!"

"If we ate what we listen to today, we'd all be dead."

That's Artie Shaw, vintage Shaw: caustic, witty, bitterly contemptuous of the mass audience that in the big band era idolized him and made him the most highly paid musician in the world. Now in his eighties, Artie occupies his own private corner of the jazz pantheon, verbally still playing solo, the most articulate exponent of America's homegrown musical idiom. To the fan-magazine public, he's the man of a thousand (actually, a mere eight) beautiful wives, ex-husband of Lana Turner, Ava Gardner and Evelyn Keyes. To knowledgeable sidemen he was the true king of the clarinet, superior in tonal warmth, intellectual grasp and improvisatory imagination to his assiduously publicized arch-rival, Benny Goodman. To a handful of intimates, he is a complex and contradictory man of acute sensibilities, masking the wounds of an almost unbearably isolated childhood behind a grimly self-protective control.

I caught my first glimpse of Artie in 1933, a black-haired young band leader captivating the coeds at a Cornell fraternity dance. I met him in Manhattan in the 1950s, when we both drifted into the Bohemian circle surrounding Meyer Levin. Artie, grown astonishingly bald, sat in deliberate solitude, an unsmiling presence. We never got beyond an exchange of nods.

Thirty years later, encountered at a writers' lunch table in Santa Barbara, he seemed more relaxed. A long psychoanalysis was behind him and a successful autobiography under his belt. But the spiky personality was still there, along with the elegantly oval head and bold features that had enhanced his Orphic charm.

"You knew Meyer?" He mellowed noticeably. Next we discovered curious parallels in our educational and political paths. Artie had been teaching at UCSB Extension a course entitled "Three Chords for Beauty and One to Pay the Rent," an exploration of the creative life virtually identical with my "Artist in Society." And, corresponding to my advisory role with Chester Bowles, he had rallied support in the entertainment world for Senator George McGovern, who ran for president against Richard Nixon in 1972 (like Earl Robinson, Artie had imperiled his career during the witch hunts of the 1950s rather than compromise his integrity).

Cautiously I steered the conversation around to music. By pure coincidence I had lately heard, and been enormously impressed by, a large collection of Shaw recordings; I mentioned some relatively obscure clarinet passages that I had liked. He seemed pleased, and more so upon learning that I had studied jazz with Lee Konitz, a stubbornly uncommercial but influential saxophone virtuoso. Artie in turn revealed that his first and continuing passion had been to write.

We exchanged visits—Artie lived in Newbury Park, about half-way down to Los Angeles—and books. I relished *The Trouble with Cinderella*, his lacerating look at fame in America; he had warm words for my biographical novel of Whistler.

In 1984, *California* magazine wanted an article on why thirty years earlier Artie had abruptly quit playing. He asked me to write it.

He had to put away his horn because he hated the ambiance of belligerent drunks; he was weary of his own perfectionist drive to conquer an instrument that in the end always eluded his grasp; and above all there was the break with his audience.

Artie wanted to stretch the musical vocabulary, break out of established harmonic combinations, find new tonal relationships. Where a popular tune ended, Artie's music began. Like all true jazzmen, he was less interested in a written melody than in its chordal underpinnings, the springboards for his solo improvisations.

"You're composing out there," he told me. "You hear something in your head and if it feels good you play it. You're like a bird darting from branch to branch; when one branch starts feeling shaky, you go to another. And when everything clicks, there's an exultation you can't get from anything else."

His fans were on a different, and to Artie, deadening track: "They wanted to hear 'Star Dust' and 'Begin the Beguine' forever."

Originally bent on a writing career, Artie had picked up the clarinet only to finance the college education that he felt an author would need—and landed on a treadmill of musical success that he couldn't leave.

In marathon telephone conversations, Artie and I disposed of world politics, Platonic philosophy, the mystery of women and the irksome surprises of aging. Artie didn't chat; his conversation was an explosion of fireworks, launched without preliminaries, often prolonged to the point of exhaustion—his listener's, not Artie's—but consistently stimulating. When the Oscar-winning documentary on his life, "Time Is All We've Got," came to Santa Barbara, we attended it together.

Mostly he was cool, disciplined, detached. But occasionally small incidents revealed a vein of tenderness, of an almost religious devotion to beauty. Once he drove half an hour to show me a splendidly proportioned fig tree in Beverly Hills. On the night of his eightieth birthday, asked by a parking attendant to hold a bouquet of flowers, he fell into a rhapsodic reverie: "Look at those colors, man! The colors!"

His tough facade, I came to realize, was essentially a survival mechanism against a world where he had early decided he could never safely drop his guard. Like the rest of us, Artie has his failings. But these are minor compared to his luminous intelligence, his musical stature and his fundamental decency. When the atonal composer Arnold Schoenberg arrived in America as a penniless refugee in 1933, it was Artie who personally and quietly guaranteed a royalty advance to him from RCA Records.

On the surface plane, Artie is hugely self-sufficient. Tossed ashore in the middle of nowhere he'd shoot some game, spear a few fish, build a cabin and in a week have the native drummers organized into a touring band. In an expansive phase, he doesn't enter a room; he storms into and occupies it. You can love Artie or be nettled by him, but you can't pretend he isn't there.

At his eighty-second birthday party in 1992 he stood tall and sturdy, wearing out a swarm of half-enchanted, half-intimidated friends. Ed Murrow had a genius for words, for the phrase that could leap across chasms. With Artie, the genius seems palpable, in the man himself.

He is a self-taught adept in French and Spanish who has run a successful dairy farm, reached national rank as a rifle champion, and qualified as an expert fly fisherman. In Spain he designed not only chess sets but his own cliff-climbing house. He is a voracious reader, with three or four books always in hand and eight thousand more crowding the shelves of the library that spreads across the upstairs floor of his house. He is also a tireless talker, able to expatiate on Hokusai woodblocks, the difference between Amish and Mennonite cultures in Pennsylvania, Flaubert's literary maxims and the biological speculations of Lewis Thomas. But for all of its bravura flights, his conversation frequently ends on a personal note.

A glimpse into his boyhood suggests why. Listen to Artie about the early years of Abraham Isaac Arshawsky, uprooted from the ghetto of New York's lower East Side to largely Gentile New Haven: "Here's this seven-year-old kid surrounded by a ring of jeering teenagers, yelling 'Christ-killer, Christ-killer!'"

"Family? I had no family. I didn't know any grandparents, aunts, uncles. I used to lie in terror at night listening to my father's threats to kill my mother and me. When I was thirteen he disappeared." All his life Artie would be haunted by the specter of that scared little boy.

He left home himself at sixteen to join a jazz group. But the dislocation of band life mirrored his friendless childhood. "It was Akron this week, Toronto the next. A one-night stand in St. Louis, then get in a car and drive to Las Vegas." His voice takes on a hoarse impatience. "Do you know how lonely that is?" His music became his life, his only passport to worldly acceptance. Growing up adrift in a world where he had no father to smooth his path, no cousins to share his confusions, where absolutely no one else was going to look out for Artie Shaw, his formula for coping was to concentrate on his music and himself. The remarkable fact about Artie is that he transcended his history to leave his mark on a world from which he felt alienated.

Nonetheless, the tightly organized adult who emerged from his adolescent nightmare lived in emotional exile, wrapped in a self-protective cocoon. In recent years Artie has broken increasingly through his shell; my late sister was deeply touched when, from a faraway town, he called her in the hospital. But for a long time, in a kind of aggressive-defensive staking out of territory, he had a tendency to gobble up conversations. If the talk turned to Scott Fitzgerald's novels or S.J. Perelman's marital miseries, Artie simply appropriated it: "I was a close friend of Scott. I knew Sid very well." End of subject. He often reminded me of Fanny, another victim of early emotional deprivation, who in a movie theater punctuated every on-screen scene with reminiscences from her own life.

A couple of years ago Artie complained to me about the lack of intellectual stimulus in his Newbury Park backwater. He would relish an evening of lively exchange.

I delivered a real plum. Dry, urbane Harry Ashmore had been brought to California by Robert Hutchins, the wunderkind president of the University of Chicago, to spark the Hutchins think-tank in Santa Barbara, the Center for Democratic Institutions. Former editor of the *Encyclopedia Brittanica*, adviser to several presidents, Harry had won a Pulitzer Prize for his coverage of the standoff in Little Rock over integration of Arkansas schools; he enjoyed national eminence as an authority on civil rights.

Ashmore never got off the ground. Artie served up a home-cooked dinner and an equally home-cooked menu of sweeping opinions. Despite his craving for energizing conversation, the years of protective self-insulation kicked in, and the only voice he could hear was his own. As I had observed to my students at Marymount, artists put the best of themselves into their work. What's left is the dregs.

Within a small circle of long standing, Artie is comfortable. Otherwise, as he puts it, "Between me and the rest of humanity is a moat filled with snakes." He is blunt in his judgments. Although conceding the towering talents of Jerome Kern and George Gershwin, he describes Kern, once his father-in-law, as a "despotic gnomish little man" who failed to protect his lyricists, and insists that Gershwin, despite a gift for melody "on a par with Schubert's," in his *Rhapsody* and *Concerto* committed a "barbarization of jazz, jazz notes without the swing."

Never boastful about his own work, Artie is nonetheless touchy about recognition of his standing. He is hurt when Elia Kazan fails to mention him in Kazan's autobiography, rails quite properly at the Oxford Dictionary of Music for by-passing him while finding room for soprano sax player Charlie Barnet, and is noticeably warmed by the abundant coverage accorded him by *Who's Who* in contrast with its passing mention of his friend Barnaby Conrad.

Something of a spiritual castaway, again and again he has tried to fill the void with women. But his string of glamour-scene marriages were, by Artie's account, simply carnal adventures, "legalized love affairs; weddings, not marriages," which collapsed of their own superficiality. In the sanctimonious self-policing days of the Hays office, the studios did not want their revered box-office queens to look like brazen hussies, cheerfully moving in with itinerant horn players; a marriage license was indispensable. Artie, brought up as "a good respectable Jewish boy," agreed to oblige. In the case of Betty Kern, he says he was groping for a home base, stability: "I wanted a family; I was marrying Jerry Kern."

His most memorable movie conquests, Artie avers, were those not formalized, such as his meetings with the number one pin-up girl of World War II. The two would rush through hotel doors, rip the clothes off each other and fling themselves onto a bed, then part in total silence. The lady's conversational powers, I gathered, were limited. But so was his interest.

By the time of my arrival in Santa Barbara, Artie had broken up with Evelyn Keyes after a long marriage, and was sharing his house with a student flutist. They were nicely matched, at least numerically; she was twenty-seven, he seventy-two. The prospect of possibly acquiring a father-in-law several years his junior didn't bother Artie, but his inamorata's preoccupation with a performing career did. So he moved on.

Well into his eighties, Artie has continued to be attractive to younger women—and continued to have trouble reconciling his requirements with theirs: "I'm looking for a pitcher big enough to contain my needs. But those needs are so pervasive that I swallow people up, overwhelm them."

Two subsequent misadventures pitched him into a period of intense misogynism: women were flighty, unpredictable, "weird;" they aged ruinously; they were "different creatures, raised on a different planet, not meant to live with us." Later he regained his balance, but for a time he was beginning to sound like a parody of Professor Higgins in *My Fair Lady*, lamenting the failure of women to keep pace with that "mahvelous sex," the male.

For me, our bonding had to overcome the ghost of Lloyd Seidman, the model-boy nemesis of my grammar-school days. Artie was Lloyd Seidman in spades, a successful version of my failed self. He had accomplished what I early yearned to do: made his mark in the musical sphere. His victories were a reminder, a rebuke; I could not resist self-denigrating comparisons.

To worsen the wound, he was now turning his energies to my one area of superiority, writing. Why couldn't he be satisfied with vanquishing the music world?

And with memories of Fanny still smarting, I winced at the prospect of a relationship where I might be reduced to a satellite, a shadow. I didn't want to play Oscar Levant to Artie's Gershwin.

However, I didn't have to. For all of the gap between us in public eminence, there were realms in which Artie and I met as equals. We had known similar boyhoods as affection-starved kids scrambling for the compensation of public acclaim. We had fought the same phantoms (loneliness, Gentile hostility, self-doubt), dreamed the same dreams (to make ourselves heard, and thereby win the love of beautiful women).

And each of us saw in the other the unfulfilled half of his own life, the career that got away, what he might have become if at a crucial point he had taken a different turning. In my case the crossroads were at Vienna, after my movie-writing stint with Korda, when I was tempted to stay in Europe and study composition; for Artie it was when he dropped plans to enroll as an English major at Columbia and instead picked up the clarinet that would carry his name around the globe.

And there was our common delight in music. We exulted together over obscure string quintets by Boccherini, the exquisite, little-noticed timing of Fred Astaire's song delivery, the jazz-flavored bounce brought by Debussy to "Golliwog's Cake Walk."

One evening after an early dinner we repaired to Artie's upstairs library-music room, where for four hours he regaled me with tapes and transcriptions, mostly small-ensemble gems, recorded in the last golden glow before his retirement. No one at the time had wanted to distribute them. For thirty years Artie had squirreled away his collection in cabinets, confident their day would come.

When I heard them, I understood why. His Gramercy Five ensemble wove a delicate, superbly coordinated filigree of sound unlike anything known to me before or since. Working without written notation, they created from such standards as "Someone to Watch Over Me" a totally new listening experience. Artie's solos overflowed with the feeling that he muzzled elsewhere. The fleet arabesques and lightning trills in "Bewitched, Bothered and Bewildered" were like the caresses of a weightless dancer; "Yesterdays" was haunting, poignant, filled with the sorrow of what a critic would later call "an alien human voice."

Late in the 1980s Artie and I were planning a trip together to Sweden, where he had a concert offer, and talked of sharing a house in Santa Barbara.

In both cases instinct told me to back off. Instinct and experience. We had agreed that after one of his drawn-out birthday bashes in Beverly Hills I would stay overnight at Newbury Park. We pulled into his driveway at 2:30 a.m., and I stumbled toward the spare bedroom. Artie headed me off. "Too much hassle," he grunted. The futon there would have to be pulled out, tugged open and fitted with bedding. "You can sleep on the living room sofa. No problem. I do it all the time."

He tossed a few cushions onto the sofa and disappeared into his bedroom.

I twisted and squirmed on the feather-soft sofa, hopelessly awake, through a miserable night. I reminded myself that Artie had been a concerned friend, extending himself to accommodate my driving problems, urging me in troubled times to "hang in there." Decades of self-contained isolation had made it difficult for him to embrace more than fleetingly any perspective but his own.

But that didn't make the sofa any firmer.

In 1991, as Artie was laboring doggedly on a long novel, "CDs"—digitally mastered compact discs—burst onto the music market. Earlier recordings, from analog signals, had been subject to distortions at every stage of the process; CDs could convert the high-speed analog tapes into recordings that virtually duplicated the fidelity of the original.

The new development brought Artie's music within reach of a whole new audience which, with the advances in electronic technology, had simply stopped buying records. That included critics for whom he had become essentially an honored name from the past. Overnight, listeners were showered with a musical bonanza, highlighted by the sleek Gramercy Five collection I had been privileged to hear. The contrast with the empty noises of heavy metal was stark; you'd have to be stone deaf not to hear the difference. Major national reviewers outdid each other with hosannas. Sales boomed.

Artie's first reaction was ambivalent. Where was this response when he had hungered for it? He might still be playing if . . .

That quickly yielded to the realization that he was luckier than countless artists, belatedly revered, who in their lifetimes knew nothing but neglect. He was being welcomed again on talk shows, featured in a glossy new Barnes-Noble publishing catalogue, proposed by the U.S. Post Office as the subject of a three-cent stamp. From Tokyo to Cape Town, affection was pouring in.

On New Year's eve of 1991-92 we attended a performance by the Santa Barbara Symphony of Artie's *Clarinet Concerto*. Asked afterward to take a bow, he was suddenly humble before the applause that swept the theater. On the way home he was uncharacteristically subdued. "It's a funny feeling. In a hundred years I won't be here but the concerto will. Little me. After all those years of struggle . . . This is what it's all about, Ted: leaving some trace of your presence that makes the scene a little richer, more bearable, for some other lonely soul. Who remembers the politicians of Mozart's day?"

CHAPTER 30

Good Morning, Judge

With my eightieth birthday came a new and welcome status. I had always felt the law might be a tolerable profession if one could by-pass the client-coddling preliminaries and start out as a judge. Suddenly I found myself knee-deep in quasi-judicial standing.

Already resident counselor for the local Screen Writers Association, I was suddenly asked by the *News-Press*, launching a short story contest, to join their panel of arbiters. A similar request, for evaluating movie treatments, came from the National Society of Arts and Letters. Cornell landed in my mailbox seeking my advice about choosing a new university president. And I was tapped to pontificate at the University of California, Santa Barbara for a video celebrating The Wisdom Of The Elders.

The contagion peaked with an invitation from PEN West, the California-based branch of the International Poets, Essayists and Novelists, to rule on the non-fiction entries in their yearly joust among writers west of the Mississippi. In my limited circle I had become an Authority.

I also became a clearing house for characters in search of authors to write their stories. Cass Sperling, the granddaughter of movie magnate Harry Warner, phoned to ask if I would undertake with her the saga of the Warner clan. Although I had known her father, Milton, when we were both stripling writers at 20th Century, I had no further yearning for the turgid waters of Hollywood. I referred her to a former protégé, Cork Millner, who was pleased to hammer out *Hollywood Be Thy Name*.

That was part of my adieu to the media scene as an active player. Mainstream movies had become a sad joke: giant conglomerates accustomed to swallowing airlines and drugstore chains and copper mines choking on indigestible sound stages; Berkeley MBAs with no background in film competing frantically for the colossal moneymaker that would shore up their sagging bottom lines. My last venture in the field had been with *The Lady and the Law*, five times optioned but never screened, a victim of unhappy timing. With the triumphant release of *Star*

Wars in 1977 the movie world had taken a radical turn toward spectacles, special effects and a space-age future, transferring car chases and the old Western gun duels to a fresh and more marketable setting. *Lady*, as a character-rooted period piece centered in the past, went in exactly the wrong direction.

Television, in search of the same sensation-hungry audience as the big screen but unable to compete in spectacle, was pulling out all the stops in mindless violence; *Playhouse 90* was a dim memory. If I felt no affinity with the Hollywood of the 1990s, I was even less at home with the television scene. Ed Murrow had despised the Madison Avenue "take" on television, but his distinguished presence, his firm grip on the tools of communication and the respect that the combination inspired had ironically paved the way for the elevation to eminence of lesser but well-publicized figures, female as well as male. Apart from the solid outpost of Public Broadcasting, with Robin McNeill and Jim Lehrer, the networks were turning out a new breed of swaggering pontificators. Their reportage reflected the influence of "infotainment": quick, superficial, accenting conflict over substance, weak on background and context. They projected an air of self-satisfaction, understandably; their top dogs commanded salaries in the millions, supplemented by extravagant fees for speaking engagements. I wondered how many of them would have survived Fiorello La Guardia's stare or the gritty newsrooms of the forties.

But they had their worshippers. For a nation raised on stars, it was an easy switch from Humphrey Bogart to Dan Rather.

I had interviewed another icon of the tube, Sam Donaldson, during the visit of the capital press corps to Santa Barbara. Donaldson was famous for his theatrical questioning of the president, shouted over the whirr of helicopter blades as Reagan made one of his quick silent exits from the White House. Upon my mention of Joe Laitin's name, Donaldson waved me readily into his office. I found myself confronting a lean, taut-faced man with intense green eyes under bristling brows. According to buzz in the press room, he had created a fearful uproar when the limousine engaged to take him to the tennis courts failed to arrive on time.

He lectured me briefly and rather condescendingly on the new arena of television reporting. “In your day, stringing words together was enough, even for radio. Now we have to synchronize eye and ear, and in any conflict the eye always wins.” He assured me his aggressiveness was in the interest of the common man, with whom he strongly identified. A decade later a reporter with the New York *Post* revealed that Donaldson had acquired 20,000 acres of ranch in New Mexico and in two years had pocketed nearly $100,000 in farm subsidies from the very government whose farm programs he had been denouncing on the air. Donaldson had his fellow-reporter thrown off his ranch. Ed Murrow he was not.

It wasn’t just the big media that had been sending me time-to-move-on signals. As a play reviewer I was finding it hard to drive to the theater at night, and harder to hear the actors when I got there. I had run out of topics for the *Monitor*, and patience with *Santa Barbara* magazine, chronically behind in its payments.

My new prestige stemmed largely from my long association with the Santa Barbara Writer’s Conference, the largest gathering of its kind in the country. Teaching had been an agreeable sideshow for me ever since Marymount days. Soon after my return to California I had a call from a Cornell classmate, Paul Lazarus, who had risen to the vice-presidency of Columbia Pictures and since retirement was on the faculty of UCSB. Paul invited me to join him in an all-day, all-Cornell weekend seminar on screenwriting at the university.

The seminar went very well; so well, in fact, that it was pointedly not repeated. Paul, despite forty years in The Industry, did not have any writing credentials of his own. He had labored hard to stake out his teaching terrain, to which he welcomed guests but not interlopers. My visa was not extended.

I shifted my sights to the local branch of Antioch University, then to the Adult Education program at City College, where I expanded my repertoire to include biography.

The Writer’s Conference had a far more distinguished aura. Founded in 1972 by Barnaby Conrad, and organized with quiet efficiency by his wife Mary, it had drawn to its lecture platforms virtually every major writer in America: Eudora Welty, John Hersey, Maya Angelou, William Styron. Among its workshop leaders was John Leggett, head of the celebrated Iowa University Writer's Workshop. Unofficial fixtures were perennial kickoff speaker Ray Bradbury, Charles Schulz of "Peanuts" fame, Alex Haley of *Roots*, and Jonathan Winters. Bradbury, white-maned and comfortably plump, could be counted on to knock the customers out of their seats with a fiery inspirational performance that was half Baptist revival meeting, half locker room appeal by a beleaguered football coach.

For hundreds of fledgling authors, the annual Conference was an oasis in the parched desert of the writing life. Every June, from nearby Lompoc and faraway Tahiti, enrollees aged 18 to 80 came to the venerable Miramar Hotel, tied up in knots of self-doubt and despair. After hearty infusions of criticism and encouragement—but mostly the companionship of kindred souls—they departed with hope miraculously renewed.

Conference director Barnaby Conrad, burly and amicable, was a respected author and painter, and until an unforgiving bull sank nine inches of horn into his thigh several decades ago, an active matador. Barnaby swam in paradoxes. Once captain of the Yale boxing team, he was proud of his Old Family lineage and his access to fellow-Yalie William Buckley—but he was closer to his disciple, *Roots* author Alex Haley, and frequently cited his claim to one sixty-fourth descent from Sephardic Jewry.

Until a drying-out at the Betty Ford Center, Barnaby had been known to get lost in his cups, leaving administration in the hands of Paul Lazarus. But wet or dry, Barnaby was a prodigious reader. He happened to have read, and much enjoyed, *To Seize the Passing Dream*. That became my passport in 1982 to the Conference staff, as leader of a new workshop on biography.

I soon developed a substantial following, along with the unexpected bonus of close contact with Jonathan Winters—screamingly funny, desperately sad, totally unpredictable—whose work I had long prized. I was surprised at his bulk, not evident in his TV impersonations. Jonathan hovered on the fringe of the weekly writers' lunches, feeling his way toward an opening. Once he had acquired the spotlight, he clung to it, "on" for a non-stop trip that careened through a half-dozen subjects and improvisations. Give him an audience—of three or three hundred—and he was a runaway locomotive, eating up the track.

Somehow Jonathan and I struck up an instant kinship. I think he perceived my awareness of the torment behind his clowning, the volcano seething within his huge powerful frame. I could sense the antennas, all but sprouting from his head, through which he picked up the vibrations around him—the unspoken messages of eyes and hands. Anne Francis had mentioned his bouts of mental illness; he himself spoke of stays in hospitals, and fearsome confrontations with a scornful father. Although his palpable tension sometimes unnerved me, I felt enormous sympathy for the loneliness of a man I considered a comic genius. Once he bawled me out genially for not turning up at the writers' lunch: "I went to the stupid lunch just to see you!"

Jonathan invited me to his home in Montecito, where an oddly nautical stairway led down to a basement studio. Here, hidden from the world, he painted small, delicately executed figures whose precision and subtle coloring brought to mind the whimsical inventions of Paul Klee, the Swiss master. I gave him my book on Whistler, and when I next saw him a few weeks later he greeted me with a new deference.

It was Jonathan's habit during Conference week to pop in on various workshops without warning, leaving them fifteen minutes later in uproarious disarray. In my case he made it a point never to intrude on the classroom proceedings, waiting instead for the coffee break to announce his presence in a nearby cubicle.

A curiously revealing incident occurred at a party where a number of guests were clustered around Barnaby and me, thumping away together at a piano. Jonathan, sitting on the sidelines with his wife Eileen, moaned in not-so-mock despair: "Piano players! Those were the guys that got the girls in college! It was always like that."

One reason Jonathan lapped up attention so hungrily was his peculiar status as a big star getting little exposure. His freewheeling antic humor discomfited the young accountants running the movie studios, and didn't fit the rigid formulas of television. One day he asked—almost begged—me to write something for him; he tossed an experimental notion or two into the air.

They fell to the ground untouched. I simply couldn't connect with his unique, off-the-wall perspective; Jonathan's imagination was wider and wilder than anything I could come up with. Only Jonathan could write for Jonathan. Within months he confirmed my point by turning out a book of inimitable short stories that made the best-seller lists.

Jonathan gradually drifted away from the local scene, spending more time in Malibu or Lake Tahoe. Now and then affectionate echoes came back to me from mutual friends who ran into him.

Slowly I began to experience a new kind of pleasure: the husbandman's joy of planting seeds and reaping a harvest. My students were finding publishers: for books on Sally Ride, America's first female astronaut; World War II correspondent Marguerite Higgins; Daniel "Chappie" James, Jr., the Pentagon's first black four-star general; and "Doc Susie" Anderson, a tiny medical pioneer in the blizzard-swept logging camps of the Rockies.

I basked in grateful acknowledgments. A.L. Lazarus, Professor Emeritus of English at Purdue University, who had more than twenty previous books under his belt and a terrifying string of degrees from William and Mary, Michigan University and UCLA, after being helped to a breakthrough on his biography of playwright George McCutcheon, wrote: "I feel blessed to have crossed your path."

A book on harnessing right-brain powers by staff member Bill Downey cited the advice of "famous writers," quoting from Saul Bellow, William Manchester, Budd Schulberg and me. Barnaby, commissioned to assemble a manual on the craft of fiction, asked me to do a segment on style.

I wove my piece around a reminiscence of William Strunk, Jr., my literary mentor at Cornell, whose *Elements of Style* has since become a miniature bible for authors:

> Willie projected an aura endearingly Victorian. His pumpkin-round head and steel-rimmed glasses, the thin, meticulously plastered gray hair, split neatly down the middle, and his cranky, half-croaked pronouncements linger in memory like the smile of the vanished Cheshire cat.
>
> His maxims on language, more relevant than ever in the semantically slovenly age of television, were delivered between pursed lips with biting precision.

In teaching and counseling I had once again found an activity that felt right, as authentically me as writing or composing or broadcasting. By the late 1980's there were more requests for advice than I could handle—and some I could not resist, like the feisty grandmother whose memoir *Growing Old Disgracefully* celebrated senior sex revels in nudist camps.

For all my productive counseling, I ran into a stone wall with my old friend Joe Laitin. Spectacled and emollient, touted as the capital's "ultimate survivor," Joe had finally been fired by Ronald Reagan after serving at the sub-cabinet level in a long string of previous administrations. Joe was a master at running political interference, one of the unsung heroes in every public enterprise who make the headliners look good. He promptly joined the Washington *Post* as their ombudsman, and I in effect became his, regularly reviewing his copy.

As Pentagon spokesman, Public Affairs chief of the Treasury, and White House press aide with Bill Moyers to Lyndon Johnson, Joe had poked into every corner of the Beltway. His French wife, Christine, had come up with the awesome opening passage from Genesis broadcast to the world by the first astronauts encircling the moon. Joe knew everybody, had seen everything, and spun a good yarn. Colin Powell refers in his memoir to Joe's "bottomless fund" of entertaining White House tales. I was sure Joe had an engrossing and amusing book in him, but I couldn't get him to write it. I felt for Joe. He was struggling against poor health, the loss of beautiful Christine, and the nagging possibility that ex-war correspondent Laitin had been crouching so long behind government barricades, deflecting arrows from his bureaucrat bosses, cultivating the nimble sidestep of the official spokesman, that he had lost contact with his early spirit as a crusading newsman and couldn't make the leap back to the other side of the news divide.

In spring of 1993, I did a *News-Press* editorial on the Serbian death squads overrunning Bosnia:

> If the establishment of the U.N. had one overriding purpose, it was to ensure that brute force would never again go unchallenged; military

> power would be subordinated to moral authority; genocidal aggression would never again be sanctioned, much less rewarded. The hand-wringing and diplomatic bargaining, the mumbling about ancient grudges "beyond solution," miss the point; Neville Chamberlain's successors propagate a peace plan that would legitimize the savagery and give a reassuring signal to future aggressors.

Later I aired some unconventional judgments on the forces behind the murder of Yitzchak Rabin, a shy, decent man so devoid of vanity that after his success in the Six-Day War he referred me for an interview to his wife. His wanton killing laid bare a long-standing but never acknowledged fault line in the Israeli landscape.

The question I had posed to Golda Meir in 1946—"What are your plans for the Arabs?" had never really been answered. In some sectors the indifference expressed by Golda had hardened dangerously. The aide to Mota Gur, driving me into the reconquered Old City of Jerusalem after the Six-Day War, had dismissed Arab squatters huddling under the battlement walls as "animals," prompting me later to write to the Los Angeles *Jewish Journal*:

> It is time to say the unsayable: an undercurrent of racist snobbery, of plain contempt for the Arab population, has—no matter how repugnant to most Israelis—been a visible if rarely acknowledged part of the national scene since my ABC days. To pretend these elements do not exist, and to defend every Israeli action with a Stephen Decatur-like "My Jewish brethren, right or wrong!" is not only an inadequate response; it is in the profoundest sense not Jewish.

With the advent to power of Menachem Begin in 1977, anti-Arab prejudice in some quarters swelled to a near-Inquisitional intolerance. Begin's right-wing administration, already backed by a hard-core bloc of Orthodox militants from Eastern Europe, had ridden into office on a wave of protest by poor "Oriental" or Sephardic Jews, descendants of those displaced from Spain in the 15th century, less educated and privileged than the European Labor/Socialists who had ruled Israel since 1948.

The Sephardis identified with the Old Testament thrust of Begin's claim to a Greater Israel stretching from the Mediterranean to the Jordan River. Suspicious of Arabs from bitter experience as a Jewish minority in Moslem lands, they were not open to an exchange of "God-given land" for peace.

When Begin urged sweeping colonization of the West Bank by his followers, the black-hatted settlers who spearheaded the response brought along a sense of divine infallibility that often matched the single-mindedness of Moslem fundamentalists. Begin, a shrewd manipulator, was not above floating the outrageous claim that Mickey Marcus was one of his comrades in the bomb-planting Irgun Zvei Leumi underground, prompting a public rebuke of the prime minister in the New York *Times* by Jerusalem Mayor Teddy Kollek.

But there was no one to challenge Begin's grip on the colonizers. Recoiling from the loss of his family in the holocost, Begin had spawned a "never again" militarism that became a virus in the Israeli bloodstream, inciting the 1982 invasion of Lebanon and feeding the excesses on the Israeli side of the *intifadah*, the Palestinian uprising of 1987. Armed settlers from the right-wing "Bloc of the Faithful" streamed into the West Bank. A former Israeli chief of staff proposed to treat Arabs like "drugged roaches in a bottle."

Jewish blood, an orthodox rabbi shrieked, was better than Arab blood because it was "sacred." From there it was a short walk to the notion that if Jewish blood ran in the veins of a secular peacemaker, it had to be spilled.

Yitzchak Rabin stands out in memory like a granite block in a verdant field, vivid by his very plainness. The Rabin who flew with me along the Jordan border thirty years ago was solid and purposeful as a cathedral: high-crested reddish hair, unblinking blue eyes, thick freckled farmer's forearms. He projected an impression of vast inner strength held tightly in reserve.

Like Harry Truman, Rabin grew to unexpected stature in office. Like Anwar Sadat, he died at the hands of a countryman fueled by a climate of fanaticism.

Can the Israeli-Arab split be healed? Not so long as terror breeds counter-terror, blotting out generous impulse everywhere. Despite their shared history of abuse—in one case by Christian zealots, in the other by conquering Turks—up to now the two peoples have dehumanized each other. Each has a case; neither has been able to rise above private sorrows to let the other's sadness in.

On the domestic front, there was the disquieting rise of Rush Limbaugh. Late night radio talk shows had been keeping insomniacs company for years. Suddenly millions more, weary of radio psychobabble, found relaxation in the midnight rambling of Larry King and his peers. The print press, in its drive for circulation, had frequently become crude, lurid; four out of five Americans, according to a *Wall Street Journal* poll, considered newspapers dishonest. This was the opening through which Limbaugh squeezed his ponderous frame, directing his fire at the "liberal" press, ignoring its overwhelmingly conservative ownership.

I first spotted the blubber-laden Limbaugh—or more accurately I smelled him, like the rotting carcass of an elephant seal—a long way off, when he was still a minor bleep on the broadcast radar screen. In a letter of November 29, 1988 to John Donovan, I reported the arrival on the airwaves of "a modernized ghost of the beloved Father Coughlin" (a rabble-rouser of the 1930s), who "makes a strong fascist appeal to the haters, greed-mongers and Birch Society crowd. And his ratings are going up—along with a lot of people's blood pressures."

I had already written to Limbaugh's radio outlet in Santa Barbara, protesting "the kind of inflammatory claptrap refined to its peak by Dr. Joseph Goebbels of Berlin." My letter went unanswered.

Limbaugh pandered to the vast audience spawned by the erosion of the American Dream. He soothed both the losers in the race for immeasurable wealth, who were as eager for scapegoats as Hitler's followers had been in collapsing Germany, and the momentary winners, furious at the prospect of parting with any of the capital that was their only reward for years of bitter struggle, and the only prop to their inner unease.

Breezily contemptuous of his listeners—"Listen to me, I'll do the thinking for you"—feeding on an apparently bottomless pit of envy and resentment, Limbaugh enlisted the nation's soreheads, bigots, and xenophobes.

He was effective because, aware that straight-out Klansmanship would no longer be tolerated, he laced his venom with humor. But anyone familiar with the World War II propaganda of Goebbels—and I was awash in it for nearly five years—could not miss under the talk-show clowning the motifs and tactics advanced in *Mein Kampf*: misquotation, innuendo, sly repetition of the Big Lie that Hitler insisted was easier to make stick than petty falsehoods (in 1940 it was "Jews own the United States" and "Jews control the media;" in Limbaugh's 1990, "liberals are out to destroy the family" and "liberals control television"). Berlin Radio had referred to President Roosevelt as "Rosenfeld;" Limbaugh jeered at "the Reverend," heavily underlined, Jesse Jackson. With incredible cheek, this devotee of Nazi techniques smeared women's rights activists as "feminazis."

Americans who did not share his enthusiasm for military solutions were branded "peace pansies," thereby in a single not-so-subtle stroke linking pacifists to homosexuality.

Limbaugh's personal claims to fuehrerhood were frequent and unmistakable. He admitted graciously to being "on loan from God," providing instruction which would relieve the faithful of any need to depend on other, more fallible sources. They were told how to react, what to read, where to write—everything but the dangerous notion of thinking for themselves. Even the "Heil Hitler" salute had its parallel in the "dittos" and "megadittos" greeting to Limbaugh from callers, signifying showers of applause, the approved genuflection before the Leader.

There was an early tendency to write Limbaugh off as a noisy buffoon, a freak, the bearded lady of the airwaves. That misgauged the degree to which our citizenry had been softened up and made ready for his soothing blather by the hypnotic escapism of the TV diet, the feel-good quackery of the Reagan years.

In my failed courtship of the Guggenheim Foundation, I had predicted that the new national toy of television would, by its methodical bludgeoning of the senses, destroy the American capacity for independent thought. Forty years later television sits enthroned in the American household, the one indispensable piece of furniture that is the main source of our information, entertainment and values, projecting a fictitious world "cynically crafted," as "Buffalo Bill" producer Dennis Klein put it, "to not disturb sleeping minds." The dismal results are in: massive apathy, plunging test scores. A third of the populace doubts that the holocaust ever happened; future generations may be open to persuasion that the moon landing was a hoax. The average American child has spent 5,000 hours in front of the tube before crossing a first grade threshold; as a teen-ager has witnessed 8,000 vividly rendered murders, then settled into a daily pattern of three hours before the electronic altar for every hour of study. By college age, only one of ten freshmen at California State Fullerton could identify Alexander Hamilton. Yet according to TV Guide, one American in four would not part with his TV set for a million dollars, although an equal number could be bought off for a paltry $25,000.

During World War II, watching a group of British officers devour their newspapers in chilly silence on the verandah of Shepheards Hotel, I was moved to scribble a poem:

Give Us This Day Our Daily Drug

The newspapers and radios have stolen our minds from us
Wrapped them up in bold black headlines and velvety manicured voices
And shipped them off to God knows where.
We used to have minds of our own—I think.
When we worked in the fields and faced the tasks that were set each day.
We weighed the color of the moon, and the sickly neigh of a colt
And we decided of our own minds whether to plant rye that year, how big to build the stable.
But that has changed. Now we are robots on an assembly line.
The printing press and science came too soon.
How many are intelligent enough
To justify the dangerous privilege
Of reading?

That was a decade before the arrival of the persuasive monster with its mesmerizing moving shadows.

Today a rising tide of entertainment conglomerates, sweeping through the windows of corporate opportunity opened up by the deregulation of the Reagan era, puts its stamp on virtually everything we see and hear. The interlocked presence on corporate boards of executives from every branch of communications enables a relative handful of people to decide for the rest of us what is "fit to print." Or to be heard, or viewed.

The mass media in which I have spent a lifetime have not only become more massive but have been crammed together under the bulging roofs of a few monoliths, each determined to synthesize its disparate properties into one vast enterprise whose every subdivision is expected to generate "product" to be systematically promoted by its corporate cousins. I see a steady wearing away of individualism as the onrushing media reduce us to a captive herd of consumers half-buried under an avalanche of images and words. We no longer have media; the media have us.

All this without the incalculable impact of the Internet. When I was a boy, we rejoiced at picking up KDKA in far off (386 miles!) Pittsburgh. Today the Internet brings the treasures of the Louvre to a Bedouin tent in the desert. It also provides a fertile forum for bigots and sociopaths.

And social interaction shrinks. The very term "user-friendly" enthrones the tool over the human. No man, John Donne warned, is an island. Marooned behind a computer, every man is. Technology without a moral base is at best meaningless, at worst destructive. Our endlessly burgeoning know-how distracts us from the still-elusive know-what and know-why for reordering a chaotic world. If computer addiction spreads, urgent realities—war, hungry children—may be shunted aside. We might see our tools running miles ahead of our objectives, and our best minds diverting themselves in the game room while the rest of the house goes up in flames.

Fifty years ago, with the arrival of television we faced a similar crossroads. As Ed Murrow then pointed out, the new instrument could be a magnificent source of pleasure and enlightenment or simply lifeless wires. We elected to leave the potentials of the tube to Madison Avenue, which promptly defined its mission as "the delivery of eyeballs" to advertisers. Unfortunately the techniques that delivered eyeballs also delivered a generation of passive button-pushers with a taste for mindless violence, and ultimately a populace unable to distinguish image from substance, fantasy from reality.

Are we willing to settle for a mountain of technical progress that brings forth Mickey Mouse? The question goes to the heart of our value system, a journey few Americans are willing to make. Are we unable or unwilling to expand our vision beyond the global marketplace, content to risk becoming so intellectually impoverished that we may wind up with the paradox of accelerated communication between people who have nothing to say?

Historian Theodore Roszak tells us the human personality is undergoing a "shift of consciousness fully as epoch-making as the appearance of speech," which will heighten awareness and unleash "visionary talents . . . on a planetary scale."

From his mouth—to quote Fanny's favorite Yiddish locution—into God's ears.

My own ears are not what they were, although the hearing aid performs miracles in restoring overtones at the piano. I have retired, or been retired from, the dating game. Most of my friends have left town, and many the planet; my phone seldom rings. I still respond to the click of high heels on the pavement outside my window, but that's a matter of genes. The last remark attributed to my maternal grandfather, Henry Holtzmann, on his death bed was a complaint about his new nurse not being up to the pulchritude level of her predecessor.

Heeding Socrates, I have spent several years examining my life. I can look back on a good share of laughter and some green oases of love; on work and friendship that have touched other lives. From hard experience I have gained a grasp of the gulf that separates troubled youth from baffled parents, and have tried to encourage each embattled side to "walk in the moccasins" of the other.

I have had my share, and more, of narrow escapes. However, I have had time and health and outlets to express a fair slice of what was on my mind. And comforting echoes trickle back. Global programming for the protection of children, in which I had an early hand, has been one of the incontestable successes of the United Nations. The FBIS, steadily expanding its reach to embrace 3,500 overseas transmitters, has become according to a China specialist at Johns Hopkins University "the biggest bang for the buck in the American intelligence community." A royalty check from ASCAP affirms that "He's Gone," composed for the Cornell varsity show of 1933 and featured several years later in my London Films movie *The Squeaker*, is after more than half a century still alive and well in Australia. Bonzo, Tony Perkins' Jim Piersall and the Kirk Douglas version of Mickey Marcus turn up periodically on the tube, and *The Lady and the Law* flourishes on Arizona bookshelves.

I have learned that even with a bad start it is possible to grow, to know many short-of-ecstasy pleasures and contribute to the fabric of one's age. If I have not learned, with Thomas à Kempis and the French philosopher Mme. Germaine de Stael to understand and therefore forgive everything (I find genocidal rape, like gas chambers, beyond pardoning), I have a far better understanding than before of the influences shaping those in my immediate circle, and of the awesome responsibility attached to parenthood. And I have learned, if not to idolize Ted Berkman, to accept him.

Could I, with Ira Gershwin, have "asked for anything more?" Yes: the pleasures of family life, the balm of an heir, immersion in a world less driven by fear, more open and mutually trusting.

Erwin Piscator, the German maestro of epic theater, exiled in New York fifty years ago, told me, "Socialism is in heaven."

If I ever find out, I'll try to let you know.

Snippets from the Cutting Room Floor

If, as Socrates insisted,"the unexamined life is not worth living," the unlived life is not worth examining.

Trivia besiege and distract us. Yes, stop and smell the roses; but first separate them from the manure.

Choose your battles carefully, lest you waste ammunition on trifles and are left to face real crises empty-handed.

Wisdom is knowing how to edit one's life, and accepting that there will always be something unavoidably left on the "overset."

The cost of living—or having lived—is engraved on our faces.

Observe reality. Fools keep tuned to the official weather report, but never look out of the window.

If you want birds in your garden, be prepared for bird dung. Every pleasure presents its bill.

In appraising our lives, we are all revisionist historians.

War shrivels man to a lethal claw.

Politicians take polls; leaders take chances.

A fire that kindles quickly is likely to die the same way;
better the long, slow-burning log.

Aging enables most of us to draw on
the accumulated ignorance of a lifetime.

Resist the temptation to respond to "How are you?" in clinical detail.
There are few subjects less riveting than other peoples' ailments.

The only ism for the nineties is humanism. Every other ism is a wasm.

Have yourself a good time.
Life will supply the requisite suffering.

❁ ❁ ❁

Acknowledgements

I want to thank Sol Stein, author, teacher and master editor, for reviewing my manuscript. And my publisher, Virginia Cornell, for a multitude of services. Also helpful were Fred Klein, Bettyann Kevles, Richard F.X. O'Connor and Lauren Roberts.

The Santa Barbara Public Library, surely one of the best of its size in the country, has been obliging beyond the call of duty.

T.B.

Index

A

B

C

D

E

F

G

H

I

J

K

L

M

N

O

S

W

Y

Z

Also From Manifest Publications

Maverick Women: Nineteenth Century Women Who Kicked Over the Traces
by FRANCES LAURENCE
They were scholars, they were saints, they were sinners . . . they were determined. In a time when a woman's mind was kept as tightly laced as her corset, these females went against family, friends and convention: Jane Barnes, Ina Coolbrith, Maria Mitchell, Pearl Hart, Nellie Cashman, Sojourner Truth, Nellie Bly, Ann Eliza W. Young, Carrie Chapman Catt, Dr. Bethenia Owens-Adair — plus. "You'll be glad to know these women and be proud they defied convention to achieve the things they did." Charles Champlin, *LA Times* **ISBN 0-9627896-7, quality paperback $18.50**

Books by VIRGINIA CORNELL:

Doc Susie: The True Story of a Country Physician in the Colorado Rockies
She was beautiful, she was smart, she was dying —
When Susan Anderson, M.D., stepped from the train into frigid Fraser, Colorado—"Icebox of the Nation"—she had everything to die for and nothing to live for. This is the true story of how Doc Susie recovered her health, then ventured forth to save the lives of lumberjacks, miners, ranchers, railroaders and their families. Over 100,000 copies of the biography of Susan Anderson, M.D., have been sold to people who love a good story.
ISBN 0-9627896-5-8, quality paperback $14.95

Ski Lodge — Millers Idlewild Inn — Adventures in Snow Business
High in the mountains, there once was a rustic, homemade ski lodge — populated by reluctant honeymooners, errant husbands, truant plumbers, youthful ski bums . . . plus one naive innkeeper. With humor and insight the author remembers when, as a single mother, she struggled to fill the gigantic footprints vacated by her frenetically energetic father.
ISBN 0-9627896-6-6, hardcover $12.95

The Latest Wrinkle — and other Signs of Aging
If you want to slam on the brakes at the first Signs of Aging, this book offers some original thoughts about how to smooth out the wrinkles caused by: fractured families, family reunions, curmudgeonly husbands, grafts on the family tree, pets that kill, obituaries, gum disease, burial plans, Chia Pets.
ISBN 0-9627896-3-1, quality paperback $9.95

ORDER FORM

The following titles are available from Manifest Publications:
Indicate number of copies ordered.

Around The World In 80 Years	$ 27.95
Maverick Women	18.50
The Latest Wrinkle	9.95
Doc Susie	14.95
Ski Lodge	12.95
Shipping and handling per order Book rate, U.S. Post Office	3.00
California residents add 7.75% tax	______
Total Amount Enclosed	**$** ______

Send to:

Name ____

Address/P.O. Box ____________________________________

City ________________________ State _____ Zip __________

Daytime Phone Number (____)________________________

Phone orders encouraged. (805) 684-4905

Or mail to:
Manifest Publications
P.O. Box 429
Carpinteria, CA 93014-0429